International Health Law ar

Basic Documents

International Health Law and Ethics

Basic Documents

Edited by

André den Exter

Maklu

Apeldoorn-Antwerpen-Portland

International Health Law and Ethics. Basic Documents
Apeldoorn - Antwerpen - Portland
Maklu
2009

488 pag. – 24 x 17 cm
ISBN 978-90-466-0259-1
D/2009/1997/15
NUR 828

Maklu Publishers
Koninginnelaan 96, 7315 EB Apeldoorn, The Netherlands, info@maklu.nl
Somersstraat 13/15, 2018 Antwerpen, Belgium, info@maklu.be
www.maklu.eu

USA & Canada
International Specialized Book Services
920 NE 58th Ave., Suite 300, Portland, OR 97213-3786, orders@isbs.com, www.isbs.com

UK and Ireland:
R. Bayliss, 81 Milehouse Road, Plymouth, Devon PL3 4AE

Contents

Foreword

The volume, '*International Health Law and Ethics. Basic Documents,*' is an initiative of the Erasmus Observatory on Health Law. The Observatory's training program covers a variety of topics on health law and ethics, including human rights and health care, public health law, health ethics, reproductive rights and pharmaceutical law. Despite the availability of numerous handbooks, collections of treaty documents and soft law on health care rights and health ethics are surprisingly absent. *International Health Law and Ethics* aims to fill this gap in the academic literature. The collection contains numerous treaty documents, declarations and recommendations on health care rights and professional ethics, from authoritative institutions such as the United Nations, World Health Organization, Council of Europe, International Labour Organization, UNESCO and the World Medical Association.

International Health Law and Ethics contains a set of normative principles and standards in health care. Following the post-WW II Nuremberg doctors' trials, there was a need to guarantee the rights of human beings in health care. Although the Human Rights Declaration (1948) and subsequent covenants – the International Covenant on Civil and Political Rights (ICCPR) and International Covenant on Economic, Social and Cultural Rights (ICESCR) – meant a major step toward safeguarding human rights in general, the health care sector, specifically, requires special standards. New developments, such as the post-war globalization of health care and liberalization of health services, new health care technologies, increasing costs of health care systems, and public health threats, revealed the need for health and human rights standards.

These standards can be found both in the WHO Constitution and in many subsequent documents that reiterate that health is a 'state of complete physical, mental and social well-being and not merely the absence of disease or infirmity'. Such a definition of health imposes government obligations in health care, reflecting three types of obligations: the obligation to respect, the obligation to protect, and the obligation to fulfil (General comment on health). The first type of obligation prohibits States themselves from acting in a manner that is contrary to the recognized rights and freedoms, i.e. the state must refrain from interfering or constraining the exercise of these rights and freedoms, while the second type of obligation requires the State to take steps (through legislation or other means) to prevent and prohibit the violation of individual rights by third parties. The third type of obligation can be considered an obligation to facilitate, provide and promote – it requires active measures that will enable and assist individuals and communities in enjoying given rights. This tripartite typology of obligations is applied in several general comments of the CESCR and the CCPR and combines both negative and positive state obligations. These obligations are related not only to the fulfilment of the right to health, but also to other human rights in health care. The typology of obligations is an important analytical tool for increasing understanding of human rights – clarifying the meaning of these rights, while, at the same time, guiding the obligations of State parties in the field of health care.

Derived from international human rights law, regional documents and explanatory reports on health care rights provide a way of "unpacking" that tripartite approach, making rights more specific, accessible and (judicially) accountable. In addition, soft law declarations and medical ethics contribute to understanding the moral meaning of human rights in health care. As such, the principles and standards provide practical guidance for the conduct of States concerning equal access to health care services, the rights of (categories of) patients, biomedical research, organ donation and transplantation, genetics and public health. These topics structure the approach of *International Health Law and Ethics*. Although not comprehensive, this guide covers basic documents, while general comments and explanatory reports amplify the principles embodied in the human rights treaties. The authoritative interpretations elucidate a 'European approach' on the State's obligations concerning health care rights and ethics.

Although it was originally meant for the Erasmus training course on Health law and ethics, I hope this volume will also be a helpful guide for all trainers, health professionals and students interested in human rights issues in health care.

As a final remark, I would like to thank Eveline Adriaanse, research assistant at the Erasmus University, for her accurate support preparing this volume, as well as my colleagues for their advice and comments on the structure and content of this book.

February 2009

The Observatory in Brief

The Erasmus Observatory on Health Law was founded to explore health law, share in its study, and help pioneer its development. It represents a network of faculties, students, fellows, lawyers and ethicists working to identify and engage with the challenges and opportunities of health law.

Mission

The Erasmus Observatory's mission is to improve and promote understanding on health law through a variety of programmatic activities, including: research, education, collaboration, and dissemination of information.

To this end, the research and education core activities of the Observatory are intertwined and mutually reinforcing components. Our method is to build out into health law, record data, self-study, and share.

The Observatory also takes an active part in the international cooperation with other universities, research centres and international organisations in order to address the increasing globalisation of health, while the dissemination of information component will be realised by publication of news letters, internet resources, and by organizing conferences and symposia on health law issues

Research

The Observatory is at the forefront of international health law research and our reputation for high standards in all that we do is crucial to our success. The scholarly mission includes the production of doctrinal, theoretical, and interdisciplinary publications in traditional academic journals or scholarly presses; pragmatic scholarship designed to assist the legal profession by reporting on important developments, gathering and organizing diverse materials that bear on a given subject, and clarifying complex areas of the law; instructional scholarship such as textbooks and instructional materials.

Research interests include a wide variety of topics including: solidarity and justice in health care; human rights and health care; patients' rights; European health law; (European) competition law and health care; pharmaceutical law; medical liability, and health ethics.

Teaching

While the core of our teaching has been courses at Erasmus Law School and other faculties, we also strive to reach and involve a much broader audience. Faculty associated with the Observatory has combined to teach courses annually as part of the curricula at the Erasmus

University Rotterdam. We have taught a generation of future lawyers and scholars and policy makers about health law, human rights and health care, anti-competition law, and public health law. These extensive offerings serve as a key means of bridging our scholarship, community-building, and educational activities. Our courses both unify and transcend these separate threads, helping to weave them into and throughout everything we do, while engaging a wide and diverse audience in the most challenging aspects of our work.

The Right to Health

PART I

Chapter 1. General

1.1. The Universal Declaration of Human Rights (1948)

ARTICLE 25

(1) Everyone has the right to a standard of living adequate for the health and well-being of himself and of his family, including … medical care and necessary social services, and the right to security in the event of unemployment, sickness, disability, widowhood, old age or other lack of livelihood in circumstances beyond his control.

(2) Motherhood and childhood are entitled to special care and assistance. All children, whether born in or out of wedlock, shall enjoy the same social protection.

1.2. International Covenant on Economic, Social and Cultural Rights, Article 12 (1966)

ARTICLE 12

1. The States Parties to the present Covenant recognize the right of everyone to the enjoyment of the highest attainable standard of physical and mental health.

2. The steps to be taken by the States Parties to the present Covenant to achieve the full realization of this right shall include those necessary for:

(a) The provision for the reduction of the stillbirth-rate and of infant mortality and for the healthy development of the child;
(b) The improvement of all aspects of environmental and industrial hygiene;
(c) The prevention, treatment and control of epidemic, endemic, occupational and other diseases;
(d) The creation of conditions which would assure to all medical service and medical attention in the event of sickness.

1.3. The right to the Highest Attainable Standard of Health: General Comment no. 14 (2000) on Health; 11/08/2000. E/C.12/2000/4.

Committee on Economic, Social and Cultural Rights
Twenty-second session Geneva, 25 April-12 May 2000

The right to the highest attainable standard of health (article 12 of the International Covenant on Economic, Social and Cultural Rights)

1. Health is a fundamental human right indispensable for the exercise of other human rights. Every human being is entitled to the enjoyment of the highest attainable standard of health conducive to living a life in dignity. The realization of the right to health may be pursued through numerous, complementary approaches, such as the formulation of health policies, or the implementation of health programmes developed by the World Health Organization (WHO), or the adoption of specific legal instruments. Moreover, the right to health includes certain components which are legally enforceable.[1]

2. The human right to health is recognized in numerous international instruments. Article 25.1 of the Universal Declaration of Human Rights affirms: "Everyone has the right to a standard of living adequate for the health of himself and of his family, including food, clothing, housing and medical care and necessary social services". The International Covenant on Economic, Social and Cultural Rights provides the most comprehensive article on the right to health in international human rights law. In accordance with article 12.1 of the Covenant, States parties recognize "the right of everyone to the enjoyment of the highest attainable standard of physical and mental health", while article 12.2 enumerates, by way of illustration, a number of "steps to be taken by the States parties ... to achieve the full realization of this right". Additionally, the right to health is recognized, inter alia, in article 5 (e) (iv) of the International Convention on the Elimination of All Forms of Racial Discrimination of 1965, in articles 11.1 (f) and 12 of the Convention on the Elimination of All Forms of Discrimination against Women of 1979 and in article 24 of the Convention on the Rights of the Child of 1989. Several regional human rights instruments also recognize the right to health, such as the European Social Charter of 1961 as revised (art. 11), the African Charter on Human and Peoples' Rights of 1981 (art. 16) and the Additional Protocol to the American Convention on Human Rights in the Area of Economic, Social and Cultural Rights of 1988 (art. 10). Similarly, the right to health has been proclaimed by the Commission on Human Rights,[2] as well as in the Vienna Declaration and Programme of Action of 1993 and other international instruments.[3]

---

1   For example, the principle of non-discrimination in relation to health facilities, goods and services is legally enforceable in numerous national jurisdictions.
2   In its resolution 1989/11.
3   The Principles for the Protection of Persons with Mental Illness and for the Improvement of Mental Health Care adopted by the United Nations General Assembly in 1991 (resolution 46/119) and the Committee's General Comment No. 5 on persons with disabilities apply to persons with mental illness; the Programme of Action of the International Conference on Population and Development

3. The right to health is closely related to and dependent upon the realization of other human rights, as contained in the International Bill of Rights, including the rights to food, housing, work, education, human dignity, life, non-discrimination, equality, the prohibition against torture, privacy, access to information, and the freedoms of association, assembly and movement. These and other rights and freedoms address integral components of the right to health.

4. In drafting article 12 of the Covenant, the Third Committee of the United Nations General Assembly did not adopt the definition of health contained in the preamble to the Constitution of WHO, which conceptualizes health as "a state of complete physical, mental and social well-being and not merely the absence of disease or infirmity". However, the reference in article 12.1 of the Covenant to "the highest attainable standard of physical and mental health" is not confined to the right to health care. On the contrary, the drafting history and the express wording of article 12.2 acknowledge that the right to health embraces a wide range of socio-economic factors that promote conditions in which people can lead a healthy life, and extends to the underlying determinants of health, such as food and nutrition, housing, access to safe and potable water and adequate sanitation, safe and healthy working conditions, and a healthy environment.

5. The Committee is aware that, for millions of people throughout the world, the full enjoyment of the right to health still remains a distant goal. Moreover, in many cases, especially for those living in poverty, this goal is becoming increasingly remote. The Committee recognizes the formidable structural and other obstacles resulting from international and other factors beyond the control of States that impede the full realization of article 12 in many States parties.

6. With a view to assisting States parties' implementation of the Covenant and the fulfilment of their reporting obligations, this General Comment focuses on the normative content of article 12 (Part I), States parties' obligations (Part II), violations (Part III) and implementation at the national level (Part IV), while the obligations of actors other than States parties are addressed in Part V. The General Comment is based on the Committee's experience in examining States parties' reports over many years.

I. Normative Content of Article 12

7. Article 12.1 provides a definition of the right to health, while article 12.2 enumerates illustrative, non-exhaustive examples of States parties' obligations.

8. The right to health is not to be understood as a right to be healthy. The right to health contains both freedoms and entitlements. The freedoms include the right to control one's health and body, including sexual and reproductive freedom, and the right to be free from interference, such as the right to be free from torture, non-consensual medical treatment and experimentation.

---

held at Cairo in 1994, as well as the Declaration and Programme for Action of the Fourth World Conference on Women held in Beijing in 1995 contain definitions of reproductive health and women's health, respectively.

By contrast, the entitlements include the right to a system of health protection which provides equality of opportunity for people to enjoy the highest attainable level of health.

9. The notion of "the highest attainable standard of health" in article 12.1 takes into account both the individual's biological and socio-economic preconditions and a State's available resources. There are a number of aspects which cannot be addressed solely within the relationship between States and individuals; in particular, good health cannot be ensured by a State, nor can States provide protection against every possible cause of human ill health. Thus, genetic factors, individual susceptibility to ill health and the adoption of unhealthy or risky lifestyles may play an important role with respect to an individual's health. Consequently, the right to health must be understood as a right to the enjoyment of a variety of facilities, goods, services and conditions necessary for the realization of the highest attainable standard of health.

10. Since the adoption of the two International Covenants in 1966 the world health situation has changed dramatically and the notion of health has undergone substantial changes and has also widened in scope. More determinants of health are being taken into consideration, such as resource distribution and gender differences. A wider definition of health also takes into account such socially-related concerns as violence and armed conflict.[4] Moreover, formerly unknown diseases, such as Human Immunodeficiency Virus and Acquired Immunodeficiency Syndrome (HIV/AIDS), and others that have become more widespread, such as cancer, as well as the rapid growth of the world population, have created new obstacles for the realization of the right to health which need to be taken into account when interpreting article 12.

11. The Committee interprets the right to health, as defined in article 12.1, as an inclusive right extending not only to timely and appropriate health care but also to the underlying determinants of health, such as access to safe and potable water and adequate sanitation, an adequate supply of safe food, nutrition and housing, healthy occupational and environmental conditions, and access to health-related education and information, including on sexual and reproductive health. A further important aspect is the participation of the population in all health-related decision-making at the community, national and international levels.

12. The right to health in all its forms and at all levels contains the following interrelated and essential elements, the precise application of which will depend on the conditions prevailing in a particular State party:
(a) Availability. Functioning public health and health-care facilities, goods and services, as well as programmes, have to be available in sufficient quantity within the State party. The precise nature of the facilities, goods and services will vary depending on numerous factors, including the State party's developmental level. They will include, however, the underlying determinants of health, such as safe and potable drinking water and adequate sanitation fa-

---

4   Common article 3 of the Geneva Conventions for the protection of war victims (1949); Additional Protocol I (1977) relating to the Protection of Victims of International Armed Conflicts, art. 75 (2) (a); Additional Protocol II (1977) relating to the Protection of Victims of Non-International Armed Conflicts, art. 4 (a).

cilities, hospitals, clinics and other health-related buildings, trained medical and professional personnel receiving domestically competitive salaries, and essential drugs, as defined by the WHO Action Programme on Essential Drugs.[5]

(b) Accessibility. Health facilities, goods and services[6] have to be accessible to everyone without discrimination, within the jurisdiction of the State party. Accessibility has four over-lapping dimensions:

Non-discrimination: health facilities, goods and services must be accessible to all, especially the most vulnerable or marginalized sections of the population, in law and in fact, without discrimination on any of the prohibited grounds.[7]

Physical accessibility: health facilities, goods and services must be within safe physical reach for all sections of the population, especially vulnerable or marginalized groups, such as ethnic minorities and indigenous populations, women, children, adolescents, older persons, persons with disabilities and persons with HIV/AIDS. Accessibility also implies that medical services and underlying determinants of health, such as safe and potable water and adequate sanitation facilities, are within safe physical reach, including in rural areas. Accessibility further includes adequate access to buildings for persons with disabilities.

Economic accessibility (affordability): health facilities, goods and services must be afford-able for all. Payment for health-care services, as well as services related to the underlying determinants of health, has to be based on the principle of equity, ensuring that these services, whether privately or publicly provided, are affordable for all, including socially disadvantaged groups. Equity demands that poorer households should not be disproportionately burdened with health expenses as compared to richer households.

Information accessibility: accessibility includes the right to seek, receive and impart information and ideas[8] concerning health issues. However, accessibility of information should not impair the right to have personal health data treated with confidentiality.

(c) Acceptability. All health facilities, goods and services must be respectful of medical ethics and culturally appropriate, i.e. respectful of the culture of individuals, minorities, peoples and communities, sensitive to gender and life-cycle requirements, as well as being designed to respect confidentiality and improve the health status of those concerned.

(d) Quality. As well as being culturally acceptable, health facilities, goods and services must also be scientifically and medically appropriate and of good quality. This requires, inter alia, skilled medical personnel, scientifically approved and unexpired drugs and hospital equipment, safe and potable water, and adequate sanitation.

---

5   See WHO Model List of Essential Drugs, revised December 1999, WHO Drug Information, vol. 13, No. 4, 1999.

6   Unless expressly provided otherwise, any reference in this General Comment to health facilities, goods and services includes the underlying determinants of health outlined in paras. 11 and 12 (a) of this General Comment.

7   See paras. 18 and 19 of this General Comment.

8   See article 19.2 of the International Covenant on Civil and Political Rights. This General Comment gives particular emphasis to access to information because of the special importance of this issue in relation to health.

13. The non-exhaustive catalogue of examples in article 12.2 provides guidance in defining the action to be taken by States. It gives specific generic examples of measures arising from the broad definition of the right to health contained in article 12.1, thereby illustrating the content of that right, as exemplified in the following paragraphs.[9]

ARTICLE 12.2 (A). THE RIGHT TO MATERNAL, CHILD AND REPRODUCTIVE HEALTH

14. "The provision for the reduction of the stillbirth rate and of infant mortality and for the healthy development of the child" (art. 12.2 (a))[10] may be understood as requiring measures to improve child and maternal health, sexual and reproductive health services, including access to family planning, pre- and post-natal care,[11]emergency obstetric services and access to information, as well as to resources necessary to act on that information.[12]

ARTICLE 12.2 (B). THE RIGHT TO HEALTHY NATURAL AND WORKPLACE ENVIRONMENTS

15. "The improvement of all aspects of environmental and industrial hygiene" (art. 12.2 (b)) comprises, inter alia, preventive measures in respect of occupational accidents and diseases; the requirement to ensure an adequate supply of safe and potable water and basic sanitation; the prevention and reduction of the population's exposure to harmful substances such as radiation and harmful chemicals or other detrimental environmental conditions that directly or indirectly

---

9   In the literature and practice concerning the right to health, three levels of health care are frequently referred to: primary health care typically deals with common and relatively minor illnesses and is provided by health professionals and/or generally trained doctors working within the community at relatively low cost; secondary health care is provided in centres, usually hospitals, and typically deals with relatively common minor or serious illnesses that cannot be managed at community level, using specialty-trained health professionals and doctors, special equipment and sometimes in-patient care at comparatively higher cost; tertiary health care is provided in relatively few centres, typically deals with small numbers of minor or serious illnesses requiring specialty-trained health professionals and doctors and special equipment, and is often relatively expensive. Since forms of primary, secondary and tertiary health care frequently overlap and often interact, the use of this typology does not always provide sufficient distinguishing criteria to be helpful for assessing which levels of health care States parties must provide, and is therefore of limited assistance in relation to the normative understanding of article 12.

10   According to WHO, the stillbirth rate is no longer commonly used, infant and under-five mortality rates being measured instead.

11   Prenatal denotes existing or occurring before birth; perinatal refers to the period shortly before and after birth (in medical statistics the period begins with the completion of 28 weeks of gestation and is variously defined as ending one to four weeks after birth); neonatal, by contrast, covers the period pertaining to the first four weeks after birth; while post-natal denotes occurrence after birth. In this General Comment, the more generic terms pre- and post-natal are exclusively employed.

12   Reproductive health means that women and men have the freedom to decide if and when to reproduce and the right to be informed and to have access to safe, effective, affordable and acceptable methods of family planning of their choice as well as the right of access to appropriate health-care services that will, for example, enable women to go safely through pregnancy and childbirth.

impact upon human health.[13] Furthermore, industrial hygiene refers to the minimization, so far as is reasonably practicable, of the causes of health hazards inherent in the working environment.[14] Article 12.2 (b) also embraces adequate housing and safe and hygienic working conditions, an adequate supply of food and proper nutrition, and discourages the abuse of alcohol, and the use of tobacco, drugs and other harmful substances.

ARTICLE 12.2 (C). THE RIGHT TO PREVENTION, TREATMENT AND CONTROL OF DISEASES

16. "The prevention, treatment and control of epidemic, endemic, occupational and other diseases" (art. 12.2 (c)) requires the establishment of prevention and education programmes for behaviour-related health concerns such as sexually transmitted diseases, in particular HIV/ AIDS, and those adversely affecting sexual and reproductive health, and the promotion of social determinants of good health, such as environmental safety, education, economic development and gender equity. The right to treatment includes the creation of a system of urgent medical care in cases of accidents, epidemics and similar health hazards, and the provision of disaster relief and humanitarian assistance in emergency situations. The control of diseases refers to States' individual and joint efforts to, inter alia, make available relevant technologies, using and improving epidemiological surveillance and data collection on a disaggregated basis, the implementation or enhancement of immunization programmes and other strategies of infectious disease control.

ARTICLE 12.2 (D). THE RIGHT TO HEALTH FACILITIES, GOODS AND SERVICES[15]

17. "The creation of conditions which would assure to all medical service and medical attention in the event of sickness" (art. 12.2 (d)), both physical and mental, includes the provision of equal and timely access to basic preventive, curative, rehabilitative health services and health education; regular screening programmes; appropriate treatment of prevalent diseases, illnesses, injuries and disabilities, preferably at community level; the provision of essential drugs; and appropriate mental health treatment and care. A further important aspect is the improvement and furtherance of participation of the population in the provision of preventive and curative health services, such as the organization of the health sector, the insurance system and, in particular, participation in political decisions relating to the right to health taken at both the community and national levels.

---

13 The Committee takes note, in this regard, of Principle 1 of the Stockholm Declaration of 1972 which states: "Man has the fundamental right to freedom, equality and adequate conditions of life, in an environment of a quality that permits a life of dignity and well-being", as well as of recent developments in international law, including General Assembly resolution 45/94 on the need to ensure a healthy environment for the well-being of individuals; Principle 1 of the Rio Declaration; and regional human rights instruments such as article 10 of the San Salvador Protocol to the American Convention on Human Rights.

14 ILO Convention No. 155, art. 4.2.

15 See para. 12 (b) and note 8 above.

ARTICLE 12. SPECIAL TOPICS OF BROAD APPLICATION

Non-discrimination and equal treatment

18. By virtue of article 2.2 and article 3, the Covenant proscribes any discrimination in access to health care and underlying determinants of health, as well as to means and entitlements for their procurement, on the grounds of race, colour, sex, language, religion, political or other opinion, national or social origin, property, birth, physical or mental disability, health status (including HIV/AIDS), sexual orientation and civil, political, social or other status, which has the intention or effect of nullifying or impairing the equal enjoyment or exercise of the right to health. The Committee stresses that many measures, such as most strategies and programmes designed to eliminate health-related discrimination, can be pursued with minimum resource implications through the adoption, modification or abrogation of legislation or the dissemination of information. The Committee recalls General Comment No. 3, paragraph 12, which states that even in times of severe resource constraints, the vulnerable members of society must be protected by the adoption of relatively low-cost targeted programmes.

19. With respect to the right to health, equality of access to health care and health services has to be emphasized. States have a special obligation to provide those who do not have sufficient means with the necessary health insurance and health-care facilities, and to prevent any discrimination on internationally prohibited grounds in the provision of health care and health services, especially with respect to the core obligations of the right to health.[16] Inappropriate health resource allocation can lead to discrimination that may not be overt. For example, investments should not disproportionately favour expensive curative health services which are often accessible only to a small, privileged fraction of the population, rather than primary and preventive health care benefiting a far larger part of the population.

Gender perspective

20. The Committee recommends that States integrate a gender perspective in their health-related policies, planning, programmes and research in order to promote better health for both women and men. A gender-based approach recognizes that biological and socio-cultural factors play a significant role in influencing the health of men and women. The disaggregation of health and socio-economic data according to sex is essential for identifying and remedying inequalities in health.

Women and the right to health

21. To eliminate discrimination against women, there is a need to develop and implement a comprehensive national strategy for promoting women's right to health throughout their life span. Such a strategy should include interventions aimed at the prevention and treatment of diseases affecting women, as well as policies to provide access to a full range of high quality

---

16   For the core obligations, see paras. 43 and 44 of the present General Comments.

and affordable health care, including sexual and reproductive services. A major goal should be reducing women's health risks, particularly lowering rates of maternal mortality and protecting women from domestic violence. The realization of women's right to health requires the removal of all barriers interfering with access to health services, education and information, including in the area of sexual and reproductive health. It is also important to undertake preventive, promotive and remedial action to shield women from the impact of harmful traditional cultural practices and norms that deny them their full reproductive rights.

Children and adolescents

22. Article 12.2 (a) outlines the need to take measures to reduce infant mortality and promote the healthy development of infants and children. Subsequent international human rights instruments recognize that children and adolescents have the right to the enjoyment of the highest standard of health and access to facilities for the treatment of illness.[17]

The Convention on the Rights of the Child directs States to ensure access to essential health services for the child and his or her family, including pre- and post-natal care for mothers. The Convention links these goals with ensuring access to child-friendly information about preventive and health-promoting behaviour and support to families and communities in implementing these practices. Implementation of the principle of non-discrimination requires that girls, as well as boys, have equal access to adequate nutrition, safe environments, and physical as well as mental health services. There is a need to adopt effective and appropriate measures to abolish harmful traditional practices affecting the health of children, particularly girls, including early marriage, female genital mutilation, preferential feeding and care of male children.[18] Children with disabilities should be given the opportunity to enjoy a fulfilling and decent life and to participate within their community.

23. States parties should provide a safe and supportive environment for adolescents, that ensures the opportunity to participate in decisions affecting their health, to build life-skills, to acquire appropriate information, to receive counselling and to negotiate the health-behaviour choices they make. The realization of the right to health of adolescents is dependent on the development of youth-friendly health care, which respects confidentiality and privacy and includes appropriate sexual and reproductive health services.

24. In all policies and programmes aimed at guaranteeing the right to health of children and adolescents their best interests shall be a primary consideration.

---

17   Article 24.1 of the Convention on the Rights of the Child.
18   See World Health Assembly resolution WHA47.10, 1994, entitled "Maternal and child health and family planning: traditional practices harmful to the health of women and children".

Older persons

25. With regard to the realization of the right to health of older persons, the Committee, in accordance with paragraphs 34 and 35 of General Comment No. 6 (1995), reaffirms the importance of an integrated approach, combining elements of preventive, curative and rehabilitative health treatment. Such measures should be based on periodical check-ups for both sexes; physical as well as psychological rehabilitative measures aimed at maintaining the functionality and autonomy of older persons; and attention and care for chronically and terminally ill persons, sparing them avoidable pain and enabling them to die with dignity.

Persons with disabilities

26. The Committee reaffirms paragraph 34 of its General Comment No. 5, which addresses the issue of persons with disabilities in the context of the right to physical and mental health. Moreover, the Committee stresses the need to ensure that not only the public health sector but also private providers of health services and facilities comply with the principle of non-discrimination in relation to persons with disabilities.

Indigenous peoples

27. In the light of emerging international law and practice and the recent measures taken by States in relation to indigenous peoples,[19] the Committee deems it useful to identify elements that would help to define indigenous peoples' right to health in order better to enable States with indigenous peoples to implement the provisions contained in article 12 of the Covenant. The Committee considers that indigenous peoples have the right to specific measures to improve their access to health services and care. These health services should be culturally appropriate, taking into account traditional preventive care, healing practices and medicines. States should provide resources for indigenous peoples to design, deliver and control such services so that they may enjoy the highest attainable standard of physical and mental health. The vital medicinal plants, animals and minerals necessary to the full enjoyment of health of indigenous peoples should also be protected. The Committee notes that, in indigenous com-

---

19   Recent emerging international norms relevant to indigenous peoples include the ILO Convention No. 169 concerning Indigenous and Tribal Peoples in Independent Countries (1989); articles 29 (c) and (d) and 30 of the Convention on the Rights of the Child (1989); article 8 (j) of the Convention on Biological Diversity (1992), recommending that States respect, preserve and maintain knowledge, innovation and practices of indigenous communities; Agenda 21 of the United Nations Conference on Environment and Development (1992), in particular chapter 26; and Part I, paragraph 20, of the Vienna Declaration and Programme of Action (1993), stating that States should take concerted positive steps to ensure respect for all human rights of indigenous people, on the basis of non-discrimination. See also the preamble and article 3 of the United Nations Framework Convention on Climate Change (1992); and article 10 (2) (e) of the United Nations Convention to Combat Desertification in Countries Experiencing Serious Drought and/or Desertification, Particularly in Africa (1994). During recent years an increasing number of States have changed their constitutions and introduced legislation recognizing specific rights of indigenous peoples.

munities, the health of the individual is often linked to the health of the society as a whole and has a collective dimension. In this respect, the Committee considers that development-related activities that lead to the displacement of indigenous peoples against their will from their traditional territories and environment, denying them their sources of nutrition and breaking their symbiotic relationship with their lands, has a deleterious effect on their health.

Limitations

28. Issues of public health are sometimes used by States as grounds for limiting the exercise of other fundamental rights. The Committee wishes to emphasize that the Covenant's limitation clause, article 4, is primarily intended to protect the rights of individuals rather than to permit the imposition of limitations by States. Consequently a State party which, for example, restricts the movement of, or incarcerates, persons with transmissible diseases such as HIV/AIDS, refuses to allow doctors to treat persons believed to be opposed to a government, or fails to provide immunization against the community's major infectious diseases, on grounds such as national security or the preservation of public order, has the burden of justifying such serious measures in relation to each of the elements identified in article 4. Such restrictions must be in accordance with the law, including international human rights standards, compatible with the nature of the rights protected by the Covenant, in the interest of legitimate aims pursued, and strictly necessary for the promotion of the general welfare in a democratic society.

29. In line with article 5.1, such limitations must be proportional, i.e. the least restrictive alternative must be adopted where several types of limitations are available. Even where such limitations on grounds of protecting public health are basically permitted, they should be of limited duration and subject to review.

II. States Parties' Obligations

General legal obligations

30. While the Covenant provides for progressive realization and acknowledges the constraints due to the limits of available resources, it also imposes on States parties various obligations which are of immediate effect. States parties have immediate obligations in relation to the right to health, such as the guarantee that the right will be exercised without discrimination of any kind (art. 2.2) and the obligation to take steps (art. 2.1) towards the full realization of article 12. Such steps must be deliberate, concrete and targeted towards the full realization of the right to health.[20]

31. The progressive realization of the right to health over a period of time should not be interpreted as depriving States parties' obligations of all meaningful content. Rather, progressive

---

20   See General Comment No. 13, para. 43.

realization means that States parties have a specific and continuing obligation to move as expeditiously and effectively as possible towards the full realization of article 12.[21]

32. As with all other rights in the Covenant, there is a strong presumption that retrogressive measures taken in relation to the right to health are not permissible. If any deliberately retrogressive measures are taken, the State party has the burden of proving that they have been introduced after the most careful consideration of all alternatives and that they are duly justified by reference to the totality of the rights provided for in the Covenant in the context of the full use of the State party's maximum available resources.[22]

33. The right to health, like all human rights, imposes three types or levels of obligations on States parties: the obligations to respect, protect and fulfil. In turn, the obligation to fulfil contains obligations to facilitate, provide and promote.[23] The obligation to respect requires States to refrain from interfering directly or indirectly with the enjoyment of the right to health. The obligation to protect requires States to take measures that prevent third parties from interfering with article 12 guarantees. Finally, the obligation to fulfil requires States to adopt appropriate legislative, administrative, budgetary, judicial, promotional and other measures towards the full realization of the right to health.

Specific legal obligations

34. In particular, States are under the obligation to respect the right to health by, inter alia, refraining from denying or limiting equal access for all persons, including prisoners or detainees, minorities, asylum seekers and illegal immigrants, to preventive, curative and palliative health services; abstaining from enforcing discriminatory practices as a State policy; and abstaining from imposing discriminatory practices relating to women's health status and needs. Furthermore, obligations to respect include a State's obligation to refrain from prohibiting or impeding traditional preventive care, healing practices and medicines, from marketing unsafe drugs and from applying coercive medical treatments, unless on an exceptional basis for the treatment of mental illness or the prevention and control of communicable diseases. Such exceptional cases should be subject to specific and restrictive conditions, respecting best practices and applicable international standards, including the Principles for the Protection of Persons with Mental Illness and the Improvement of Mental Health Care.[24]

In addition, States should refrain from limiting access to contraceptives and other means of maintaining sexual and reproductive health, from censoring, withholding or intentionally misrepresenting health-related information, including sexual education and information, as

---

21 See General Comment No. 3, para. 9; General Comment No. 13, para. 44.
22 See General Comment No. 3, para. 9; General Comment No. 13, para. 45.
23 According to General Comments Nos. 12 and 13, the obligation to fulfil incorporates an obligation to facilitate and an obligation to provide. In the present General Comment, the obligation to fulfil also incorporates an obligation to promote because of the critical importance of health promotion in the work of WHO and elsewhere.
24 General Assembly resolution 46/119 (1991).

well as from preventing people's participation in health-related matters. States should also refrain from unlawfully polluting air, water and soil, e.g. through industrial waste from State-owned facilities, from using or testing nuclear, biological or chemical weapons if such testing results in the release of substances harmful to human health, and from limiting access to health services as a punitive measure, e.g. during armed conflicts in violation of international humanitarian law.

35. Obligations to protect include, inter alia, the duties of States to adopt legislation or to take other measures ensuring equal access to health care and health-related services provided by third parties; to ensure that privatization of the health sector does not constitute a threat to the availability, accessibility, acceptability and quality of health facilities, goods and services; to control the marketing of medical equipment and medicines by third parties; and to ensure that medical practitioners and other health professionals meet appropriate standards of education, skill and ethical codes of conduct. States are also obliged to ensure that harmful social or traditional practices do not interfere with access to pre- and post-natal care and family-planning; to prevent third parties from coercing women to undergo traditional practices, e.g. female genital mutilation; and to take measures to protect all vulnerable or marginalized groups of society, in particular women, children, adolescents and older persons, in the light of gender-based expressions of violence. States should also ensure that third parties do not limit people's access to health-related information and services.

36. The obligation to fulfil requires States parties, inter alia, to give sufficient recognition to the right to health in the national political and legal systems, preferably by way of legislative implementation, and to adopt a national health policy with a detailed plan for realizing the right to health. States must ensure provision of health care, including immunization programmes against the major infectious diseases, and ensure equal access for all to the underlying determinants of health, such as nutritiously safe food and potable drinking water, basic sanitation and adequate housing and living conditions. Public health infrastructures should provide for sexual and reproductive health services, including safe motherhood, particularly in rural areas. States have to ensure the appropriate training of doctors and other medical personnel, the provision of a sufficient number of hospitals, clinics and other health-related facilities, and the promotion and support of the establishment of institutions providing counselling and mental health services, with due regard to equitable distribution throughout the country. Further obligations include the provision of a public, private or mixed health insurance system which is affordable for all, the promotion of medical research and health education, as well as information campaigns, in particular with respect to HIV/AIDS, sexual and reproductive health, traditional practices, domestic violence, the abuse of alcohol and the use of cigarettes, drugs and other harmful substances. States are also required to adopt measures against environmental and occupational health hazards and against any other threat as demonstrated by epidemiological data. For this purpose they should formulate and implement national policies aimed at reducing and eliminating pollution of air, water and soil, including pollution by heavy metals such as lead from gasoline. Furthermore, States parties are required to formulate, implement and periodically

review a coherent national policy to minimize the risk of occupational accidents and diseases, as well as to provide a coherent national policy on occupational safety and health services.[25]

37. The obligation to fulfil (facilitate) requires States inter alia to take positive measures that enable and assist individuals and communities to enjoy the right to health. States parties are also obliged to fulfil (provide) a specific right contained in the Covenant when individuals or a group are unable, for reasons beyond their control, to realize that right themselves by the means at their disposal. The obligation to fulfil (promote) the right to health requires States to undertake actions that create, maintain and restore the health of the population. Such obligations include: (i) fostering recognition of factors favouring positive health results, e.g. research and provision of information; (ii) ensuring that health services are culturally appropriate and that health care staff are trained to recognize and respond to the specific needs of vulnerable or marginalized groups; (iii) ensuring that the State meets its obligations in the dissemination of appropriate information relating to healthy lifestyles and nutrition, harmful traditional practices and the availability of services; (iv) supporting people in making informed choices about their health.

International obligations

38. In its General Comment No. 3, the Committee drew attention to the obligation of all States parties to take steps, individually and through international assistance and cooperation, especially economic and technical, towards the full realization of the rights recognized in the Covenant, such as the right to health. In the spirit of article 56 of the Charter of the United Nations, the specific provisions of the Covenant (articles 12, 2.1, 22 and 23) and the Alma-Ata Declaration on primary health care, States parties should recognize the essential role of international cooperation and comply with their commitment to take joint and separate action to achieve the full realization of the right to health. In this regard, States parties are referred to the Alma-Ata Declaration which proclaims that the existing gross inequality in the health status of the people, particularly between developed and developing countries, as well as within countries, is politically, socially and economically unacceptable and is, therefore, of common concern to all countries.[26]

---

25 Elements of such a policy are the identification, determination, authorization and control of dangerous materials, equipment, substances, agents and work processes; the provision of health information to workers and the provision, if needed, of adequate protective clothing and equipment; the enforcement of laws and regulations through adequate inspection; the requirement of notification of occupational accidents and diseases, the conduct of inquiries into serious accidents and diseases, and the production of annual statistics; the protection of workers and their representatives from disciplinary measures for actions properly taken by them in conformity with such a policy; and the provision of occupational health services with essentially preventive functions. See ILO Occupational Safety and Health Convention, 1981 (No. 155) and Occupational Health Services Convention, 1985 (No. 161).

26 Article II, Alma-Ata Declaration, Report of the International Conference on Primary Health Care, Alma-Ata, 6-12 September 1978, in: World Health Organization, "Health for All" Series, No. 1, WHO, Geneva, 1978.

39. To comply with their international obligations in relation to article 12, States parties have to respect the enjoyment of the right to health in other countries, and to prevent third parties from violating the right in other countries, if they are able to influence these third parties by way of legal or political means, in accordance with the Charter of the United Nations and applicable international law. Depending on the availability of resources, States should facilitate access to essential health facilities, goods and services in other countries, wherever possible and provide the necessary aid when required.[27] States parties should ensure that the right to health is given due attention in international agreements and, to that end, should consider the development of further legal instruments. In relation to the conclusion of other international agreements, States parties should take steps to ensure that these instruments do not adversely impact upon the right to health. Similarly, States parties have an obligation to ensure that their actions as members of international organizations take due account of the right to health. Accordingly, States parties which are members of international financial institutions, notably the International Monetary Fund, the World Bank, and regional development banks, should pay greater attention to the protection of the right to health in influencing the lending policies, credit agreements and international measures of these institutions.

40. States parties have a joint and individual responsibility, in accordance with the Charter of the United Nations and relevant resolutions of the United Nations General Assembly and of the World Health Assembly, to cooperate in providing disaster relief and humanitarian assistance in times of emergency, including assistance to refugees and internally displaced persons. Each State should contribute to this task to the maximum of its capacities. Priority in the provision of international medical aid, distribution and management of resources, such as safe and potable water, food and medical supplies, and financial aid should be given to the most vulnerable or marginalized groups of the population. Moreover, given that some diseases are easily transmissible beyond the frontiers of a State, the international community has a collective responsibility to address this problem. The economically developed States parties have a special responsibility and interest to assist the poorer developing States in this regard.

41. States parties should refrain at all times from imposing embargoes or similar measures restricting the supply of another State with adequate medicines and medical equipment. Restrictions on such goods should never be used as an instrument of political and economic pressure. In this regard, the Committee recalls its position, stated in General Comment No. 8, on the relationship between economic sanctions and respect for economic, social and cultural rights.

42. While only States are parties to the Covenant and thus ultimately accountable for compliance with it, all members of society – individuals, including health professionals, families, local communities, intergovernmental and non-governmental organizations, civil society organizations, as well as the private business sector – have responsibilities regarding the realization of the right to health. State parties should therefore provide an environment which facilitates the discharge of these responsibilities.

---

27   See para. 45 of this General Comment.

Core obligations

43. In General Comment No. 3, the Committee confirms that States parties have a core obligation to ensure the satisfaction of, at the very least, minimum essential levels of each of the rights enunciated in the Covenant, including essential primary health care. Read in conjunction with more contemporary instruments, such as the Programme of Action of the International Conference on Population and Development,[28] the Alma-Ata Declaration provides compelling guidance on the core obligations arising from article 12. Accordingly, in the Committee's view, these core obligations include at least the following obligations:

(a) To ensure the right of access to health facilities, goods and services on a non-discriminatory basis, especially for vulnerable or marginalized groups;
(b) To ensure access to the minimum essential food which is nutritionally adequate and safe, to ensure freedom from hunger to everyone;
(c) To ensure access to basic shelter, housing and sanitation, and an adequate supply of safe and potable water;
(d) To provide essential drugs, as from time to time defined under the WHO Action Programme on Essential Drugs;
(e) To ensure equitable distribution of all health facilities, goods and services;
(f) To adopt and implement a national public health strategy and plan of action, on the basis of epidemiological evidence, addressing the health concerns of the whole population; the strategy and plan of action shall be devised, and periodically reviewed, on the basis of a participatory and transparent process; they shall include methods, such as right to health indicators and benchmarks, by which progress can be closely monitored; the process by which the strategy and plan of action are devised, as well as their content, shall give particular attention to all vulnerable or marginalized groups.

44. The Committee also confirms that the following are obligations of comparable priority:

(a) To ensure reproductive, maternal (pre-natal as well as post-natal) and child health care;
(b) To provide immunization against the major infectious diseases occurring in the community;
(c) To take measures to prevent, treat and control epidemic and endemic diseases;
(d) To provide education and access to information concerning the main health problems in the community, including methods of preventing and controlling them;
(e) To provide appropriate training for health personnel, including education on health and human rights.

45. For the avoidance of any doubt, the Committee wishes to emphasize that it is particularly incumbent on States parties and other actors in a position to assist, to provide "international

---

28   Report of the International Conference on Population and Development, Cairo, 5-13 September 1994 (United Nations publication, Sales No. E.95.XIII.18), chap. I, resolution 1, annex, chaps. VII and VIII.

assistance and cooperation, especially economic and technical"[29] which enable developing countries to fulfil their core and other obligations indicated in paragraphs 43 and 44 above.

III. Violations

46. When the normative content of article 12 (Part I) is applied to the obligations of States parties (Part II), a dynamic process is set in motion which facilitates identification of violations of the right to health. The following paragraphs provide illustrations of violations of article 12.

47. In determining which actions or omissions amount to a violation of the right to health, it is important to distinguish the inability from the unwillingness of a State party to comply with its obligations under article 12. This follows from article 12.1, which speaks of the highest attainable standard of health, as well as from article 2.1 of the Covenant, which obliges each State party to take the necessary steps to the maximum of its available resources. A State which is unwilling to use the maximum of its available resources for the realization of the right to health is in violation of its obligations under article 12. If resource constraints render it impossible for a State to comply fully with its Covenant obligations, it has the burden of justifying that every effort has nevertheless been made to use all available resources at its disposal in order to satisfy, as a matter of priority, the obligations outlined above. It should be stressed, however, that a State party cannot, under any circumstances whatsoever, justify its non-compliance with the core obligations set out in paragraph 43 above, which are non-derogable.

48. Violations of the right to health can occur through the direct action of States or other entities insufficiently regulated by States. The adoption of any retrogressive measures incompatible with the core obligations under the right to health, outlined in paragraph 43 above, constitutes a violation of the right to health. Violations through acts of commission include the formal repeal or suspension of legislation necessary for the continued enjoyment of the right to health or the adoption of legislation or policies which are manifestly incompatible with pre-existing domestic or international legal obligations in relation to the right to health.

49. Violations of the right to health can also occur through the omission or failure of States to take necessary measures arising from legal obligations. Violations through acts of omission include the failure to take appropriate steps towards the full realization of everyone's right to the enjoyment of the highest attainable standard of physical and mental health, the failure to have a national policy on occupational safety and health as well as occupational health services, and the failure to enforce relevant laws.

Violations of the obligation to respect

50. Violations of the obligation to respect are those State actions, policies or laws that contravene the standards set out in article 12 of the Covenant and are likely to result in bodily harm, unnecessary morbidity and preventable mortality. Examples include the denial of access to

---

29   Covenant, art. 2.1.

health facilities, goods and services to particular individuals or groups as a result of de jure or de facto discrimination; the deliberate withholding or misrepresentation of information vital to health protection or treatment; the suspension of legislation or the adoption of laws or policies that interfere with the enjoyment of any of the components of the right to health; and the failure of the State to take into account its legal obligations regarding the right to health when entering into bilateral or multilateral agreements with other States, international organizations and other entities, such as multinational corporations.

Violations of the obligation to protect

51. Violations of the obligation to protect follow from the failure of a State to take all necessary measures to safeguard persons within their jurisdiction from infringements of the right to health by third parties. This category includes such omissions as the failure to regulate the activities of individuals, groups or corporations so as to prevent them from violating the right to health of others; the failure to protect consumers and workers from practices detrimental to health, e.g. by employers and manufacturers of medicines or food; the failure to discourage production, marketing and consumption of tobacco, narcotics and other harmful substances; the failure to protect women against violence or to prosecute perpetrators; the failure to discourage the continued observance of harmful traditional medical or cultural practices; and the failure to enact or enforce laws to prevent the pollution of water, air and soil by extractive and manufacturing industries.

Violations of the obligation to fulfil

52. Violations of the obligation to fulfil occur through the failure of States parties to take all necessary steps to ensure the realization of the right to health. Examples include the failure to adopt or implement a national health policy designed to ensure the right to health for everyone; insufficient expenditure or misallocation of public resources which results in the non-enjoyment of the right to health by individuals or groups, particularly the vulnerable or marginalized; the failure to monitor the realization of the right to health at the national level, for example by identifying right to health indicators and benchmarks; the failure to take measures to reduce the inequitable distribution of health facilities, goods and services; the failure to adopt a gender-sensitive approach to health; and the failure to reduce infant and maternal mortality rates.

IV. Implementation at the National Level

Framework legislation

53. The most appropriate feasible measures to implement the right to health will vary significantly from one State to another. Every State has a margin of discretion in assessing which measures are most suitable to meet its specific circumstances. The Covenant, however, clearly imposes a duty on each State to take whatever steps are necessary to ensure that everyone has access to health facilities, goods and services so that they can enjoy, as soon as possible, the highest attainable standard of physical and mental health. This requires the adoption of a

national strategy to ensure to all the enjoyment of the right to health, based on human rights principles which define the objectives of that strategy, and the formulation of policies and corresponding right to health indicators and benchmarks. The national health strategy should also identify the resources available to attain defined objectives, as well as the most cost-effective way of using those resources.

54. The formulation and implementation of national health strategies and plans of action should respect, inter alia, the principles of non-discrimination and people's participation. In particular, the right of individuals and groups to participate in decision-making processes, which may affect their development, must be an integral component of any policy, programme or strategy developed to discharge governmental obligations under article 12. Promoting health must involve effective community action in setting priorities, making decisions, planning, implementing and evaluating strategies to achieve better health. Effective provision of health services can only be assured if people's participation is secured by States.

55. The national health strategy and plan of action should also be based on the principles of accountability, transparency and independence of the judiciary, since good governance is essential to the effective implementation of all human rights, including the realization of the right to health. In order to create a favourable climate for the realization of the right, States parties should take appropriate steps to ensure that the private business sector and civil society are aware of, and consider the importance of, the right to health in pursuing their activities.

56. States should consider adopting a framework law to operationalize their right to health national strategy. The framework law should establish national mechanisms for monitoring the implementation of national health strategies and plans of action. It should include provisions on the targets to be achieved and the time-frame for their achievement; the means by which right to health benchmarks could be achieved; the intended collaboration with civil society, including health experts, the private sector and international organizations; institutional responsibility for the implementation of the right to health national strategy and plan of action; and possible recourse procedures. In monitoring progress towards the realization of the right to health, States parties should identify the factors and difficulties affecting implementation of their obligations.

Right to health indicators and benchmarks

57. National health strategies should identify appropriate right to health indicators and benchmarks. The indicators should be designed to monitor, at the national and international levels, the State party's obligations under article 12. States may obtain guidance on appropriate right to health indicators, which should address different aspects of the right to health, from the ongoing work of WHO and the United Nations Children's Fund (UNICEF) in this field. Right to health indicators require disaggregation on the prohibited grounds of discrimination.

58. Having identified appropriate right to health indicators, States parties are invited to set appropriate national benchmarks in relation to each indicator. During the periodic reporting

procedure the Committee will engage in a process of scoping with the State party. Scoping involves the joint consideration by the State party and the Committee of the indicators and national benchmarks which will then provide the targets to be achieved during the next reporting period. In the following five years, the State party will use these national benchmarks to help monitor its implementation of article 12. Thereafter, in the subsequent reporting process, the State party and the Committee will consider whether or not the benchmarks have been achieved, and the reasons for any difficulties that may have been encountered.

Remedies and accountability

59. Any person or group victim of a violation of the right to health should have access to effective judicial or other appropriate remedies at both national and international levels.[30] All victims of such violations should be entitled to adequate reparation, which may take the form of restitution, compensation, satisfaction or guarantees of non-repetition. National ombudsmen, human rights commissions, consumer forums, patients' rights associations or similar institutions should address violations of the right to health.

60. The incorporation in the domestic legal order of international instruments recognizing the right to health can significantly enhance the scope and effectiveness of remedial measures and should be encouraged in all cases.[31] Incorporation enables courts to adjudicate violations of the right to health, or at least its core obligations, by direct reference to the Covenant.

61. Judges and members of the legal profession should be encouraged by States parties to pay greater attention to violations of the right to health in the exercise of their functions.

62. States parties should respect, protect, facilitate and promote the work of human rights advocates and other members of civil society with a view to assisting vulnerable or marginalized groups in the realization of their right to health.

V. Obligations of Actors other than States Parties

63. The role of the United Nations agencies and programmes, and in particular the key function assigned to WHO in realizing the right to health at the international, regional and country levels, is of particular importance, as is the function of UNICEF in relation to the right to health of children. When formulating and implementing their right to health national strategies, States parties should avail themselves of technical assistance and cooperation of WHO. Further, when preparing their reports, States parties should utilize the extensive information and advisory

---

30 Regardless of whether groups as such can seek remedies as distinct holders of rights, States parties are bound by both the collective and individual dimensions of article 12. Collective rights are critical in the field of health; modern public health policy relies heavily on prevention and promotion which are approaches directed primarily to groups.

31 See General Comment No. 2, para. 9.

services of WHO with regard to data collection, disaggregation, and the development of right to health indicators and benchmarks.

64. Moreover, coordinated efforts for the realization of the right to health should be maintained to enhance the interaction among all the actors concerned, including the various components of civil society. In conformity with articles 22 and 23 of the Covenant, WHO, The International Labour Organization, the United Nations Development Programme, UNICEF, the United Nations Population Fund, the World Bank, regional development banks, the International Monetary Fund, the World Trade Organization and other relevant bodies within the United Nations system, should cooperate effectively with States parties, building on their respective expertise, in relation to the implementation of the right to health at the national level, with due respect to their individual mandates. In particular, the international financial institutions, notably the World Bank and the International Monetary Fund, should pay greater attention to the protection of the right to health in their lending policies, credit agreements and structural adjustment programmes. When examining the reports of States parties and their ability to meet the obligations under article 12, the Committee will consider the effects of the assistance provided by all other actors. The adoption of a human rights-based approach by United Nations specialized agencies, programmes and bodies will greatly facilitate implementation of the right to health. In the course of its examination of States parties' reports, the Committee will also consider the role of health professional associations and other non-governmental organizations in relation to the States' obligations under article 12.

65. The role of WHO, the Office of the United Nations High Commissioner for Refugees, the International Committee of the Red Cross/Red Crescent and UNICEF, as well as non governmental organizations and national medical associations, is of particular importance in relation to disaster relief and humanitarian assistance in times of emergencies, including assistance to refugees and internally displaced persons. Priority in the provision of international medical aid, distribution and management of resources, such as safe and potable water, food and medical supplies, and financial aid should be given to the most vulnerable or marginalized groups of the population.

1.4. ILO C130 Medical Care and Sickness Benefits Convention, 1969

ARTICLE 7

The contingencies covered shall include:

(a) need for medical care of a curative nature and, under prescribed conditions, need for medical care of a preventive nature;

...

Part II. Medical Care

ARTICLE 8

Each Member shall secure to the persons protected, subject to prescribed conditions, the provision of medical care of a curative or preventive nature in respect of the contingency referred to in subparagraph (a) of Article 7.

ARTICLE 9

The medical care referred to in Article 8 shall be afforded with a view to maintaining, restoring or improving the health of the person protected and his ability to work and to attend to his personal needs.

ARTICLE 10

The persons protected in respect of the contingency referred to in subparagraph (a) of Article 7 shall comprise:

(a) all employees, including apprentices, and the wives and children of such employees; or
(b) prescribed classes of the economically active population, constituting not less than 75 per cent of the whole economically active population, and the wives and children of persons in the said classes; or
(c) prescribed classes of residents constituting not less than 75 per cent of all residents.

ARTICLE 13

The medical care referred to in Article 8 shall comprise at least:

(a) general practitioner care, including domiciliary visiting;
(b) specialist care at hospitals for in-patients and out-patients, and such specialist care as may be available outside hospitals;

(c) the necessary pharmaceutical supplies on prescription by medical or other qualified practitioners;

(d) hospitalisation where necessary;

(e) dental care, as prescribed; and

(f) medical rehabilitation, including the supply, maintenance and renewal of prosthetic and orthopaedic appliances, as prescribed.

1.5. International Convention on the Elimination of all forms of Racial Discrimination

ARTICLE 5

… States Parties undertake to prohibit and to eliminate racial discrimination in all its forms and to guarantee the right of everyone, without distinction as to race, colour, or national or ethnic origin, to equality before the law, notably in the enjoyment of the following rights:

…

(e) Economic, social and cultural rights, in particular:

(iv) The right to public health, medical care, social security and social services;

1.6. International Convention on the Protection of the Rights of All Migrant Workers and Members of their Families (1990)

ARTICLE 28

Migrant workers and members of their families shall have the right to receive any medical care that is urgently required for the preservation of their life or the avoidance of irreparable harm to their health on the basis of equality of treatment with nationals of the State concerned. Such emergency medical care shall not be refused them by reason of any irregularity with regard to stay or employment.

1.7. Universal Declaration Bioethics UNESCO (2005)

ARTICLE 14. SOCIAL RESPONSIBILITY AND HEALTH

1. The promotion of health and social development for their people is a central purpose of governments that all sectors of society share.

2. Taking into account that the enjoyment of the highest attainable standard of health is one of the fundamental rights of every human being without distinction of race, religion, political belief, economic or social condition, progress in science and technology should advance:

(a) access to quality health care and essential medicines, especially for the health of women and children, because health is essential to life itself and must be considered to be a social and human good;
(b) access to adequate nutrition and water;
(c) improvement of living conditions and the environment;
(d) elimination of the marginalization and the exclusion of persons on the basis of any grounds;
(e) reduction of poverty and illiteracy.

1.8. European Social Charter (1961)

ARTICLE 11. THE RIGHT TO PROTECTION OF HEALTH

With a view to ensuring the effective exercise of the right to protection of health, the Contracting Parties undertake, either directly or in co operation with public or private organisations, to take appropriate measures designed inter alia:

1 to remove as far as possible the causes of ill health;
2 to provide advisory and educational facilities for the promotion of health and the encouragement of individual responsibility in matters of health;
3 to prevent as far as possible epidemic, endemic and other diseases.

ARTICLE 13. THE RIGHT TO SOCIAL AND MEDICAL ASSISTANCE

With a view to ensuring the effective exercise of the right to social and medical assistance, the Contracting Parties undertake:

1 to ensure that any person who is without adequate resources and who is unable to secure such resources either by his own efforts or from other sources, in particular by benefits under a social security scheme, be granted adequate assistance, and, in case of sickness, the care necessitated by his condition;
2 to ensure that persons receiving such assistance shall not, for that reason, suffer from a diminution of their political or social rights;
3 to provide that everyone may receive by appropriate public or private services such advice and personal help as may be required to prevent, to remove, or to alleviate personal or family want;
4 to apply the provisions referred to in paragraphs 1, 2 and 3 of this article on an equal footing with their nationals to nationals of other Contracting Parties lawfully within their territories, in accordance with their obligations under the European Convention on Social and Medical Assistance, signed at Paris on 11th December 1953.

1.9. European Social Charter (Revised), 1996, ETS No. 163

ARTICLE 11. THE RIGHT TO PROTECTION OF HEALTH

With a view to ensuring the effective exercise of the right to protection of health, the Parties undertake, either directly or in co operation with public or private organisations, to take appropriate measures designed inter alia:

1 to remove as far as possible the causes of ill health;
2 to provide advisory and educational facilities for the promotion of health and the encouragement of individual responsibility in matters of health;
3 to prevent as far as possible epidemic, endemic and other diseases, as well as accidents.

ARTICLE 13. THE RIGHT TO SOCIAL AND MEDICAL ASSISTANCE

With a view to ensuring the effective exercise of the right to social and medical assistance, the Parties undertake:

1 to ensure that any person who is without adequate resources and who is unable to secure such resources either by his own efforts or from other sources, in particular by benefits under a social security scheme, be granted adequate assistance, and, in case of sickness, the care necessitated by his condition;
2 to ensure that persons receiving such assistance shall not, for that reason, suffer from a diminution of their political or social rights;
3 to provide that everyone may receive by appropriate public or private services such advice and personal help as may be required to prevent, to remove, or to alleviate personal or family want;
4 to apply the provisions referred to in paragraphs 1, 2 and 3 of this article on an equal footing with their nationals to nationals of other Parties lawfully within their territories, in accordance with their obligations under the European Convention on Social and Medical Assistance, signed at Paris on 11 December 1953.

1.10. European Code of Social Security (Revised)

Rome, 6.XI.1990, ETS No. 139

Part II – Medical care

ARTICLE 8

The contingency covered shall comprise the need for medical care of a curative nature and, under prescribed conditions, the need for medical care of a preventive nature.

ARTICLE 10

1   Medical care shall comprise:

    a general practitioner care and specialist care, inside or outside hospitals, including the necessary diagnoses and tests, as well as domiciliary visits;

    b care provided by a member of a profession legally recognised as allied to the medical profession, under the supervision of a medical or other qualified practitioner;

    c the provision of the necessary pharmaceutical supplies on prescription by a medical practitioner or other qualified practitioner;

    d maintenance in a hospital or any other medical institution;

    e dental care including the necessary dental prostheses;

    f medical rehabilitation, including the supply, maintenance and renewal of prosthetic and orthopaedic appliances as well as medical aids as may be prescribed;

    g transport of the patient as may be prescribed.

2   Where a Party's legislation requires the beneficiary or the beneficiary's breadwinner to share in the cost of medical care, the rules governing such cost sharing shall be such as not to impose hardship or render medical and social protection less effective.

3   Medical care shall aim at preserving, restoring or improving the health of the person protected and his ability to work and to meet his personal needs.

1.11. Explanatory report on the European Code of Social Security (Revised) 1998

Medical Care

ARTICLE 8

102. This provision reproduces Article 7 (a) of ILO Convention No. 130.

103. The contingency covered is the need for medical care by reason of a morbid state whether this results from an accident or disease.

104. The contingency does not extend to pregnancy, confinement or their sequelae, these being dealt with in Part VIII on maternity benefits.

105. The types of medical care of a curative nature that must be provided, and which represent minimum standards, are enumerated in Article 10.

106. The types of medical care of a preventive nature to be given to the persons protected are for national legislations to prescribe.

ARTICLE 10

123. This paragraph is based on Article 10, paragraph 1 of ILO Convention No. 121 and Article 13 of ILO Convention No. 130.

124. This paragraph shows a list of medical benefits that must be covered by the legislation of a Party that accepts the obligations laid down in Part II (medical care). Nonetheless, the paragraph leaves the Party freedom of policy with regard to the implementation of these standards, as the paragraph confines itself to indicating the nature of the medical care that must be covered, not to fixing a precise level of such benefits. However, the level of the benefits should be in accordance with what is generally recognized and accepted as good medical practice.

125. This means, for instance, that newly developing specialisms or specialist care that is not considered to be usual within the profession do not have to be included in the legislation of a Party. Furthermore, this article leaves the Party the possibility to restrict the provision of the treatment (i.e. by way of waiting list), or to limit the number of treatments subject to compliance with the provisions of paragraph 3 of the Article.

126. With regard to the provision of necessary pharmaceutical supplies, the word "necessary" indicates that not all medicines that are legally for sale in the territory of a Party must be provided under the national legislation. If there is a choice between a relatively cheap and a relatively expensive medicine, and both have equivalent pharmaceutical value for a certain treatment, a Party is allowed to provide only the cheaper one.

Paragraph 2

127. This paragraph is based on Article 17 of ILO Convention No. 130.

128. The European Code of Social Security permits by the beneficiary or the breadwinner of a share of the costs of the medical treatment of morbid conditions.

129. The Protocol lays down the upper limit of the share payable; it must not exceed 25% of the costs except in the case of routine dental care, for which it may be fixed at a maximum of 331/3%.

130. No precise figures for the degree of cost-sharing appear in the (revised) Code since the sharing of cost may vary for example according to whether it is calculated as a flat rate or as a proportion of the cost of the products and services. Cost-sharing may be higher than mentioned in the Protocol.

131. The concept of cost-sharing implies that part of the cost is borne by the insured person, which rules out the full burden of medical costs being borne by the person protected. This paragraph is designed to limit the beneficiaries' share: the financial burden must not impose hardship and so risk detracting from the effectiveness of medical and social protection. The risk is especially high for persons with chronic disease or destitute persons.

132. In overall terms, the risk of hardship can therefore be averted, for example, by limiting the insured person's share to an overall amount or a restricted number of medical benefits, by exempting certain groups, such as those receiving welfare assistance, from paying any share, or by drawing up a list of chronic and especially costly diseases whose treatment will be fully covered.

Paragraph 3

133. This paragraph reflects the main objectives assigned to the Parties who have accepted Part II (Medical care) of the (revised) Code and testifies to the importance of prevention and rehabilitation in this instrument.

134. Medical care should indeed be aimed at the simultaneous:

- prevention of the occurrence of any contingency covered by Article 8 of the (revised) Code;
- prevention of the worsening of the condition or situation of the person concerned, resulting from the occurrence of the contingency;
- improvement of the patient's state of health;
- reduction of the social and financial consequences of the occurrence of the contingency, in particular by implementing measures such as medical rehabilitation.

1.12. Convention for the Protection of Human Rights and Dignity of the Human Being with regard to the Application of Biology and Medicine: Convention on Human Rights and Biomedicine

Oviedo, 1997, European Treaty Series – No. 164

ARTICLE 3. EQUITABLE ACCESS TO HEALTH CARE

Parties, taking into account health needs and available resources, shall take appropriate measures with a view to providing, within their jurisdiction, equitable access to health care of appropriate quality.

Explanatory report

ARTICLE 3. EQUITABLE ACCESS TO HEALTH CARE

23. This article defines an aim and imposes an obligation on States to use their best endeavours to reach it.

24. The aim is to ensure equitable access to health care in accordance with the person's medical needs. "Health care" means the services offering diagnostic, preventive, therapeutic and rehabilitative interventions, designed to maintain or improve a person's state of health or alleviate a person's suffering. This care must be of a fitting standard in the light of scientific progress and be subject to a continuous quality assessment.

25. Access to health care must be equitable. In this context, "equitable" means first and foremost the absence of unjustified discrimination. Although not synonymous with absolute equality, equitable access implies effectively obtaining a satisfactory degree of care.

26. The Parties to the Convention are required to take appropriate steps to achieve this aim as far as the available resources permit. The purpose of this provision is not to create an individual right on which each person may rely in legal proceedings against the State, but rather to prompt the latter to adopt the requisite measures as part of its social policy in order to ensure equitable access to health care.

27. Although States are now making substantial efforts to ensure a satisfactory level of health care, the scale of this effort largely depends on the volume of available resources. Moreover, State measures to ensure equitable access may take many different forms and a wide variety of methods may be employed to this end.

1.13. Charter of Fundamental Rights of the European Union (2007/C 303/01)

Title IV. Solidarity

ARTICLE 34. SOCIAL SECURITY AND SOCIAL ASSISTANCE

1. The Union recognises and respects the entitlement to social security benefits and social services providing protection in cases such as maternity, illness, industrial accidents, dependency or old age, and in the case of loss of employment, in accordance with the rules laid down by Union law and national laws and practices.

2. Everyone residing and moving legally within the European Union is entitled to social security benefits and social advantages in accordance with Union law and national laws and practices.

3. ...

ARTICLE 35. HEALTH CARE

Everyone has the right of access to preventive health care and the right to benefit from medical treatment under the conditions established by national laws and practices. A high level of human health protection shall be ensured in the definition and implementation of all the Union's policies and activities.

1.14. Council Regulation (EC) No 1408/71 of 14 June 1971 on the application of social security schemes to employed persons, to self-employed persons and to members of their families moving within the Community (Consolidated version OJ No L 28 of 30. 1. 1997, p. 1 (OJ L 149, 5.7.1971, p. 2)

Title III. Special provisions relating to the various categories of benefits

Chapter I. Sickness and Maternity

Article 22 Stay outside the competent State – Return to or transfer of residence to another Member State during sickness or maternity —Need to go to another Member State in order to receive appropriate treatment

1. An employed or self-employed person who satisfies the conditions of the legislation of the competent State for entitlement to benefits, taking account where appropriate of the provisions of Article 18, and:

(a) whose condition requires benefits in kind which become necessary on medical grounds during a stay in the territory of another Member State, taking into account the nature of the benefits and the expected length of the stay;
(b) who, having become entitled to benefits chargeable to the competent institution, is authorized by that institution to return to the territory of the Member State where he resides, or to transfer his residence to the territory of another Member State; or
(c) who is authorized by the competent institution to go to the territory of another Member State to receive there the treatment appropriate to his condition, shall be entitled:
(i) to benefits in kind provided on behalf of the competent institution by the institution of the place of stay or residence in accordance with the provisions of the legislation which it administers, as though he were insured with it; the length of the period during which benefits are provided shall be governed, however, by the legislation of the competent State;
(ii) to cash benefits provided by the competent institution in accordance with the provisions of the legislation which it administers. However, by agreement between the competent institution and the institution of the place of stay or residence, such benefits may be provided by the latter institution on behalf of the former, in accordance with the provisions of the legislation of the competent State.

1a. The Administrative Commission shall establish a list of benefits in kind which, in order to be provided during a stay in another Member State, require, for practical reasons, a prior agreement between the person concerned and the institution providing the care;

2. The authorization required under paragraph 1 (b) may be refused only if it is established that movement of the person concerned would be prejudicial to his state of health or the receipt of medical treatment. The authorization required under paragraph 1 (c) may not be refused

where the treatment in question is among the benefits provided for by the legislation of the Member State on whose territory the person concerned resided and where he cannot be given such treatment within the time normally necessary for obtaining the treatment in question in the Member State of residence taking account of his current state of health and the probable course of the disease.

3. Paragraphs 1, 1a and 2 shall apply by analogy to members of the family of an employed or self-employed person. However, for the purpose of applying paragraph 1 (a) and (c) (i) to the members of the family referred to in Article 19 (2) who reside in the territory of a Member State other than the one in whose territory the employed or self-employed person resides:

(a) benefits in kind shall be provided on behalf of the institution of the Member State in whose territory the members of the family are residing by the institution of the place of stay in accordance with the provisions of the legislation which it administers as if the employed or self-employed person were insured there. The period during which benefits are provided shall, however, be that laid down under the legislation of the Member State in whose territory the members of the family are residing;
(b) the authorization required under paragraph 1 (c) shall be issued by the institution of the Member State in whose territory the members of the family are residing.

4. The fact that the provisions of paragraph 1 apply to an employed or self-employed person shall not affect the right to benefit of members of his family.

ARTICLE 22A. SPECIAL RULES FOR CERTAIN CATEGORIES OF PERSONS

Notwithstanding Article 2, Article 22(1)(a) and (c) and (1a) shall also apply to persons who are nationals of one of the Member States and who are insured under the legislation of a Member State and to the members of their families residing with them.

1.15. Regulation (EC) No 883/2004 of the European Parliament and of the Council of 29 April 2004 on the coordination of social security systems

Title III. Special provisions concerning the various categories of benefits

Chapter 1. Sickness, maternity and equivalent paternity benefits

Section 1. Insured persons and members of their families

ARTICLE 17. RESIDENCE IN A MEMBER STATE OTHER THAN THE COMPETENT MEMBER STATE

An insured person or members of his family who reside in a Member State other than the competent Member State shall receive in the Member State of residence benefits in kind provided, on behalf of the competent institution, by the institution of the place of residence, in accordance with the provisions of the legislation it applies, as though they were insured under the said legislation.

Article 18 Stay in the competent Member State when residence is in another Member State – Special rules for the members of the families of frontier workers

1. Unless otherwise provided for by paragraph 2, the insured person and the members of his family referred to in Article 17 shall also be entitled to benefits in kind while staying in the competent Member State. The benefits in kind shall be provided by the competent institution and at its own expense, in accordance with the provisions of the legislation it applies, as though the persons concerned resided in that Member State.

2. The members of the family of a frontier worker shall be entitled to benefits in kind during their stay in the competent Member State, unless this Member State is listed in Annex III. In this event, the members of the family of a frontier worker shall be entitled to benefits in kind in the competent Member State under the conditions laid down in Article 19(1).

ARTICLE 19. STAY OUTSIDE THE COMPETENT MEMBER STATE

1. Unless otherwise provided for by paragraph 2, an insured person and the members of his family staying in a Member State other than the competent Member State shall be entitled to the benefits in kind which become necessary on medical grounds during their stay, taking into account the nature of the benefits and the expected length of the stay. These benefits shall be provided on behalf of the competent institution by the institution of the place of stay, in accordance with the provisions of the legislation it applies, as though the persons concerned were insured under the said legislation.

2. The Administrative Commission shall establish a list of benefits in kind which, in order to be provided during a stay in another Member State, require for practical reasons a prior agreement between the person concerned and the institution providing the care.

Article 20. Travel with the purpose of receiving benefits in kind – Authorisation to receive appropriate treatment outside the Member State of residence

1. Unless otherwise provided for by this Regulation, an insured person travelling to another Member State with the purpose of receiving benefits in kind during the stay shall seek authorization from the competent institution.

2. An insured person who is authorised by the competent institution to go to another Member State with the purpose of receiving the treatment appropriate to his condition shall receive the benefits in kind provided, on behalf of the competent institution, by the institution of the place of stay, in accordance with the provisions of the legislation it applies, as though he were insured under the said legislation. The authorisation shall be accorded where the treatment in question is among the benefits provided for by the legislation in the Member State where the person concerned resides and where he cannot be given such treatment within a time-limit which is medically justifiable, taking into account his current state of health and the probable course of his illness.

3. Paragraphs 1 and 2 shall apply mutatis mutandis to the members of the family of an insured person.

4. If the members of the family of an insured person reside in a Member State other than the Member State in which the insured person resides, and this Member State has opted for reimbursement on the basis of fixed amounts, the cost of the benefits in kind referred to in paragraph 2 shall be borne by the institution of the place of residence of the members of the family. In this case, for the purposes of paragraph 1, the institution of the place of residence of the members of the family shall be considered to be the competent institution.

Article 21. Cash benefits

1. An insured person and members of his family residing or staying in a Member State other than the competent Member State shall be entitled to cash benefits provided by the competent institution in accordance with the legislation it applies. By agreement between the competent institution and the institution of the place of residence or stay, such benefits may, however, be provided by the institution of the place of residence or stay at the expense of the competent institution in accordance with the legislation of the competent Member State.

2. The competent institution of a Member State whose legislation stipulates that the calculation of cash benefits shall be based on average income or on an average contribution basis shall determine such average income or average contribution basis exclusively by reference to

the incomes confirmed as having been paid, or contribution bases applied, during the periods completed under the said legislation.

3. The competent institution of a Member State whose legislation provides that the calculation of cash benefits shall be based on standard income shall take into account exclusively the standard income or, where appropriate, the average of standard incomes for the periods completed under the said legislation.

4. Paragraphs 2 and 3 shall apply mutatis mutandis to cases where the legislation applied by the competent institution lays down a specific reference period which corresponds in the case in question either wholly or partly to the periods which the person concerned has completed under the legislation of one or more other Member States.

1.16. Proposal for a Directive of the European Parliament and of the Council on the application of patients' rights in cross-border healthcare. Commission of the European Communities

Brussels, 2.7.2008 COM(2008) 414 final 2008/0142

General Provision

ARTICLE I. AIM

This Directive establishes a general framework for the provision of safe, high quality and efficient cross-border healthcare.

ARTICLE 2. SCOPE

This Directive shall apply to provision of healthcare regardless of how it is organised, delivered and financed or whether it is public or private.

ARTICLE 3. RELATIONSHIP WITH OTHER COMMUNITY PROVISIONS

1. This Directive shall apply without prejudice to:

(a) Directive 95/46/EC on the protection of individuals with regard to the processing of personal data and on the free movement of such data and Directive 2002/58/EC concerning the processing of personal data and the protection of privacy in the electronic communications sector;

…

(c) Directive 2001/20/EC of the European Parliament and of the Council of 4 April 2001 on the approximation of the laws, regulations and administrative provisions of the Member States relating to the implementation of good clinical practice in the conduct of clinical trials on medicinal products for human use;

…

(e) Directive 2000/43/EC of the Council of 29 June 2000 implementing the principle of equal treatment between persons irrespective of racial or ethnic origin.

(f) Regulations on coordination of social security schemes, in particular Article 22 of Regulation (EC) No 1408/71 of the Council of 14 June 1971 on the application of social security schemes to employed persons and their families moving within the Community and Council Regulation (EC) No 883/2004 of the European Parliament and of the Council of 29 April 2004 on the coordination of social security systems.

...

2. When the circumstances under which an authorisation to go to another Member State in order to receive appropriate treatment under Article 22 of Regulation (EC) No 1408/71 must be granted are met, the provisions of that Regulation shall apply and the provisions of Articles 6, 7, 8 and 9 of this Directive shall not apply. Conversely, when an insured person seeks healthcare in another Member State in other circumstances, Articles 6, 7, 8 and 9 of this Directive apply and Article 22 of Council Regulation (EC) No 1408/71 shall not apply. However, whenever the conditions for granting an authorisation set out in Article 22(2) of Regulation (EC) No 1408/71 are fulfilled, the authorisation shall be accorded and the benefits provided in accordance with that Regulation. In that case Articles 6, 7, 8 and 9 of this Directive shall not apply.

3. If the provisions of this Directive conflict with a provision of another Community act governing specific aspects of healthcare, the provision of the other Community act shall prevail and shall apply to those specific situations concerned. These include:

(a) Directive 2005/36/EC on the recognition of professional qualifications;

(b) Directive 2000/31/EC of the European Parliament and of the Council of 8 June 2000 on certain legal aspects of information society services, in particular electronic commerce, in the Internal Market.

4. Member States shall apply the provisions of this Directive in compliance with the rules of the EC Treaty.

ARTICLE 4. DEFINITIONS

For the purposes of this Directive, the following definitions shall apply:

(a) "healthcare" means a health service provided by or under the supervision of a health professional in exercise of his profession, and regardless of the ways in which it is organised, delivered and financed at national level or whether it is public or private;
(b) "cross-border healthcare" means healthcare provided in a Member State other than that where the patient is an insured person or healthcare provided in a Member State other than that where the healthcare provider resides, is registered or is established;
(c) "use of healthcare in another Member State" means healthcare provided in the Member State other than that where the patient is an insured person;
(d) "health professional" means a doctor of medicine or a nurse responsible for general care or a dental practitioner or a midwife or a pharmacist within the meaning of Directive 2005/36/EC or another professional exercising activities in the healthcare sector which are restricted to a regulated profession as defined in Article 3(1)(a) of Directive 2005/36/EC;
(e) "healthcare provider" means any natural or legal person legally providing healthcare on the territory of a Member State;

(f) "patient" means any natural person who receives or wishes to receive healthcare in a Member State;

(g) "insured person" means:

i) until the date of application of Regulation (EC) No 883/2004: a person who is insured in accordance with the provisions of Articles 1, 2 and 4 of Regulation (EC) No 1408/71,

ii) as from the date of application of Regulation (EC) No 883/2004: a person who is an insured person within the meaning of Article 1(c) of Regulation (EC) No 883/2004;

(h) "Member State of affiliation" means the Member State where the patient is an insured person;

(i) "Member State of treatment" means the Member State on whose territory cross-border healthcare is actually provided;

(j) "medicinal product" means a medicinal product as defined by Directive 2001/83/EC;

(k) "prescription" means a medicinal prescription as defined by the Directive 2001/83/EC including prescriptions issued and transmitted electronically (ePrescriptions);

(l) "harm" means adverse outcomes or injuries stemming from the provision of healthcare.

Chapter II. Member State Authorities Responsible for Compliance with Common Principles for Healthcare

Article 5. Responsibilities of authorities of the Member State of treatment

1. The Member States of treatment shall be responsible for the organisation and the delivery of healthcare. In such a context and taking into account principles of universality, access to good quality care, equity and solidarity, they shall define clear quality and safety standards for healthcare provided on their territory, and ensure that:

(a) mechanisms are in place for ensuring that healthcare providers are able to meet such standards, taking into account international medical science and generally recognised good medical practices;

(b) the application of such standards by healthcare providers in practice is regularly monitored and corrective action is taken when appropriate standards are not met, taking into account progress in medical science and health technology;

(c) healthcare providers provide all relevant information to enable patients to make an informed choice, in particular on availability, prices and outcomes of the healthcare provided and details of their insurance cover or other means of personal or collective protection with regard to professional liability;

(d) patients have a means of making complaints and are guaranteed remedies and compensation when they suffer harm arising from the healthcare they receive;

(e) systems of professional liability insurance or a guarantee or similar arrangement, which are equivalent or essentially comparable as regards their purpose and which are appropriate to the nature and the extent of the risk are in place for treatment provided on their territory;

(f) the fundamental right to privacy with respect to the processing of personal data is protected in conformity with national measures implementing Community provisions on the protection of personal data, in particular Directives 95/46/EC and 2002/58/EC;

(g) patients from other Member States shall enjoy equal treatment with the nationals of the Member State of treatment, including the protection against discrimination provided for according to Community law and national legislation in force in the Member State of treatment.

2. Any measures taken by Member States, when implementing this Article, shall respect the provisions of Directive 2005/36/EC on the recognition of professional qualifications and Directive 2000/31/EC on certain legal aspects of information society services, in particular electronic commerce.

3. In so far as it is necessary to facilitate the provision of cross-border healthcare and taking as a basis a high level of protection of health, the Commission, in cooperation with the Member States, shall develop guidelines to facilitate the implementation of paragraph 1.

Chapter III. Use of healthcare in another Member State

ARTICLE 6. HEALTHCARE PROVIDED IN ANOTHER MEMBER STATE

1. Subject to the provisions of this Directive, in particular Articles 7, 8 and 9, the Member State of affiliation shall ensure that insured persons travelling to another Member State with the purpose of receiving healthcare there or seeking to receive healthcare provided in another Member State, will not be prevented from receiving healthcare provided in another Member State where the treatment in question is among the benefits provided for by the legislation of the Member State of affiliation to which the insured person is entitled. The Member State of affiliation shall reimburse the costs to the insured person, which would have been paid for by its statutory social security system had the same or similar healthcare been provided in its territory. In any event, it is for the Member State of affiliation to determine the healthcare that is paid for regardless of where it is provided.

2. The costs of healthcare provided in another Member State shall be reimbursed by the Member State of affiliation in accordance with the provisions of this Directive up to the level of costs that would have been assumed had the same or similar healthcare been provided in the Member State of affiliation, without exceeding the actual costs of healthcare received.

3. The Member State of affiliation may impose on a patient seeking healthcare provided in another Member State, the same conditions, criteria of eligibility and regulatory and administrative formalities for receiving healthcare and reimbursement of healthcare costs as it would impose if the same or similar healthcare was provided in its territory, in so far as they are neither discriminatory nor an obstacle to freedom of movement of persons.

4. Member States shall have a mechanism for calculation of costs that are to be reimbursed to the insured person by the statutory social security system for healthcare provided in another

Member State. This mechanism shall be based on objective, non-discriminatory criteria known in advance and the costs reimbursed according to this mechanism shall be not less than what would have been assumed had the same or similar healthcare been provided in the territory of the Member State of affiliation.

5. Patients travelling to another Member State with the purpose of receiving healthcare there or seeking to receive healthcare provided in another Member State shall be guaranteed access to their medical records, in conformity with national measures implementing Community provisions on the protection of personal data, in particular Directives 95/46/EC and 2002/58/EC.

ARTICLE 7. NON-HOSPITAL CARE

The Member State of affiliation shall not make the reimbursement of the costs of non-hospital care provided in another Member State subject to prior authorisation, where the cost of that care, if it had been provided in its territory, would have been paid for by its social security system.

ARTICLE 8. HOSPITAL AND SPECIALISED CARE

1. For the purposes of reimbursement of healthcare provided in another Member State in accordance with this Directive, hospital care shall mean:

(a) healthcare which requires overnight accommodation of the patient in question for at least one night;
(b) healthcare, included in a specific list, that does not require overnight accommodation of the patient for at least one night. This list shall be limited to:

– healthcare that requires use of highly specialised and cost-intensive medical infrastructure or medical equipment; or
– healthcare involving treatments presenting a particular risk for the patient or the population.

2. This list shall be set up and may be regularly updated by the Commission. Those measures, designed to amend non-essential elements of this Directive by supplementing it, shall be adopted in accordance with the regulatory procedure with scrutiny referred to in Article 19(3).

3. The Member State of affiliation may provide for a system of prior authorisation for reimbursement by its social security system of the cost of hospital care provided in another Member State where the following conditions are met:

(a) had the healthcare been provided in its territory, it would have been assumed by the Member State's social security system; and

(b) the purpose of the system is to address the consequent outflow of patients due to the implementation of the present Article and to prevent it from seriously undermining, or being likely to seriously undermine:

(i) the financial balance of the Member State's social security system; and/or (ii) the planning and rationalisation carried out in the hospital sector to avoid hospital overcapacity, imbalance in the supply of hospital care and logistical and financial wastage, the maintenance of a balanced medical and hospital service open to all, or the maintenance of treatment capacity or medical competence on the territory of the concerned Member State.

4. The prior authorisation system shall be limited to what is necessary and proportionate to avoid such impact, and shall not constitute a means of arbitrary discrimination.

5. The Member State shall make publicly available all relevant information on the prior authorisation systems introduced pursuant to the provisions of paragraph 3.

ARTICLE 9. PROCEDURAL GUARANTEES REGARDING THE USE OF HEALTHCARE IN ANOTHER MEMBER STATE

1. The Member State of affiliation shall ensure that administrative procedures regarding the use of healthcare in another Member State related to any prior authorization referred to in Article 8(3), reimbursement of costs of healthcare incurred in another Member State and other conditions and formalities referred to in Article 6(3), are based on objective, non-discriminatory criteria which are published in advance, and which are necessary and proportionate to the objective to be achieved. In any event, an insured person shall always be granted the authorisation pursuant to Regulations on coordination of social security referred to in Art. 3.1 f) whenever the conditions of Art.22.1 c) and Art. 22.2 of Regulation 1408/71 are met.

2. Any such procedural systems shall be easily accessible and capable of ensuring that requests are dealt with objectively and impartially within time limits set out and made public in advance by the Member States.

3. Member States shall specify in advance and in a transparent way the criteria for refusal of the prior authorisation referred to in Article 8(3).

4. Member States shall, when setting out the time limits within which requests for the use of healthcare in another Member State must be dealt with, take into account:

(a) the specific medical condition,
(b) the patient's degree of pain,
(c) the nature of the patient's disability, and
(d) the patient's ability to carry out a professional activity.

5. Member States shall ensure that any administrative decisions regarding the use of healthcare in another Member State are subject to administrative review and also capable of being challenged in judicial proceedings, which include provision for interim measures.

ARTICLE 10. INFORMATION FOR PATIENTS CONCERNING THE USE OF HEALTHCARE IN ANOTHER MEMBER STATE

1. The Member States of affiliation shall ensure that there are mechanisms in place to provide patients on request with information on receiving healthcare in another Member State, and the terms and conditions that would apply, inter alia, whenever harm is caused as a result of healthcare received in another Member State.

2. The information referred to in paragraph 1 shall be made easily accessible, including by electronic means, and shall include information on patients' entitlements, on procedures for accessing those entitlements and on systems of appeal and redress if the patient is deprived of such entitlements.

3. The Commission may, in accordance with the procedure referred to in Article 19(2), develop a standard Community format for the prior information referred to in paragraph 1.

ARTICLE 11. APPLICABLE RULES TO HEALTHCARE PROVIDED IN ANOTHER MEMBER STATE

1. When healthcare is provided in a Member State other than that where the patient is an insured person, or in a Member State other than that where the healthcare provider resides, is registered or established, such healthcare service is provided according to the legislation of the Member State of treatment in accordance with Art.5.

2. This article does not apply as far as the recognition of the professional qualifications is concerned.

ARTICLE 12. NATIONAL CONTACT POINTS FOR CROSS-BORDER HEALTHCARE

1. Member States shall designate national contact points for cross-border healthcare and communicate their names and contact details to the Commission.

2. The national contact point in the Member State of affiliation shall, in close cooperation with other competent national authorities, and with national contact points in other Member States, in particular in the Member State of treatment, and with the Commission:

(a) provide and disseminate information to patients in particular on their rights related to cross-border healthcare and the guarantees of quality and safety, protection of personal data, procedures for complaints and means of redress available for healthcare provided in another Member State, and on the terms and conditions applicable;

(b) help patients to protect their rights and seek appropriate redress in the event of harm caused by the use of healthcare in another Member State; the national contact point shall in particular inform patients about the options available to settle any dispute, help to identify the appropriate out-of-court settlement scheme for the specific case and help patients to monitor their dispute where necessary;
(c) gather detailed information on national bodies operating out-of-court settlement of disputes and facilitate co-operation with those bodies;
(d) facilitate the development of international out-of-court settlement scheme for disputes arising from cross-border healthcare;

3. The Commission shall, in accordance with the procedure referred to in Article 19(2), adopt:

(a) measures necessary for the management of the network of national contact points provided for in this Article;
(b) the nature and type of data to be collected and exchanged within the network;
(c) guidelines on information to patients provided for in paragraph 2(a) of this Article.

Chapter IV. Cooperation on Health Care

ARTICLE 13. DUTY OF COOPERATION

1. Member States shall render such mutual assistance as is necessary for the implementation of this Directive.

2. Member States shall facilitate cooperation in cross-border healthcare provision at regional and local level as well as through information and communication technologies, cross-border healthcare provided on a temporary or ad hoc basis and other forms of cross-border cooperation.

ARTICLE 14. RECOGNITION OF PRESCRIPTIONS ISSUED IN ANOTHER MEMBER STATE

1. If a medicinal product is authorised to be marketed on their territory in accordance with Article 6(1) of Directive 2001/83/EC, Member States shall ensure that prescriptions issued by an authorised person in another Member State for a named patient can be used in their territory and that any restrictions on recognition of individual prescriptions are prohibited unless they:

(a) are limited to what is necessary and proportionate to safeguard human health and are non-discriminatory or (b) are based on legitimate and justified doubts about the authenticity or content of an individual prescription.

2. For facilitating the implementation of paragraph 1, the Commission shall adopt:

(a) measures enabling a pharmacist or other health professional to verify the authenticity of the prescription and whether the prescription was issued in another Member State by an authorised person through developing a Community prescription template, and supporting interoperability of ePrescriptions;
(b) measures to ensure that medicinal products prescribed in one Member State and dispensed in another are correctly identified and that the information to patients concerning the product is comprehensible;
(c) measures to exclude specific categories of medicinal products from the recognition of prescriptions provided for under this article where necessary in order to safeguard public health.

3. The measures referred to in points (a) and (b) of paragraph 2 shall be adopted in accordance with the regulatory procedure referred to in Article 19(2). The measures referred to in point (c) of paragraph 2, designed to amend non-essential elements of this Directive, by supplementing it, shall be adopted in accordance with the regulatory procedure with scrutiny referred to in Article 19(3).

4. Paragraph 1 shall not apply to medicinal products subject to special medical prescription as provided for in Article 71(2) of Directive 2001/83/EC.

ARTICLE 15. EUROPEAN REFERENCE NETWORKS

1. Member States shall facilitate the development of the European reference networks of healthcare providers. Those networks shall at all times be open for new healthcare providers which might wish to join them, provided that such healthcare providers fulfil all the required conditions and criteria

2. The objective of European reference networks shall be:

(a) to help to realise the potential of European cooperation regarding highly specialised healthcare for patients and for healthcare systems from innovations in medical science and health technologies;
(b) to help to promote access to high quality and cost-effective healthcare for all patients with a medical condition requiring a particular concentration of resources or expertise;
(c) to maximise cost-effective use of resources by concentrating them where appropriate;
(d) to help to share knowledge and provide training for health professionals;
(e) to provide quality and safety benchmarks and to help develop and spread best practice within and outside the network;
(f) to help Member States with an insufficient number of patients with a particular medical condition or lacking technology or expertise to provide a full range of highly specialised services of the highest quality.

3. The Commission shall adopt:

(a) a list of specific criteria and conditions that the European reference networks must fulfil, including the conditions and criteria required from healthcare providers wishing to join the European reference networks, in order to ensure, in particular, that the European reference networks:

(i)   have appropriate capacities to diagnose, to follow-up and manage patients with evidence of good outcomes so far as applicable;
(ii)   have sufficient capacity and activity to provide relevant services and maintain quality of the services provided;
(iii)   have capacity to provide expert advice, diagnosis or confirmation of diagnosis, to produce and adhere to good practice guidelines and to implement outcome measures and quality control;
(iv)   can demonstrate a multi-disciplinary approach;
(v)   provide high level of expertise and experience documented through publications, grants or honorific positions, teaching and training activities;
(vi)   provide strong contribution to research;
(vii)   are involved in epidemiological surveillance, such as registries;
(viii) have close links and collaboration with other expert centres and networks at national and international level and capacity to network;
(ix)   have close links and collaboration with patients associations where such associations exist.

(b) the procedure for establishing European reference networks.

4. The measures referred to in paragraph 3, designed to amend non-essential elements of this Directive by supplementing it, shall be adopted in accordance with the regulatory procedure with scrutiny referred to in Article 19(3).

ARTICLE 16. E-HEALTH

The Commission shall, in accordance with the procedure referred to in Article 19(2), adopt specific measures necessary for achieving the interoperability of information and communication technology systems in the healthcare field, applicable whenever Member States decide to introduce them. Those measures shall reflect developments in health technologies and medical science and respect the fundamental right to the protection of personal data in accordance with the applicable law. They shall specify in particular the necessary standards and terminologies for inter-operability of relevant information and communication technology systems to ensure safe, high-quality and efficient provision of cross-border health services.

Article 17. Cooperation on management of new health technologies

1. Member States shall facilitate development and functioning of a network connecting the national authorities or bodies responsible for health technology assessment.

2. The objective of the health technology assessment network shall be:

(a) to support cooperation between national authorities or bodies;
(b) to support provision of objective, reliable, timely, transparent and transferable information on the short- and long-term effectiveness of health technologies and enable an effective exchange of this information between national authorities or bodies.

3. Member States shall designate the authorities or bodies participating in the network as referred to in paragraph 1 and communicate to the Commission names and contact details of those authorities or bodies.

4. The Commission shall, in accordance with the procedure referred to in Article 19(2), adopt the necessary measures for the establishment and the management of this network and specifying the nature and type of the information to be exchanged.

Article 18. Data collection for statistical and monitoring purposes

1. Member States shall collect statistical and other additional data needed for monitoring purposes on the provision of cross-border healthcare, the care provided, its providers and patients, the cost and the outcomes. They shall collect such data as part of their general systems for collecting healthcare data, in accordance with national and Community law for the production of statistics and on the protection of personal data.

2. Member States shall transmit the data referred to in paragraph 1 to the Commission at least annually, except for data that are already collected pursuant to Directive 2005/36/EC.

3. Without prejudice to the measures adopted for the implementation of the Community Statistical Programme as well as to those adopted for the implementation of Regulation (EC) No .../...of the European Parliament and of the Council on Community statistics on public health and health and safety at work [COM(2007)46], the Commission shall, in accordance with the procedure referred to in Article 19(2), adopt measures for the implementation of this Article.

Chapter V. Implementing and Final Provisions

...

ARTICLE 22. TRANSPOSITION

Member States shall bring into force the laws, regulations and administrative provisions necessary to comply with this Directive by ... [one year after its entry into force]. They shall forthwith communicate to the Commission the text of those provisions and a correlation table between those provisions and this Directive. When Member States adopt those provisions, they shall contain a reference to this Directive or be accompanied by such a reference on the occasion of their official publication. Member States shall determine how such reference is to be made.

1.17. A Declaration on the Promotion of Patients' Rights in Europe, WHO 1994

1. Human Rights and Values in Health Care

The instruments cited in the introduction should be understood as applying also specifically in the health care setting, and it should therefore be noted that the human values expressed in these instruments shall be reflected in the health care system. It should also be noted that where exceptional limitations are imposed on the rights of patients, these must be in accordance with human rights instruments and have a legal base in the law of the country. It may be further observed that the rights specified below carry a matching responsibility to act with due concern for the health of others and for their same rights.

1.1 – 1.5 ...

1.6 Everyone has the right to such protection of health as is afforded by appropriate measures for disease prevention and health care, and to the opportunity to pursue his or her own highest attainable level of health.

1.18. World Medical Association Statement on Access to Health Care

Adopted by the 40th World Medical Assembly Vienna, Austria, September 1988 and revised by the WMA General Assembly, Pilanesberg, South Africa, October 2006

Preamble

1. The Constitution of the World Health Organization states that the "enjoyment of the highest attainable standard of health is one of the fundamental rights of every human being...." Access to health care is a multi-dimensional concept that involves a balancing of factors within the practical constraints of a specific country's resources and capabilities. The factors include health human resources, financing, transportation, freedom of choice, public education, quality, and allocation of technology.

Guidelines

Health Human Resources

2. National Medical Associations should join with other concerned groups from both the private and public sectors to address issues related to the supply and distribution of health human resources. Data should be collected to assess supply and distribution and determine the appropriate mix of health professionals and health workers that can effectively meet the needs of the population. Special efforts should be made to attract physicians and allied health care providers to underserved geographic areas through a variety of incentives and programs. Punitive or coercive models should not be employed. Looking ahead to long-term needs, incentives should also be created to attract medical school students who wish to work in regions where there are health human resource shortages.

Financing

3. A pluralistic financing system should be developed that contains elements of both public and private funding. The exact mix of financing may vary significantly from country to country. The system should be based on standards of uniform eligibility and benefits, and it should include adequate payment mechanisms for this purpose. These mechanisms should be clearly explained to the public so that all concerned understand the payment options available to them. Where appropriate, incentives should be provided for those in the private sector to provide care to patients who otherwise would not have access to it. No one who needs care should be denied it because of inability to pay. Society has an obligation to provide a reasonable subsidy for care of the needy, and physicians have an obligation to participate to a reasonable degree in such subsidized care. Governments have an obligation to ensure that such plans are administered fairly and objectively.

Transportation

4. Society has an obligation to provide adequate access to medical facilities for patients who live in remote areas. Transportation should also be provided to isolated rural patients who require a sophisticated level of care that can be found only in metropolitan medical centres. Telemedicine can sometimes be an acceptable substitute for transportation of patients.

Freedom of Choice

5. All health care delivery systems should provide each individual with the greatest possible personal freedom of choice in selecting a physician. To promote informed personal choice, adequate information concerning both private and public sector options should be made available to the public, employers and other payers of health care.

Public Education

6. Educational programs that assist people in making informed choices about their personal health and about the appropriate uses of both self-care and professional care should be established. These programs should include information about the costs and benefits associated with alternative courses of treatment; the use of professional services that permit early detection and treatment or prevention of illnesses; personal responsibilities in preventing illnesses; and the effective use of the health care system. Patients should be given access to, and retain, copies of their own medical records.

7. In local communities, it is important that the public understand health care plans designed for their benefit and how these plans affect everyone concerned. Physicians have an obligation to actively participate in such educational efforts.

Quality

8. Quality assurance mechanisms should be part of every system of health care delivery. Physicians, in particular, should accept a responsibility for being guardians for the quality of medical care and should not allow other considerations to jeopardize the quality of care provided.

Allocation of Technology

9. Guidelines should be developed for the allocation of scarce health care technologies in order to meet the needs of all patients and heath care practitioners and to ensure the fair and equitable allocation of technology and resources across the health care sector.

Conclusion

10. Access is maximized when the following conditions exist:

1. Adequate medical care is available to every individual, regardless of ability to pay.
2. There is maximum freedom of choice of health care providers and payment systems to accommodate the diverse needs of the population.
3. The entire population has easy access to adequate and comprehensive information on health care providers.
4. There is adequate opportunity for active participation by all parties in healthcare systems design and administration.
5. Physicians are provided with transparent and efficient ethical criteria for working in over-crowded health systems that endanger health care.
6. Medical associations promote equal access to health care, both locally and nationally, through dialogue and common activities with health authorities.

1.19. African Charter on Human and People's Rights (1981)

adopted June 27, 1981, OAU Doc. CAB/LEG/67/3 rev. 5, 21 I.L.M. 58 (1982), entered into force Oct. 21, 1986

ARTICLE 16

1. Every individual shall have the right to enjoy the best attainable state of physical and mental health.

2. States Parties to the present Charter shall take the necessary measures to protect the health of their people and to ensure that they receive medical attention when they are sick.

Chapter 2.
Prisoners and the right to health

2.1. Standard Minimum Rules for the Treatment of Prisoners

Adopted by the First United Nations Congress on the Prevention of Crime and the Treatment of Offenders, held at Geneva in 1955, and approved by the Economic and Social Council by its resolution 663 C (XXIV) of 31 July 1957 and 2076 (LXII) of 13 May 1977

22. (1) At every institution there shall be available the services of at least one qualified medical officer who should have some knowledge of psychiatry. The medical services should be organized in close relationship to the general health administration of the community or nation. They shall include a psychiatric service for the diagnosis and, in proper cases, the treatment of states of mental abnormality.

(2) Sick prisoners who require specialist treatment shall be transferred to specialized institutions or to civil hospitals. Where hospital facilities are provided in an institution, their equipment, furnishings and pharmaceutical supplies shall be proper for the medical care and treatment of sick prisoners, and there shall be a staff of suitable trained officers.

(3) The services of a qualified dental officer shall be available to every prisoner.

23. (1) In women's institutions there shall be special accommodation for all necessary pre-natal and post-natal care and treatment. Arrangements shall be made wherever practicable for children to be torn in a hospital outside the institution. If a child is born in prison, this fact shall not be mentioned in the birth certificate.

(2) Where nursing infants are allowed to remain in the institution with their mothers, provision shall be made for a nursery staffed by qualified persons, where the infants shall be placed when they are not in the care of their mothers.

24. The medical officer shall see and examine every prisoner as soon as possible after his admission and thereafter as necessary, with a view particularly to the discovery of physical or mental illness and the taking of all necessary measures; the segregation of prisoners suspected of infectious or contagious conditions; the noting of physical or mental defects which might hamper rehabilitation, and the determination of the physical capacity of every prisoner for work.

25. (1) The medical officer shall have the care of the physical and mental health of the prisoners and should daily see all sick prisoners, all who complain of illness, and any prisoner to whom his attention is specially directed.

(2) The medical officer shall report to the director whenever he considers that a prisoner's physical or mental health has been or will be injuriously affected by continued imprisonment or by any condition of imprisonment.

26. (I) The medical officer shall regularly inspect and advise the director upon:

...

(b) The hygiene and cleanliness of the institution and the prisoners;
(c) The sanitation, heating, lighting and ventilation of the institution;

...

(2) The director shall take into consideration the reports and advice that the medical officer submits according to rules 25 (2) and 26 and, in case he concurs with the recommendations made, shall take immediate steps to give effect to those recommendations; if they are not within his competence or if he does not concur with them, he shall immediately submit his own report and the advice of the medical officer to higher authority.

Rules applicable to Special Categories, Insane and Mentally Abnormal Prisoners

82. (1) Persons who are found to be insane shall not be detained in prisons and arrangements shall be made to remove them to mental institutions as soon as possible.

(2) Prisoners who suffer from other mental diseases or abnormalities shall be observed and treated in specialized institutions under medical management.

(3) During their stay in a prison, such prisoners shall be placed under the special supervision of a medical officer.

(4) The medical or psychiatric service of the penal institutions shall provide for the psychiatric treatment of all other prisoners who are in need of such treatment.

83. It is desirable that steps should be taken, by arrangement with the appropriate agencies, to ensure if necessary the continuation of psychiatric treatment after release and the provision of social-psychiatric after-care.

2.2. United Nations Rules for the Protection of Juveniles Deprived of their Liberty

Adopted by General Assembly resolution 45/113 of 14 December 1990

H. Medical care

49. Every juvenile shall receive adequate medical care, both preventive and remedial, including dental, ophthalmological and mental health care, as well as pharmaceutical products and special diets as medically indicated. All such medical care should, where possible, be provided to detained juveniles through the appropriate health facilities and services of the community in which the detention facility is located, in order to prevent stigmatization of the juvenile and promote self-respect and integration into the community.

50. Every juvenile has a right to be examined by a physician immediately upon admission to a detention facility, for the purpose of recording any evidence of prior ill-treatment and identifying any physical or mental condition requiring medical attention.51. The medical services provided to juveniles should seek to detect and should treat any physical or mental illness, substance abuse or other condition that may hinder the integration of the juvenile into society. Every detention facility for juveniles should have immediate access to adequate medical facilities and equipment appropriate to the number and requirements of its residents and staff trained in preventive health care and the handling of medical emergencies. Every juvenile who is ill, who complains of illness or who demonstrates symptoms of physical or mental difficulties, should be examined promptly by a medical officer.

52. Any medical officer who has reason to believe that the physical or mental health of a juvenile has been or will be injuriously affected by continued detention, a hunger strike or any condition of detention should report this fact immediately to the director of the detention facility in question and to the independent authority responsible for safeguarding the well-being of the juvenile.

53. A juvenile who is suffering from mental illness should be treated in a specialized institution under independent medical management. Steps should be taken, by arrangement with appropriate agencies, to ensure any necessary continuation of mental health care after release.

54. Juvenile detention facilities should adopt specialized drug abuse prevention and rehabilitation programmes administered by qualified personnel. These programmes should be adapted to the age, sex and other requirements of the juveniles concerned, and detoxification facilities and services staffed by trained personnel should be available to drug- or alcohol-dependent juveniles.

55. Medicines should be administered only for necessary treatment on medical grounds and, when possible, after having obtained the informed consent of the juvenile concerned. In particular, they must not be administered with a view to eliciting information or a confession, as

a punishment or as a means of restraint. Juveniles shall never be testees in the experimental use of drugs and treatment. The administration of any drug should always be authorized and carried out by qualified medical personnel.

Council of Europe Committee of Ministers Recommendation (2006)2 of the Committee of Ministers to member states on the European Prison Rules

Adopted by the Committee of Ministers on 11 January 2006

Part III Health

Health care

39. Prison authorities shall safeguard the health of all prisoners in their care.

40.1 Medical services in prison shall be organised in close relation with the general health administration of the community or nation.

40.2 Health policy in prisons shall be integrated into, and compatible with, national health policy.

40.3 Prisoners shall have access to the health services available in the country without discrimination on the grounds of their legal situation.

40.4 Medical services in prison shall seek to detect and treat physical or mental illnesses or defects from which prisoners may suffer.

40.5 All necessary medical, surgical and psychiatric services including those available in the community shall be provided to the prisoner for that purpose.

Health care provision

46.1 Sick prisoners who require specialist treatment shall be transferred to specialised institutions or to civil hospitals, when such treatment is not available in prison.

46.2 Where a prison service has its own hospital facilities, they shall be adequately staffed and equipped to provide the prisoners referred to them with appropriate care and treatment.

Mental health

47.1 Specialised prisons or sections under medical control shall be available for the observation and treatment of prisoners suffering from mental disorder or abnormality who do not necessarily fall under the provisions of Rule 12.

47.2 The prison medical service shall provide for the psychiatric treatment of all prisoners who are in need of such treatment and pay special attention to suicide prevention.

Other matters

48.1 Prisoners shall not be subjected to any experiments without their consent.

48.2 Experiments involving prisoners that may result in physical injury, mental distress or other damage to health shall be prohibited.

2.3. Recommendation No. R (98) 71 of the Committee of Ministers to Member States concerning the ethical and organizational aspects of health care in prison

Adopted by the Committee of Ministers on 8 April 1998

The Committee of Ministers, under the terms of Article 15.b of the Statute of the Council of Europe, Considering that medical practice in the community and in the prison context should be guided by the same ethical principles; Aware that the respect for the fundamental rights of prisoners entails the provision to prisoners of preventive treatment and health care equivalent to those provided to the community in general; Recognising that the medical practitioner in prison often faces difficult problems which stem from conflicting expectations from the prison administration and prisoners, the consequences of which require that the practitioner should adhere to very strict ethical guidelines; Considering that it is in the interests of the prison doctor, the other health care staff, the inmates and the prison administration to proceed on a clear vision of the right to health care in prison and the specific role of the prison doctor and the other health care staff; Considering that specific problem situations in prisons such as overcrowding, infectious diseases, drug addiction, mental disturbance, violence, cellular confinement or body searches require sound ethical principles in the conduct of medical practice; Bearing in mind the European Convention on Human Rights, the European Social Charter and the Convention on Human Rights and Biomedicine; Bearing in mind the European Convention for the Prevention of Torture and Inhuman or Degrading Treatment or Punishment, and the recommendations on health care service in prisons summarised in the 3rd general report on the activities of the European Committee for the Prevention of Torture and Inhuman or Degrading Treatment or Punishment; Referring to its Recommendation No. R (87) 3 on the European Prison Rules which help to guarantee minimum standards of humanity and dignity in prisons; Recalling Recommendation No. R (90) 3 on medical research on human beings and Recommendation No. R (93) 6 concerning prison and criminological aspects of the control of transmissible diseases including Aids and related health problems in prison, as well as the 1993 WHO guidelines on HIV infection and Aids in prison; Mindful of Recommendations 1235 (1994) on psychiatry and human rights and 1257 (1995) on the conditions of detention in Council of Europe member states, prepared by the Parliamentary Assembly of the Council of Europe; Referring to the Principles of Medical Ethics for the Protection of Detained Persons and Prisoners against Torture and other Cruel, Inhuman or Degrading Treatment or Punishment, adopted by United Nations General Assembly in 1982; Referring to the specific declarations of the World Medical Association (WMA) concerning medical ethics, in particular the Declaration of Tokyo (1975), the Declaration of Malta on hunger strikers (1991) and the Statement on body searches of prisoners (1993); Taking note of recent reforms in structure, organisation and regulation of prison health care services in several member states, in particular in connection with reforms of their health care systems; Taking into account the different administrative structures of member states which require the implementation of recommendations both at federal and state levels,

Recommends that the governments of member states:

- take into account, when reviewing their legislation and in their practice in the area of health care provision in prison, the principles and recommendations set out in the appendix to this recommendation;
- ensure the widest possible dissemination of the recommendation and its explanatory memorandum, paying special attention to all individuals and bodies responsible for the organisation and provision of preventive treatment and health care in prison.

Appendix to Recommendation No. R (98) 7

I. Main characteristics of the right to health in prison

A. Access to a doctor

1. When entering prison and later on while in custody, prisoners should be able at any time to have access to a doctor or a fully qualified nurse, irrespective of their detention regime and without undue delay, if required by their state of health. All detainees should benefit from appropriate medical examinations on admission. Special emphasis should be put on the screening of mental disorders, of psychological adaptation to prison, of withdrawal symptoms resulting from use of drugs, medication or alcohol, and of contagious and chronic conditions.

2. In order to satisfy the health requirements of the inmates, doctors and qualified nurses should be available on a full-time basis in the large penal institutions, depending on the number and the turnover of inmates and their average state of health.

3. A prison's health care service should at least be able to provide out-patient consultations and emergency treatment. When the state of health of the inmates requires treatment which cannot be guaranteed in prison, everything possible should be done to ensure that treatment is given, in all security in health establishments outside the prison.

4. Prisoners should have access to a doctor, when necessary, at any time during the day and the night. Someone competent to provide first aid should always be present on the prison premises. In case of serious emergencies, the doctor, a member of the nursing staff and the prison management should be warned; active participation and commitment of the custodial staff is essential.

5. An access to psychiatric consultation and counselling should be secured. There should be a psychiatric team in larger penal institutions. If this is not available as in the smaller establishments, consultations should be assured by a psychiatrist, practising in hospital or in private.

6. The services of a qualified dental surgeon should be available to every prisoner.

7. The prison administration should make arrangements for ensuring contacts and co-operation with local public and private health institutions. Since it is not easy to provide appropriate treatment in prison for certain inmates addicted to drugs, alcohol or medication, external consultants belonging to the system providing specialist assistance to addicts in the general community should be called on for counselling and even care purposes.

8. Where appropriate, specific services should be provided to female prisoners. Pregnant inmates should be medically monitored and should be able to deliver in an external hospital service most appropriate to their condition.

9. In being escorted to hospital the patient should be accompanied by medical or nursing staff, as required.

B. Equivalence of care

10. Health policy in custody should be integrated into, and compatible with, national health policy. A prison health care service should be able to provide medical, psychiatric and dental treatment and to implement programmes of hygiene and preventive medicine in conditions comparable to those enjoyed by the general public. Prison doctors should be able to call upon specialists. If a second opinion is required, it is the duty of the service to arrange it.

11. The prison health care service should have a sufficient number of qualified medical, nursing and technical staff, as well as appropriate premises, installations and equipment of a quality comparable, if not identical, to those which exist in the outside environment.

12. The role of the ministry responsible for health should be strengthened in the domain of quality assessment of hygiene, health care and organisation of health services in custody, in accordance with national legislation. A clear division of responsibilities and authority should be established between the ministry responsible for health or other competent ministries, which should co-operate in implementing an integrated health policy in prison.

Chapter 3.
Women and the right to health

3.1. Convention on the Elimination of all Forms of Discrimination against Women

General Assembly Res. 34/180, 34 U.N. GAOR Supp. (No. 46) at 193, U.N. Doc. A/34/46, entered into force Sept. 3, 1981.

ARTICLE 12

1. States Parties shall take all appropriate measures to eliminate discrimination against women in the field of health care in order to ensure, on a basis of equality of men and women, access to health care services, including those related to family planning.

2. Notwithstanding the provisions of paragraph 1 of this article, States Parties shall ensure to women appropriate services in connection with pregnancy, confinement and the post-natal period, granting free services where necessary, as well as adequate nutrition during pregnancy and lactation.

3.2. World Medical Association Statement on Family Planning and the Right of a Woman to Contraception

Adopted by the 48th General Assembly, Somerset West, Republic of South Africa, October 1996 and amended by the General Assembly, Copenhagen, Denmark, October 2007

The WMA recognizes that unwanted pregnancies and pregnancies that are too closely spaced can have a serious adverse effect on the health of a woman and of her children. These adverse effects can include the premature deaths of women. Existing children in the family can also suffer starvation, neglect or abandonment resulting in their death or impaired health, when families are unable to provide for all their children. Social functioning and the ability to reach their full potential can also be impaired.

The WMA recognizes the benefits for women who are able to control their fertility. They should be helped to make such choices themselves, as well as in discussion with their partners. The ability to do so by choice and not chance is a principal component of women's physical and mental health and social well being.

Access to adequate fertility control methods is not universal; many of the poorest women in the world have the least access. Knowledge about how their bodies work, information on how to control their fertility and the materials necessary to make those choices are universal and basic human rights for all women.

The role of family planning and secure access to appropriate methods is recognized in the 5th Millennium Development goal as a major factor promoting maternal and child health.

The WMA recommends that National Medical Associations:

Promote family planning education by working with governments, NGOs and others to provide secure and high-quality services and assistance

Attempt to ensure that such information, materials, products and services are available without regard to nationality, creed, race, religion or socioeconomic status.

Chapter 4. Disabled persons and the right to health

4.1. Convention on the Rights of Persons with Disabilities

adopted on 13 December 2006

ARTICLE 25. HEALTH

States Parties recognize that persons with disabilities have the right to the enjoyment of the highest attainable standard of health without discrimination on the basis of disability. States Parties shall take all appropriate measures to ensure access for persons with disabilities to health services that are gender-sensitive, including health-related rehabilitation. In particular, States Parties shall:

(a) Provide persons with disabilities with the same range, quality and standard of free or affordable health care and programmes as provided to other persons, including in the area of sexual and reproductive health and population-based public health programmes;
(b) Provide those health services needed by persons with disabilities specifically because of their disabilities, including early identification and intervention as appropriate, and services designed to minimize and prevent further disabilities, including among children and older persons;
(c) Provide these health services as close as possible to people's own communities, including in rural areas;
(d) Require health professionals to provide care of the same quality to persons with disabilities as to others, including on the basis of free and informed consent by, inter alia, raising awareness of the human rights, dignity, autonomy and needs of persons with disabilities through training and the promulgation of ethical standards for public and private health care;
(e) Prohibit discrimination against persons with disabilities in the provision of health insurance, and life insurance where such insurance is permitted by national law, which shall be provided in a fair and reasonable manner;
(f) Prevent discriminatory denial of health care or health services or food and fluids on the basis of disability.

Chapter 5. Children and the right to health

5.1. Convention on the Rights of the Child

Adopted and opened for signature, ratification and accession by General Assembly resolution 44/25 of 20 November 1989

ARTICLE 24

1. States Parties recognize the right of the child to the enjoyment of the highest attainable standard of health and to facilities for the treatment of illness and rehabilitation of health. States Parties shall strive to ensure that no child is deprived of his or her right of access to such health care services.

2. States Parties shall pursue full implementation of this right and, in particular, shall take appropriate measures:

(a) To diminish infant and child mortality;
(b) To ensure the provision of necessary medical assistance and health care to all children with emphasis on the development of primary health care;
(c) To combat disease and malnutrition, including within the framework of primary health care, through, inter alia, the application of readily available technology and through the provision of adequate nutritious foods and clean drinking water, taking into consideration the dangers and risks of environmental pollution;
(d) To ensure appropriate pre-natal and post-natal health care for mothers;
(e) To ensure that all segments of society, in particular parents and children, are informed, have access to education and are supported in the use of basic knowledge of child health and nutrition, the advantages of breast-feeding, hygiene and environmental sanitation and the prevention of accidents;
(f) To develop preventive health care, guidance for parents and family planning education and services.

3. States Parties shall take all effective and appropriate measures with a view to abolishing traditional practices prejudicial to the health of children.

4. States Parties undertake to promote and encourage international co-operation with a view to achieving progressively the full realization of the right recognized in the present article. In this regard, particular account shall be taken of the needs of developing countries.

Article 26

1. States Parties shall recognize for every child the right to benefit from social security, including social insurance, and shall take the necessary measures to achieve the full realization of this right in accordance with their national law.

2. The benefits should, where appropriate, be granted, taking into account the resources and the circumstances of the child and persons having responsibility for the maintenance of the child, as well as any other consideration relevant to an application for benefits made by or on behalf of the child.

5.2. African Charter on the Rights and Welfare of the Child (1990)

OAU Doc. CAB/LEG/24.9/49 (1990), entered into force Nov. 29, 1999

ARTICLE 14. HEALTH AND HEALTH SERVICES

1. Every child shall have the right to enjoy the best attainable state of physical, mental and spiritual health.

2. States Parties to the present Charter shall undertake to pursue the full implementation of this right and in particular shall take measures:

(a) to reduce infant and child morality rate;
(b) to ensure the provision of necessary medical assistance and health care to all children with emphasis on the development of primary health care;
(c) to ensure the provision of adequate nutrition and safe drinking water;
(d) to combat disease and malnutrition within the framework of primary health care through the application of appropriate technology;
(e) to ensure appropriate health care for expectant and nursing mothers;
(f) to develop preventive health care and family life education and provision of service;
(g) to integrate basic health service programmes in national development plans;
(h) to ensure that all sectors of the society, in particular, parents, children, community leaders and community workers are informed and supported in the use of basic knowledge of child health and nutrition, the advantages of breastfeeding, hygiene and environmental sanitation and the prevention of domestic and other accidents;
(i) to ensure the meaningful participation of non-governmental organizations, local communities and the beneficiary population in the planning and management of a basic service programme for children;
(j) to support through technical and financial means, the mobilization of local community resources in the development of primary health care for children.

Patients' Rights

PART II

Chapter 1. General

1.1. Universal Declaration of Human Rights (1948)

adopted and proclaimed by General Assembly resolution 217 A (III) of 10 December 1948.

ARTICLE 3

Everyone has the right to life, liberty and security of person.

ARTICLE 5

No one shall be subjected to torture or to cruel, inhuman or degrading treatment or punishment.

1.2. International Covenant on Civil and Political Rights (1966)

ARTICLE 6

1. Every human being has the inherent right to life. This right shall be protected by law. No one shall be arbitrarily deprived of his life.

…

ARTICLE 7

No one shall be subjected to torture or to cruel, inhuman or degrading treatment or punishment. In particular, no one shall be subjected without his free consent to medical or scientific experimentation.

ARTICLE 9

1. Everyone has the right to liberty and security of person. No one shall be subjected to arbitrary arrest or detention. No one shall be deprived of his liberty except on such grounds and in accordance with such procedure as are established by law.

…

3. Anyone arrested or detained on a criminal charge shall be brought promptly before a judge or other officer authorized by law to exercise judicial power and shall be entitled to trial within a reasonable time or to release. It shall not be the general rule that persons awaiting trial shall be detained in custody, but release may be subject to guarantees to appear for trial, at any other stage of the judicial proceedings, and, should occasion arise, for execution of the judgement.

4. Anyone who is deprived of his liberty by arrest or detention shall be entitled to take proceedings before a court, in order that that court may decide without delay on the lawfulness of his detention and order his release if the detention is not lawful.

…

ARTICLE 10

1. All persons deprived of their liberty shall be treated with humanity and with respect for the inherent dignity of the human person.

…

1.3. European Convention for Protection of Human Rights and Fundamental Freedoms

Rome, 4.XI.1950, ETS No. 5

ARTICLE 2. RIGHT TO LIFE

1. Everyone's right to life shall be protected by law. No one shall be deprived of his life intentionally save in the execution of a sentence of a court following his conviction of a crime for which this penalty is provided by law.

2. Deprivation of life shall not be regarded as inflicted in contravention of this article when it results from the use of force which is no more than absolutely necessary:

a. in defence of any person from unlawful violence;
b. in order to effect a lawful arrest or to prevent the escape of a person lawfully detained;
c. in action lawfully taken for the purpose of quelling a riot or insurrection.

ARTICLE 3. PROHIBITION OF TORTURE

No one shall be subjected to torture or to inhuman or degrading treatment or punishment.

ARTICLE 8. RIGHT TO RESPECT FOR PRIVATE AND FAMILY LIFE

1. Everyone has the right to respect for his private and family life, his home and his correspondence.

2. There shall be no interference by a public authority with the exercise of this right except such as is in accordance with the law and is necessary in a democratic society in the interests of national security, public safety or the economic well being of the country, for the prevention of disorder or crime, for the protection of health or morals, or for the protection of the rights and freedoms of others.

1.4. Convention for the Protection of Human Rights and Dignity of the Human Being with regard to the Application of Biology and Medicine: Convention on Human Rights and Biomedicine

Oviedo, 4.IV.1997, ETS 164

Preamble

The member States of the Council of Europe, the other States and the European Community, signatories hereto, Bearing in mind the Universal Declaration of Human Rights proclaimed by the General Assembly of the United Nations on 10 December 1948; Bearing in mind the Convention for the Protection of Human Rights and Fundamental Freedoms of 4 November 1950; Bearing in mind the European Social Charter of 18 October 1961; Bearing in mind the International Covenant on Civil and Political Rights and the International Covenant on Economic, Social and Cultural Rights of 16 December 1966; Bearing in mind the Convention for the Protection of Individuals with regard to Automatic Processing of Personal Data of 28 January 1981; Bearing also in mind the Convention on the Rights of the Child of 20 November 1989; Considering that the aim of the Council of Europe is the achievement of a greater unity between its members and that one of the methods by which that aim is to be pursued is the maintenance and further realisation of human rights and fundamental freedoms; Conscious of the accelerating developments in biology and medicine; Convinced of the need to respect the human being both as an individual and as a member of the human species and recognising the importance of ensuring the dignity of the human being; Conscious that the misuse of biology and medicine may lead to acts endangering human dignity; Affirming that progress in biology and medicine should be used for the benefit of present and future generations; Stressing the need for international co-operation so that all humanity may enjoy the benefits of biology and medicine; Recognising the importance of promoting a public debate on the questions posed by the application of biology and medicine and the responses to be given thereto; Wishing to remind all members of society of their rights and responsibilities. Taking account of the work of the Parliamentary Assembly in this field, including Recommendation 1160 (1991) on the preparation of a convention on bioethics; Resolving to take such measures as are necessary to safeguard human dignity and the fundamental rights and freedoms of the individual with regard to the application of biology and medicine, Have agreed as follows:

Chapter I – General provisions

ARTICLE 1. PURPOSE AND OBJECT

Parties to this Convention shall protect the dignity and identity of all human beings and guarantee everyone, without discrimination, respect for their integrity and other rights and fundamental freedoms with regard to the application of biology and medicine.

Each Party shall take in its internal law the necessary measures to give effect to the provisions of this Convention.

ARTICLE 2. PRIMACY OF THE HUMAN BEING

The interests and welfare of the human being shall prevail over the sole interest of society or science.

ARTICLE 3. EQUITABLE ACCESS TO HEALTH CARE

Parties, taking into account health needs and available resources, shall take appropriate measures with a view to providing, within their jurisdiction, equitable access to health care of appropriate quality.

ARTICLE 4. PROFESSIONAL STANDARDS

Any intervention in the health field, including research, must be carried out in accordance with relevant professional obligations and standards.

Chapter II. Consent

ARTICLE 5. GENERAL RULE

An intervention in the health field may only be carried out after the person concerned has given free and informed consent to it. This person shall beforehand be given appropriate information as to the purpose and nature of the intervention as well as on its consequences and risks. The person concerned may freely withdraw consent at any time.

ARTICLE 6. PROTECTION OF PERSONS NOT ABLE TO CONSENT

1. Subject to Articles 17 and 20 below, an intervention may only be carried out on a person who does not have the capacity to consent, for his or her direct benefit.

2. Where, according to law, a minor does not have the capacity to consent to an intervention, the intervention may only be carried out with the authorisation of his or her representative or an authority or a person or body provided for by law. The opinion of the minor shall be taken into consideration as an increasingly determining factor in proportion to his or her age and degree of maturity.

3. Where, according to law, an adult does not have the capacity to consent to an intervention because of a mental disability, a disease or for similar reasons, the intervention may only be carried out with the authorisation of his or her representative or an authority or a person or body provided for by law. The individual concerned shall as far as possible take part in the authorisation procedure.

4. The representative, the authority, the person or the body mentioned in paragraphs 2 and 3 above shall be given, under the same conditions, the information referred to in Article 5.

5. The authorisation referred to in paragraphs 2 and 3 above may be withdrawn at any time in the best interests of the person concerned.

ARTICLE 7. PROTECTION OF PERSONS WHO HAVE A MENTAL DISORDER

Subject to protective conditions prescribed by law, including supervisory, control and appeal procedures, a person who has a mental disorder of a serious nature may be subjected, without his or her consent, to an intervention aimed at treating his or her mental disorder only where, without such treatment, serious harm is likely to result to his or her health.

ARTICLE 8. EMERGENCY SITUATION

When because of an emergency situation the appropriate consent cannot be obtained, any medically necessary intervention may be carried out immediately for the benefit of the health of the individual concerned.

ARTICLE 9. PREVIOUSLY EXPRESSED WISHES

The previously expressed wishes relating to a medical intervention by a patient who is not, at the time of the intervention, in a state to express his or her wishes shall be taken into account.

Chapter III. Private life and right to information

ARTICLE 10. PRIVATE LIFE AND RIGHT TO INFORMATION

1. Everyone has the right to respect for private life in relation to information about his or her health.

2. Everyone is entitled to know any information collected about his or her health. However, the wishes of individuals not to be so informed shall be observed.

3. In exceptional cases, restrictions may be placed by law on the exercise of the rights contained in paragraph 2 in the interests of the patient.

Chapter IV. Human genome

ARTICLE 11. NON-DISCRIMINATION

Any form of discrimination against a person on grounds of his or her genetic heritage is prohibited.

ARTICLE 12. PREDICTIVE GENETIC TESTS

Tests which are predictive of genetic diseases or which serve either to identify the subject as a carrier of a gene responsible for a disease or to detect a genetic predisposition or susceptibility to a disease may be performed only for health purposes or for scientific research linked to health purposes, and subject to appropriate genetic counselling.

ARTICLE 13. INTERVENTIONS ON THE HUMAN GENOME

An intervention seeking to modify the human genome may only be undertaken for preventive, diagnostic or therapeutic purposes and only if its aim is not to introduce any modification in the genome of any descendants.

ARTICLE 14. NON-SELECTION OF SEX

The use of techniques of medically assisted procreation shall not be allowed for the purpose of choosing a future child's sex, except where serious hereditary sex-related disease is to be avoided.

Chapter V. Scientific research

ARTICLE 15. GENERAL RULE

Scientific research in the field of biology and medicine shall be carried out freely, subject to the provisions of this Convention and the other legal provisions ensuring the protection of the human being.

ARTICLE 16. PROTECTION OF PERSONS UNDERGOING RESEARCH

Research on a person may only be undertaken if all the following conditions are met:

i   there is no alternative of comparable effectiveness to research on humans;
ii   the risks which may be incurred by that person are not disproportionate to the potential benefits of the research;
iii the research project has been approved by the competent body after independent examination of its scientific merit, including assessment of the importance of the aim of the research, and multidisciplinary review of its ethical acceptability,
iv   the persons undergoing research have been informed of their rights and the safeguards prescribed by law for their protection;
v   the necessary consent as provided for under Article 5 has been given expressly, specifically and is documented. Such consent may be freely withdrawn at any time.

Article 17. Protection of persons not able to consent to research

1. Research on a person without the capacity to consent as stipulated in Article 5 may be undertaken only if all the following conditions are met:

i   the conditions laid down in Article 16, sub-paragraphs i to iv, are fulfilled;
ii the results of the research have the potential to produce real and direct benefit to his or her health;
iii research of comparable effectiveness cannot be carried out on individuals capable of giving consent;
iv the necessary authorisation provided for under Article 6 has been given specifically and in writing; and
v   the person concerned does not object.

2. Exceptionally and under the protective conditions prescribed by law, where the research has not the potential to produce results of direct benefit to the health of the person concerned, such research may be authorised subject to the conditions laid down in paragraph 1, sub-paragraphs i, iii, iv and v above, and to the following additional conditions:

i   the research has the aim of contributing, through significant improvement in the scientific understanding of the individual's condition, disease or disorder, to the ultimate attainment of results capable of conferring benefit to the person concerned or to other persons in the same age category or afflicted with the same disease or disorder or having the same condition;
ii the research entails only minimal risk and minimal burden for the individual concerned.

Article 18. Research on embryos in vitro

1. Where the law allows research on embryos in vitro, it shall ensure adequate protection of the embryo.

2. The creation of human embryos for research purposes is prohibited.

Chapter VI. Organ and tissue removal from living donors for transplantation purposes

Article 19. General rule

1. Removal of organs or tissue from a living person for transplantation purposes may be carried out solely for the therapeutic benefit of the recipient and where there is no suitable organ or tissue available from a deceased person and no other alternative therapeutic method of comparable effectiveness.

2. The necessary consent as provided for under Article 5 must have been given expressly and specifically either in written form or before an official body.

ARTICLE 20. PROTECTION OF PERSONS NOT ABLE TO CONSENT TO ORGAN REMOVAL

1. No organ or tissue removal may be carried out on a person who does not have the capacity to consent under Article 5.

2. Exceptionally and under the protective conditions prescribed by law, the removal of regenerative tissue from a person who does not have the capacity to consent may be authorised provided the following conditions are met:

i   there is no compatible donor available who has the capacity to consent;
ii   the recipient is a brother or sister of the donor;
iii   the donation must have the potential to be life-saving for the recipient;
iv   the authorisation provided for under paragraphs 2 and 3 of Article 6 has been given specifically and in writing, in accordance with the law and with the approval of the competent body;
v   the potential donor concerned does not object.

Chapter VII. Prohibition of financial gain and disposal of a part of the human body

ARTICLE 21. PROHIBITION OF FINANCIAL GAIN

The human body and its parts shall not, as such, give rise to financial gain.

ARTICLE 22. DISPOSAL OF A REMOVED PART OF THE HUMAN BODY

When in the course of an intervention any part of a human body is removed, it may be stored and used for a purpose other than that for which it was removed, only if this is done in conformity with appropriate information and consent procedures.

Chapter VIII. Infringements of the provisions of the Convention

ARTICLE 23. INFRINGEMENT OF THE RIGHTS OR PRINCIPLES

The Parties shall provide appropriate judicial protection to prevent or to put a stop to an unlawful infringement of the rights and principles set forth in this Convention at short notice.

ARTICLE 24. COMPENSATION FOR UNDUE DAMAGE

The person who has suffered undue damage resulting from an intervention is entitled to fair compensation according to the conditions and procedures prescribed by law.

ARTICLE 25. SANCTIONS

Parties shall provide for appropriate sanctions to be applied in the event of infringement of the provisions contained in this Convention.

Chapter IX. Relation between this Convention and other provisions

ARTICLE 26. RESTRICTIONS ON THE EXERCISE OF THE RIGHTS

1. No restrictions shall be placed on the exercise of the rights and protective provisions contained in this Convention other than such as are prescribed by law and are necessary in a democratic society in the interest of public safety, for the prevention of crime, for the protection of public health or for the protection of the rights and freedoms of others.

2. The restrictions contemplated in the preceding paragraph may not be placed on Articles 11, 13, 14, 16, 17, 19, 20 and 21.

ARTICLE 27. WIDER PROTECTION

None of the provisions of this Convention shall be interpreted as limiting or otherwise affecting the possibility for a Party to grant a wider measure of protection with regard to the application of biology and medicine than is stipulated in this Convention.

Chapter X . Public debate

ARTICLE 28. PUBLIC DEBATE

Parties to this Convention shall see to it that the fundamental questions raised by the developments of biology and medicine are the subject of appropriate public discussion in the light, in particular, of relevant medical, social, economic, ethical and legal implications, and that their possible application is made the subject of appropriate consultation.

Chapter XI. Interpretation and follow-up of the Convention

ARTICLE 29. INTERPRETATION OF THE CONVENTION

The European Court of Human Rights may give, without direct reference to any specific proceedings pending in a court, advisory opinions on legal questions concerning the interpretation of the present Convention at the request of:

– the Government of a Party, after having informed the other Parties;
– the Committee set up by Article 32, with membership restricted to the Representatives of the Parties to this Convention, by a decision adopted by a two-thirds majority of votes cast.

Article 30. Reports on the application of the Convention

On receipt of a request from the Secretary General of the Council of Europe any Party shall furnish an explanation of the manner in which its internal law ensures the effective implementation of any of the provisions of the Convention.

Chapter XII. Protocols

Article 31. Protocols

Protocols may be concluded in pursuance of Article 32, with a view to developing, in specific fields, the principles contained in this Convention. The Protocols shall be open for signature by Signatories of the Convention. They shall be subject to ratification, acceptance or approval. A Signatory may not ratify, accept or approve Protocols without previously or simultaneously ratifying accepting or approving the Convention.

Chapter XIII. Amendments to the Convention

Article 32. Amendments to the Convention

1. The tasks assigned to "the Committee" in the present article and in Article 29 shall be carried out by the Steering Committee on Bioethics (CDBI), or by any other committee designated to do so by the Committee of Ministers.

2. Without prejudice to the specific provisions of Article 29, each member State of the Council of Europe, as well as each Party to the present Convention which is not a member of the Council of Europe, may be represented and have one vote in the Committee when the Committee carries out the tasks assigned to it by the present Convention.

3. Any State referred to in Article 33 or invited to accede to the Convention in accordance with the provisions of Article 34 which is not Party to this Convention may be represented on the Committee by an observer. If the European Community is not a Party it may be represented on the Committee by an observer.

4. In order to monitor scientific developments, the present Convention shall be examined within the Committee no later than five years from its entry into force and thereafter at such intervals as the Committee may determine.

5. Any proposal for an amendment to this Convention, and any proposal for a Protocol or for an amendment to a Protocol, presented by a Party, the Committee or the Committee of Ministers shall be communicated to the Secretary General of the Council of Europe and forwarded by him to the member States of the Council of Europe, to the European Community, to any Signatory, to any Party, to any State invited to sign this Convention in accordance with the

provisions of Article 33 and to any State invited to accede to it in accordance with the provisions of Article 34.

6. The Committee shall examine the proposal not earlier than two months after it has been forwarded by the Secretary General in accordance with paragraph 5. The Committee shall submit the text adopted by a two-thirds majority of the votes cast to the Committee of Ministers for approval. After its approval, this text shall be forwarded to the Parties for ratification, acceptance or approval.

7. Any amendment shall enter into force, in respect of those Parties which have accepted it, on the first day of the month following the expiration of a period of one month after the date on which five Parties, including at least four member States of the Council of Europe, have informed the Secretary General that they have accepted it.

In respect of any Party which subsequently accepts it, the amendment shall enter into force on the first day of the month following the expiration of a period of one month after the date on which that Party has informed the Secretary General of its acceptance.

Chapter XIV. Final clauses

ARTICLE 33. SIGNATURE, RATIFICATION AND ENTRY INTO FORCE

ARTICLE 34. NON MEMBER STATES

1. After the entry into force of this Convention, the Committee of Ministers of the Council of Europe may, after consultation of the Parties, invite any non-member State of the Council of Europe to accede to this Convention by a decision taken by the majority provided for in Article 20, paragraph d, of the Statute of the Council of Europe, and by the unanimous vote of the representatives of the Contracting States entitled to sit on the Committee of Ministers.

2. In respect of any acceding State, the Convention shall enter into force on the first day of the month following the expiration of a period of three months after the date of deposit of the instrument of accession with the Secretary General of the Council of Europe.

...

ARTICLE 36. RESERVATIONS

1. Any State and the European Community may, when signing this Convention or when depositing the instrument of ratification, acceptance, approval or accession, make a reservation in respect of any particular provision of the Convention to the extent that any law then in force in its territory is not in conformity with the provision. Reservations of a general character shall not be permitted under this article.

2. Any reservation made under this article shall contain a brief statement of the relevant law.

3. Any Party which extends the application of this Convention to a territory mentioned in the declaration referred to in Article 35, paragraph 2, may, in respect of the territory concerned, make a reservation in accordance with the provisions of the preceding paragraphs.

4. Any Party which has made the reservation mentioned in this article may withdraw it by means of a declaration addressed to the Secretary General of the Council of Europe. The withdrawal shall become effective on the first day of the month following the expiration of a period of one month after the date of its receipt by the Secretary General.

...

1.5. Convention for the protection of Human Rights and dignity of the human being with regard to the application of biology and medicine: Convention on Human Rights and Biomedicine

(ETS No. 164)

Explanatory Report

This Explanatory Report to the Convention on human rights and biomedicine was drawn up under the responsibility of the Secretary General of the Council of Europe, on the basis of a draft prepared, at the request of the Steering Committee on Bioethics (CDBI), by Mr Jean MICHAUD (France), Chairman of the CDBI. It takes into account the discussions held in the CDBI and its Working Group entrusted with the drafting of the Convention; it also takes into account the remarks and proposals made by Delegations. The Explanatory Report is not an authoritative interpretation of the Convention. Nevertheless it covers the main issues of the preparatory work and provides information to clarify the object and purpose of the Convention and to better understand the scope of its provisions.

Introduction

1. For several years now, the Council of Europe, through the work of the Parliamentary Assembly and of the ad hoc Committee of Experts on Bioethics (CAHBI), later renamed the Steering Committee on Bioethics (CDBI), has concerned itself with the problems confronting mankind as a result of advances in medicine and biology. At the same time, a number of countries have done their own internal work on these topics, and this work is proceeding. So far, therefore, two types of endeavour have been undertaken, one at a national and the other at international level.

2. Basically, these studies are the fruit of observation and concern: observation of the radical developments in science and their applications to medicine and biology, that is fields in which people are directly involved and concern about the ambivalent nature of many of these advances. The scientists and practitioners behind them have worthy aims and often attain them. But some of the known or alleged developments of their work are taking or could potentially take a dangerous turn, as a result of a distortion of the original objectives. Science, with its new complexity and extensive ramifications, thus presents a dark side or a bright side according to how it is used.

3. It has subsequently become necessary to ensure that the beneficial side prevails by developing awareness of what is at stake and constantly reviewing all the possible consequences. No doubt the ethics committees and other national bodies and legislators, as well as the international organisations, have already applied themselves to this task, but their efforts have remained either restricted to a particular geographical area or incomplete because of their focus on a particular topic. On the other hand, common values are more often than not claimed as a basis for the various texts, opinions and recommendations. But differences may, nonetheless,

become apparent in connection with certain aspects of the problems dealt with. Even simple definitions may give rise to profound differences.

Drafting of a Convention

4. It has consequently become apparent that there was a need to make a greater effort to harmonise existing standards. In 1990, at their 17th Conference (Istanbul, 5-7 June 1990), the European Ministers of Justice, following the proposal of Ms Catherine Lalumière, Secretary General of the Council of Europe, adopted Resolution No. 3 on bioethics which recommended that the Committee of Ministers instruct the CAHBI to examine the possibility of preparing a framework convention "setting out common general standards for the protection of the human person in the context of the development of the biomedical sciences".

...

Structure of the Convention

7. The Convention sets out only the most important principles. Additional standards and more detailed questions should be dealt with in additional protocols. The Convention as a whole will thus provide a common framework for the protection of human rights and human dignity in both longstanding and developing areas concerning the application of biology and medicine.

Comments on the provisions of the Convention

Title

8. The title of the instrument is "Convention for the Protection of Human Rights and Dignity of the Human Being with regard to the Application of Biology and Medicine: Convention on Human Rights and Biomedicine".

9. The term "Human Rights" refers to the principles laid down in the Convention for the Protection of Human Rights and Fundamental Freedoms of 4 November 1950, which guarantee protection of such rights. The two Conventions share not only the same underlying approach but also many ethical principles and legal concepts. Indeed, this Convention elaborates some of the principles enshrined in the European Convention for the Protection of Human Rights. The concept of the human being has been used because of its general character. The concept of human dignity, which is also highlighted, constitutes the essential value to be upheld. It is at the basis of most of the values emphasised in the Convention.

10. The phrase "application of biology and medicine", was preferred to "life sciences" in particular, which was considered too broad. It is used in Article 1 and restricts the scope of the Convention to human medicine and biology, thereby excluding animal and plant biology insofar as they do not concern human medicine or biology. The Convention thus covers all

medical and biological applications concerning human beings, including preventive, diagnostic, therapeutic and research applications.

Preamble

11. Various international instruments already provide protection and guarantees in the field of human rights, both individual and social: the Universal Declaration of Human Rights, the International Covenant on Civil and Political Rights, the International Covenant on Economic, Social and Cultural Rights, the Convention on the Rights of the Child, the Convention for the Protection of Human Rights and Fundamental Freedoms, the European Social Charter. Several instruments of a more specific nature prepared by the Council of Europe are also relevant, such as the Convention for the Protection of Individuals with regard to Automatic Processing of Personal Data.

12. They must now be supplemented by other texts so that full account is taken of the potential implications of scientific actions.

13. The principles enshrined in these instruments remain the basis of our conception of human rights; hence they are set out at the beginning of the preamble to the Convention, of which they are the cornerstone.

14. Starting with the preamble, however, it was necessary to take account of the actual developments in medicine and biology, while indicating the need for them to be used solely for the benefit of present and future generations. This concern has been affirmed at three levels:

–   The first is that of the individual, who had to be shielded from any threat resulting from the improper use of scientific developments. Several articles of the Convention illustrate the wish to make it clear that pride of place ought to be given to the individual: protection against unlawful interference with the human body, prohibition of the use of all or part of the body for financial gain, restriction of the use of genetic testing, etc.
–   The second level relates to society. Indeed, in this particular field, to a greater extent than in many others, the individual must also be considered to constitute part of a social corpus sharing a number of ethical principles and governed by legal standards. Whenever choices are involved in regard to the application of certain developments, the latter must be recognised and endorsed by the community. This is why public debate is so important and is given a place in the Convention. Nevertheless, the interests at stake are not equal; as indicated in Article 2, they are graded to reflect the priority in principle attached to the interests of the individual as opposed to those of science or society solely. The adjective "alone" makes it clear that care must be taken not to neglect the latter; they must come immediately after the interests of the individual. It is only in very precise situations, and subject to the respect of strict conditions that the general interest, as it is defined in Article 26, would take priority.
–   The third and final concern relates to the human species. Many of the current achievements and forthcoming advances are based on genetics. Progress in knowledge of the genome

is producing more ways of influencing and acting on it. This knowledge already enables considerable progress to take place in the diagnosis and, sometimes, in the prevention of an increasing number of diseases. There are reasons to hope that it could also enable therapeutic progress to take place. However, the risks associated with this growing area of expertise should not be ignored. It is no longer the individual or society that may be at risk but the human species itself. The Convention sets up safeguards, starting with the preamble where reference is made to the benefits to future generations and to all humanity, while provision is made throughout the text for the necessary legal guarantees to protect the identity of the human being.

15. The preamble refers to the developments in medicine and biology which should be used only for the benefit of present and future generations and not be diverted in ways that run counter to their proper objective. It proclaims the respect due to man as an individual and as a member of the human species. It concludes that progress, human benefit and protection can be reconciled if public awareness is aroused as a result of an international instrument devised by the Council of Europe in line with its vocation. Stress is laid on the need for international co-operation to extend the benefits of progress to the whole of mankind.

Chapter I. General provisions

ARTICLE 1. PURPOSE AND OBJECT

16. This article defines the Convention's scope and purpose.

17. The aim of the Convention is to guarantee everyone's rights and fundamental freedoms and, in particular, their integrity and to secure the dignity and identity of human beings in this sphere.

18. The Convention does not define the term "everyone" (in French "toute personne"). These two terms are equivalent and found in the English and French versions of the European Convention on Human Rights, which however does not define them. In the absence of a unanimous agreement on the definition of these terms among member States of the Council of Europe, it was decided to allow domestic law to define them for the purposes of the application of the present Convention.

19. The Convention also uses the expression "human being" to state the necessity to protect the dignity and identity of all human beings. It was acknowledged that it was a generally accepted principle that human dignity and the identity of the human being had to be respected as soon as life began.

20. The second paragraph of the Article specifies that each Party shall take in its internal law the necessary measures to give effect to the provisions of this Convention. This paragraph indicates that the internal law of the Parties shall conform to the Convention. Conformity between the Convention and domestic law may be achieved either by applying directly the Convention's

provisions in domestic law or by enacting the necessary legislation to give effect to them. With regard to each provision, the means will have to be determined by each Party in accordance with its constitutional law and taking into account the nature of the provision in question. In this respect, it should be noted that the Convention contains a number of provisions which may, under the domestic law of many States, qualify as directly applicable ("self-executing provisions"). This is the case, particularly, of the provisions formulating individual rights. Other provisions contain more general principles which may require the enactment of legislation in order that effect be given to them in domestic law.

ARTICLE 2. PRIMACY OF THE HUMAN BEING

21. This article affirms the primacy of the human being over the sole interest of science or society. Priority is given to the former, which must in principle take precedence over the latter in the event of a conflict between them. One of the important fields of application of this principle concerns research, as covered by the provisions of Chapter V of this Convention.

22. The whole Convention, the aim of which is to protect human rights and dignity, is inspired by the principle of the primacy of the human being, and all its articles must be interpreted in this light.

ARTICLE 3. EQUITABLE ACCESS TO HEALTH CARE

23. This article defines an aim and imposes an obligation on States to use their best endeavours to reach it.

24. The aim is to ensure equitable access to health care in accordance with the person's medical needs. "Health care" means the services offering diagnostic, preventive, therapeutic and rehabilitative interventions, designed to maintain or improve a person's state of health or alleviate a person's suffering. This care must be of a fitting standard in the light of scientific progress and be subject to a continuous quality assessment.

25. Access to health care must be equitable. In this context, "equitable" means first and foremost the absence of unjustified discrimination. Although not synonymous with absolute equality, equitable access implies effectively obtaining a satisfactory degree of care.

26. The Parties to the Convention are required to take appropriate steps to achieve this aim as far as the available resources permit. The purpose of this provision is not to create an individual right on which each person may rely in legal proceedings against the State, but rather to prompt the latter to adopt the requisite measures as part of its social policy in order to ensure equitable access to health care.

27. Although States are now making substantial efforts to ensure a satisfactory level of health care, the scale of this effort largely depends on the volume of available resources. Moreover,

State measures to ensure equitable access may take many different forms and a wide variety of methods may be employed to this end.

Article 4. Professional standards

28. This article applies to doctors and health care professionals generally, including psychologists whose interactions with patients in clinical and research settings can have profound effects and social workers who are members of teams involved in the decision making process or in the carrying out of interventions. From the term "professional standards" it follows that it does not concern persons other than health care professionals called upon to perform medical acts, for example in an emergency.

29. The term "intervention" must be understood here in a broad sense; it covers all medical acts, in particular interventions performed for the purpose of preventive care, diagnosis, treatment or rehabilitation or in a research context.

30. All interventions must be performed in accordance with the law in general, as supplemented and developed by professional rules. In some countries these rules take the form of professional codes of ethics (drawn up by the State or by the profession), in others codes of medical conduct, health legislation, medical ethics or any other means of guaranteeing the rights and interests of the patient, and which may take account of any right of conscientious objection by health care professionals. The Article covers both written and unwritten rules. When there is a contradiction between different rules, the law provides the means of resolving the conflict.

31. The content of professional standards, obligations and rules of conduct is not identical in all countries. The same medical duties may vary slightly from one society to another. However, the fundamental principles of the practice of medicine apply in all countries. Doctors and, in general, all professionals who participate in a medical act are subject to legal and ethical imperatives. They must act with care and competence, and pay careful attention to the needs of each patient.

32. It is the essential task of the doctor not only to heal patients but also to take the proper steps to promote health and relieve pain, taking into account the psychological well-being of the patient. Competence must be determined primarily in relation to the scientific knowledge and clinical experience appropriate to a profession or speciality at a given time. The current state of the art determines the professional standard and skill to be expected of health care professionals in the performance of their work. In following the progress of medicine, it changes with new developments and eliminates methods which do not reflect the state of the art. Nevertheless, it is accepted that professional standards do not necessarily prescribe one line of action as being the only one possible: recognised medical practice may, indeed, allow several possible forms of intervention, thus leaving some freedom of choice as to methods or techniques.

33. Further, a particular course of action must be judged in the light of the specific health problem raised by a given patient. In particular, an intervention must meet criteria of relevance and

proportionality between the aim pursued and the means employed. Another important factor in the success of medical treatment is the patient's confidence in his or her doctor. This confidence also determines the duties of the doctor towards the patient. An important element of these duties is the respect of the rights of the patient. The latter creates and increases mutual trust. The therapeutic alliance will be strengthened if the rights of the patient are fully respected.

Chapter II. Consent

Article 5. General rule

34. This article deals with consent and affirms at the international level an already well-established rule, that is that no one may in principle be forced to undergo an intervention without his or her consent. Human beings must therefore be able freely to give or refuse their consent to any intervention involving their person. This rule makes clear patients' autonomy in their relationship with health care professionals and restrains the paternalist approaches which might ignore the wish of the patient. The word "intervention" is understood in its widest sense, as in Article 4 – that is to say, it covers all medical acts, in particular interventions performed for the purpose of preventive care, diagnosis, treatment, rehabilitation or research.

35. The patient's consent is considered to be free and informed if it is given on the basis of objective information from the responsible health care professional as to the nature and the potential consequences of the planned intervention or of its alternatives, in the absence of any pressure from anyone. Article 5, paragraph 2, mentions the most important aspects of the information which should precede the intervention but it is not an exhaustive list: informed consent may imply, according to the circumstances, additional elements. In order for their consent to be valid the persons in question must have been informed about the relevant facts regarding the intervention being contemplated. This information must include the purpose, nature and consequences of the intervention and the risks involved. Information on the risks involved in the intervention or in alternative courses of action must cover not only the risks inherent in the type of intervention contemplated, but also any risks related to the individual characteristics of each patient, such as age or the existence of other pathologies. Requests for additional information made by patients must be adequately answered.

36. Moreover, this information must be sufficiently clear and suitably worded for the person who is to undergo the intervention. The patient must be put in a position, through the use of terms he or she can understand, to weigh up the necessity or usefulness of the aim and methods of the intervention against its risks and the discomfort or pain it will cause.

37. Consent may take various forms. It may be express or implied. Express consent may be either verbal or written. Article 5, which is general and covers very different situations, does not require any particular form. The latter will largely depend on the nature of the intervention. It is agreed that express consent would be inappropriate as regards many routine medical acts. The consent is therefore often implicit, as long as the person concerned is sufficiently informed. In some cases, however, for example invasive diagnostic acts or treatments, express

consent may be required. Moreover, the patient's express, specific consent must be obtained for participation in research or removal of body parts for transplantation purposes (see Articles 16 and 19).

38. Freedom of consent implies that consent may be withdrawn at any time and that the decision of the person concerned shall be respected once he or she has been fully informed of the consequences. However, this principle does not mean, for example, that the withdrawal of a patient's consent during an operation should always be followed. Professional standards and obligations as well as rules of conduct which apply in such cases under Article 4 may oblige the doctor to continue with the operation so as to avoid seriously endangering the health of the patient.

39. Furthermore, Article 26 of the Convention, as well as Article 6 concerning protection of persons not able to consent, Article 7 concerning protection of persons who have mental disorders and Article 8 concerning emergency situations, define the instances in which the exercise of the rights contained in the Convention and hence the need for consent may be limited.

40. Information is the patient's right, but as provided for in Article 10, the patient's possible wish not to be informed must be observed. This does not, however, obviate the need to seek consent to the intervention proposed to the patient.

ARTICLE 6. PROTECTION OF PERSONS NOT ABLE TO CONSENT

41. Some individuals may not be able to give full and valid consent to an intervention due to either their age (minors) or their mental incapacity. It is therefore necessary to specify the conditions under which an intervention may be carried out on these people in order to ensure their protection.

42. The incapacity to consent referred to in this article must be understood in the context of a given intervention. However, account has been taken of the diversity of legal systems in Europe: in some countries the patient's capacity to consent must be verified for each intervention taken individually, while in others the system is based on the institution of legal incapacitation, whereby a person may be declared incapable of consenting to one or several types of act. Since the purpose of the Convention is not to introduce a single system for the whole of Europe but to protect persons who are not able to give their consent, the reference in the text to domestic law seems necessary: it is for domestic law in each country to determine, in its own way, whether or not persons are capable of consenting to an intervention and taking account of the need to deprive persons of their capacity for autonomy only where it is necessary in their best interests.

43. However, in order to protect the fundamental rights of the human being, and in particular to avoid the application of discriminatory criteria, paragraph 3 lists the reasons why an adult may be considered incapable of consenting under domestic law, namely a mental disability, a disease or similar reasons. The term "similar reasons" refers to such situations as accidents

or states of coma, for example, where the patient is unable to formulate his or her wishes or to communicate them (see also paragraph 57 below on emergency situations). If adults have been declared incapable but at a certain time do not suffer from a reduced mental capacity (for example because their illness improves favourably), they must, according to Article 5, themselves consent.

44. Whenever a person is acknowledged to be incapable of giving consent, the Convention establishes the principle of protection whereby, according to paragraph 1, the intervention must be for the direct benefit of the person. Deviation from this rule is possible in only two cases, covered by Articles 17 and 20 of the Convention, on medical research and the removal of regenerative tissue respectively.

45. As indicated before, the second and third paragraphs prescribe that when a minor (paragraph 2) or an adult (paragraph 3) is not capable of consenting to an intervention, the intervention may be carried out only with the consent of parents who have custody of the minor, his or her legal representative or any person or body provided for by law. However, as far as possible, with a view to the preservation of the autonomy of persons with regard to interventions affecting their health, the second part of paragraph 2 states that the opinion of minors should be regarded as an increasingly determining factor in proportion to their age and capacity for discernment. This means that in certain situations which take account of the nature and seriousness of the intervention as well as the minor's age and ability to understand, the minor's opinion should increasingly carry more weight in the final decision. This could even lead to the conclusion that the consent of a minor should be necessary, or at least sufficient for some interventions. Note that the provision of the second sub-paragraph of paragraph 2 is consistent with Article 12 of the United Nations Convention on the Rights of the Child, which stipulates that "States Parties shall assure the child, who is capable of forming his or her own views the right to express those views freely in all matters affecting the child, the views of the child being given due weight in accordance with the age and maturity of the child".

46. Furthermore, the participation of adults not able to consent in decisions must not be totally ruled out. This idea is reflected in the obligation to involve the adult in the authorisation procedure whenever possible. Thus, it will be necessary to explain to them the significance and circumstances of the intervention and then obtain their opinion.

47. Paragraph 4 of this article draws a parallel with Article 5 concerning consent in general, stating that the person or body whose authorisation is required for the intervention to take place must be given adequate information about the consequences and risks involved.

48. According to paragraph 5, the person or body concerned may withdraw their authorisation at any time, provided that this is done in the interest of the person not able to consent. The first duty of doctors or other health care professionals is to their patient and it is also part of the professional standard (Article 4) to act in the interest of the patient. It is, in fact, a duty of the doctor to protect the patient against decisions taken by a person or body whose authorisation is required, which are not in the interest of the patient; in this respect, national law should

provide adequate recourse procedures. The subordination of consent (or its withdrawal) to the interest of the patient is in keeping with the objective of protecting the person. While a person capable of giving consent to an intervention has the right to withdraw that consent freely, even if this appears to be contrary to the person's interest, the same right must not apply to an authorisation given for an intervention on another person, which should be retractable only if this is in the interest of that third party person.

49. It was not considered necessary to provide in this article for a right of appeal against the decision of the legal representative to authorise or refuse to authorise an intervention. In the very terms of paragraphs 2 and 3 of this article, the intervention may be carried out only "with the authorisation of his or her representative or an authority or a person or body provided for by law", which in itself implies the possibility of appealing to a body or authority in the manner provided for in domestic law.

ARTICLE 7. PROTECTION OF PERSONS WHO HAVE MENTAL DISORDER

50. This article deals with the specific question of the treatment of patients suffering from mental disorders. On the one hand it constitutes an exception to the general rule of consent for persons able to consent (Article 5), but whose ability to decide on a proposed treatment is severely impaired by their very mental disorder. On the other hand, it guarantees the protection of these people by limiting the number of instances in which they may be subjected to treatment for their mental disorders without their consent, by subjecting such interventions to specific conditions. Moreover, this Article does not provide for the specific emergency situations mentioned in Article 8.

51. The first condition is that the person must be suffering from a mental disorder (trouble mental in French). In order for the article to apply, an impairment of the person's mental faculties must be observed.

52. The second condition is that the intervention is necessary to treat specifically these mental disorders. For every other type of intervention, the practitioner must therefore seek the consent of the patient, insofar as this is possible, and the assent or refusal of the patient must be followed. The refusal to consent to an intervention may only be disregarded under those circumstances prescribed by law and where a failure to intervene would result in serious harm to the health of the individual (or to the health and safety of others). In other words, if persons capable of consent refuse an intervention not aimed at treating their mental disorder, their opposition must be respected in the same way as for other patients capable of consent.

53. A number of member States have laws about the treatment of patients with mental illness of a serious nature who either are compulsorily detained or have a life-threatening medical emergency. They permit intervention for certain serious situations, such as the treatment of a serious somatic illness in a psychotic patient or also for certain serious medical emergencies (for example acute appendicitis, an overdose of medication or the case of a woman with a severe psychotic illness who has a ruptured ectopic pregnancy). In such cases the legislation

permits a life-saving treatment, so long as the physician concerned believes it is proper to do so. The procedure is covered by Article 6 (Protection of persons not able to consent) or Article 8 (Emergency situations).

54. The third condition is that, without treatment of his or her mental disorder, serious harm is likely to result to the person's health. Such a risk exists, for example, when a person suffers from a suicidal tendency and is therefore a danger to himself or herself. The article is concerned only with the risk to the patient's own health, whereas Article 26 of the Convention permits patients to be treated against their will in order to protect other people's rights and freedoms (for example, in the event of violent behaviour). On the one hand, therefore, the article protects the person's health (in so far as treatment of the mental disorder without consent is allowed when failure to administer the treatment would seriously harm the person's health), and on the other hand it protects their autonomy (since treatment without consent is prohibited when failure to administer the treatment represents no serious risk to the person's health).

55. The last condition is that the protective conditions laid down in national law must be observed. The article specifies that these conditions must include appropriate supervisory, control and appeal procedures, such as mediation by a judicial authority. This requirement is understandable in view of the fact that it will be possible for an intervention to be carried out on a person who has not consented to it; it is therefore necessary to provide an arrangement for adequately protecting the rights of that person. In this connection, Recommendation No. R (83) 2 of the Committee of Ministers of the Council of Europe concerning the legal protection of persons suffering from mental disorder placed as involuntary patients establishes a number of principles which must be respected during psychiatric treatment and placement. The Hawaii Declaration of the World Psychiatric Association of 10 July 1983 and its revised versions and the Madrid Declaration of 25 August 1996, as well as Parliamentary Assembly Recommendation 1235 (1994) on psychiatry and human rights, should also be mentioned.

ARTICLE 8. EMERGENCY SITUATIONS

56. In emergencies, doctors may be faced with a conflict of duties between their obligations to provide care and seek the patient's consent. This article allows the practitioner to act immediately in such situations without waiting until the consent of the patient or the authorisation of the legal representative where appropriate can be given. As it departs from the general rule laid down in Articles 5 and 6, it is accompanied by conditions.

57. First, this possibility is restricted to emergencies which prevent the practitioner from obtaining the appropriate consent. The article applies both to persons who are capable and to persons who are unable either de jure or de facto to give consent. An example that might be put forward is that of a patient in a coma who is thus unable to give his consent (see also paragraph 43 above), or that of a doctor who is unable to contact an incapacitated person's legal representative who would normally have to authorise an urgent intervention. Even in emergency situations, however, health care professionals must make every reasonable effort to determine what the patient would want.

58. Next, the possibility is limited solely to medically necessary interventions which can not be delayed. Interventions for which a delay is acceptable are excluded. However, this possibility is not reserved for life-saving interventions.

59. Lastly, the article specifies that the intervention must be carried out for the immediate benefit of the individual concerned.

ARTICLE 9. PREVIOUSLY EXPRESSED WISHES

60. Whereas Article 8 obviates the need for consent in emergencies, this article is designed to cover cases where persons capable of understanding have previously expressed their consent (that is either assent or refusal) with regard to foreseeable situations where they would not be in a position to express an opinion about the intervention.

61 The article therefore covers not only the emergencies referred to in Article 8 but also situations where individuals have foreseen that they might be unable to give their valid consent, for example in the event of a progressive disease such as senile dementia.

62. The article lays down that when persons have previously expressed their wishes, these shall be taken into account. Nevertheless, taking previously expressed wishes into account does not mean that they should necessarily be followed. For example, when the wishes were expressed a long time before the intervention and science has since progressed, there may be grounds for not heeding the patient's opinion. The practitioner should thus, as far as possible, be satisfied that the wishes of the patient apply to the present situation and are still valid, taking account in particular of technical progress in medicine.

Chapter III – Private life and right to information

ARTICLE 10. PRIVATE LIFE AND RIGHT TO INFORMATION

63. The first paragraph establishes the right to privacy of information in the health field, thereby reaffirming the principle introduced in Article 8 of the European Convention on Human Rights and reiterated in the Convention for the Protection of Individuals with regard to Automatic Processing of Personal Data. It should be pointed out that, under Article 6 of the latter Convention, personal data concerning health constitute a special category of data and are as such subject to special rules.

64. However, certain restrictions to the respect of privacy are possible for one of the reasons and under the conditions provided for in under Article 26.1. For example, a judicial authority may order that a test be carried out in order to identify the author of a crime (exception based on the prevention of a crime) or to determine the filiation link (exception based on the protection of the rights of others).

65. The first sentence of the second paragraph lays down that individuals are entitled to know any information collected about their health, if they wish to know. This right is of fundamental importance in itself but also conditions the effective exercise of other rights such as the right of consent set forth in Article 5.

66. A person's "right to know" encompasses all information collected about his or her health, whether it be a diagnosis, prognosis or any other relevant fact.

67. The right to know goes hand in hand with the "right not to know", which is provided for in the second sentence of the second paragraph. Patients may have their own reasons for not wishing to know about certain aspects of their health. A wish of this kind must be observed. The patient's exercise of the right not to know this or that fact concerning his health is not regarded as an impediment to the validity of his consent to an intervention; for example, he can validly consent to the removal of a cyst despite not wishing to know its nature.

68. In some circumstances, the right to know or not to know may be restricted in the patient's own interest or else on the basis of Article 26.1, for example, in order to protect the rights of a third party or of society.

69. Therefore, the last paragraph of Article 10 sets out that in exceptional cases domestic law may place restrictions on the right to know or not to know in the interests of the patient's health (for example a prognosis of death which might, in certain cases if immediately passed on to the patient, seriously worsen his or her condition). In some cases, the doctor's duty to provide information which is also covered under Article 4 conflicts with the interests of the patient's health. It is for domestic law, taking account of the social and cultural background, to solve this conflict. Where appropriate under judicial control, domestic law may justify the doctor sometimes withholding part of the information or, at all events, disclosing it with circumspection ("therapeutic necessity").

70. Furthermore, it may be of vital importance for patients to know certain facts about their health, even though they have expressed the wish not to know them. For example, the knowledge that they have a predisposition to a disease might be the only way to enable them to take potentially effective (preventive) measures. In this case, a doctor's duty to provide care, as laid down in Article 4, might conflict with the patient's right not to know. It could also be appropriate to inform an individual that he or she has a particular condition when there is a risk not only to that person but also to others. Here too it will be for domestic law to indicate whether the doctor, in the light of the circumstances of the particular case, may make an exception to the right not to know. At the same time, certain facts concerning the health of a person who has expressed a wish not to be told about them may be of special interest to a third party, as in the case of a disease or a particular condition transmissible to others, for example. In such a case, the possibility for prevention of the risk to the third party might, on the basis of Article 26, warrant his or her right taking precedence over the patient's right to privacy, as laid down in paragraph 1, and as a result the right not to know, as laid down in paragraph 2. In any case,

the right not to know of the person concerned may be opposed to the interest to be informed of another person and the interests of these two persons should be balanced by internal law.

Chapter IV. Human genome

71. Genetic science has undergone dramatic changes in recent years. In human medicine, apart from the pharmaceutical field, there are other areas in which, it can be applied, namely: genetic testing, gene therapy and the scientific elucidation of disease causes and mechanisms.

72. Genetic testing consists of medical examinations aimed at detecting or ruling out the presence of hereditary illnesses or predisposition to such illnesses in a person by directly or indirectly analysing their genetic heritage (chromosomes, genes).

73. The aim of gene therapy is to correct changes to the human genetic heritage which may result in hereditary diseases. The difference between gene therapy and the analysis of the genome lies in the fact that the latter does not modify the genetic heritage but simply studies its structure and its relationship with the symptoms of the illness. In theory, there are two distinct forms of gene therapy. Somatic gene therapy aims to correct the genetic defects in the somatic cells and to produce an effect restricted to the person treated. Were it possible to undertake gene therapy on germ cells, the disease of the person who has provided the cells would not be cured, as the correction would be carried out on the cells whose sole function is to transmit genetic information to future generations.

ARTICLE 11. NON-DISCRIMINATION

74. The mapping out of the human genome, which is advancing rapidly, as well as the development of the genetic tests which are linked with it are likely to bring substantial advances in the prevention of illnesses and the administration of treatment. But genetic testing also raises considerable concerns. Among these the most widespread is probably the concern that genetic testing, which can detect a genetic disease, a predisposition or a susceptibility to a genetic disease, may become a means of selection and discrimination.

75. The fundamental principle established in Article 11 is that any form of discrimination against an individual on grounds of his or her genetic heritage is prohibited.

76. Under Article 14 of the European Convention on Human Rights, the enjoyment of the rights and freedoms set forth in the Convention must be secured without discrimination on any ground such as sex, race, colour, language, religion, political or other opinion, national or social origin, association with a national minority, property, birth or other status. Article 11 adds to this list a person's genetic heritage. The prohibition of discrimination set out thus applies to all areas included in the field of application of this Convention. This notion also includes non-discrimination on grounds of race as understood by the 1965 United Nations Convention on the Elimination of all Forms of Racial Discrimination and as it has been interpreted by the Convention Committee (CERD).

77. Whereas the term "discrimination" has usually a negative connotation in French, this is not necessarily the case in English (where one must use the expression "unfair discrimination"); it has, however, been decided to keep the same term in both languages, as it is in the European Convention of Human Rights and in the case law of the Court. Discrimination here must, therefore, in French as in English, be understood as unfair discrimination. In particular, it cannot prohibit positive measures which may be implemented with the aim of re-establishing a certain balance in favour of those at a disadvantage because of their genetic inheritance.

ARTICLE 12. PREDICTIVE GENETIC TESTS

78. Progress in the study of human genetics has occurred at a remarkable rate over the course of the last ten years. Developments in the field now make it possible to identify with much greater precision than ever before those who carry specific genes for major single gene disorders (for example cystic fibrosis, haemophilia, Huntington's disease, retinitis pigmentosa etc) and also those who carry genes which may increase their risk of developing major disorders later in life (for example heart disease, cancer and Alzheimer's disease). It has been possible to identify those who were destined or likely to develop certain single gene disorders on the basis of a clear mendelian pattern of inheritance or through the identification of phenotypic characteristics (either through clinical observation or through standard laboratory biochemical tests) which permit action to be taken to prevent the onset of clinical disease. Advances in genetics have led to much more sophisticated and precise techniques for testing for some disorders. However, the identification of a particular abnormal gene does not necessarily imply that the carrier will develop the disease nor does it predict the pattern or severity of the disease.

79. Modern techniques have also made it possible to identify genes which contribute to the development of major disorders later in life – and to which other genes and environmental and lifestyle factors also made a contribution. It has also been possible to identify some of these genetically determined risk factors in the past through the identification of phenotypic characteristics. The probability of individuals developing the disease later in life is, however, much less certain than in the case of the single gene disorders, since the probability of doing so depends upon factors which are outside individuals' control (for example other genetic characteristics) as well as factors which may be modified by individuals in ways which will alter the risk (for example diet, smoking, lifestyle factors etc).

80. Tests which are predictive of certain genetic diseases may offer considerable benefits to an individual's health by allowing timely preventive treatment to be instituted or by offering opportunities to diminish the risks through modifications in behaviour, lifestyle or environment. This, however, is not possible at present in many genetically determined disorders. The right to know as well as the right not to know and proper informed consent are, therefore, of particular importance in this field since problems may clearly arise for the individual resulting from tests predictive of genetic disease for which there is currently no effective treatment.

A further complicating factor is that tests predictive of genetically determined diseases may also have implications for members of the family and the offspring of the person who has undergone testing. It is essential that appropriate professional standards are developed in this field.

81. The situation is even more complicated with predictive testing for serious late onset diseases, when there is at present no treatment available. Screening for serious late onset diseases should remain exceptional, even when screening is related to scientific research: it would put too much strain on the free participation and on the privacy of individuals.

82. Because of the particular problems which are related to predictive testing, it is necessary to strictly limit its applicability to health purposes for the individual. Scientific research likewise should be carried out in the context of developing medical treatment and enhancing our ability to prevent disease.

83. Article 12 as such does not imply any limitation of the right to carry out diagnostic interventions at the embryonic stage to find out whether an embryo carries hereditary traits that will lead to serious diseases in the future child.

84. Because there is an apparent risk that use is made of genetic testing possibilities outside health care (for instance in the case of medical examination prior to an employment or insurance contract), it is of importance to clearly distinguish between health care purposes for the benefit of the individual on the one hand and third parties' interests, which may be commercial, on the other hand.

85. Article 12 prohibits the carrying out of predictive tests for reasons other than health or health-related research, even with the assent of the person concerned. Therefore, it is forbidden to do predictive genetic testing as part of pre-employment medical examinations, whenever it does not serve a health purpose of the individual. This means that in particular circumstances, when the working environment could have prejudicial consequences on the health of an individual because of a genetic predisposition, predictive genetic testing may be offered without prejudice to the aim of improving working conditions. The test should be clearly used in the interest of the individual's health. The right not to know should also be respected.

86. Insofar as predictive genetic testing, in the case of employment or private insurance contracts, does not have a health purpose, it entails a disproportionate interference in the rights of the individual to privacy. An insurance company will not be entitled to subject the conclusion or modification of an insurance policy to the holding of a predictive genetic test. Nor will it be able to refuse the conclusion or modification of such a policy on the ground that the applicant has not submitted to a test, as the conclusion of a policy cannot reasonably be made conditional on the performance of an illegal act.

87. However, national law may allow for the performance of a test predictive of a genetic disease outside the health field for one of the reasons and under the conditions provided for in Article 26.1 of the Convention.

88. According to Article 5, a genetic test may only be carried out after the person concerned has given free and informed consent. Article 12 adds a supplementary condition which is that predictive tests must be accompanied by appropriate genetic counselling.

ARTICLE 13. INTERVENTIONS ON THE HUMAN GENOME

89. The progress of science, in particular in knowledge of the human genome and its application, has raised very positive perspectives, but also questions and even great fears. Whilst developments in this field may lead to great benefit for humanity, misuse of these developments may endanger not only the individual but the species itself. The ultimate fear is of intentional modification of the human genome so as to produce individuals or entire groups endowed with particular characteristics and required qualities. In Article 13, the Convention provides the answer to these fears in several ways.

90. In every case, any intervention which aims to modify the human genome must be carried out for preventive, diagnostic or therapeutic purposes. Interventions aimed at modifying genetic characteristics not related to a disease or to an ailment are prohibited. As long as somatic cell gene therapy is currently at the research stage, its application can be allowed only if it complies with the standards of protection provided for in Article 15 and the following Articles.

91. Interventions seeking to introduce any modification in the genome of any descendants are prohibited. Consequently, in particular genetic modifications of spermatozoa or ova for fertilisation are not allowed. Medical research aiming to introduce genetic modifications in spermatozoa or ova which are not for procreation is only permissible if carried out in vitro with the approval of the appropriate ethical or regulatory body.

92. On the other hand the article does not rule out interventions for a somatic purpose which might have unwanted side-effects on the germ cell line. Such may be the case, for example, for certain treatments of cancer by radiotherapy or chemotherapy, which may affect the reproductive system of the person undergoing the treatment.

ARTICLE 14. NON-SELECTION OF SEX

93. Medically-assisted procreation includes artificial insemination, in vitro fertilisation and any technique having the same effect which permits procreation beyond the natural process. According to this Article, it is not permissible to use a technique of medically-assisted procreation in order to choose a future child's sex, except where serious hereditary sex-related disease is to be avoided.

94. It is for internal law to determine, according to the procedures applied in each state, the seriousness of a hereditary sex-related disease. In some countries, guidelines are laid down by political or administrative authorities or by national ethics committees, ad hoc committees, professional bodies, etc. In every case, appropriate genetic counselling of the persons concerned is necessary.

Chapter V – Scientific research

ARTICLE 15. GENERAL RULE

95. Freedom of scientific research in the field of biology and medicine is justified not only by humanity's right to knowledge, but also by the considerable progress its results may bring in terms of the health and well-being of patients.

96. Nevertheless, such freedom is not absolute. In medical research it is limited by the fundamental rights of individuals expressed, in particular, by the provisions of the Convention and by other legal provisions which protect the human being. In this connection, it should be pointed out that the first Article of the Convention specifies that its aim is to protect the dignity and identity of human being and guarantee to everyone, without discrimination, respect for their integrity as well as for other rights and fundamental freedoms. Any research will therefore have to observe these principles.

ARTICLE 16. PROTECTION OF PERSONS UNDERGOING RESEARCH

97. This Article lays down the conditions for all research on human beings. These conditions were largely inspired by Recommendation No. R (90) 3 of the Committee of Ministers to member States on medical research on the human being.

98. The first condition is that there must be no alternative of comparable effectiveness to research on humans. Consequently, research will not be allowed if comparable results can be obtained by other means. Invasive methods will not be authorised if other less invasive or non-invasive methods can be used with comparable effect.

99. The second condition is that the risks which may be incurred by that person are not disproportionate to the potential benefits of the research.

100. The third condition is the need for an independent examination of the scientific merit as well as of the ethical, including legal, social and economic acceptability of the research project. The examination of the latter aspects have to be carried out by independent multi-disciplinary ethics committees.

101. Paragraph iv underlines the obligation to inform the person in advance of their legal rights and guarantees, for example their right to freely withdraw their consent at any time.

102. Paragraph v reinforces conditions set forth in Article 5 concerning consent. In the sphere of research, implicit consent is insufficient. For this reason the Article requires not only the person's free and informed consent, but their express, specific and written consent. The words "specific consent" are to be understood here as meaning consent which is given to one particular intervention carried out in the framework of research.

ARTICLE 17. PROTECTION OF PERSONS NOT ABLE TO CONSENT TO RESEARCH

Paragraph 1

103. In its first paragraph this Article establishes a principle with regard to research on a person who is not able to consent: the research must be potentially beneficial to the health of the person concerned. The benefit must be real and follow from the potential results of the research, and the risk must not be disproportionate to the potential benefit.

104. Moreover, to allow such research, there should be no alternative subject with full capacity. It is not sufficient that there should be no capable volunteers. Recourse to research on persons not able to consent must be, scientifically, the sole possibility. This will apply, for instance, to research aimed at improving the understanding of development in children or improving the understanding of diseases affecting these people specifically, such as infant diseases or certain psychiatric disorders such as dementia in adults. Such research can only be carried out, respectively, on children or the adults concerned.

105. Protection of the person not able to consent is also strengthened by the requirement that the necessary authorisation as provided for under Article 6 be given specifically and in writing. It is also stipulated that such authorisation may be freely withdrawn at any time.

106. The research must not be carried out if the person concerned objects. In the case of infants or very young children, it is necessary to evaluate their attitude taking account of their age and maturity. The rule prohibiting the carrying out of the research against the wish of the subject reflects concern, in research, for the autonomy and dignity of the person in all circumstances, even if the person is considered legally incapable of giving consent. This provision is also a means of guaranteeing that the burden of the research is acceptable to the person at all times.

Paragraph 2

107. Under the protective conditions prescribed by domestic law, paragraph 2 provides, exceptionally, for the possibility of waiving the direct benefit rule on certain very strict conditions. Were such research to be banned altogether, progress in the battles to maintain and improve health and to combat diseases only afflicting children, mentally disabled persons or persons suffering from senile dementia would become impossible. The group of people concerned may in the end benefit from this kind of research.

108. As well as the general conditions of research on persons not able to consent, a certain number of supplementary conditions must be fulfilled. In this way the Convention enables these people to enjoy the benefits of science in the fight against disease, while guaranteeing the individual protection of the person who undergoes the research. The required conditions imply that:

- in order to obtain the necessary results for the patient group concerned, there is neither an alternative method of comparable effectiveness to research on humans, nor research of comparable effectiveness on individuals capable of giving informed consent;
- the research has the aim of contributing to the ultimate attainment of results capable of conferring a benefit to the person concerned or to other persons in the same age category, or afflicted with the same disease or disorder or having the same condition, through significant improvements in the scientific understanding of the individual's conditions, disease or disorder;
- the research entails only minimal risk and minimal burden for the individual concerned (for example blood sampling – see paragraphs 111 and 113 below);
- the research project not only has scientific merit but is also ethically and legally acceptable and has been given prior approval by the competent bodies;
- the person's representative or an authority or a person or body provided for by law has given authorisation (adequate representation of the interests of the patient);
- the person concerned does not object (the wish of the person concerned prevails and is always decisive);
- authorisation for this research may be withdrawn at any time throughout a research project.

109. One of the first supplementary conditions is that this research should be likely to significantly improve the scientific understanding of a person's health condition, disease or disorder and obtain, in the end, results benefitting the health of the person undergoing research or the health of persons in the same category. This means, for example, that a minor may participate in research on an ailment from which he or she suffers even if the minor would not benefit by the results of the research, provided that the research might be of significant benefit to other children suffering from the same disease. In the case of healthy minors undergoing research it is obvious that the result of the research might be of benefit only to other children. In cases where healthy minors participate in research, clearly it is to obtain results of benefit to other children; however such research may well be of ultimate benefit to healthy children taking part in this research.

110. The research on "the individual's condition" might cover, with regard to research on children, not only diseases or abnormalities peculiar to childhood or certain aspects of common diseases that are specific to childhood, but also the normal development of the child where knowledge is necessary for the understanding of these diseases or abnormalities.

111. While Article 16.ii restricts research in general by establishing a criterion of risk/benefit proportionality, Article 17 lays down a more stringent requirement for research without direct benefit to persons incapable of giving consent, namely only minimal risk and minimal burden for the individual concerned. Indeed, it is only in respecting these conditions that such research may be carried out without constituting an instrumentalisation of these persons contrary to their dignity. For example, taking a single blood sample from a child would generally only present a minimal risk, and might therefore be regarded as acceptable.

112. Diagnostic and therapeutic progress for the benefit of sick children depends to a large extent on new knowledge and insight regarding the normal biology of the human organism and calls for research on the age-related functions and development of normal children before it can be applied in the treatment of sick children. Moreover, paediatric research concerns not only the diagnosis and treatment of serious pathological conditions but also the maintenance and improvement of the state of health of children who are not ill, or who are only slightly ill. In this connection mention should be made of prophylaxis through vaccination or immunisation, dietary measures or preventive treatments whose effectiveness, especially in terms of costs and possible risks, urgently requires evaluation by means of scientifically controlled studies. Any restriction based on the requirement of "potential direct benefit" for the person undergoing the test would make such studies impossible in the future.

113. As examples, the following fields of research can be mentioned, provided all conditions outlined above are met (including the condition that it is impossible to obtain the same results through research carried out on capable persons and the condition of minimal risk and minimal burden):

– in respect of children: replacing X-ray examinations or invasive diagnostic measures for children by ultrasonic scanning; analyses of incidental blood samples from newborn infants without respiratory problems in order to establish the necessary oxygen content for premature infants; discovering the causes and improving treatment of leukaemia in children (for example by taking a blood sample);
– in respect of adults not able to consent: research on patients in intensive care or in a coma to improve the understanding of the causes of coma or the treatment in intensive care.

114. The above-mentioned examples of medical research cannot be described as routine treatment. They are in principle without direct therapeutic benefit for the patient. However, they may be ethically acceptable if the above highly protective conditions, resulting from the combined effect of Articles 6, 7, 16 and 17, are fulfilled.

ARTICLE 18. RESEARCH ON EMBRYOS IN VITRO

115. The first paragraph of Article 18 stresses the necessity to protect the embryo in the framework of research: where national law allows research on embryos in vitro the law must ensure adequate protection of the embryo.

116. The article does not take a stand on the admissibility of the principle of research on in vitro embryos. However, paragraph 2 of the Article prohibits the creation of human embryos with the aim to carry out research on them.

Chapter VI. Organ and tissue removal from living donors for transplantation purposes

ARTICLE 19. GENERAL RULE

117. Organ transplants are current medical techniques helping to save, prolong or greatly fa-cilitate the lives of persons suffering from certain serious disorders. The purpose of this chapter is to establish a framework to protect living donors in the context of organ (in particular liver, kidney, lung, pancreas) or tissue removal (for instance, skin). The provisions in this chapter do not apply to blood transfusions.

118. According to the first principle of the text, organs or tissues should be removed from deceased donors rather than from living donors whenever possible. Removing organs or tissue from living donors always represents a risk for the donors, if only because of the anaesthesia they sometimes have to undergo. This implies that organs from living persons should not be used where an appropriate organ from a deceased person is available.

119. The second condition in the case of living donors is that there exists no alternative thera-peutic method of comparable effectiveness. In view of the risk involved in any organ removal, there is no justification for resorting to this if there is another way of bringing the same benefit to the recipient. The transplant must therefore be necessary in the sense that there is no other solution that would produce similar results, such as "conventional" treatment, or tissues of animal origin, cultured tissues or tissues transplanted from the recipient. In this respect dialysis treatment is not considered to provide results in terms of the patient's quality of life comparable with those obtained by a kidney transplant.

120. In order for an organ to be removed, the express and specific consent of the donor must be given, in accordance with Article 5 of the Convention. Moreover, Article 19, paragraph 2, stipulates that this consent must be specific and given in written form or before an official body, making the conditions set forth in Article 5 more stringent for this particular type of intervention. The official body concerned could be a court or a notary, for example.

121. The removal of organs may only be carried out for the therapeutic benefit of the recipient where the need was known before the removal. Tissue, for its part, can be stored in tissue banks for future needs (it should be stressed that this concerns, in most cases, unused tissue – for example tissue removed after an intervention – see Article 22); in this case the provisions of Recommendation No. R (94) 1 of the Committee of Ministers to the member States on human tissue banks are applicable.

ARTICLE 20. PROTECTION OF PERSONS NOT ABLE TO CONSENT TO ORGAN REMOVAL

122. Article 20 deals specifically with the question of the removal of organs or tissue from persons incapable of giving consent. The principle is that this practice is prohibited.

123. Only in very exceptional circumstances may exceptions be made to this rule, and only for the removal of regenerative tissue. Within the meaning of this Article, regenerative tissue is that capable of reconstituting its tissue mass and function after partial removal. These exceptions are justified by the fact that regenerative tissue, in particular bone marrow, can only be transplanted between genetically compatible persons, often brothers and sisters.

124. If, at the present time, bone marrow transplants among brothers and sisters is the most important situation which meets with the condition of this article, the formula "regenerative tissue" takes into account future developments in medicine.

125. Paragraph 2 therefore permits removal of bone marrow from a minor for the benefit of his or her brother or sister. It is the principle of mutual aid between very close members of a family which, subject to certain conditions, can justify an exception to the prohibition of removal which is intended to protect the persons who are not able to give their consent. This exception to the general rule is qualified by a number of conditions set forth in Article 20, designed to protect the person who is incapable of giving consent, and these may be supplemented by national law. The conditions of Article 19, paragraph 1, also apply.

126. The first condition is the absence, within reasonable limits, of a compatible donor who is able to consent.

127. Moreover, the removal is only authorised on the condition that, in the absence of the donation, the life of the recipient is in danger. It goes without saying that the risks to the donor should be acceptable; the professional standards of Article 4 naturally apply, in particular as regards the balance between risk and benefit.

128. It is also required that the beneficiary be a brother or sister. This restriction is intended to avoid both family and doctors going to extreme lengths to find a donor at any price, even if the level of kinship is distant and the chances for a successful transplant are not very likely, because of tissue incompatibility.

129. Furthermore, in keeping with Article 6, the authorisation of the representative of the person not able to consent or the authorisation of the authority or body provided for by law is needed before the removal can be carried out (see under 38 above for withdrawal). The agreement of the competent body mentioned in Article 20, iv is also required. The intervention of such a body (which might be a court, a professionally qualified body, an ethics committee, etc.) aims to guarantee that the decision to be taken is impartial.

130. Finally, the removal may not be carried out if the potential donor objects in any way. As in the case of research, this opposition, in whatever form, is decisive and must always be observed.

Chapter VII. Prohibition of financial gain and disposal of a part of the human body

ARTICLE 21. PROHIBITION OF FINANCIAL GAIN

131. This article applies the principle of human dignity set forth in the preamble and in Article 1.

132. It states in particular that the human body and its parts must not, as such, give rise to financial gain. Under this provision organs and tissues proper, including blood, should not be bought or sold or give rise to financial gain for the person from whom they have been removed or for a third party, whether an individual or a corporate entity such as, for example, a hospital. However, technical acts (sampling, testing, pasteurisation, fractionation, purification, storage, culture, transport, etc.) which are performed on the basis of these items may legitimately give rise to reasonable remuneration. For instance, this Article does not prohibit the sale of a medical device incorporating human tissue which has been subjected to a manufacturing process as long as the tissue is not sold as such. Further, this Article does not prevent a person from whom an organ or tissue has been taken from receiving compensation which, while not constituting remuneration, compensates that person equitably for expenses incurred or loss of income (for example as a result of hospitalisation).

133. The provision does not refer to such products as hair and nails, which are discarded tissues, and the sale of which is not an affront to human dignity.

134. The question of patents was not considered in connection with this provision; accordingly the latter was not intended to apply to the question of the patentability of biotechnological inventions. Such was the complexity of the problem of patents that a detailed study was necessary before any regulations were drawn up. If such a study led to the conclusion that regulations on the subject were desirable, the regulations should include principles and rules suited to the specific nature of the subject. In this respect, it has been noted that the European Community has issued a proposal for a Directive containing the principle according to which "the human body and its elements in their natural state shall not be considered patentable inventions".

ARTICLE 22. DISPOSAL OF A REMOVED PART OF THE HUMAN BODY

135. Parts of the human body are often removed in the course of interventions, for example surgery. The aim of this article is to ensure the protection of individuals with regard to parts of their body which are thus removed and then stored or used for a purpose different from that for which they have been removed. Such a provision is necessary in particular, because much information on the individual may be derived from any part of the body, however small (for example blood, hair, bone, skin, organ). Even when the sample is anonymous the analysis may yield information about identity.

136. This provision thus establishes a rule consistent with the general principle in Article 5 on consent, ie that parts of the body which have been removed during an intervention for a

specified purpose must not be stored or used for a different purpose unless the relevant conditions governing information and consent have been observed.

137. The information and consent arrangements may vary according to the circumstances, thus allowing for flexibility since the express consent of an individual to the use of parts of his body is not systematically needed. Thus, sometimes, it will not be possible, or very difficult, to find the persons concerned again in order to ask for their consent. In some cases, it will be sufficient for a patient or his or her representative, who have been duly informed (for instance, by means of leaflets handed to the persons concerned at the hospital), not to express their opposition. In other cases, depending on the nature of the use to which the removed parts are to be put, express and specific consent will be necessary, in particular where sensitive information is collected about identifiable individuals.

138. This article must not be understood to authorise an exception to the principle in Article 19 that removal of organs for transplantation purposes may be carried out only for the benefit of the recipient. However, in a case where the organ appears not to be suitable for transplantation purposes, because of its condition, it may then exceptionally be used for research in transplantation medicine specifically related to the particular organ.

Chapter VIII. Infringements of the provisions of the Convention

ARTICLE 23. INFRINGEMENT OF THE RIGHTS OR PRINCIPLES

139. This article requires the Parties to make available a judicial procedure to prevent or put a stop to an infringement of the principles set forth in the Convention. It therefore covers not only infringements which have already begun and are ongoing but also the threat of an infringement.

140. The judicial protection requested must be appropriate and proportionate to the infringement or the threats of infringement of the principles. Such is the case, for example, with proceedings initiated by a public prosecutor in cases of infringements affecting several persons unable to defend themselves, in order to put an end to the violation of their rights.

141. Under the Convention, the appropriate protective machinery must be capable of operating rapidly as it has to allow an infringement to be prevented or halted at short notice. This requirement can be explained by the fact that, in many cases, the very integrity of an individual has to be protected and an infringement of this right might have irreversible consequences.

142. The judicial protection thus provided by the Convention applies only to unlawful infringements or to threats thereof.

The reason for this qualifying adjective is that the Convention itself, in Article 26.1, permits restrictions to the free exercise of the rights it recognises.

ARTICLE 24. COMPENSATION FOR UNDUE DAMAGE

143. This Article sets forth the principle that any person who has suffered undue damage resulting from an intervention is entitled to fair compensation. The Convention uses the expression "undue damage" because in medicine some damage, such as amputation, is inherent in the therapeutic intervention itself.

144. The due or undue nature of the damage will have to be determined in the light of the circumstances of each case. The cause of the damage must be an intervention in the widest sense, taking the form of either an act or an omission. The intervention may or may not constitute an offence. In order to give entitlement to compensation, the damage must result from the intervention.

145. Compensation conditions and procedures are prescribed by national law. In many cases, this establishes a system of individual liability based either on fault or on the notion of risk or strict liability. In other cases, the law may provide for a collective system of compensation irrespective of individual liability.

146. On the subject of fair compensation, reference can be made to Article 50 of the European Convention on Human Rights, which allows the Court to afford just satisfaction to the injured party.

ARTICLE 25. SANCTIONS

147. Since the aim of the sanctions provided for in Article 25 is to guarantee compliance with the provisions of the Convention, they must be in keeping with certain criteria, particularly those of necessity and proportionality. As a result, in order to measure the expediency and determine the nature and scope of the sanction, the domestic law must pay special attention to the content and importance of the provision to be complied with, the seriousness of the offence and the extent of its possible repercussions for the individual and for society.

Chapter IX. Relation between this Convention and other provisions

ARTICLE 26. RESTRICTIONS ON THE EXERCISE OF RIGHTS

Paragraph 1

148. This article lists the only possible exceptions to the rights and protective provisions contained in all the provisions of the Convention, without prejudice to any specific restrictions which this or that Article may involve.

149. It echoes partially the provisions of Article 8, paragraph 2, of the European Convention on Human Rights. The exceptions made in Article 8, paragraph 2, of the European Convention on Human Rights have not all been considered relevant to this Convention. The exceptions

defined in the article are aimed at protecting collective interests (public safety, the prevention of crime, and the protection of public health) or the rights or freedoms of others.

150. Compulsory isolation of a patient with a serious infectious disease, where necessary, is a typical example of an exception for reason of the protection of public health.

151. A person who may, due to his or her mental disorder, be a possible source of serious harm to others may, according to the law, be subjected to a measure of confinement or treatment without his or her consent. Here, in addition to the cases contemplated in Article 7, the restriction may be applicable in order to protect other people's rights and freedom.

152. Protection of the rights of others may also, for example, justify an order by a judicial authority for a test to be carried out to establish parentage.

153. It may also be justified to use genetic assessments (DNA tests) for the identification of persons in connection with criminal investigation.

154. Certain legislations provide for court-ordered psychiatric treatment of an accused person who, failing such treatment, would be unfit to stand trial, with the object of enabling the accused to make a proper defence. Such court-ordered treatment, with attached appropriate safeguards, may be considered as relevant within the scope of Article 26, which refers namely to necessary measures for the fair administration of justice ("prevention of crime") which, in a democratic society, include the defence of the accused.

155. The protection of the patient's health is not mentioned in this paragraph as one of the factors justifying an exception to the provisions of the Convention as a whole. In order to clarify its scope, it seemed preferable to define this exception in each of the provisions expressly alluding to it. Article 7, for example, specifies the conditions on which individuals suffering from mental disorders may, without their consent, be given treatment if their health might seriously suffer otherwise.

156. Moreover, defending the economic well-being of the country, public order or morals and national security are not included amongst the general exceptions referred to in the first paragraph of this article, unlike Article 8 of the European Convention on Human Rights. It did not appear desirable, in the context of this Convention, to make the exercise of fundamental rights chiefly concerned with the protection of a person's rights in the health sphere subject to the economic well-being of the country, to public order, to morals or to national security.

157. The economic aspect is however referred to in Article 3 by the words "available resources"; however, within the meaning of this article this notion does not represent a reason for allowing for an exception to the rights secured in other provisions of the Convention.

158. War and armed conflict were also ruled out as possible grounds for exceptions. However, this is not meant as preventing the law from taking specific measures in the military aiming at protecting public health in that particular context.

159. The reasons mentioned in Article 26.1 should not be regarded as justifying an absolute exception to the rights secured by the Convention. To be admissible, restrictions must be prescribed by law and be necessary in a democratic society for the protection of the collective interest in question or for the protection of individual interests, that is the rights and freedom of others. These conditions must be interpreted in the light of the criteria established with regard to the same concepts by the case-law of the European Court of Human Rights. In particular, the restrictions must meet the criteria of necessity, proportionality and subsidiarity, taking into account the social and cultural conditions proper to each State. The term "prescribed by law" should be interpreted in accordance with the meaning usually given to it by the European Court of Human Rights, that is a formal law is not required and each State may adopt the form of domestic law it considers most appropriate.

Paragraph 2

160. The restrictions set out in the first paragraph of the Article shall not apply to the provisions mentioned in the second paragraph. It concerns the following provisions: Article 11 (Non-discrimination), Article 13 (Interventions on human genome), Article 14 (Non selection of sex), Article 16 (Protection of persons undergoing research), Article 17 (Protection of persons not able to consent to research), Articles 19 and 20 (Organ and tissue removal from living donors for transplantation purposes) and Article 21 (Prohibition of financial gain).

ARTICLE 27. WIDER PROTECTION

161. In pursuance of this article, the Parties may apply rules of a more protective nature than those contained in the Convention. In other words, the text lays down common standards with which States must comply, while allowing them to provide greater protection of the human being and of human rights with regard to applications of biology and medicine.

162. A conflict may arise between the various rights established by the Convention, for example between a scientist's right of freedom of research and the rights of a person submitting to the research. However, the expression "wider protection" must be interpreted in the light of the purpose of the Convention, as defined in Article 1, namely the protection of the human being with regard to the application of biology and medicine.

In the example quoted, any additional statutory protection can only mean greater protection for a person submitting to research.

Chapter X. Public debate

ARTICLE 28. PUBLIC DEBATE

163. The purpose of this article is to prompt the Parties to create greater public awareness of the fundamental questions raised by the application of biology and medicine. Society's views must be ascertained as far as possible with regard to problems concerning its members as a whole. To this end, appropriate public discussion and consultation are recommended. The word "appropriate" leaves the Parties free to select the most suitable procedures. Where appropriate, for example, States may organise ethics committees and have recourse to the teaching of ethics in the field of medicine, biology and health to health care professionals, teachers and the general public.

Chapter XI. Interpretation and follow-up of the Convention

ARTICLE 29. INTERPRETATION OF THE CONVENTION

164. This article allows the possibility of requesting the European Court of Human Rights' advisory opinion on legal questions concerning the interpretation of the Convention. The opinion shall be without direct reference to any specific proceedings in a court.

165. This Convention does not itself give individuals a right to bring proceedings before the European Court of Human Rights. However, facts which are an infringement of the rights contained in this Convention may be considered in proceedings under the European Convention of Human Rights, if they also constitute a violation of one of the rights contained in the latter Convention.

ARTICLE 30. (REPORTS ON THE APPLICATION OF THE CONVENTION)

166. According to the model of Article 57 of the European Convention of Human Rights, this Article stipulates that any Party, on the request of the Secretary General of the Council of Europe, shall furnish an explanation of the manner in which its internal law ensures the effective implementation of any of the provisions of the Convention.

Chapter XII. Protocols

ARTICLE 31. PROTOCOLS

167. The Convention establishes principles valid for all applications of biology and medicine in human beings. This article makes provision for the immediate drawing up of protocols containing rules on specific fields. As the purpose of the protocols is to develop further the principles contained in the Convention, their provisions should not depart from those therein. In particular, they cannot lay down rules affording human beings less protection than that resulting from the principles of the Convention.

168. To be able to sign or ratify a protocol, a State must have simultaneously or previously signed or ratified the Convention. On the other hand, States which have signed or ratified the Convention will not be obliged to sign or ratify a protocol.

Chapter XIII. Amendments to the Convention

Article 32. Amendments to the Convention

169. Amendments to the Convention shall be examined by the CDBI, or by any other committee designated by the Committee of Ministers. Accordingly, each member State of the Council of Europe, as well as each Party to the Convention which is not a member of the Council of Europe, will have the right to vote concerning the proposed amendments.

170. This article provides that the Convention shall be re-examined no later than five years from its entry into force and thereafter at such intervals as the Committee in charge of the re-examination may determine.

Chapter XIV. Final clauses

Article 33. Signature, ratification and entry into force

171. Other than the member States of the Council of Europe, the following States, which took part in its preparation, may sign the Convention: Australia, Canada, the Holy See, Japan and the United States of America.

Article 35. Territories

172. Since this provision is mainly aimed at overseas territories, it was agreed that it would be clearly against the philosophy of the Convention for any Party to exclude parts of its main territory from the application of this instrument, and that there would be no need to lay this down explicitly in the Convention.

Article 36. Reservations

173. This article, on the model of Article 64 of the European Convention of Human Rights, permits reservations in respect of any particular provision of the Convention, to the extent that any law in force is not in conformity with the provision.

174. The term law does not imply that a formal law is required (for example, in some countries, the professional bodies issue their own deontological rules which are applicable to their members to the extent that they do not contradict State norms). However, according to paragraph 1, a reservation of a general character, that is couched in terms too vague or broad for it to be possible to determine its exact meaning and scope, is not permitted.

175. Furthermore, according to paragraph 2, any reservation made shall contain a brief statement of the law concerned; this statement constitutes an evidential factor and contributes to legal certainty, and is not a purely formal requirement but a condition of substance (see European Court of Human Rights, Belilos Case, sections 55 and 59).

176. It was agreed that any declaration, even described as interpretative, made by the State or the European Community relating to any provision of the Convention, which seeks to modify for the declaring State the obligations deriving from such provision should meet, in order to be valid, the requirements set out in Article 36.

1.6. Charter of Fundamental Rights of the European Union (2007/C 303/01)

Preamble

The peoples of Europe, in creating an ever closer union among them, are resolved to share a peaceful future based on common values. Conscious of its spiritual and moral heritage, the Union is founded on the indivisible, universal values of human dignity, freedom, equality and solidarity; it is based on the principles of democracy and the rule of law. It places the individual at the heart of its activities, by establishing the citizenship of the Union and by creating an area of freedom, security and justice. The Union contributes to the preservation and to the development of these common values while respecting the diversity of the cultures and traditions of the peoples of Europe as well as the national identities of the Member States and the organisation of their public authorities at national, regional and local levels; it seeks to promote balanced and sustainable development and ensures free movement of persons, services, goods and capital, and the freedom of establishment. To this end, it is necessary to strengthen the protection of fundamental rights in the light of changes in society, social progress and scientific and technological developments by making those rights more visible in a Charter.

This Charter reaffirms, with due regard for the powers and tasks of the Union and for the principle of subsidiarity, the rights as they result, in particular, from the constitutional traditions and international obligations common to the Member States, the European Convention for the Protection of Human Rights and Fundamental Freedoms, the Social Charters adopted by the Union and by the Council of Europe and the case-law of the Court of Justice of the European Union and of the European Court of Human Rights. In this context the Charter will be interpreted by the courts of the Union and the Member States with due regard to the explanations prepared under the authority of the Praesidium of the Convention which drafted the Charter and updated under the responsibility of the Praesidium of the European Convention.

Enjoyment of these rights entails responsibilities and duties with regard to other persons, to the human community and to future generations. The Union therefore recognises the rights, freedoms and principles set out hereafter.

Title I. Dignity

ARTICLE 1. HUMAN DIGNITY

Human dignity is inviolable. It must be respected and protected.

ARTICLE 2. RIGHT TO LIFE

1. Everyone has the right to life.

2. No one shall be condemned to the death penalty, or executed.

ARTICLE 3. RIGHT TO THE INTEGRITY OF THE PERSON

1. Everyone has the right to respect for his or her physical and mental integrity.

2. In the fields of medicine and biology, the following must be respected in particular:

(a) the free and informed consent of the person concerned, according to the procedures laid down by law;
(b) the prohibition of eugenic practices, in particular those aiming at the selection of persons;
(c) the prohibition on making the human body and its parts as such a source of financial gain;
(d) the prohibition of the reproductive cloning of human beings.

ARTICLE 4. PROHIBITION OF TORTURE AND INHUMAN OR DEGRADING TREATMENT OR PUNISHMENT

No one shall be subjected to torture or to inhuman or degrading treatment or punishment.

ARTICLE 7. RESPECT FOR PRIVATE AND FAMILY LIFE

Everyone has the right to respect for his or her private and family life, home and communications.

ARTICLE 8. PROTECTION OF PERSONAL DATA

1. Everyone has the right to the protection of personal data concerning him or her.

2. Such data must be processed fairly for specified purposes and on the basis of the consent of the person concerned or some other legitimate basis laid down by law. Everyone has the right of access to data which has been collected concerning him or her, and the right to have it rectified.

3. Compliance with these rules shall be subject to control by an independent authority.

1.7. A Declaration on the Promotion of Patients' Rights in Europe (1994)

A WHO European Consultation on the Rights of Patients, meeting in Amsterdam from 28 to 30 March 1994, endorsed the document Principles of the rights of patients in Europe as a set of principles for the promotion and implementation of patients' rights in WHO's European Member States.

The meeting gave detailed consideration to a wide range of possible strategies based on the principles presented in the document and on the recent and current experiences of participants. The essence of these strategies is presented below.

Strategies for the Promotion of Patients' Rights

The development of a strategy to promote patients' rights and responsibilities has to be carefully prepared, in order to ensure that the intention is translated into practical action which Commands the support of all parties involved. Such action does not follow automatically, but takes time to become fully effective. National situations vary in respect of legal frameworks, health care systems, economic conditions, and social, cultural and ethical values, but there are certain common approaches which can be appropriately adapted to the circumstances of each country. We encourage all interested parties in our countries to initiate or renew multiple strategies of implementation, which will likely need most or all of the following components:

– legislation or regulations, specifying the rights, entitlements and responsibilities of patients, health professionals and health care institutions;
– medical and other professional codes, patients' charters and similar instruments, drawn up in the light of agreed common understandings between the representatives of citizens, patients, health professionals and policy-makers, and periodically revised in response to changing circumstances;
– networking between and among patient and health care provider groups, recognizing the distinction between citizen and user participation;
– government support for the establishment and effective running of nongovernmental organizations (NGOs) in the field of patients' rights;
– national colloquia and conferences to bring the parties together to create and promote a shared sense of understanding;
– involvement of the media in informing the public, stimulating constructive debate and sustaining awareness of the rights and responsibilities of patients and users and their representative organs;
– better training in communication and advocacy skills for health professionals as well as for patient and other user groups, in order to further the development of a proper understanding of the perspective and role of all parties;
– promotion of research to evaluate and document the effectiveness of legal and other provisions and the various initiatives taken in the diverse contexts of the different countries.

International Action

Cooperation between WHO, the Council of Europe and the European Union in support of patients' rights would be further enhanced by action taken as a result of this Consultation. Consistency of policy positions, coordinated strategies of implementation and an understanding of how their respective resources and competences can best be used are essential components of a sustained European movement to promote and protect the rights of patients and their professional providers and advisers. International NGOs also have a critical role to play in promoting the rights of patients. The forthcoming WHO Regional Conference on Health Policy (Copenhagen, 5-9 December 1994) will provide an important opportunity for further promoting patients' rights in Europe. The proposed WHO Regional Conference on Health Care Systems in Transition in Europe, to be held in Vienna on 23-28 March 1996, will also explore issues concerning the rights, roles and responsibilities of both patients and providers. We propose to WHO that the Regional Office should establish an appropriate mechanism to monitor developments in countries and to present the findings to the Vienna Conference.

Principles of the Rights of Patients in Europe: A Common Framework

Introduction

1. Background

Social, economic, cultural, ethical and political developments have given rise to a movement in Europe towards the fuller elaboration and fulfilment of the rights of patients. New and more positive concepts of patients' rights have been advocated. In part, this has been a reflection of the central place given both to full implementation of the concept of respect for persons and to equity in health as a policy objective in Member States. As a consequence there is now greater emphasis on the encouragement of individual choice and the opportunity to exercise it freely, and the commitment to build mechanisms for ensuring quality of care. Developments within health care systems such as their increasing complexity, the fact that medical practice has become more hazardous and in many cases more impersonal and dehumanized, often involving bureaucracy, and no less the progress made in medical and health science and technology have all placed new emphasis on the importance of recognizing the individual's right to self-determination and often on the need to reformulate guarantees of other rights of patients.

Simultaneously, the human rights movement has gathered importance in the world since 1945 when, in the Charter of the United Nations, Member States reaffirmed their faith in fundamental human rights. This was followed, on 10 December 1948, by the adoption of the Universal Declaration of Human Rights and, on 4 November 1950, by the signature of the European Convention of Human Rights. Governments are more and more giving their active consideration to such issues. The World Health Organization's study of patients' rights in Europe shows that increasingly there are shared principles that are being adopted in a number of countries and which seem to be independent of the characteristics of a given country's health system. It seems timely to give this policy trend further momentum.

The present document is an attempt to formulate a set of patients' rights which reflects the evolving concepts and is relevant to the context in which health care will be provided in future.

These principles of the rights of patients in Europe have been drafted in full awareness of the work of others who have already been engaged in drawing up instruments specific to patients' rights. For the most part though, such earlier efforts were directed at particular groups or concerned with specific activities in health care or approached patients' rights from the perspective of the duties and responsibilities of health care providers and establishments. The present text is the result of an attempt to refocus these concerns from the patient's point of view as the user of and partner in health care in all its various forms. It has been deliberately couched in general terms, so far as possible avoiding reference to the circumstances of particular groups or illustrative examples. It is felt, however, that this exposition of general considerations embraces the basic principles and concepts to be adopted when promoting and guaranteeing patients' rights in a particular country or other situation. particular needs and circumstances. The text does not directly cover questions of implementation, since these are necessarily specific to a country or situation; it has nevertheless been drafted in the belief that these guidelines can be further elaborated within countries to suit their particular needs and circumstances.

Guiding Principles

In this text, the concept of health care is derived from the principles of the World Health Assembly resolution on health for all (HFA) (WHA30.43, 19 May 1977) and the related model of health care set out in the Declaration of Alma-Ata (12 September 1978). Health care thus embraces a full range of services covering health promotion and protection, disease prevention, diagnosis, treatment, care and rehabilitation. Accordingly, the patient encounters a wide variety of health care providers and fulfils a variety of roles, from sick and dependent person to client receiving advice to consumer or customer obtaining health products for self-administration. Furthermore, this variety of patient roles implies a continuum of health states from high-level wellness to permanent disability and terminal illness.

In the treatment of patients' rights, a distinction should be made between social and individual rights. Social rights in health care relate to the societal obligation undertaken or otherwise enforced by government and other public or private bodies to make reasonable provision of health care for the whole population. What is reasonable in terms of the volume and range of services available and the degree of sophistication of technology and specialization will be dependent on political, social, cultural and economic factors. Social rights also relate to equal access to health care for all those living in a country or other geopolitical area and the elimination of unjustified discriminatory barriers, whether financial, geographical, cultural or social and psychological.

Social rights are enjoyed collectively and are relative to the level of development of the particular society; they are also in some measure subject to political judgment regarding priorities for development in a society.

In contrast, individual rights in patient care are more readily expressed in absolute terms and when made operational can be made enforceable on behalf of an individual patient. These rights cover such areas as the integrity of the person, privacy and religious convictions. Although this text does address social rights, the main focus is on individual rights. The conceptual foundations for this treatment of patients' rights are for the most part laid on a number of intergovernmental declarations relating to human rights and freedoms. The intention is not to create new rights but to apply them in one coherent, comprehensive statement to the field of patients and health care. For similar reasons the text does not address general rights, obligations and liabilities, which are covered by the statutes and case law of each country.

A further issue arises concerning the place of exceptional limitations to particular rights of patients. For the most part these have been kept out of the text, in order to state the proposed rights as clearly and simply as possible. It is therefore pertinent to clarify here at the outset the nature of the principal forms of limitation. Exceptions to the rights of patients are usually anticipated in law. The guiding rule in such exceptions is always that patients can be subjected only to such limitations as are compatible with human rights instruments and in accordance with a procedure prescribed by law. In practice, this means limitations which apply for reasons of public order, public health and other persons' human rights. In some situations, the reason for restricting the rights of the patient is an overriding interest of a third party (the so-called conflict of duties doctrine), i.e. the unfettered application of the patient's right would cause serious harm to a third party, there is no other means to avoid the harm and there is a reasonable expectation that the restriction would prevent the harm. In other situations a similar justification applies when the purpose is to avoid serious harm to the patient (the so-called therapeutic exception). As this document addresses general principles, these exceptional limitations to the rights of patients have mostly not been included.

Purpose of the Document

The principles of the rights of patients in Europe are offered as a contribution to support the growing interest in many Member States in the issues of patients' rights. In its scope and focus, this document seeks to reflect and express people's aspirations not only for improvements in their health care but also for fuller recognition of their rights as patients. In so doing, it keeps in mind the perspectives of health care providers as well as of patients. This implies the complementary nature of rights and responsibilities: patients have responsibilities both to themselves for their own self-care and to health care providers, and health care providers enjoy the same protection of their human rights as all other people. There is a basic assumption in the text that the articulation of patients' rights will in turn make people more conscious of their responsibilities when seeking and receiving or providing health care, and that this will ensure that patient/provider relationships are marked by mutual support and respect.

Patients should be aware of the practical contributions they can make to the optimal functioning of the health system. Their active participation in the diagnosis and treatment process is often desirable and sometimes indispensable. It is always important that they provide the relevant health professionals with all the information required for the purposes of diagnosis and treatment, The patient has an essential role, the reciprocal of the providers, in ensuring that the dialogue between them is carried out in good faith.

Indeed, the role patients play in the appropriate delivery of health care should be underlined, especially in today's complex health systems which are largely supported by collective financial mechanisms and where the economic and equitable use of resources allocated to health care is an objective which can be shared by health professionals and patients alike. Equally, while patients' participation in clinical teaching must be subject to their informed consent, they should also be aware that the competence of future professionals in par depends on patients agreeing to be involved in their training.

Implementation

It is a matter for decision by countries how they might make use of a document such as this when reviewing their present policies on, practices in and legislative support to, patients' rights.

Although for the purposes of clarity of presentation some proposals are made in a clear-cut way, the text is a set of guidelines which could be used in policy discussions within countries and in the formulation or reformulation, as the case may be, of national policies, laws or official statements on any or all of the issues covered. However, it is hoped that this document will be of direct value to all parties, including patient and consumer bodies involved in health care, professional associations of physicians and of other health care providers, and associations of hospitals and other health care establishments.

2. Objectives

Against this background, the Principles of the rights of patients in Europe can be seen, in terms of content, as a document which seeks:

– to reaffirm fundamental human rights in health care, and in particular to protect the dignity and integrity of the person and to promote respect of the patient as a person;
– to offer for the consideration of Member States a set of common basic principles underlying the rights of patients, which might be used when framing or reviewing patient care policies;
– to help patients obtain the fullest benefit from their use of the services of the health care system, and mitigate the effects of any problems which they may experience with that system;
– to promote and sustain beneficial relationships between patients and health care providers, and in particular to encourage a more active form of patient participation;
– to strengthen existing and afford new opportunities for dialogue between patients' organizations, health care providers, health administrations and wider societal interests;
– to focus national, regional and international attention on evolving needs in patients' rights and to foster closer international cooperation in this field;

– to ensure the protection of fundamental human rights and to promote the humanization of assistance to all patients, including the most vulnerable such as children, psychiatric patients,
– the elderly or the severely ill.

3. Conceptual Foundations

In drafting these Principles of the rights of patients in Europe, the following intergovernmental instruments, which together offer a framework and a set of basic concepts which can be applied to the rights of patients, have been taken into account:

– the Universal Declaration of Human Rights (1948)
– the International Covenant on Civil and Political Rights (1966)
– the International Covenant on Economic, Social and Cultural Rights (1966)
– the European Convention for the Protection of Human Rights and Fundamental Freedoms (1950)
– the European Social Charter (1961)
– the Rights of Patients

1. Human Rights and Values in Health Care.

The instruments cited in the introduction should be understood as applying also specifically in the health care setting, and it should therefore be noted that the human values expressed in these instruments shall be reflected in the health care system. It should also be noted that where exceptional limitations are imposed on the rights of patients, these must be in accordance with human rights instruments and have a legal base in the law of the country. It may be further observed that the rights specified below carry a matching responsibility to act with due concern for the health of others and for their same rights.

1.1 Everyone has the right to respect of his or her person as a human being.

1.2 Everyone has the right to self-determination.

1.3 Everyone has the right to physical and mental integrity and to the security of his or her person.

1.4 Everyone has the right to respect for his or her privacy.

1.5 Everyone has the right to have his or her moral and cultural values and religious and philosophical convictions respected

1.6 Everyone has the right to such protection of health as is afforded by appropriate measures for disease prevention and health care, and to the opportunity to pursue his or her own highest attainable level of health.

2. Information

2.1 Information about health services and how best to use them is to be made available to the public in order to benefit all those concerned.

2.2 Patients have the right to be fully informed about their health status, including the medical facts about their condition; about the proposed medical procedures, together with the potential risks and benefits of each procedure; about alternatives to the proposed procedures, including the effect of non-treatment; and about the diagnosis, prognosis and progress of treatment.

2.3 Information may only be withheld from patients exceptionally when there is good reason to believe that this information would without any expectation of obvious positive effects cause them serious harm.

2.4 Information must be communicated to the patient in a way appropriate to the latter's capacity for understanding, minimizing the use of unfamiliar technical terminology. If the patient does not speak the common language, some form of interpreting should be available.

2.5 Patients have the right not to be informed, at their explicit request.

2.6 Patients have the right to choose who, if any one, should be informed on their behalf.

2.7 Patients should have the possibility of obtaining a second opinion.

2.8 When admitted to a health care establishment, patients should be informed of the identity and professional status of the health care providers taking care of them and of any rules and routines which would bear on their stay and care.

2.9 Patients should be able to request and be given a written summary of their diagnosis, treatment and care on discharge from a health care establishment.

3. Consent

3.1 The informed consent of the patient is a prerequisite for any medical intervention.

3.2 A patient has the right to refuse or to halt a medical intervention. The implications of refusing or halting such an intervention must be carefully explained to the patient.

3.3 When a patient is unable to express his or her will and a medical intervention is urgently needed, the consent of the patient may be presumed, unless it is obvious from a previous declared expression of will that consent would be refused in the situation.

3.4 When the consent of a legal representative is required and the proposed intervention is urgently needed, that intervention may be made if it is not possible to obtain, in time, the representative's consent.

3.5 When the consent of a legal representative is required, patients (whether minor or adult) must nevertheless be involved in the decision-making process to the fullest extent which their capacity allows.

3.6 If a legal representative refuses to give consent and the physician or other provider is of the opinion that the intervention is in the interest of the patient, then the decision must be referred to a court or some form of arbitration.

3.7 In all other situations where the patient is unable to give informed consent and where there is no legal representative or representative designated by the patient for this purpose, appropriate measures should be taken to provide for a substitute decision making process, taking into account what is known and, to the greatest extent possible, what may be presumed about the wishes of the patient.

3.8 The consent of the patient is required for the preservation and use of all substances of the human body. Consent may be presumed when the substances are to be used in the current course of diagnosis, treatment and care of that patient.

3.9 The informed consent of the patient is needed for participation in clinical teaching.

3.10 The informed consent of the patient is a prerequisite for participation in scientific research. All protocols must be submitted to proper ethical review procedures. Such research should not be carried out on those who are unable to express their will, unless the consent of a legal representative has been obtained and the research would likely be in the interest of the patient. As an exception to the requirement of involvement being in the interest of the patient, an incapacitated person may be involved in observational research which is not of direct benefit to his or her health provided that that person offers no objection, that the risk and/or burden is minimal, that the research is of significant value and that no alternative methods and other research subjects are available.

4. Confidentiality and Privacy

4.1 All information about a patient's health status, medical condition, diagnosis, prognosis and treatment and all other information of a personal kind must be kept confidential, even after death.

4.2 Confidential information can only be disclosed if the patient gives explicit consent or if the law expressly provides for this. Consent may be presumed where disclosure is to other health care providers involved in that patient's treatment.

4.3 All identifiable patient data must be protected. The protection of the data must be appropriate to the manner of their storage. Human substances from which identifiable data can be derived must be likewise protected.

4.4 Patients have the right of access to their medical files and technical records and to any other files and records pertaining to their diagnosis, treatment and care and to receive a copy of their own files and records or parts thereof. Such access excludes data concerning third parties.

4.5 Patients have the right to require the correction, completion, deletion, clarification and/ or updating of personal and medical data concerning them which are inaccurate, incomplete, ambiguous or outdated, or which are not relevant to the purposes of diagnosis, treatment and care

4.6 There can be no intrusion into a patient's private and family life unless and only if, in addition to the patient consenting to it, it can be justified as necessary to the patient's diagnosis, treatment and care.

4.7 Medical interventions may only be carried out when there is proper respect shown for the privacy of the individual. This means that a given intervention may be carried out only in the presence of those persons who are necessary for the intervention unless the patient consents or requests otherwise.

4.8 Patients admitted to health care establishments have the right to expect physical facilities which ensure privacy, particularly when health care providers are offering them personal care or carrying out examinations and treatment.

5. Care and Treatment

5.1 Everyone has the right to receive such health care as is appropriate to his or her health needs, including preventive care and activities aimed at health promotion. Services should be continuously available and accessible to all equitably, without discrimination and according to the financial, human and material resources which can be made available in a given society.

5.2 Patients have a collective right to some form of representation at each level of the health care system in matters pertaining to the planning and evaluation of services, including the range, quality and functioning of the care provided.

5.3 Patients have the right to a quality of care which is marked both by high technical standards and by a humane relationship between the patient and health care providers.

5.4 Patients have the right to continuity of care, including cooperation between all health care providers and/or establishments which may be involved in their diagnosis, treatment and care.

5.5 In circumstances where a choice must be made by providers between potential patients for a particular treatment which is in limited supply, all such patients are entitled to a fair selection procedure for that treatment. That choice must be based on medical criteria and made without discrimination.

5.6 Patients have the right to choose and change their own physician or other health care provider and health care establishment, provided that it is compatible with the functioning of the health care system.

5.7 Patients for whom there are no longer medical grounds for continued stay in a health care establishment are entitled to a full explanation before they can be transferred to another establishment or sent home. Transfer can only take place after another health care establishment has agreed to accept the patient. Where the patient is discharged to home and when his or her condition so requires, community and domiciliary services should be available.

5.8 Patients have the right to be treated with dignity in relation to their diagnosis, treatment and care, which should be rendered with respect for their culture and values.

5.9 Patients have the right to enjoy support from family, relatives and friends during the course of care and treatment and to receive spiritual support and guidance at all times.

5.10 Patients have the right to relief of their suffering according to the current state of knowledge.

5.11 Patients have the right to humane terminal care and to die in dignity.

6. Application

6.1 The exercise of the rights set forth in this document implies that appropriate means are established for this purpose.

6.2 The enjoyment of these rights shall be secured without discrimination.

6.3 In the exercise of these rights, patients shall be subjected only to such limitations as are compatible with human rights instruments and in accordance with a procedure prescribed by law.

6.4 If patients cannot avail themselves of the rights set forth in this document, these rights should be exercised by their legal representative or by a person designated by the patient for that purpose; where neither a legal representative nor a personal Surrogate has been appointed, other measures for representation of those patients should be taken.

6.5 Patients must have access to such information and advice as will enable them to exercise the rights set forth in this document. Where patients feel that their rights have not been respected they should be enabled to lodge a complaint. In addition to recourse to the courts, there should be independent mechanisms at institutional and other levels to facilitate the processes of lodging, mediating and adjudicating complaints. These mechanisms would, inter alia, ensure that information relating to complaints procedures was available to patients and that an independent person was available and accessible to them for consultation regarding the most appropriate course of action to take. These mechanisms should further ensure that, where necessary, assistance and advocacy on behalf of the patient would be made available. Patients have the right to have their complaints examined and dealt with in a thorough, just, effective and prompt way and to be informed about their outcome.

...

1.8. African Charter on Human and Peoples' Rights

adopted June 27, 1981, OAU Doc. AB/LEG/67/3 rev. 5, 21 I.L.M. 58 (1982), entered into force Oct. 21, 1986

ARTICLE 4

Human beings are inviolable. Every human being shall be entitled to respect for his life and the integrity of his person. No one may be arbitrarily deprived of this right.

ARTICLE 5

Every individual shall have the right to the respect of the dignity inherent in a human being and to the recognition of his legal status. All forms of exploitation and degradation of man particularly slavery, slave trade, torture, cruel, inhuman or degrading punishment and treatment shall be prohibited.

ARTICLE 6

Every individual shall have the right to liberty and to the security of his person. No one may be deprived of his freedom except for reasons and conditions previously laid down by law. In particular, no one may be arbitrarily arrested or detained.

1.9. Additional Protocol to the Convention for the Protection of Human Rights and Dignity of the Human Being with regard to the Application of Biology and Medicine, on the Prohibition of Cloning Human Beings (ETS No. 168)

The member States of the Council of Europe, the other States and the European Community Signatories to this Additional Protocol to the Convention for the Protection of Human Rights and Dignity of the Human Being with regard to the Application of Biology and Medicine, Noting scientific developments in the field of mammal cloning, particularly through embryo splitting and nuclear transfer; Mindful of the progress that some cloning techniques themselves may bring to scientific knowledge and its medical application; Considering that the cloning of human beings may become a technical possibility; Having noted that embryo splitting may occur naturally and sometimes result in the birth of genetically identical twins; Considering however that the instrumentalisation of human beings through the deliberate creation of genetically identical human beings is contrary to human dignity and thus constitutes a misuse of biology and medicine; Considering also the serious difficulties of a medical, psychological and social nature that such a deliberate biomedical practice might imply for all the individuals involved; Considering the purpose of the Convention on Human Rights and Biomedicine, in particular the principle mentioned in Article 1 aiming to protect the dignity and identity of all human beings,

Have agreed as follows:

ARTICLE 1

1. Any intervention seeking to create a human being genetically identical to another human being, whether living or dead, is prohibited.

2. For the purpose of this article, the term human being "genetically identical" to another human being means a human being sharing with another the same nuclear gene set.

ARTICLE 2

No derogation from the provisions of this Protocol shall be made under Article 26, paragraph 1, of the Convention.

ARTICLE 3

As between the Parties, the provisions of Articles 1 and 2 of this Protocol shall be regarded as additional articles to the Convention and all the provisions of the Convention shall apply accordingly.

ARTICLE 4

This Protocol shall be open for signature by Signatories to the Convention. It is subject to ratification, acceptance or approval. A Signatory may not ratify, accept or approve this Protocol unless it has previously or simultaneously ratified, accepted or approved the Convention. Instruments of ratification, acceptance or approval shall be deposited with the Secretary General of the Council of Europe.

1.10. Additional Protocol to the Convention on Human Rights and Biomedicine on the Prohibition of Cloning Human Beings (ETS No. 168)

Explanatory Report

I. The Additional Protocol to the Convention on Human Rights and Biomedicine on the Prohibition of Cloning Human Beings was opened to signature by Signatories to the Convention, in Paris, on 12 January 1998.

II. The text of the Explanatory Report does not constitute an instrument providing an authoritative interpretation of the text of the Protocol, although it might be of such nature as to facilitate the understanding of the provisions contained therein.

Commentary

1. This Protocol builds on certain provisions of the Convention on Human Rights and Biomedicine, in particular the following: Article 1 provides that Parties to this Convention shall protect the dignity and identity of all human beings and guarantee everyone, without discrimination, respect for their integrity and other rights and fundamental freedoms with regard to the application of biology and medicine; Article 13, which provides that an intervention seeking to modify the human genome may only be undertaken for preventive, diagnostic or therapeutic purposes and only if its aim is not to introduce any modification in the genome of any descendants; Article 18.1, which ensures the protection of the embryo in vitro in the framework of research and Article 18.2 which prohibits the creation of embryos for research purposes.

2. Cloning of cells and tissue is considered worldwide to be an ethically acceptable valuable biomedical technique. However, there are different views about the ethical acceptability of cloning undifferentiated cells of embryonic origin. Whatever attitudes towards such cloning techniques exist, the standards set forth in the Convention on Human Rights and Biomedicine as mentioned above form clear barriers against the misuse of human embryos, as their adequate protection is guaranteed and their creation for research purposes is prohibited by Article 18 of the Convention. Therefore, one has to distinguish between three situations: cloning of cells as a technique, use of embryonic cells in cloning techniques, and cloning of human beings, for example by utilising the techniques of embryo splitting or nuclear transfer. Whereas the first situation is fully acceptable ethically, the second should be examined in the protocol on embryo protection. The consequences of the third situation, that is the prohibition of cloning human beings, are within the scope of this Protocol.

3. Deliberately cloning humans is a threat to human identity, as it would give up the indispensable protection against the predetermination of the human genetic constitution by a third party. Further ethical reasoning for a prohibition to clone human beings is based first and foremost on human dignity which is endangered by instrumentalisation through artificial human cloning. Even if in the future, in theory, a situation could be conceived, which might seem to

exclude the instrumentalisation of artificially cloned human offspring, this is not considered a sufficient ethical justification for the cloning of human beings. As naturally occurring genetic recombination is likely to create more freedom for the human being than a predetermined genetic make up, it is in the interest of all persons to keep the essentially random nature of the composition of their own genes.

4. This Protocol does not take a specific stand on the admissibility of cloning cells and tissue for research purposes resulting in medical applications. However, it can be said that cloning as a biomedical technique is an important tool for the development of medicine, especially for the development of new therapies. The provisions in this Protocol shall not be understood as prohibiting cloning techniques in cell biology.

5. However, the Protocol does enshrine clear barriers against any attempt artificially to produce genetically identical human beings. The Protocol is not concerned with hormone stimulation to treat infertility in women and which might result in the birth of twins. It explicitly restricts genetic identity to sharing the same nuclear gene set, meaning that any intervention by embryo splitting or nuclear transfer techniques seeking to create a human being genetically identical to another human being, whether living or dead, is prohibited.

6. In conformity with the approach followed in the preparation of the Convention on Human Rights and Biomedicine, it was decided to leave it to domestic law to define the scope of the expression "human being" for the purposes of the application of the present Protocol.

7. The term "nuclear" means that only genes of the nucleus – not the mitochondrial genes – are looked at with respect to identity, which is why the prohibition of cloning human beings also covers all nuclear transfer methods seeking to create identical human beings. The term "the same nuclear gene set" takes into account the fact that during development some genes may undergo somatic mutation. Thus monozygotic twins developed from a single fertilised egg will share the same nuclear gene set, but may not be 100% identical with respect to all their genes. It is important to note that the Protocol does not intend to discriminate in any fashion against natural monozygotic twins.

8. This Protocol is an important step in drawing up clear ethical and legal provisions in the area of reproductive medicine. Together with the provisions in Articles 1, 13, 14 and 18 of the Convention, it enshrines important ethical principles which should form the basis for further developments of biology and medicine in this field not only today but also in the future.

1.11. World Medical Association Declaration on the Rights of the Patient

Adopted by the 34th World Medical Assembly, Lisbon, Portugal, September/October 1981, and amended by the 47th WMA General Assembly, Bali, Indonesia, September 1995, and editorially revised at the 171st Council Session, Santiago, Chile, October 2005

Preamble

The relationship between physicians, their patients and broader society has undergone significant changes in recent times. While a physician should always act according to his/her conscience, and always in the best interests of the patient, equal effort must be made to guarantee patient autonomy and justice. The following Declaration represents some of the principal rights of the patient that the medical profession endorses and promotes. Physicians and other persons or bodies involved in the provision of health care have a joint responsibility to recognize and uphold these rights. Whenever legislation, government action or any other administration or institution denies patients these rights, physicians should pursue appropriate means to assure or to restore them.

Principles

1. Right to medical care of good quality

a. Every person is entitled without discrimination to appropriate medical care.

b. Every patient has the right to be cared for by a physician whom he/she knows to be free to make clinical and ethical judgements without any outside interference.

c. The patient shall always be treated in accordance with his/her best interests. The treatment applied shall be in accordance with generally approved medical principles.

d. Quality assurance should always be a part of health care. Physicians, in particular, should accept responsibility for being guardians of the quality of medical services.

e. In circumstances where a choice must be made between potential patients for a particular treatment that is in limited supply, all such patients are entitled to a fair selection procedure for that treatment. That choice must be based on medical criteria and made without discrimination.

f. The patient has the right to continuity of health care. The physician has an obligation to cooperate in the coordination of medically indicated care with other health care providers treating the patient. The physician may not discontinue treatment of a patient as long as further treatment is medically indicated, without giving the patient reasonable assistance and sufficient opportunity to make alternative arrangements for care.

2. Right to freedom of choice

a. The patient has the right to choose freely and change his/her physician and hospital or health service institution, regardless of whether they are based in the private or public sector.

b. The patient has the right to ask for the opinion of another physician at any stage.

3. Right to self-determination

a. The patient has the right to self-determination, to make free decisions regarding himself/herself. The physician will inform the patient of the consequences of his/her decisions.

b. A mentally competent adult patient has the right to give or withhold consent to any diagnostic procedure or therapy. The patient has the right to the information necessary to make his/her decisions. The patient should understand clearly what is the purpose of any test or treatment, what the results would imply, and what would be the implications of withholding consent.

c. The patient has the right to refuse to participate in research or the teaching of medicine.

4. The unconscious patient

a. If the patient is unconscious or otherwise unable to express his/her will, informed consent must be obtained whenever possible, from a legally entitled representative.

b. If a legally entitled representative is not available, but a medical intervention is urgently needed, consent of the patient may be presumed, unless it is obvious and beyond any doubt on the basis of the patient's previous firm expression or conviction that he/she would refuse consent to the intervention in that situation.

c. However, physicians should always try to save the life of a patient unconscious due to a suicide attempt.

5. The legally incompetent patient

a. If a patient is a minor or otherwise legally incompetent, the consent of a legally entitled representative is required in some jurisdictions. Nevertheless the patient must be involved in the decision-making to the fullest extent allowed by his/her capacity.

b. If the legally incompetent patient can make rational decisions, his/her decisions must be respected, and he/she has the right to forbid the disclosure of information to his/her legally entitled representative.

c. If the patient's legally entitled representative, or a person authorized by the patient, forbids treatment which is, in the opinion of the physician, in the patient's best interest, the physician should challenge this decision in the relevant legal or other institution. In case of emergency, the physician will act in the patient's best interest.

6. Procedures against the patient's will

Diagnostic procedures or treatment against the patient's will can be carried out only in exceptional cases, if specifically permitted by law and conforming to the principles of medical ethics.

7. Right to information

a. The patient has the right to receive information about himself/herself recorded in any of his/her medical records, and to be fully informed about his/her health status including the medical facts about his/her condition. However, confidential information in the patient's records about a third party should not be given to the patient without the consent of that third party.

b. Exceptionally, information may be withheld from the patient when there is good reason to believe that this information would create a serious hazard to his/her life or health.

c. Information should be given in a way appropriate to the patient's culture and in such a way that the patient can understand.

d. The patient has the right not to be informed on his/her explicit request, unless required for the protection of another person's life.

e. The patient has the right to choose who, if anyone, should be informed on his/her behalf.

8. Right to confidentiality

a. All identifiable information about a patient's health status, medical condition, diagnosis, prognosis and treatment and all other information of a personal kind must be kept confidential, even after death. Exceptionally, descendants may have a right of access to information that would inform them of their health risks.

b. Confidential information can only be disclosed if the patient gives explicit consent or if expressly provided for in the law. Information can be disclosed to other health care providers only on a strictly "need to know" basis unless the patient has given explicit consent.

c. All identifiable patient data must be protected. The protection of the data must be appropriate to the manner of its storage. Human substances from which identifiable data can be derived must be likewise protected.

9. Right to Health Education

Every person has the right to health education that will assist him/her in making informed choices about personal health and about the available health services. The education should include information about healthy lifestyles and about methods of prevention and early detection of illnesses. The personal responsibility of everybody for his/her own health should be stressed. Physicians have an obligation to participate actively in educational efforts.

10. Right to dignity

a. The patient's dignity and right to privacy shall be respected at all times in medical care and teaching, as shall his/her culture and values.

b. The patient is entitled to relief of his/her suffering according to the current state of knowledge.

c. The patient is entitled to humane terminal care and to be provided with all available assistance in making dying as dignified and comfortable as possible.

...

Chapter 2. Prisoners and patients' rights

2.1. Recommendation No. R (98) 71 of the Committee of Ministers to Member States concerning the ethical and organisational aspects of health care in prison

(Adopted by the Committee of Ministers on 8 April 1998)

...

C. Patient's consent and confidentiality

13. Medical confidentiality should be guaranteed and respected with the same rigour as in the population as a whole.

14. Unless inmates suffer from any illness which renders them incapable of understanding the nature of their condition, they should always be entitled to give the doctor their informed consent before any physical examination of their person or their body products can be undertaken, except in cases provided for by law. The reasons for each examination should be clearly explained to, and understood by, the inmates. The indication for any medication should be explained to the inmates, together with any possible side effects likely to be experienced by them.

15. Informed consent should be obtained in the case of mentally ill patients as well as in situations when medical duties and security requirements may not coincide, for example refusal of treatment or refusal of food.

16. Any derogation from the principle of freedom of consent should be based upon law and be guided by the same principles which are applicable to the population as a whole.

17. Remand prisoners should be entitled to ask for a consultation with their own doctor or another outside doctor at their own expense.

Sentenced prisoners may seek a second medical opinion and the prison doctor should give this proposition sympathetic consideration. However, any decision as to the merits of this request is ultimately his responsibility.

18. All transfers to other prisons should be accompanied by full medical records. The records should be transferred under conditions ensuring their confidentiality. Prisoners should be

informed that their medical record will be transferred. They should be entitled to object to the transfer, in accordance with national legislation.

All released prisoners should be given relevant written information concerning their health for the benefit of their family doctor.

E. Refusal of treatment, hunger strike

60. In the case of refusal of treatment, the doctor should request a written statement signed by the patient in the presence of a witness. The doctor should give the patient full information as to the likely benefits of medication, possible therapeutic alternatives, and warn him/her about risks associated with his/her refusal. It should be ensured that the patient has a full understanding of his/her situation. If there are difficulties of comprehension due to the language used by the patient, the services of an experienced interpreter must be sought.

61. The clinical assessment of a hunger striker should be carried out only with the express permission of the patient, unless he or she suffers from serious mental disorders which require the transfer to a psychiatric service.

62. Hunger strikers should be given an objective explanation of the harmful effects of their action upon their physical well-being, so that they understand the dangers of prolonged hunger striking.

63. If, in the opinion of the doctor, the hunger striker's condition is becoming significantly worse, it is essential that the doctor report this fact to the appropriate authority and take action in accordance with national legislation (including professional standards).

H. Body searches, medical reports, medical research

74. Medical research on prisoners should be carried out in accordance with the principles set out in Recommendations No. R (87) 3 on the European Prison Rules, No. R (90) 3 on medical research in human beings and No. R (93) 6 on prison and criminological aspects of the control of transmissible diseases including Aids and related health problems in prison.

...

Chapter 3. Mentally ill and patients' rights

3.1. Declaration on the Rights of Mentally Retarded Persons

Proclaimed by General Assembly resolution 2856 (XXVI) of 20 December 1971

The General Assembly,

Mindful of the pledge of the States Members of the United Nations under the Charter to take joint and separate action in co-operation with the Organization to promote higher standards of living, full employment and conditions of economic and social progress and development, Reaffirming faith in human rights and fundamental freedoms and in the principles of peace, of the dignity and worth of the human person and of social justice proclaimed in the Charter, Recalling the principles of the Universal Declaration of Human Rights, the International Covenants on Human Rights, the Declaration of the Rights of the Child and the standards already set for social progress in the constitutions, conventions, recommendations and resolutions of the International Labour Organisation, the United Nations Educational, Scientific and Cultural Organization, the World Health Organization, the United Nations Children's Fund and other organizations concerned, Emphasizing that the Declaration on Social Progress and Development has proclaimed the necessity of protecting the rights and assuring the welfare and rehabilitation of the physically and mentally disadvantaged, Bearing in mind the necessity of assisting mentally retarded persons to develop their abilities in various fields of activities and of promoting their integration as far as possible in normal life, Aware that certain countries, at their present stage of development, can devote only limited efforts to this end, Proclaims this Declaration on the Rights of Mentally Retarded Persons and calls for national and international action to en sure that it will be used as a common basis and frame of reference for the protection of these rights:

1. The mentally retarded person has, to the maximum degree of feasibility, the same rights as other human beings.

2. The mentally retarded person has a right to proper medical care and physical therapy and to such education, training, rehabilitation and guidance as will enable him to develop his ability and maximum potential.

3. The mentally retarded person has a right to economic security and to a decent standard of living. He has a right to perform productive work or to engage in any other meaningful occupation to the fullest possible extent of his capabilities.

4. Whenever possible, the mentally retarded person should live with his own family or with foster parents and participate in different forms of community life. The family with which he lives should receive assistance. If care in an institution becomes necessary, it should be provided in surroundings and other circumstances as close as possible to those of normal life.

5. The mentally retarded person has a right to a qualified guardian when this is required to protect his personal well-being and interests.

6. The mentally retarded person has a right to protection from exploitation, abuse and degrading treatment. If prosecuted for any offence, he shall have a right to due process of law with full recognition being given to his degree of mental responsibility.

7. Whenever mentally retarded persons are unable, because of the severity of their handicap, to exercise all their rights in a meaningful way or it should become necessary to restrict or deny some or all of these rights, the procedure used for that restriction or denial of rights must contain proper legal safeguards against every form of abuse. This procedure must be based on an evaluation of the social capability of the mentally retarded person by qualified experts and must be subject to periodic review and to the right of appeal to higher authorities.

3.2. Madrid Declaration on Ethical Standards for psychiatric practice (Declaration of Madrid)

Approved by the General Assembly of the World Psychiatric Association in Madrid, Spain, on August 25, 1996, and enhanced by the WPA General Assemblies in Hamburg, Germany on August 8, 1999, in Yokohama, Japan, on August 26, 2002, and in Cairo, Egypt, on September 12, 2005.

In 1977, the World Psychiatric Association approved the Declaration of Hawaii which set out ethical guidelines for the practice of psychiatry. The Declaration was updated in Vienna in 1983. To reflect the impact of changing social attitudes and new medical developments on the psychiatric profession, the World Psychiatric Association has once again undertaken a review of ethical standards that should be abided to by all its members and all persons practicing psychiatry.

Medicine is both a healing art and a science. The dynamics of this combination are best reflected in psychiatry, the branch of medicine that specializes in the care and protection of those who are ill or infirm, because of a mental disorder or impairment. Although there may be cultural, social and national differences, the need for ethical conduct and continual review of ethical standards is universal.

As practitioners of medicine, psychiatrists must be aware of the ethical implications of being a physician, and of the specific ethical demands of the specialty of psychiatry. As members of society, psychiatrists must advocate for fair and equal treatment of the mentally ill, for social justice and equity for all.

Ethical practice is based on the psychiatrist's individual sense of responsibility to the patient and judgment in determining what is correct and appropriate conduct. External standards and influences such as professional codes of conduct, the study of ethics, or the rule of law by themselves will not guarantee the ethical practice of medicine.

Psychiatrists should keep in mind at all times the boundaries of the psychiatrist-patient relationship, and be guided primarily by the respect for patients and concern for their welfare and integrity.

It is in this spirit that the World Psychiatric Association approved at the General Assembly on August 25th, 1996, amended on August 8th 1999 and on August 26th 2002 the following ethical standards that should govern the practice of psychiatrists universally.

1. Psychiatry is a medical discipline concerned with the prevention of mental disorders in the population, the provision of the best possible treatment for mental disorders, the rehabilitation of individuals suffering from mental illness and the promotion of mental health. Psychiatrists serve patients by providing the best therapy available consistent with accepted scientific knowledge and ethical principles. Psychiatrists should devise therapeutic interventions that

are least restrictive to the freedom of the patient and seek advice in areas of their work about which they do not have primary expertise. While doing so, psychiatrists should be aware of and concerned with the equitable allocation of health resources.

2. It is the duty of psychiatrists to keep abreast of scientific developments of the specialty and to convey updated knowledge to others. Psychiatrists trained in research should seek to advance the scientific frontiers of psychiatry.

3. The patient should be accepted as a partner by right in the therapeutic process. The psychiatrist-patient relationship must be based on mutual trust and respect to allow the patient to make free and informed decisions. It is the duty of psychiatrists to provide the patient with all relevant information so as to empower the patient to come to a rational decision according to personal values and preferences.

4. When the patient is gravely disabled, incapacitated and/or incompetent to exercise proper judgment because of a mental disorder, the psychiatrists should consult with the family and, if appropriate, seek legal counsel, to safeguard the human dignity and the legal rights of the patient. No treatment should be provided against the patient's will, unless withholding treatment would endanger the life of the patient and/or the life of others. Treatment must always be in the best interest of the patient.

5. When psychiatrists are requested to assess a person, it is their duty first to inform and advise the person being assessed about the purpose of the intervention, the use of the findings, and the possible repercussions of the assessment. This is particularly important when psychiatrists are involved in third party situations.

6. Information obtained in the therapeutic relationship is private to the patient and should be kept in confidence and used, only and exclusively, for the purpose of improving the mental health of the patient. Psychiatrists are prohibited from making use of such information for personal reasons, or personal benefit. Breach of confidentiality may only be appropriate when required by law (as in obligatory reporting of child abuse) or when serious physical or mental harm to the patient or to a third person would ensue if confidentiality were maintained; whenever possible, psychiatrists should first advise the patient about the action to be taken.

7. Research that is not conducted in accordance with the canons of science and that is not scientifically valid is unethical. Research activities should be approved by an appropriately constituted ethics committee. Psychiatrists should follow national and international rules for the conduct of research. Only individuals properly trained for research should undertake or direct it. Because psychiatric patients constitute a particularly vulnerable research population, extra caution should be taken to assess their competence to participate as research subjects and to safeguard their autonomy and their mental and physical integrity. Ethical standards should also be applied in the selection of population groups, in all types of research including epidemiological and sociological studies and in collaborative research involving other disciplines or several investigating centres.

Guidelines concerning specific situations

The World Psychiatric Association Ethics Committee recognizes the need to develop a number of specific guidelines on a number of specific situations. The first five were approved by the General Assembly in Madrid, Spain, on August 25, 1996, the 6 through 8 by the General Assembly in Hamburg, Germany, on August 8, 1999, the 9 through 12 by the General Assembly in Yokohama, Japan, on August 26, 2002, and the 13 through 15 at the General Assembly in Cairo, Egypt, on September 12, 2005.

1. Euthanasia: A physician's duty, first and foremost, is the promotion of health, the reduction of suffering, and the protection of life. The psychiatrist, among whose patients are some who are severely incapacitated and incompetent to reach an informed decision, should be particularly careful of actions that could lead to the death of those who cannot protect themselves because of their disability. The psychiatrist should be aware that the views of a patient may be distorted by mental illness such as depression. In such situations, the psychiatrist's role is to treat the illness.

2. Torture: Psychiatrists shall not take part in any process of mental or physical torture, even when authorities attempt to force their involvement in such acts.

3. Death Penalty: Under no circumstances should psychiatrists participate in legally authorized executions nor participate in assessments of competency to be executed.

4. Selection of Sex: Under no circumstances should a psychiatrist participate in decisions to terminate pregnancy for the purpose of sex selection.

5. Organ Transplantation: The role of the psychiatrist is to clarify the issues surrounding organ donations and to advise on religious, cultural, social and family factors to ensure that informed and proper decisions be made by all concerned. The psychiatrists should not act as a proxy decision maker for patients nor use psychotherapeutic skills to influence the decision of a patient in these matters. Psychiatrists should seek to protect their patients and help them exercise self-determination to the fullest extent possible in situations of organ transplantation.

6. Psychiatrists addressing the media. In all contacts with the media psychiatrists shall ensure that people with mental illness are presented in a manner which preserves their dignity and pride, and which reduces stigma and discrimination against them.

An important role of psychiatrists is to advocate for those people who suffer from mental disorders. As the public perception of psychiatrists and psychiatry reflects on patients, psychiatrists shall ensure that in their contact with the media they represent the profession of psychiatry with dignity.

Psychiatrists shall not make announcements to the media about presumed psychopathology on any individuals.

In presenting research findings to the media, psychiatrists shall ensure the scientific integrity of the information given and be mindful of the potential impact of their statements on the public perception of mental illness and on the welfare of people with mental disorders.

7. Psychiatrists and discrimination on ethnic or cultural grounds. Discrimination by psychiatrists on the basis of ethnicity or culture, whether directly or by aiding others is unethical. Psychiatrists shall never be involved or endorse, directly or indirectly, any activity related to ethnic cleansing.

8. Psychiatrists and genetic research and counseling: Research on the genetic bases of mental disorders is rapidly increasing and more people suffering from mental illness are participating in such research.

Psychiatrists involved in genetic research or counseling shall be mindful of the fact that the implication of genetic information are not limited to the individual from whom it was obtained and that its disclosure can have negative and disruptive effects on the families and communities of the individuals concerned.

Psychiatrist shall therefore ensure that:

- People and families who participate in genetic research do so with a fully informed consent;
- Any genetic information in their possession is adequately protected against unauthorized access, misinterpretation or misuse;
- Care is taken in communication with patients and families to make clear that current genetic knowledge is incomplete and may be altered by future findings.

Psychiatrists shall only refer people to facilities for diagnostic genetic testing if that facility has:
- Demonstrated satisfactory quality assurance, procedures for such testing;
- Adequate and easily accessible resources for genetic counseling.

Genetic counseling with regard to family planning or abortion shall be respectful of the patients' value system, while providing sufficient medical and psychiatric information to aid patients make decisions they consider best for them.

9. Ethics of Psychotherapy in Medicine: Medical treatments of any nature should be administered under the provisions of good practice guidelines regarding their indications, effectiveness, safety, and quality control. Psychotherapy, in its broadest sense, is an accepted component of many medical interactions. In a more specific and restricted sense, psychotherapy utilizes techniques involving verbal and non-verbal communication and interaction to achieve specified treatment goals in the care of specific disorders. Psychiatrists providing specific forms of psychotherapy must have appropriate training in such techniques. The general guidelines that apply to any medical treatment also apply to specific forms of psychotherapy in regard to

its indications and outcomes, positive or negative. The effectiveness of psychotherapy and its place in a treatment plan are important subjects for both researchers and clinicians.

Psychotherapy by psychiatrists is a form of treatment for mental and other illnesses and emotional problems. The treatment approach utilized is determined in concert by the doctor and patient and/or the patient's family and/or guardians following a careful history and examination employing all relevant clinical and laboratory studies. The approach employed should be specific to the disease and patient's needs and sensitive to personal, familial, religious and cultural factors. It should be based on sound research and clinical wisdom and have the purpose of removing, modifying or retarding symptoms or disturbed patterns of behavior. It should promote positive adaptations including personal growth and development.

Psychiatrists and other clinicians responsible for a patient have to ensure that these guidelines are fully applied. Therefore, the psychiatrist or other delegated qualified clinician should determine the indications for psychotherapy and follow its development. In this context the essential notion is that the treatment is the consequence of a diagnosis and both are medical acts performed to take care of an ill person. These two levels of decisions, interventions and responsibilities are similar to other situations in clinical medicine; however, this does not exclude other interventions such as rehabilitation, which can be administered by non-medical personnel.

1. Like any other treatment in medicine, the prescription of psychotherapy should follow accepted guidelines for obtaining informed consent prior to the initiation of treatment as well as updating it in the course of treatment if goals and objectives of treatment are modified in a significant way.
2. If clinical wisdom, long standing and well-established practice patterns (this takes into consideration cultural and religious issues) and scientific evidence suggest potential clinical benefits to combining medication treatment with psychotherapy this should be brought to the patient's attention and fully discussed.
3. Psychotherapy explores intimate thoughts, emotions and fantasies, and as such may engender intense transference and counter-transference. In a psychotherapy relationship the power is unequally shared between the therapist and patient, and under no circumstances shall the psychotherapist use this relationship to personal advantage or transgress the boundaries established by the professional relationship.
4. At the initiation of psychotherapy, the patient shall be advised that information shared and health records will be kept in confidence except where the patient gives specific informed consent for release of information to third parties, or where a court order may require the production of records. The other exception is where there is a legal requirement to report certain information as in the case of child abuse.

10. Conflict of Interest in Relationship with Industry: Although most organizations and institutions, including the WPA, have rules and regulations governing their relationship with industry and donors, individual physicians are often involved in interactions with the pharmaceutical

industry, or other granting agencies that could lead to ethical conflict In these situations psychiatrists should be mindful of and apply the following guidelines.

1. The practitioner must diligently guard against accepting gifts that could have an undue influence on professional work.
2. Psychiatrists conducting clinical trials are under an obligation to disclose to the Ethics Review Board and their research subjects their financial and contractual obligations and benefits related to the sponsor of the study. Every effort should be made to set up review boards composed of researchers, ethicists and community representatives to assure the rights of research subjects are protected.
3. Psychiatrists conducting clinical trials have to ensure that their patients have understood all aspects of the informed consent. The level of education or sophistication of the patient is no excuse for bypassing this commitment. If the patient is deemed incompetent the same rules would apply in obtaining informed consent from the substitute decision maker. Psychiatrists must be cognizant that covert commercial influence on the trial design, promotion of drugs trials without scientific value, breach of confidentiality, and restrictive contractual clauses regarding publication of results may each in different ways encroach upon the freedom of science and scientific information.

11. Conflicts Arising with Third Party Players: The obligations of organizations toward shareholders or the administrator regarding maximization of profits and minimization of costs can be in conflict with the principles of good practice Psychiatrists working in such potentially conflicting environments, should uphold the rights of the patients to receive the best treatment possible.

1. In agreement with the UN Resolution 46/119 of the "Principles for the Protection of Persons with Mental Illness, psychiatrists should oppose discriminatory practices which limit their benefits and entitlements, deny parity curb the scope of treatment, or limit their access to proper medications for patients with a mental disorder.
2. Professional independence to apply best practice guidelines and clinical wisdom in upholding the welfare of the patient should be the primary considerations for the psychiatrist. It is also the duty of the psychiatrist to protect the patient privacy and confidentiality as part of preserving the sanctity and healing potential of the doctor-patient relationship.

12. Violating the Clinical Boundaries and Trust Between Psychiatrists and Patients: The psychiatrist-patient relationship may be the only relationship that permits an exploration of the deeply personal and emotional space, as granted by the patient. Within this relationship, the psychiatrist's respect for the humanity and dignity of the patient builds a foundation of trust that is essential for a comprehensive treatment plan. The relationship encourages the patient to explore deeply held strengths, weaknesses, fears, and desires, and many of these might be related to sexuality. Knowledge of these characteristics of the patient places the psychiatrist in a position of advantage that the patient allows on the expectation of trust and respect. Taking advantage of that knowledge by manipulating the patient's sexual fears and desires in order to obtain sexual access is a breach of the trust, regardless of consent. In the therapeutic

relationship, consent on the part of the patient is considered vitiated by the knowledge the psychiatrists possesses about the patient and by the power differential that vests the psychiatrist with special authority over the patient. Consent under these circumstances will be tantamount to exploitation of the patient.

The latent sexual dynamics inherent in all relationships can become manifest in the course of the therapeutic relationship and if they are not properly handled by the therapist can produce anguish to the patient. This anguish is likely to become more pronounced if seductive statements and inappropriate non-verbal behavior are used by the therapist. Under no circumstances, therefore, should a psychiatrist get involved with a patient in any form of sexual behavior, irrespective of whether this behavior is initiated by the patient or the therapist.

13. Protection of the Rights of Psychiatrists:

0. Psychiatrists need to protect their right to live up to the obligations of their profession and to the expectations the public has of them to treat and to advocate for the welfare of their patients.
1. Psychiatrists ought to have the right to practice their specialty at the highest level of excellence by providing independent assessments of a persons' mental condition and by instituting effective treatment and management protocols in accordance to best practices and evidence-based medicine.
2. There are aspects in the history of psychiatry and in present working expectations in some totalitarian political regimes and profit driven economical systems that increase psychiatrists' vulnerabilities to be abused in the sense of having to acquiesce to inappropriate demands to provide inaccurate psychiatric reports that help the system, but damage the interests of the person being assessed.
3. Psychiatrists also share the stigma of their patients and, similarly, can become victims of discriminatory practices. It should be the right and the obligation of psychiatrists to practice their profession and to advocate for the medical needs and the social and political rights of their patients without suffering being outcast by the profession, being ridiculed in the media or persecuted.

14. Disclosing the Diagnosis of Alzheimer's Disease (AD) and Other Dementias: AD patient's right to know is now a well established priority, recognised by healthcare professionals. Most patients want all information available and to be actively involved in making decision about treatments. At the same time, patients have the right also not to know if that is their wish. All must be given the opportunity to learn as much or as little as they want to know.

The alteration of patient's cognition makes the ability to make judgements and insight more difficult. Patients with dementia are also often brought by family members which introduces into the doctor-patient relationship a third partner.

Doctors, patients and families who share the responsibilities for fighting and coping with Alzheimer's disease for years all require access to information on the disease, including the diagnosis.

In addition to the "patient's right to know", telling the patient has many benefits. Patients and/or families should be told the diagnosis as early as possible in the disease process. Having family (or informal carer) involved in the discussion of the disclosure process is highly beneficial.

The physician should give accurate and reliable information, using simple language. He also should assess the patient's and the family's understanding of the situation. As usual, the bad news should be accompanied by information on a treatment and management plan. Information on physical or speech therapy, support groups, day care centres, and other interventions should be provided. It should also be emphasised that a reorganised family network can alleviate the carer's burden and maintain quality of life as far as possible.

There are some exceptions, some of them transitory, to the disclosure of the diagnosis to a patient with dementia: 1) severe dementia where understanding the diagnosis is unlikely, 2) when a phobia about the condition is likely, or 3) when a patient is severely depressed;

15. Dual Responsibilities of Psychiatrists: These situations may arise as part of legal proceedings (i.e. fitness to stand trial, criminal responsibility, dangerousness, testamentary capacity) or other competency related needs, such as for insurance purposes when evaluating claims for benefits, or for employment purposes when evaluating fitness to work or suitability for a particular employment or specific task.

During therapeutic interactions conflicting situations may arise if the physician's knowledge of the patient's condition cannot be kept private or when clinical notes or medical records are part of a larger employment dossier, hence not confidential to the clinical personnel in charge of the case (i.e. the military, correctional systems, medical services for employees of large corporations, treatment protocols paid by third parties).

It is the duty of a psychiatrist confronted with dual obligations and responsibilities at assessment time to disclose to the person being assessed the nature of the triangular relationship and the absence of a therapeutic doctor-patient relationship, besides the obligation to report to a third party even if the findings are negative and potentially damaging to the interests of the person under assessment. Under these circumstances, the person may choose not to proceed with the assessment.

Additionally, psychiatrists should advocate for separation of records and for limits to exposure of information such that only elements of information that are essential for purposes of the agency can be revealed.

3.3. Principles for the protection of persons with mental illness and the improvement of mental health care

Adopted by the (UN) General Assembly resolution 46/119 of 17 December 1991

Application

These Principles shall be applied without discrimination of any kind such as on grounds of disability, race, colour, sex, language, religion, political or other opinion, national, ethnic or social origin, legal or social status, age, property or birth.

Definitions

In these Principles:

- "Counsel" means a legal or other qualified representative;
- "Independent authority" means a competent and independent authority prescribed by domestic law;
- "Mental health care" includes analysis and diagnosis of a person's mental condition, and treatment, care and rehabilitation for a mental illness or suspected mental illness;
- "Mental health facility" means any establishment, or any unit of an establishment, which as its primary function provides mental health care;
- "Mental health practitioner" means a medical doctor, clinical psychologist, nurse, social worker or other appropriately trained and qualified person with specific skills relevant to mental health care;
- "Patient" means a person receiving mental health care and includes all persons who are admitted to a mental health facility;
- "Personal representative" means a person charged by law with the duty of representing a patient's interests in any specified respect or of exercising specified rights on the patient's behalf, and includes the parent or legal guardian of a minor unless otherwise provided by domestic law;

"The review body" means the body established in accordance with Principle 17 to review the involuntary admission or retention of a patient in a mental health facility.

General limitation clause

The exercise of the rights set forth in these Principles may be subject only to such limitations as are prescribed by law and are necessary to protect the health or safety of the person concerned or of others, or otherwise to protect public safety, order, health or morals or the fundamental rights and freedoms of others.

PRINCIPLE 1

Fundamental freedoms and basic rights

1. All persons have the right to the best available mental health care, which shall be part of the health and social care system.

2. All persons with a mental illness, or who are being treated as such persons, shall be treated with humanity and respect for the inherent dignity of the human person.

3. All persons with a mental illness, or who are being treated as such persons, have the right to protection from economic, sexual and other forms of exploitation, physical or other abuse and degrading treatment.

4. There shall be no discrimination on the grounds of mental illness. "Discrimination" means any distinction, exclusion or preference that has the effect of nullifying or impairing equal enjoyment of rights. Special measures solely to protect the rights, or secure the advancement, of persons with mental illness shall not be deemed to be discriminatory. Discrimination does not include any distinction, exclusion or preference undertaken in accordance with the provisions of these Principles and necessary to protect the human rights of a person with a mental illness or of other individuals.

5. Every person with a mental illness shall have the right to exercise all civil, political, economic, social and cultural rights as recognized in the Universal Declaration of Human Rights, the International Covenant on Economic, Social and Cultural Rights, the International Covenant on Civil and Political Rights, and in other relevant instruments, such as the Declaration on the Rights of Disabled Persons and the Body of Principles for the Protection of All Persons under Any Form of Detention or Imprisonment.

6. Any decision that, by reason of his or her mental illness, a person lacks legal capacity, and any decision that, in consequence of such incapacity, a personal representative shall be appointed, shall be made only after a fair hearing by an independent and impartial tribunal established by domestic law. The person whose capacity is at issue shall be entitled to be represented by a counsel. If the person whose capacity is at issue does not himself or herself secure such representation, it shall be made available without payment by that person to the extent that he or she does not have sufficient means to pay for it. The counsel shall not in the same proceedings represent a mental health facility or its personnel and shall not also represent a member of the family of the person whose capacity is at issue unless the tribunal is satisfied that there is no conflict of interest. Decisions regarding capacity and the need for a personal representative shall be reviewed at reasonable intervals prescribed by domestic law. The person whose capacity is at issue, his or her personal representative, if any, and any other interested person shall have the right to appeal to a higher court against any such decision.

7. Where a court or other competent tribunal finds that a person with mental illness is unable to manage his or her own affairs, measures shall be taken, so far as is necessary and appropriate to that person's condition, to ensure the protection of his or her interest.

Principle 2. Protection of minors

Special care should be given within the purposes of these Principles and within the context of domestic law relating to the protection of minors to protect the rights of minors, including, if necessary, the appointment of a personal representative other than a family member.

Principle 3. Life in the community

Every person with a mental illness shall have the right to live and work, as far as possible, in the community.

Principle 4. Determination of mental illness

1. A determination that a person has a mental illness shall be made in accordance with internationally accepted medical standards.

2. A determination of mental illness shall never be made on the basis of political, economic or social status, or membership of a cultural, racial or religious group, or any other reason not directly relevant to mental health status.

3. Family or professional conflict, or non-conformity with moral, social, cultural or political values or religious beliefs prevailing in a person's community, shall never be a determining factor in diagnosing mental illness.

4. A background of past treatment or hospitalization as a patient shall not of itself justify any present or future determination of mental illness.

5. No person or authority shall classify a person as having, or otherwise indicate that a person has, a mental illness except for purposes directly relating to mental illness or the consequences of mental illness.

Principle 5. Medical examination

No person shall be compelled to undergo medical examination with a view to determining whether or not he or she has a mental illness except in accordance with a procedure authorized by domestic law.

Principle 6. Confidentiality

The right of confidentiality of information concerning all persons to whom these Principles apply shall be respected.

Principle 7. Role of community and culture

1. Every patient shall have the right to be treated and cared for, as far as possible, in the community in which he or she lives.

2. Where treatment takes place in a mental health facility, a patient shall have the right, whenever possible, to be treated near his or her home or the home of his or her relatives or friends and shall have the right to return to the community as soon as possible.

3. Every patient shall have the right to treatment suited to his or her cultural background.

Principle 8. Standards of care

1. Every patient shall have the right to receive such health and social care as is appropriate to his or her health needs, and is entitled to care and treatment in accordance with the same standards as other ill persons.

2. Every patient shall be protected from harm, including unjustified medication, abuse by other patients, staff or others or other acts causing mental distress or physical discomfort.

Principle 9. Treatment

1. Every patient shall have the right to be treated in the least restrictive environment and with the least restrictive or intrusive treatment appropriate to the patient's health needs and the need to protect the physical safety of others.

2. The treatment and care of every patient shall be based on an individually prescribed plan, discussed with the patient, reviewed regularly, revised as necessary and provided by qualified professional staff.

3. Mental health care shall always be provided in accordance with applicable standards of ethics for mental health practitioners, including internationally accepted standards such as the Principles of Medical Ethics adopted by the United Nations General Assembly. Mental health knowledge and skills shall never be abused.

4. The treatment of every patient shall be directed towards preserving and enhancing personal autonomy.

PRINCIPLE 10. MEDICATION

1. Medication shall meet the best health needs of the patient, shall be given to a patient only for therapeutic or diagnostic purposes and shall never be administered as a punishment or for the convenience of others. Subject to the provisions of paragraph 15 of Principle 11, mental health practitioners shall only administer medication of known or demonstrated efficacy.

2. All medication shall be prescribed by a mental health practitioner authorized by law and shall be recorded in the patient's records.

PRINCIPLE 11. CONSENT TO TREATMENT

1. No treatment shall be given to a patient without his or her informed consent, except as provided for in paragraphs 6, 7, 8, 13 and 15 below.

2. Informed consent is consent obtained freely, without threats or improper inducements, after appropriate disclosure to the patient of adequate and understandable information in a form and language understood by the patient on:

(a) The diagnostic assessment;
(b) The purpose, method, Likely duration and expected benefit of the proposed treatment;
(c) Alternative modes of treatment, including those less intrusive; and
(d) Possible pain or discomfort, risks and side-effects of the proposed treatment.

3. A patient may request the presence of a person or persons of the patient's choosing during the procedure for granting consent.

4. A patient has the right to refuse or stop treatment, except as provided for in paragraphs 6, 7, 8, 13 and 15 below. The consequences of refusing or stopping treatment must be explained to the patient.

5. A patient shall never be invited or induced to waive the right to informed consent. If the patient should seek to do so, it shall be explained to the patient that the treatment cannot be given without informed consent.

6. Except as provided in paragraphs 7, 8, 12, 13, 14 and 15 below, a proposed plan of treatment may be given to a patient without a patient's informed consent if the following conditions are satisfied:

(a) The patient is, at the relevant time, held as an involuntary patient;
(b) An independent authority, having in its possession all relevant information, including the information specified in paragraph 2 above, is satisfied that, at the relevant time, the patient lacks the capacity to give or withhold informed consent to the proposed plan of treatment or,

if domestic legislation so provides, that, having regard to the patient's own safety or the safety of others, the patient unreasonably withholds such consent; and

(c) The independent authority is satisfied that the proposed plan of treatment is in the best interest of the patient's health needs.

7. Paragraph 6 above does not apply to a patient with a personal representative empowered by law to consent to treatment for the patient; but, except as provided in paragraphs 12, 13, 14 and 15 below, treatment may be given to such a patient without his or her informed consent if the personal representative, having been given the information described in paragraph 2 above, consents on the patient's behalf.

8. Except as provided in paragraphs 12, 13, 14 and 15 below, treatment may also be given to any patient without the patient's informed consent if a qualified mental health practitioner authorized by law determines that it is urgently necessary in order to prevent immediate or imminent harm to the patient or to other persons. Such treatment shall not be prolonged beyond the period that is strictly necessary for this purpose.

9. Where any treatment is authorized without the patient's informed consent, every effort shall nevertheless be made to inform the patient about the nature of the treatment and any possible alternatives and to involve the patient as far as practicable in the development of the treatment plan.

10. All treatment shall be immediately recorded in the patient's medical records, with an indication of whether involuntary or voluntary.

11. Physical restraint or involuntary seclusion of a patient shall not be employed except in accordance with the officially approved procedures of the mental health facility and only when it is the only means available to prevent immediate or imminent harm to the patient or others. It shall not be prolonged beyond the period which is strictly necessary for this purpose. All instances of physical restraint or involuntary seclusion, the reasons for them and their nature and extent shall be recorded in the patient's medical record. A patient who is restrained or secluded shall be kept under humane conditions and be under the care and close and regular supervision of qualified members of the staff. A personal representative, if any and if relevant, shall be given prompt notice of any physical restraint or involuntary seclusion of the patient.

12. Sterilization shall never be carried out as a treatment for mental illness.

13. A major medical or surgical procedure may be carried out on a person with mental illness only where it is permitted by domestic law, where it is considered that it would best serve the health needs of the patient and where the patient gives informed consent, except that, where the patient is unable to give informed consent, the procedure shall be authorized only after independent review.

14. Psychosurgery and other intrusive and irreversible treatments for mental illness shall never be carried out on a patient who is an involuntary patient in a mental health facility and, to the extent that domestic law permits them to be carried out, they may be carried out on any other patient only where the patient has given informed consent and an independent external body has satisfied itself that there is genuine informed consent and that the treatment best serves the health needs of the patient.

15. Clinical trials and experimental treatment shall never be carried out on any patient without informed consent, except that a patient who is unable to give informed consent may be admitted to a clinical trial or given experimental treatment, but only with the approval of a competent, independent review body specifically constituted for this purpose.

16. In the cases specified in paragraphs 6, 7, 8, 13, 14 and 15 above, the patient or his or her personal representative, or any interested person, shall have the right to appeal to a judicial or other independent authority concerning any treatment given to him or her.

PRINCIPLE 12. NOTICE OF RIGHTS

1. A patient in a mental health facility shall be informed as soon as possible after admission, in a form and a language which the patient understands, of all his or her rights in accordance with these Principles and under domestic law, which information shall include an explanation of those rights and how to exercise them.

2. If and for so long as a patient is unable to understand such information, the rights of the patient shall be communicated to the personal representative, if any and if appropriate, and to the person or persons best able to represent the patient's interests and willing to do so.

3. A patient who has the necessary capacity has the right to nominate a person who should be informed on his or her behalf, as well as a person to represent his or her interests to the authorities of the facility.

PRINCIPLE 13. RIGHTS AND CONDITIONS IN MENTAL HEALTH FACILITIES

1. Every patient in a mental health facility shall, in particular, have the right to full respect for his or her:

(a) Recognition everywhere as a person before the law;
(b) Privacy;
(c) Freedom of communication, which includes freedom to communicate with other persons in the facility; freedom to send and receive uncensored private communications; freedom to receive, in private, visits from a counsel or personal representative and, at all reasonable times, from other visitors; and freedom of access to postal and telephone services and to newspapers, radio and television;

(d) Freedom of religion or belief.

2. The environment and living conditions in mental health facilities shall be as close as possible to those of the normal life of persons of similar age and in particular shall include:

(a) Facilities for recreational and leisure activities;
(b) Facilities for education;
(c) Facilities to purchase or receive items for daily living, recreation and communication;
(d) Facilities, and encouragement to use such facilities, for a patient's engagement in active occupation suited to his or her social and cultural background, and for appropriate vocational rehabilitation measures to promote reintegration in the community. These measures should include vocational guidance, vocational training and placement services to enable patients to secure or retain employment in the community.

3. In no circumstances shall a patient be subject to forced labour. Within the limits compatible with the needs of the patient and with the requirements of institutional administration, a patient shall be able to choose the type of work he or she wishes to perform.

4. The labour of a patient in a mental health facility shall not be exploited. Every such patient shall have the right to receive the same remuneration for any work which he or she does as would, according to domestic law or custom, be paid for such work to a non-patient. Every such patient shall, in any event, have the right to receive a fair share of any remuneration which is paid to the mental health facility for his or her work.

PRINCIPLE 14. RESOURCES FOR MENTAL HEALTH FACILITIES

1. A mental health facility shall have access to the same level of resources as any other health establishment, and in particular:

(a) Qualified medical and other appropriate professional staff in sufficient numbers and with adequate space to provide each patient with privacy and a programme of appropriate and active therapy;
(b) Diagnostic and therapeutic equipment for the patient;
(c) Appropriate professional care; and
(d) Adequate, regular and comprehensive treatment, including supplies of medication.

2. Every mental health facility shall be inspected by the competent authorities with sufficient frequency to ensure that the conditions, treatment and care of patients comply with these Principles.

PRINCIPLE 15. ADMISSION PRINCIPLES

1. Where a person needs treatment in a mental health facility, every effort shall be made to avoid involuntary admission.

2. Access to a mental health facility shall be administered in the same way as access to any other facility for any other illness.

3. Every patient not admitted involuntarily shall have the right to leave the mental health facility at any time unless the criteria for his or her retention as an involuntary patient, as set forth in Principle 16, apply, and he or she shall be informed of that right.

PRINCIPLE 16. INVOLUNTARY ADMISSION

1. A person may (a) be admitted involuntarily to a mental health facility as a patient; or (b) having already been admitted voluntarily as a patient, be retained as an involuntary patient in the mental health facility if, and only if, a qualified mental health practitioner authorized by law for that purpose determines, in accordance with Principle 4, that person has a mental illness and considers:

(a) That, because of that mental illness, there is a serious likelihood of immediate or imminent harm to that person or to other persons; or
(b) That, in the case of a person whose mental illness is severe and whose judgement is impaired, failure to admit or retain that person is likely to lead to a serious deterioration in his or her condition or will prevent the giving of appropriate treatment that can only be given by admission to a mental health facility in accordance with the principle of the least restrictive alternative. In the case referred to in subparagraph (b), a second such mental health practitioner, independent of the first, should be consulted where possible. If such consultation takes place, the involuntary admission or retention may not take place unless the second mental health practitioner concurs.

2. Involuntary admission or retention shall initially be for a short period as specified by domestic law for observation and preliminary treatment pending review of the admission or retention by the review body. The grounds of the admission shall be communicated to the patient without delay and the fact of the admission and the grounds for it shall also be communicated promptly and in detail to the review body, to the patient's personal representative, if any, and, unless the patient objects, to the patient's family.

3. A mental health facility may receive involuntarily admitted patients only if the facility has been designated to do so by a competent authority prescribed by domestic law.

PRINCIPLE 17. REVIEW BODY

1. The review body shall be a judicial or other independent and impartial body established by domestic law and functioning in accordance with procedures laid down by domestic law. It shall, in formulating its decisions, have the assistance of one or more qualified and independent mental health practitioners and take their advice into account.

2. The review body's initial review, as required by paragraph 2 of Principle 16, of a decision to admit or retain a person as an involuntary patient shall take place as soon as possible after that decision and shall be conducted in accordance with simple and expeditious procedures as specified by domestic law.

3. The review body shall periodically review the cases of involuntary patients at reasonable intervals as specified by domestic law.

4. An involuntary patient may apply to the review body for release or voluntary status, at reasonable intervals as specified by domestic law.

5. At each review, the review body shall consider whether the criteria for involuntary admission set out in paragraph 1 of Principle 16 are still satisfied, and, if not, the patient shall be discharged as an involuntary patient.

6. If at any time the mental health practitioner responsible for the case is satisfied that the conditions for the retention of a person as an involuntary patient are no longer satisfied, he or she shall order the discharge of that person as such a patient.

7. A patient or his personal representative or any interested person shall have the right to appeal to a higher court against a decision that the patient be admitted to, or be retained in, a mental health facility.

PRINCIPLE 18. PROCEDURAL SAFEGUARDS

1. The patient shall be entitled to choose and appoint a counsel to represent the patient as such, including representation in any complaint procedure or appeal. If the patient does not secure such services, a counsel shall be made available without payment by the patient to the extent that the patient lacks sufficient means to pay.

2. The patient shall also be entitled to the assistance, if necessary, of the services of an interpreter. Where such services are necessary and the patient does not secure them, they shall be made available without payment by the patient to the extent that the patient lacks sufficient means to pay.

3. The patient and the patient's counsel may request and produce at any hearing an independent mental health report and any other reports and oral, written and other evidence that are relevant and admissible.

4. Copies of the patient's records and any reports and documents to be submitted shall be given to the patient and to the patient's counsel, except in special cases where it is determined that a specific disclosure to the patient would cause serious harm to the patient's health or put at risk the safety of others. As domestic law may provide, any document not given to the patient should, when this can be done in confidence, be given to the patient's personal representative

and counsel. When any part of a document is withheld from a patient, the patient or the patient's counsel, if any, shall receive notice of the withholding and the reasons for it and shall be subject to judicial review.

5. The patient and the patient's personal representative and counsel shall be entitled to attend, participate and be heard personally in any hearing.

6. If the patient or the patient's personal representative or counsel requests that a particular person be present at a hearing, that person shall be admitted unless it is determined that the person's presence could cause serious harm to the patient's health or put at risk the safety of others.

7. Any decision whether the hearing or any part of it shall be in public or in private and may be publicly reported shall give full consideration to the patient's own wishes, to the need to respect the privacy of the patient and of other persons and to the need to prevent serious harm to the patient's health or to avoid putting at risk the safety of others.

8. The decision arising out of the hearing and the reasons for it shall be expressed in writing. Copies shall be given to the patient and his or her personal representative and counsel. In deciding whether the decision shall be published in whole or in part, full consideration shall be given to the patient's own wishes, to the need to respect his or her privacy and that of other persons, to the public interest in the open administration of justice and to the need to prevent serious harm to the patient's health or to avoid putting at risk the safety of others.

PRINCIPLE 19. ACCESS TO INFORMATION

1. A patient (which term in this Principle includes a former patient) shall be entitled to have access to the information concerning the patient in his or her health and personal records maintained by a mental health facility. This right may be subject to restrictions in order to prevent serious harm to the patient's health and avoid putting at risk the safety of others. As domestic law may provide, any such information not given to the patient should, when this can be done in confidence, be given to the patient's personal representative and counsel. When any of the information is withheld from a patient, the patient or the patient's counsel, if any, shall receive notice of the withholding and the reasons for it and it shall be subject to judicial review.

2. Any written comments by the patient or the patient's personal representative or counsel shall, on request, be inserted in the patient's file.

PRINCIPLE 20. CRIMINAL OFFENDERS

1. This Principle applies to persons serving sentences of imprisonment for criminal offences, or who are otherwise detained in the course of criminal proceedings or investigations against them, and who are determined to have a mental illness or who it is believed may have such an illness.

2. All such persons should receive the best available mental health care as provided in Principle 1. These Principles shall apply to them to the fullest extent possible, with only such limited modifications and exceptions as are necessary in the circumstances. No such modifications and exceptions shall prejudice the persons' rights under the instruments noted in paragraph 5 of Principle 1.

3. Domestic law may authorize a court or other competent authority, acting on the basis of competent and independent medical advice, to order that such persons be admitted to a mental health facility.

4. Treatment of persons determined to have a mental illness shall in all circumstances be consistent with Principle 11.

PRINCIPLE 21. COMPLAINTS

Every patient and former patient shall have the right to make a complaint through procedures as specified by domestic law.

PRINCIPLE 22. MONITORING AND REMEDIES

States shall ensure that appropriate mechanisms are in force to promote compliance with these Principles, for the inspection of mental health facilities, for the submission, investigation and resolution of complaints and for the institution of appropriate disciplinary or judicial proceedings for professional misconduct or violation of the rights of a patient.

PRINCIPLE 23. IMPLEMENTATION

1. States should implement these Principles through appropriate legislative, judicial, administrative, educational and other measures, which they shall review periodically.

2. States shall make these Principles widely known by appropriate and active means.

PRINCIPLE 24. SCOPE OF PRINCIPLES RELATING TO MENTAL HEALTH FACILITIES

These Principles apply to all persons who are admitted to a mental health facility.

PRINCIPLE 25. SAVING OF EXISTING RIGHTS

There shall be no restriction upon or derogation from any existing rights of patients, including rights recognized in applicable international or domestic law, on the pretext that these Principles do not recognize such rights or that they recognize them to a lesser extent.

Medical Research

PART III

1. Nuremberg Code (1947)

1. The voluntary consent of the human subject is absolutely essential. This means that the person involved should have legal capacity to give consent; should be so situated as to be able to exercise free power of choice, without the intervention of any element of force, fraud, deceit, duress, over-reaching, or other ulterior form of constraint or coercion; and should have sufficient knowledge and comprehension of the elements of the subject matter involved as to enable him to make an understanding and enlightened decision. This latter element requires that before the acceptance of an affirmative decision by the experimental subject there should be made known to him the nature, duration, and purpose of the experiment; the method and means by which it is to be conducted; all inconveniences and hazards reasonable to be expected; and the effects upon his health or person which may possibly come from his participation in the experiment.

The duty and responsibility for ascertaining the quality of the consent rests upon each individual who initiates, directs or engages in the experiment. It is a personal duty and responsibility which may not be delegated to another with impunity.

2. The experiment should be such as to yield fruitful results for the good of society, unprocurable by other methods or means of study, and not random and unnecessary in nature.

3. The experiment should be so designed and based on the results of animal experimentation and a knowledge of the natural history of the disease or other problem under study that the anticipated results will justify the performance of the experiment.

4. The experiment should be so conducted as to avoid all unnecessary physical and mental suffering and injury.

5. No experiment should be conducted where there is an a priori reason to believe that death or disabling injury will occur; except, perhaps, in those experiments where the experimental physicians also serve as subjects.

6. The degree of risk to be taken should never exceed that determined by the humanitarian importance of the problem to be solved by the experiment.

7. Proper preparations should be made and adequate facilities provided to protect the experimental subject against even remote possibilities of injury, disability, or death.

8. The experiment should be conducted only by scientifically qualified persons. The highest degree of skill and care should be required through all stages of the experiment of those who conduct or engage in the experiment.

9. During the course of the experiment the human subject should be at liberty to bring the experiment to an end if he has reached the physical or mental state where continuation of the experiment seems to him to be impossible.

10. During the course of the experiment the scientist in charge must be prepared to terminate the experiment at any stage, if he has probable cause to believe, in the exercise of the good faith, superior skill and careful judgment required of him that a continuation of the experiment is likely to result in injury, disability, or death to the experimental subject.

2. International Covenant on Civil and Political Rights, 1966

ARTICLE 7. PROHIBITION OF TORTURE OR CRUEL, INHUMAN OR DEGRADING TREATMENT OR PUNISHMENT

No one shall be subjected to torture or to cruel, inhuman or degrading treatment or punishment. In particular, no one shall be subjected without his free consent to medical or scientific experimentation.

3. General Comment No. 20: Replaces general comment 7 concerning prohibition of torture and cruel treatment or punishment (Art. 7)

10/03/92. CCPR General Comment No. 20. (General Comments)

1. This general comment replaces general comment 7 (the sixteenth session, 1982) reflecting and further developing it.

2. The aim of the provisions of article 7 of the International Covenant on Civil and Political Rights is to protect both the dignity and the physical and mental integrity of the individual. It is the duty of the State party to afford everyone protection through legislative and other measures as may be necessary against the acts prohibited by article 7, whether inflicted by people acting in their official capacity, outside their official capacity or in a private capacity. The prohibition in article 7 is complemented by the positive requirements of article 10, paragraph 1, of the Covenant, which stipulates that "All persons deprived of their liberty shall be treated with humanity and with respect for the inherent dignity of the human person".

3. The text of article 7 allows of no limitation. The Committee also reaffirms that, even in situations of public emergency such as those referred to in article 4 of the Covenant, no derogation from the provision of article 7 is allowed and its provisions must remain in force. The Committee likewise observes that no justification or extenuating circumstances may be invoked to excuse a violation of article 7 for any reasons, including those based on an order from a superior officer or public authority.

4. The Covenant does not contain any definition of the concepts covered by article 7, nor does the Committee consider it necessary to draw up a list of prohibited acts or to establish sharp distinctions between the different kinds of punishment or treatment; the distinctions depend on the nature, purpose and severity of the treatment applied.

5. The prohibition in article 7 relates not only to acts that cause physical pain but also to acts that cause mental suffering to the victim. In the Committee's view, moreover, the prohibition must extend to corporal punishment, including excessive chastisement ordered as punishment for a crime or as an educative or disciplinary measure. It is appropriate to emphasize in this regard that article 7 protects, in particular, children, pupils and patients in teaching and medical institutions.

6. The Committee notes that prolonged solitary confinement of the detained or imprisoned person may amount to acts prohibited by article 7. As the Committee has stated in its general comment No. 6 (16), article 6 of the Covenant refers generally to abolition of the death penalty in terms that strongly suggest that abolition is desirable. Moreover, when the death penalty is applied by a State party for the most serious crimes, it must not only be strictly limited in accordance with article 6 but it must be carried out in such a way as to cause the least possible physical and mental suffering.

7. Article 7 expressly prohibits medical or scientific experimentation without the free consent of the person concerned. The Committee notes that the reports of States parties generally contain little information on this point. More attention should be given to the need and means to ensure observance of this provision. The Committee also observes that special protection in regard to such experiments is necessary in the case of persons not capable of giving valid consent, and in particular those under any form of detention or imprisonment. Such persons should not be subjected to any medical or scientific experimentation that may be detrimental to their health.

8. The Committee notes that it is not sufficient for the implementation of article 7 to prohibit such treatment or punishment or to make it a crime. States parties should inform the Committee of the legislative, administrative, judicial and other measures they take to prevent and punish acts of torture and cruel, inhuman and degrading treatment in any territory under their jurisdiction.

9. In the view of the Committee, States parties must not expose individuals to the danger of torture or cruel, inhuman or degrading treatment or punishment upon return to another country by way of their extradition, expulsion or refoulement. States parties should indicate in their reports what measures they have adopted to that end.

10. The Committee should be informed how States parties disseminate, to the population at large, relevant information concerning the ban on torture and the treatment prohibited by article 7. Enforcement personnel, medical personnel, police officers and any other persons involved in the custody or treatment of any individual subjected to any form of arrest, detention or imprisonment must receive appropriate instruction and training. States parties should inform the Committee of the instruction and training given and the way in which the prohibition of article 7 forms an integral part of the operational rules and ethical standards to be followed by such persons.

11. In addition to describing steps to provide the general protection against acts prohibited under article 7 to which anyone is entitled, the State party should provide detailed information on safeguards for the special protection of particularly vulnerable persons. It should be noted that keeping under systematic review interrogation rules, instructions, methods and practices as well as arrangements for the custody and treatment of persons subjected to any form of arrest, detention or imprisonment is an effective means of preventing cases of torture and ill-treatment. To guarantee the effective protection of detained persons, provisions should be made for detainees to be held in places officially recognized as places of detention and for their names and places of detention, as well as for the names of persons responsible for their detention, to be kept in registers readily available and accessible to those concerned, including relatives and friends. To the same effect, the time and place of all interrogations should be recorded, together with the names of all those present and this information should also be available for purposes of judicial or administrative proceedings. Provisions should also be made against incommunicado detention. In that connection, States parties should ensure that any places of detention be free from any equipment liable to be used for inflicting torture or

ill-treatment. The protection of the detainee also requires that prompt and regular access be given to doctors and lawyers and, under appropriate supervision when the investigation so requires, to family members.

12. It is important for the discouragement of violations under article 7 that the law must prohibit the use of admissibility in judicial proceedings of statements or confessions obtained through torture or other prohibited treatment.

13. States parties should indicate when presenting their reports the provisions of their criminal law which penalize torture and cruel, inhuman and degrading treatment or punishment, specifying the penalties applicable to such acts, whether committed by public officials or other persons acting on behalf of the State, or by private persons. Those who violate article 7, whether by encouraging, ordering, tolerating or perpetrating prohibited acts, must be held responsible. Consequently, those who have refused to obey orders must not be punished or subjected to any adverse treatment.

14. Article 7 should be read in conjunction with article 2, paragraph 3, of the Covenant. In their reports, States parties should indicate how their legal system effectively guarantees the immediate termination of all the acts prohibited by article 7 as well as appropriate redress. The right to lodge complaints against maltreatment prohibited by article 7 must be recognized in the domestic law. Complaints must be investigated promptly and impartially by competent authorities so as to make the remedy effective. The reports of States parties should provide specific information on the remedies available to victims of maltreatment and the procedure that complainants must follow, and statistics on the number of complaints and how they have been dealt with.

15. The Committee has noted that some States have granted amnesty in respect of acts of torture. Amnesties are generally incompatible with the duty of States to investigate such acts; to guarantee freedom from such acts within their jurisdiction; and to ensure that they do not occur in the future. States may not deprive individuals of the right to an effective remedy, including compensation and such full rehabilitation as may be possible.

4. Additional Protocol to the Convention on Human Rights and Biomedicine, concerning Biomedical Research (ETS No. 195)

Preamble

The member States of the Council of Europe, the other States and the European Community signatories to this Additional Protocol to the Convention for the Protection of Human Rights and Dignity of the Human Being with regard to the Application of Biology and Medicine (hereinafter referred to as "the Convention"), Considering that the aim of the Council of Europe is the achievement of greater unity between its members and that one of the methods by which this aim is pursued is the maintenance and further realisation of human rights and fundamental freedoms; Considering that the aim of the Convention, as defined in Article 1, is to protect the dignity and identity of all human beings and guarantee everyone, without discrimination, respect for their integrity and other rights and fundamental freedoms with regard to the application of biology and medicine; Considering that progress in medical and biological sciences, in particular advances obtained through biomedical research, contributes to saving lives and improving quality of life; Conscious of the fact that the advancement of biomedical science and practice is dependent on knowledge and discovery which necessitates research on human beings; Stressing that such research is often transdisciplinary and international; Taking into account national and international professional standards in the field of biomedical research and the previous work of the Committee of Ministers and the Parliamentary Assembly of the Council of Europe in this field; Convinced that biomedical research that is contrary to human dignity and human rights should never be carried out; Stressing the paramount concern to be the protection of the human being participating in research; Affirming that particular protection shall be given to human beings who may be vulnerable in the context of research; Recognising that every person has a right to accept or refuse to undergo biomedical research and that no one should be forced to undergo such research; Resolving to take such measures as are necessary to safeguard human dignity and the fundamental rights and freedoms of the individual with regard to biomedical research,

Have agreed as follows:

Chapter I – Object and scope

ARTICLE 1. OBJECT AND PURPOSE

Parties to this Protocol shall protect the dignity and identity of all human beings and guarantee everyone, without discrimination, respect for their integrity and other rights and fundamental freedoms with regard to any research involving interventions on human beings in the field of biomedicine.

ARTICLE 2. SCOPE

1. This Protocol covers the full range of research activities in the health field involving interventions on human beings.

2. This Protocol does not apply to research on embryos in vitro. It does apply to research on foetuses and embryos in vivo.

3. For the purposes of this Protocol, the term "intervention" includes:

i. a physical intervention, and
ii. any other intervention in so far as it involves a risk to the psychological health of the person concerned.

Chapter II – General provisions

ARTICLE 3. PRIMACY OF THE HUMAN BEING

The interests and welfare of the human being participating in research shall prevail over the sole interest of society or science.

ARTICLE 4. GENERAL RULE

Research shall be carried out freely, subject to the provisions of this Protocol and the other legal provisions ensuring the protection of the human being.

ARTICLE 5. ABSENCE OF ALTERNATIVES

Research on human beings may only be undertaken if there is no alternative of comparable effectiveness.

ARTICLE 6. RISKS AND BENEFITS

1. Research shall not involve risks and burdens to the human being disproportionate to its potential benefits.

2. In addition, where the research does not have the potential to produce results of direct benefit to the health of the research participant, such research may only be undertaken if the research entails no more than acceptable risk and acceptable burden for the research participant. This shall be without prejudice to the provision contained in Article 15 paragraph 2, sub-paragraph ii for the protection of persons not able to consent to research.

ARTICLE 7. APPROVAL

Research may only be undertaken if the research project has been approved by the competent body after independent examination of its scientific merit, including assessment of the importance of the aim of research, and multidisciplinary review of its ethical acceptability.

ARTICLE 8. SCIENTIFIC QUALITY

Any research must be scientifically justified, meet generally accepted criteria of scientific quality and be carried out in accordance with relevant professional obligations and standards under the supervision of an appropriately qualified researcher.

Chapter III – Ethics committee

ARTICLE 9. INDEPENDENT EXAMINATION BY AN ETHICS COMMITTEE

1. Every research project shall be submitted for independent examination of its ethical acceptability to an ethics committee. Such projects shall be submitted to independent examination in each State in which any research activity is to take place.

2. The purpose of the multidisciplinary examination of the ethical acceptability of the research project shall be to protect the dignity, rights, safety and well-being of research participants. The assessment of the ethical acceptability shall draw on an appropriate range of expertise and experience adequately reflecting professional and lay views.

3. The ethics committee shall produce an opinion containing reasons for its conclusion.

ARTICLE 10. INDEPENDENCE OF THE ETHICS COMMITTEE

1. Parties to this Protocol shall take measures to assure the independence of the ethics committee. That body shall not be subject to undue external influences.

2. Members of the ethics committee shall declare all circumstances that might lead to a conflict of interest. Should such conflicts arise, those involved shall not participate in that review.

ARTICLE 11. INFORMATION FOR THE ETHICS COMMITTEE

1. All information which is necessary for the ethical assessment of the research project shall be given in written form to the ethics committee.

2. In particular, information on items contained in the appendix to this Protocol shall be provided, in so far as it is relevant for the research project. The appendix may be amended by the Committee set up by Article 32 of the Convention by a two-thirds majority of the votes cast.

ARTICLE 12. UNDUE INFLUENCE

The ethics committee must be satisfied that no undue influence, including that of a financial nature, will be exerted on persons to participate in research. In this respect, particular attention must be given to vulnerable or dependent persons.

Chapter IV – Information and consent

ARTICLE 13. INFORMATION FOR RESEARCH PARTICIPANTS

1. The persons being asked to participate in a research project shall be given adequate information in a comprehensible form. This information shall be documented.

2. The information shall cover the purpose, the overall plan and the possible risks and benefits of the research project, and include the opinion of the ethics committee. Before being asked to consent to participate in a research project, the persons concerned shall be specifically informed, according to the nature and purpose of the research:

i.   of the nature, extent and duration of the procedures involved, in particular, details of any burden imposed by the research project;
ii.   of available preventive, diagnostic and therapeutic procedures;
iii. of the arrangements for responding to adverse events or the concerns of research participants;
iv.   of arrangements to ensure respect for private life and ensure the confidentiality of personal data;
v.   of arrangements for access to information relevant to the participant arising from the research and to its overall results;
vi.   of the arrangements for fair compensation in the case of damage;
vii. of any foreseen potential further uses, including commercial uses, of the research results, data or biological materials;
viii. of the source of funding of the research project.

3. In addition, the persons being asked to participate in a research project shall be informed of the rights and safeguards prescribed by law for their protection, and specifically of their right to refuse consent or to withdraw consent at any time without being subject to any form of discrimination, in particular regarding the right to medical care.

ARTICLE 14. CONSENT

1. No research on a person may be carried out, subject to the provisions of both Chapter V and Article 19, without the informed, free, express, specific and documented consent of the person. Such consent may be freely withdrawn by the person at any phase of the research.

2. Refusal to give consent or the withdrawal of consent to participation in research shall not lead to any form of discrimination against the person concerned, in particular regarding the right to medical care.

3. Where the capacity of the person to give informed consent is in doubt, arrangements shall be in place to verify whether or not the person has such capacity.

Chapter V – Protection of persons not able to consent to research

ARTICLE 15. PROTECTION OF PERSONS NOT ABLE TO CONSENT TO RESEARCH

1. Research on a person without the capacity to consent to research may be undertaken only if all the following specific conditions are met:

i.   the results of the research have the potential to produce real and direct benefit to his or her health;
ii. research of comparable effectiveness cannot be carried out on individuals capable of giving consent;
iii. the person undergoing research has been informed of his or her rights and the safeguards prescribed by law for his or her protection, unless this person is not in a state to receive the information;
iv. the necessary authorisation has been given specifically and in writing by the legal representative or an authority, person or body provided for by law, and after having received the information required by Article 16, taking into account the person's previously expressed wishes or objections. An adult not able to consent shall as far as possible take part in the authorisation procedure. The opinion of a minor shall be taken into consideration as an increasingly determining factor in proportion to age and degree of maturity;
v.   the person concerned does not object.

2. Exceptionally and under the protective conditions prescribed by law, where the research has not the potential to produce results of direct benefit to the health of the person concerned, such research may be authorised subject to the conditions laid down in paragraph 1, sub-paragraphs ii, iii, iv, and v above, and to the following additional conditions:

i.   the research has the aim of contributing, through significant improvement in the scientific understanding of the individual's condition, disease or disorder, to the ultimate attainment of results capable of conferring benefit to the person concerned or to other persons in the same age category or afflicted with the same disease or disorder or having the same condition;
ii. the research entails only minimal risk and minimal burden for the individual concerned; and any consideration of additional potential benefits of the research shall not be used to justify an increased level of risk or burden.

3. Objection to participation, refusal to give authorisation or the withdrawal of authorisation to participate in research shall not lead to any form of discrimination against the person concerned, in particular regarding the right to medical care.

ARTICLE 16. INFORMATION PRIOR TO AUTHORISATION

1. Those being asked to authorise participation of a person in a research project shall be given adequate information in a comprehensible form. This information shall be documented.

2. The information shall cover the purpose, the overall plan and the possible risks and benefits of the research project, and include the opinion of the ethics committee. They shall further be informed of the rights and safeguards prescribed by law for the protection of those not able to consent to research and specifically of the right to refuse or to withdraw authorisation at any time, without the person concerned being subject to any form of discrimination, in particular regarding the right to medical care. They shall be specifically informed according to the nature and purpose of the research of the items of information listed in Article 13.

3. The information shall also be provided to the individual concerned, unless this person is not in a state to receive the information.

ARTICLE 17. RESEARCH WITH MINIMAL RISK AND MINIMAL BURDEN

1. For the purposes of this Protocol it is deemed that the research bears a minimal risk if, having regard to the nature and scale of the intervention, it is to be expected that it will result, at the most, in a very slight and temporary negative impact on the health of the person concerned.

2. It is deemed that it bears a minimal burden if it is to be expected that the discomfort will be, at the most, temporary and very slight for the person concerned. In assessing the burden for an individual, a person enjoying the special confidence of the person concerned shall assess the burden where appropriate.

Chapter VI – Specific situations

ARTICLE 18. RESEARCH DURING PREGNANCY OR BREASTFEEDING

1. Research on a pregnant woman which does not have the potential to produce results of direct benefit to her health, or to that of her embryo, foetus or child after birth, may only be undertaken if the following additional conditions are met:

i.   the research has the aim of contributing to the ultimate attainment of results capable of conferring benefit to other women in relation to reproduction or to other embryos, foetuses or children;
ii. research of comparable effectiveness cannot be carried out on women who are not pregnant;

iii. the research entails only minimal risk and minimal burden.

2. Where research is undertaken on a breastfeeding woman, particular care shall be taken to avoid any adverse impact on the health of the child.

Article 19. Research on persons in emergency clinical situations

1. The law shall determine whether, and under which protective additional conditions, research in emergency situations may take place when:

i.   a person is not in a state to give consent, and
ii. because of the urgency of the situation, it is impossible to obtain in a sufficiently timely manner, authorisation from his or her representative or an authority or a person or body which would in the absence of an emergency situation be called upon to give authorisation.

2. The law shall include the following specific conditions:

i.   research of comparable effectiveness cannot be carried out on persons in non-emergency situations;
ii. the research project may only be undertaken if it has been approved specifically for emergency situations by the competent body;
iii. any relevant previously expressed objections of the person known to the researcher shall be respected;
iv. where the research has not the potential to produce results of direct benefit to the health of the person concerned, it has the aim of contributing, through significant improvement in the scientific understanding of the individual's condition, disease or disorder, to the ultimate attainment of results capable of conferring benefit to the person concerned or to other persons in the same category or afflicted with the same disease or disorder or having the same condition, and entails only minimal risk and minimal burden.

3. Persons participating in the emergency research project or, if applicable, their representatives shall be provided with all the relevant information concerning their participation in the research project as soon as possible. Consent or authorisation for continued participation shall be requested as soon as reasonably possible.

Article 20. Research on persons deprived of liberty

Where the law allows research on persons deprived of liberty, such persons may participate in a research project in which the results do not have the potential to produce direct benefit to their health only if the following additional conditions are met:

i.   research of comparable effectiveness cannot be carried out without the participation of persons deprived of liberty;

ii. the research has the aim of contributing to the ultimate attainment of results capable of conferring benefit to persons deprived of liberty;

iii. the research entails only minimal risk and minimal burden.

Chapter VII – Safety and supervision

ARTICLE 21. MINIMISATION OF RISK AND BURDEN

1. All reasonable measures shall be taken to ensure safety and to minimise risk and burden for the research participants.

2. Research may only be carried out under the supervision of a clinical professional who possesses the necessary qualifications and experience.

ARTICLE 22. ASSESSMENT OF HEALTH STATUS

1. The researcher shall take all necessary steps to assess the state of health of human beings prior to their inclusion in research, to ensure that those at increased risk in relation to participation in a specific project be excluded.

2. Where research is undertaken on persons in the reproductive stage of their lives, particular consideration shall be given to the possible adverse impact on a current or future pregnancy and the health of an embryo, foetus or child.

ARTICLE 23. NON-INTERFERENCE WITH NECESSARY CLINICAL INTERVENTIONS

1. Research shall not delay nor deprive participants of medically necessary preventive, diagnostic or therapeutic procedures.

2. In research associated with prevention, diagnosis or treatment, participants assigned to control groups shall be assured of proven methods of prevention, diagnosis or treatment.

3. The use of placebo is permissible where there are no methods of proven effectiveness, or where withdrawal or withholding of such methods does not present an unacceptable risk or burden.

ARTICLE 24. NEW DEVELOPMENTS

1. Parties to this Protocol shall take measures to ensure that the research project is re-examined if this is justified in the light of scientific developments or events arising in the course of the research.

2. The purpose of the re-examination is to establish whether:

i. the research needs to be discontinued or if changes to the research project are necessary for the research to continue;
ii. research participants, or if applicable their representatives, need to be informed of the developments or events;
iii. additional consent or authorisation for participation is required.

3. Any new information relevant to their participation shall be conveyed to the research participants, or, if applicable, to their representatives, in a timely manner.

4. The competent body shall be informed of the reasons for any premature termination of a research project.

Chapter VIII – Confidentiality and right to information

ARTICLE 25. CONFIDENTIALITY

1. Any information of a personal nature collected during biomedical research shall be considered as confidential and treated according to the rules relating to the protection of private life.

2. The law shall protect against inappropriate disclosure of any other information related to a research project that has been submitted to an ethics committee in compliance with this Protocol.

ARTICLE 26. RIGHT TO INFORMATION

1. Research participants shall be entitled to know any information collected on their health in conformity with the provisions of Article 10 of the Convention.

2. Other personal information collected for a research project will be accessible to them in conformity with the law on the protection of individuals with regard to processing of personal data.

ARTICLE 27. DUTY OF CARE

If research gives rise to information of relevance to the current or future health or quality of life of research participants, this information must be offered to them. That shall be done within a framework of health care or counselling. In communication of such information, due care must be taken in order to protect confidentiality and to respect any wish of a participant not to receive such information.

ARTICLE 28. AVAILABILITY OF RESULTS

1. On completion of the research, a report or summary shall be submitted to the ethics committee or the competent body.

2. The conclusions of the research shall be made available to participants in reasonable time, on request.

3. The researcher shall take appropriate measures to make public the results of research in reasonable time.

Chapter IX – Research in States not parties to this Protocol

ARTICLE 29. RESEARCH IN STATES NOT PARTIES TO THIS PROTOCOL

Sponsors or researchers within the jurisdiction of a Party to this Protocol that plan to undertake or direct a research project in a State not party to this Protocol shall ensure that, without prejudice to the provisions applicable in that State, the research project complies with the principles on which the provisions of this Protocol are based. Where necessary, the Party shall take appropriate measures to that end.

Chapter X – Infringement of the provisions of the Protocol

ARTICLE 30. INFRINGEMENT OF THE RIGHTS OR PRINCIPLES

The Parties shall provide appropriate judicial protection to prevent or to put a stop to an unlawful infringement of the rights or principles set forth in this Protocol at short notice.

ARTICLE 31. COMPENSATION FOR DAMAGE

The person who has suffered damage as a result of participation in research shall be entitled to fair compensation according to the conditions and procedures prescribed by law.

ARTICLE 32. SANCTIONS

Parties shall provide for appropriate sanctions to be applied in the event of infringement of the provisions contained in this Protocol.

Chapter XI – Relation between this Protocol and other provisions and re-examination of the Protocol

ARTICLE 33. RELATION BETWEEN THIS PROTOCOL AND THE CONVENTION

As between the Parties, the provisions of Articles 1 to 32 of this Protocol shall be regarded as additional articles to the Convention, and all the provisions of the Convention shall apply accordingly.

ARTICLE 34. WIDER PROTECTION

None of the provisions of this Protocol shall be interpreted as limiting or otherwise affecting the possibility for a Party to grant research participants a wider measure of protection than is stipulated in this Protocol.

ARTICLE 35. RE-EXAMINATION OF THE PROTOCOL

In order to monitor scientific developments, the present Protocol shall be examined within the Committee referred to in Article 32 of the Convention no later than five years from the entry into force of this Protocol and thereafter at such intervals as the Committee may determine.

Chapter XII – Final clauses

ARTICLE 36. SIGNATURE AND RATIFICATION

This Protocol shall be open for signature by Signatories to the Convention. It is subject to ratification, acceptance or approval. A Signatory may not ratify, accept or approve this Protocol unless it has previously or simultaneously ratified, accepted or approved the Convention. Instruments of ratification, acceptance or approval shall be deposited with the Secretary General of the Council of Europe.

ARTICLE 37. ENTRY INTO FORCE

1. This Protocol shall enter into force on the first day of the month following the expiration of a period of three months after the date on which five States, including at least four member States of the Council of Europe, have expressed their consent to be bound by the Protocol in accordance with the provisions of Article 36.

2. In respect of any Signatory which subsequently expresses its consent to be bound by it, the Protocol shall enter into force on the first day of the month following the expiration of a period of three months after the date of the deposit of the instrument of ratification, acceptance or approval.

ARTICLE 38. ACCESSION

1. After the entry into force of this Protocol, any State which has acceded to the Convention may also accede to this Protocol.

2. Accession shall be effected by the deposit with the Secretary General of the Council of Europe of an instrument of accession which shall take effect on the first day of the month following the expiration of a period of three months after the date of its deposit.

Article 39. Denunciation

1. Any Party may at any time denounce this Protocol by means of a notification addressed to the Secretary General of the Council of Europe.

2. Such denunciation shall become effective on the first day of the month following the expiration of a period of three months after the date of receipt of such notification by the Secretary General.

Appendix

Information to be given to the ethics committee

Information on the following items shall be provided to the ethics committee, in so far as it is relevant for the research project:

Description of the project

i.   the name of the principal researcher, qualifications and experience of researchers and, where appropriate, the clinically responsible person, and funding arrangements;
ii.   the aim and justification for the research based on the latest state of scientific knowledge;
iii. methods and procedures envisaged, including statistical and other analytical techniques;
iv.   a comprehensive summary of the research project in lay language;
v.   a statement of previous and concurrent submissions of the research project for assessment or approval and the outcome of those submissions;

Participants, consent and information

vi.   justification for involving human beings in the research project;
vii. the criteria for inclusion or exclusion of the categories of persons for participation in the research project and how those persons are to be selected and recruited;
viii. reasons for the use or the absence of control groups;
ix.   – a description of the nature and degree of foreseeable risks that may be incurred through participating in research;
      – the nature, extent and duration of the interventions to be carried out on the research participants, and details of any burden imposed by the research project;
xi.   arrangements to monitor, evaluate and react to contingencies that may have consequences for the present or future health of research participants;
xii. the timing and details of information for those persons who would participate in the research project and the means proposed for provision of this information;
xiii. documentation intended to be used to seek consent or, in the case of persons not able to consent, authorisation for participation in the research project;

xiv. arrangements to ensure respect for the private life of those persons who would participate in research and ensure the confidentiality of personal data;

xv. arrangements foreseen for information which may be generated and be relevant to the present or future health of those persons who would participate in research and their family members;

Other information

xvi. details of all payments and rewards to be made in the context of the research project;

xvii. details of all circumstances that might lead to conflicts of interest that may affect the independent judgement of the researchers;

xviii. details of any foreseen potential further uses, including commercial uses, of the research results, data or biological materials;

xix. details of all other ethical issues, as perceived by the researcher;

xx. details of any insurance or indemnity to cover damage arising in the context of the research project.

The ethics committee may request additional information necessary for evaluation of the research project.

5. Explanatory Report. Additional Protocol to the Convention on Human Rights and Biomedicine, concerning Biomedical Research (ETS No. 195).

Introduction

1. This Additional Protocol to the Convention on Human Rights and Biomedicine on Biomedical Research builds on the principles embodied in the Convention, with a view to protecting human rights and dignity in the specific field of biomedical research. The benefits for human health of the acquisition of knowledge from research utilising systematic methodologies in the sphere of biomedicine are widely acknowledged. The distinction between medical research and innovative medical practice derives from the intent behind the intervention. In medical practice the sole intention is to benefit the individual patient, not to gain knowledge of general benefit, though such knowledge may emerge from the clinical experience gained. In an intervention for the purpose of biomedical research the primary intention is to advance knowledge so that patients in general may benefit. An individual research participant may or may not benefit directly.

2. The purpose of the Protocol is to define and safeguard fundamental rights in the field of biomedical research, in particular of those participating in research. Biomedical research is a powerful tool to improve human health. Freedom of research is important in and of itself, but also because of the practical benefits it brings to the healthcare field. At the same time, it is always necessary to protect human beings participating in research. Research participants are contributing their time to the research and may be subjecting themselves to risks and burdens. Particular attention must be paid to ensuring that their human rights are always protected and their altruism is not exploited.

Drafting of the Protocol

3. In Recommendation 1160 in 1991, the Council of Europe Parliamentary Assembly recommended that the Committee of Ministers "envisage a framework convention comprising a main text with general principles and additional protocols on specific aspects." Also in 1991, the Committee of Ministers instructed the CAHBI (ad hoc Committee of Experts on Bioethics), re-designated the CDBI in 1992 (Steering Committee on Bioethics) "to prepare, ...Protocols to this Convention, relating to, in a preliminary phase: organ transplants and the use of substances of human origin; medical research on human beings." The Additional Protocol was drafted with the inclusion of the relevant provisions of the Convention concerning biomedical research. This was done to facilitate its use by practitioners in the field of biomedical research, avoiding the need for them to consult a number of interlinked legal instruments.

...

The Protocol is accompanied by this Explanatory Report, drawn up under the responsibility of the Secretary General of the Council of Europe. It takes into account the discussions held in the CDBI and its Working Party entrusted with the drafting of the Protocol; it also takes into account the remarks and proposals made by delegations. The Committee of Ministers has authorised its publication on 30 June 2004. The Explanatory Report is not an authoritative interpretation of the Protocol. Nevertheless it covers the main issues of the preparatory work and provides information to clarify the object and purpose of the Protocol and make the scope of its provisions more comprehensible.

Comments on the provisions of the Protocol

Title

8. The title identifies this instrument as the "Additional Protocol to the Convention on Human Rights and Biomedicine, on Biomedical Research."

9. The term "biomedical research" is used in order to be consistent with the Convention (Convention for the Protection of Human Rights and Dignity of the Human Being with regard to the Application of Biology and Medicine) and in order to stress that the Protocol covers all areas of research involving interventions on human beings in the field of biomedicine, which may also be carried out by biologists and other professionals such as psychologists.

Preamble

10. Protection and guarantees in the fields of biology and medicine, including biomedical research, are provided by the Convention for the Protection of Human Rights and Dignity of the Human Being with Regard to the Application of Biology and Medicine (Convention on Human Rights and Biomedicine), hereafter the "Convention".

11. After the Protocol on the prohibition of cloning human beings and the Protocol concerning transplantation of organs and tissues of human origin, this Additional Protocol on biomedical research supplements further the provisions of the Convention. The Protocols are designed to address the ethical and legal issues raised by present or future scientific advances through the further development, in specific fields such as biomedical research, of the principles contained in the Convention. The preamble to this Protocol reaffirms the aims of the Council of Europe and the Convention. It recognises the role of progress in medical and biological sciences and the contribution that it has made to reducing morbidity and mortality and improving the quality of life. It also takes due regard of the previous work of the Committee of Ministers and the Parliamentary Assembly concerning biomedical research and this has been taken into account in the preparation of this Additional Protocol.

12. The preamble affirms the commitment of the Parties to take necessary measures to safeguard human dignity and the fundamental rights and freedoms of human beings with regard to biomedical research. It highlights some of the fundamental principles that underlie that commitment:

- biomedical research shall never be carried out contrary to human dignity;
- the protection of the human being must always be of paramount concern;
- every person has a right to accept or refuse to undergo biomedical research and no one shall be forced to participate; and
- particular protection shall be given to human beings vulnerable in the context of biomedical research.

Chapter I – Object and scope

Article 1. (Object and purpose)

13. This article specifies that the object of the Protocol is to protect the dignity and identity of all human beings and guarantee everyone, without discrimination, respect for their integrity and other fundamental rights and freedoms with regard to any research in the field of biomedicine involving interventions on human beings. Research should not be carried out in a manner, which, owing to its aim, nature or realisation, would infringe human dignity. It closely follows the approach of Article 1 in the Convention, narrowing its application to a research context. The Convention does not define the term "everyone" (in French "toute personne"). These two terms are equivalent and found in the English and French versions of the European Convention on Human Rights, which however does not define them. In the absence of a unanimous agreement on the definition of these terms among member States of the Council of Europe, it was decided to allow domestic law to define them for the purposes of the application of the Convention on Human Rights and Biomedicine. The Convention also uses the expression "human being" to state the necessity to protect the dignity and identity of all human beings. It was acknowledged that it was a generally accepted principle that human dignity and the identity of the human being had to be respected as soon as life began.

Article 2. (Scope)

14. The scope of the Protocol is set out in this article.

15. In paragraph 1, it states that the Protocol covers the full range of research activities in the health field involving interventions on human beings. This includes all aspects of the research project from start to finish, including selection and recruitment of the participants. It lays out the principles for all types of biomedical research involving interventions on human beings. It is difficult to exactly delimit the health field. The Protocol covers research into molecular, cellular and other mechanisms in health, disorders and disease; and diagnostic, therapeutic, preventive and epidemiological studies involving interventions. This list is not meant to be exhaustive. Insofar as a human being is involved in research, this Protocol applies, not withstanding the fact that provisions of other protocols could apply to research in specific spheres.

16. The scope of the Protocol does not extend to studies whose purpose is not to gain new scientific knowledge but to collect or to process information for purely statistical purposes such as for audits or monitoring of the healthcare system.

17. Paragraph 3 states that, for the purposes of this Protocol, the term "intervention" covers physical interventions. It covers other interventions in so far as they involve a risk to the psychological health of the person concerned. The term "intervention" must be understood here in a broad sense; in the context of this Protocol it includes all medical acts and interactions relating to the health or well being of persons in the framework of health care systems or any other setting for scientific research purposes. The Protocol covers all interventions performed for the purposes of research in the fields of preventive care, diagnosis, treatment, or rehabilitation. The Protocol merely follows the definition of intervention used by the Convention, applying it here to the specific field of biomedical research. Questionnaires, interviews and observational research taking place in the context of a biomedical research protocol constitute interventions when they involve a risk to the psychological health of the person concerned. Questionnaires or interviews could carry a risk to the psychological health of the research participant, if they include questions of an intimate nature capable of resulting in psychological harm. In this context, slight and temporary emotional distress would not be regarded as psychological harm. However, such questionnaires could be related to enquiries into sexual history or to certain psychiatric disorders. Studies in the field of genetics that involve probing into past and family medical histories are another example of sensitive areas of research. Small groups of patients with rare genetic diseases or patients with discernible, and sometimes sensitive, social markers in an individual or group context could be particularly at risk of discrimination or stigmatisation. Such risk may exist even if the data is anonymised because the group to which the source belongs to is still identifiable. This potential would have to be evaluated. Member States would be able to choose the criteria for making this distinction. A possible method of doing so would be by the development of guidelines as to the type of questionnaires, interviews and observations which have this potential. It should not be forgotten that even observation, questions or interviews could be profoundly troubling to a patient if they address a sensitive sphere of that person's private life, such as a previous or current illness. One ramification of defining such research as coming within the scope of this Protocol is that it would be reviewed by an ethics committee, which could point out any potential problems in the research project. The Protocol does not address established medical interventions independent of a research project, even if they result in biological materials or personal data that might later be used in biomedical research. However, research interventions designed to procure biological materials or data are covered under this Protocol.

18. This Protocol does not address research on the body or body parts of deceased persons.

19. Research on foetuses and embryos in vivo, and pregnant women is covered by the Protocol. As women should not be excluded from the protections envisaged by the Protocol by virtue of the fact they are pregnant, and the impact on the embryo or foetus must always be considered when research is undertaken on such women, it is therefore necessary for both to be covered by this Protocol. However, research on embryos in vitro is excluded, this type of research being covered by Article 18 of the Convention. The CAHBI decided at its 15th meeting (24-27 March 1992, Madrid) to exclude the embryo from the draft Protocol on Medical Research. It was foreseen that this type of research would be addressed in another Protocol on the protection of the human embryo and foetus. This Protocol does not address research

on archived biological materials or personal data. However, this does not necessarily exclude biomedical research based on archived personal data or biological materials from submission to an ethics committee. The Protocol was not prepared with the intention of regulating interventions to collect biological materials which would be stored for future research, for instance in biobanks.

Chapter II – General provisions

Article 3. (Primacy of the human being)

20. This article affirms the primacy of the human being participating in research over the sole interest of science or society. Priority is given to the former and this must as a matter of principle take precedence over the latter in the event of a conflict between them.

21. The whole Additional Protocol, the aim of which is to protect human rights and dignity, is inspired by the principle of the primacy of the human being, and all its Articles must be interpreted in this light.

Article 4. (General rule)

22. Freedom of biomedical research is justified not only by humanity's right to knowledge, but also by the considerable progress its results may bring in terms of the health and well-being of patients and the general population.

23. Nevertheless, such freedom is not absolute. In biomedical research it is limited by the fundamental rights of individuals expressed, in particular, by the provisions of the Additional Protocol and the Convention and by other legal provisions that protect the human being. In this regard, it should be noted that the first Article of the Protocol specifies that its aim is to protect the dignity and identity of all human beings and guarantee everyone, without discrimination, respect for their integrity as well as for other fundamental rights and freedoms with regard to any research involving interventions on human beings in the field of biomedicine.

Article 5. (Absence of alternatives)

24. The Article sets out the requirement that research on human beings can only be undertaken if there is no alternative of comparable effectiveness. Comparable effectiveness refers to the foreseen results of the research, not to individual benefits for a participant. Invasive methods will not be authorised if other less invasive or non-invasive methods can be used with comparable effect. Consequently, research on human beings will not be allowed if comparable results can be obtained by other means unless this is clearly unreasonable. Such alternatives include computer modelling or research on animals. This does not imply that the Protocol authorises using alternatives that are unethical. The Protocol does not evaluate the ethical acceptability of research on animals or other alternatives. These matters are addressed by other legal instruments, such as the Council of Europe Convention for the Protection of Vertebrate

Animals used for Experimental and Other Scientific Purposes (ETS No. 123), national law and professional obligations and standards.

ARTICLE 6. (RISKS AND BENEFITS)

25. The principle that research shall not involve risk and burden disproportionate to its potential benefits is set out in this article. When medical research may be of direct benefit to the health of the person undergoing research, a higher degree of risk and burden may be acceptable provided that it is in proportion to the possible benefit. For example, a higher degree of risk and burden may be acceptable on a new treatment for advanced cancer, whereas the same risk and burden would be quite unacceptable where the aim is to improve the treatment of a mild infection. The notions of risk and burden include not only physical risks and burdens but also social or psychological risks to the participant. A direct benefit to a person's health signifies not only treatment to cure the patient but also treatment that may alleviate his/her suffering thus improving his/her quality of life. However, it must be noted that benefits referred to in this article include not only direct benefits but also the benefits of the research to science or society. This is particularly relevant in the case of research that has not the potential to produce results of direct benefit for the health of the person concerned. It should be recalled that such research may entail, for a person able to consent, only acceptable risk and acceptable burden for the person concerned.

26. An individual may choose to take part in research a number of times or regularly, provided that continued participation in research does not endanger the participant's health.

27. The Article also addresses the participation in research of persons who are able to consent but who would gain no potential direct benefit from the research. This category includes all non-therapeutic research, including that on the so-called "healthy volunteers." The Article sets out the additional preconditions for this type of research. Whether or not the risk and burden are acceptable will be considered carefully by the ethics committee and competent body that approves the research project. The final decision on whether or not the risk and burden are acceptable will be made by the persons concerned when they decide to give or withhold consent. Because these participants are able to consent to research, the level of risk and burden permitted (acceptable) is higher than that allowed for persons not able to consent (minimal risk and minimal burden).

ARTICLE 7. (APPROVAL)

28. Article 16 of the Convention sets out the conditions that must be met before research on a person may be undertaken, and includes the condition that the research project has been approved by the competent body after independent examination of its scientific merit, including assessment of the importance of the aim of the research, and multidisciplinary review of its ethical acceptability. This article of the Protocol sets out the requirements for such approval. It is acknowledged that in some countries, the ethics committee could also act as the competent body while in other cases or in other countries, the competent body might be a Ministry or

a regulatory agency (for pharmaceuticals, for instance), which would take the opinion of the ethics committee into account. Research must comply with the relevant legal requirements. The Article does not set out a specific procedure or sequence for the submission of research projects to the relevant bodies.

29. This provision does not contradict the principle of freedom of research. In fact, Article 4 of this Protocol states that biomedical research shall be carried out freely. However, this freedom is not absolute. It is qualified by the legal provisions ensuring the protection of the human being. Independent examination of the ethical acceptability of the research project by an ethics committee, and the approval of that project is one such protective provisions. Allowing unethical research to utilise human beings would contravene their fundamental rights. It is the responsibility of Parties to designate within the framework of their legal system the ethics committee or a different competent body as the decision making organ in order to protect the participants taking part in the research.

30. The relevance of the research to the health needs of the local community may be relevant to the ethical assessment of a research project. In most cases, such relevance, along with the fulfilment of the other conditions, will be a factor in a positive opinion on the research project by an ethics committee and approval by the competent body. However, this does not mean that only research that is relevant to local health needs can be approved. The example may be given of a phase of research undertaken in an urban European setting where the results may be of relevance to a cure for a tropical disease; especially where the research would involve volunteers capable of giving consent, there should be no strict prohibition on participating in such research out of solidarity. However, the aim of considering this issue is to prevent the "export" of research in order to avoid stringent ethical standards or in order to find volunteers in another country when they cannot be found in the country where the research would be relevant to local health needs.

ARTICLE 8. (SCIENTIFIC QUALITY)

31. This article applies to all researchers in the biomedical field, including doctors and other healthcare professionals. It is understood that researchers engaging in biomedical research may also be biologists, psychologists, computer experts, medical students or members of other professions outside of the health care field (sociologists, educationalists etc.). The requirement of supervision by an appropriately qualified researcher makes it clear that the suitability of the person supervising must be assessed in relation to the particular project concerned. It is intended not to foreclose on the possibility of students, for example, being part of a biomedical research team as long as their work is supervised by an appropriately qualified researcher.

32. The term "research" must be understood here as corresponding to the scope set out in Article 2.

33. All research must be carried out in accordance with the law in general, as supplemented and developed by professional standards.

34. The current state of the art of scientific knowledge and clinical experience determines the professional standards and skill to be expected of professionals in the performance of research. In following the progress of biology and medicine, it changes with new developments and eliminates methods that do not reflect the state of the art. Nevertheless, it is accepted that professional standards do not necessarily prescribe one line of action as being the only one possible or foreclose research seeking to improve or replace an intervention.

35. Furthermore, in cases where the research has the possibility of producing a real and direct benefit for the health of a research participant, a particular course of action must be judged in the light of the participant's specific health problem.

36. In particular, an intervention must meet criteria of relevance and proportionality between the aim pursued and the means employed. This is particularly relevant in the case of research that does not have the potential of producing a real and direct benefit for the health of a research participant. The issue of proportionality is addressed specifically in Article 6 of this Protocol.

37. The Article states that research must be scientifically justified and meet generally accepted criteria of scientific quality. This would ordinarily be done by independent peer review or scientific advisors. The assessment of scientific quality will in particular take into account the appropriateness of the research design, the objectives of the research, the technical feasibility, statistical methods (including sample size calculation where relevant), and the potential for reaching valid conclusions with the smallest possible number of research participants. It has to be recognised that there may be different types of research projects requiring their own kind of assessment, e.g. a study to develop new methods or a pilot study proving the suitability of a project, which may include tools such as questionnaires. The scientific design of such a study has to be appropriate in respect to its limited aim, e.g. only to derive a statistically based tendency or probability, so that a subsequent study to prove or refute a scientific hypothesis could be justified. However, for a study to be able to reach valid conclusions, there must be a sufficient number of participants to demonstrate, for example, that there is a statistically significant difference between the outcome for the group of patients who received a new drug treatment compared to those who received standard treatment. It is considered that research that does not meet these criteria is, by definition, unethical and should not be approved by the ethics committee or competent body reviewing the research. The participation of persons in research of sub-standard scientific quality is not considered permissible. Scientific quality must be present in the project before its approval and throughout the implementation of the research.

Chapter III – Ethics committee

ARTICLE 9. (INDEPENDENT EXAMINATION BY AN ETHICS COMMITTEE)

38. The Article requires that all research projects within the scope of this Protocol be submitted for independent examination of their scientific merit and ethical acceptability in each State

in which any research activity is to take place. This may include States from which research participants are to be recruited for research physically carried out in another State. Best practice is to also submit research projects to an ethics committee in every research location within each State. Although each committee will reach an independent view on the appropriateness of carrying out the research in that particular location, it is acceptable for such committees to endorse the conclusions of one "lead" ethics committee within that State on the science and ethics of the research project.

39. Due to the differing systems in use in various States, the Article refers to ethics committees. It is considered that this term covers ethics committees or other bodies authorised to review biomedical research involving interventions on human beings. In many States this would refer to a multidisciplinary ethics committee but review by a scientific committee might also be required. The Article does not require a positive assessment by the ethics committee being that the role of such bodies or committees in many States is advisory. The conclusion of this assessment may have legal force in some jurisdictions while in others it serves to advise the competent body (for example, a regulatory body) which will rule on the commencement of the research project.

40. The second paragraph sets out the purpose of the multidisciplinary examination after the precondition of scientific quality has been met. This purpose, in accordance with the aim of the Convention and Protocol to protect the dignity and identity of all human beings, is to protect the dignity, rights, safety and well being of the research participants. If participants are to be included during the reproductive stage of their lives, care should be taken, within the framework of the ethics committee opinion, that if the research project could have an impact on reproductive health or on a future child (for example, in a project concerning the use of a new drug, the effect of which on an unborn child is not known) the duty of the researcher to provide birth control advice, is fulfilled. Both paragraphs 1 and 2 of this article refer to the examination of the "ethical acceptability" of the research project. The requirement for multidisciplinary review of the ethical acceptability of research projects was first set out in the Convention's Article 16, indent iii, and a number of the provisions of this Protocol develop this principle by establishing more precise rules.

41. Further, the second paragraph of the Article states that the assessment of the ethical acceptability shall draw on an appropriate range of expertise and experience adequately reflecting professional and lay views. This combination of different types of expertise, experience, and viewpoints gives an ethics committee its multidisciplinary character, though the specific competences to be included may differ, for example in accordance with the type of research to be reviewed. The existence of an independent ethics committee ensures that the interests and concerns of the community are represented, and the participation of laypersons is important in ensuring that the public can have confidence in the system for oversight of biomedical research. Such laypersons will be neither healthcare professionals nor have experience in carrying out biomedical research. The fact that a person is an expert in an unrelated field, such as engineering or accountancy, does not preclude a person from being able to express lay views within the meaning of this article. Thus this paragraph further details what is meant by the

term "multidisciplinary" In order to satisfy the spirit of the requirement of multidisciplinarity, thought should also be given to gender and cultural balance in the bodies carrying out the assessment. In creating this body, the nature of the projects that are likely to be presented for review should also be taken into account. The ethics committee may need to invite experts to assist it in evaluating a project from a specific sphere of biomedicine. It may be appropriate for ethics committees to consult with patients' organisations familiar with a particular condition and/or situation.

42. Paragraph 3 requires that after the multidisciplinary review of the ethical acceptability of a research project, the ethics committee give clearly stated reasons for its positive or negative conclusions. This is a general principle of administrative law. Whether the reasoning and conclusions are further considered by the competent body in granting or denying approval, or they are regarded as the final say on the research project, the basis for the conclusion should be clearly comprehensible both to specialists in the field and to laypersons. Clear reasoning and conclusions are also necessary if an appeals process is provided for.

ARTICLE 10. (INDEPENDENCE OF THE ETHICS COMMITTEE)

43. The Article first addresses the independence of the ethics committee on the group level. Parties to the Protocol shall take measures to assure the operational independence of their ethics committees, ensuring that they are not subject to undue external influences to come to a specific conclusion.

44. Next, in the second paragraph, the article addresses the independence of the individuals making up the ethics committee. It requires members to declare any direct or indirect conflicts of interest related to submitted research projects and requires that members with such conflicts shall not participate in the discussion and decision making related to the project in question. A conflict arises when a person's judgement concerning a primary interest, such as scientific knowledge, could be unduly influenced by secondary interests, which may include financial gain, personal advancement, or personal, family, academic or political interests. It is not inherently unethical to find oneself in a position of conflict of interest; what is required is to recognise the fact and deal with it appropriately. Potential conflicts of interest, as well as the perception of the existence of such conflicts, may be as important as actual conflicts, to the point that they may affect the credibility of ethical review.

45. The independence of the ethics committee as a whole and its individual members may be reinforced by provision of insurance for the ethics committee and its members for civil liability. Such insurance could be particularly important for lay members, who would not be covered by insurance that might already cover the participation of employees of universities or research institutes or medical professionals.

ARTICLE 11. (INFORMATION FOR THE ETHICS COMMITTEE)

46. The Article requires that all information that is necessary to the ethical assessment of the research project must be submitted in written form to the ethics committee. This information is necessary for the proper evaluation of biomedical research projects by the entrusted committee in order to protect the dignity, rights, safety and well-being of those participating.

47. The Article states that, in so far as it is relevant for the research project, the information listed in the Appendix shall be provided. The Appendix is an integral part of the Protocol. It is noted that, in conformity with paragraph 2 of this article, amendments to the items of information found in the Appendix can be made if adopted by a two-thirds majority of the Committee foreseen by Article 32 of the Convention. These amendments will enter into force following their adoption.

Appendix

48. Indent i of the Appendix to this article requires submission of the name of the principal researcher. In the case of there being a single researcher, that person is logically the principal researcher. In cases of multiple researchers being involved, this would be the responsible researcher to whom the collaborators report. The other researchers should provide information on issues related to the research project to the principal researcher, who will usually maintain contacts with the ethics committee regarding the project. However, all the researchers are responsible for the implementation of the research project, particularly concerning safety and ethical issues.

49. The information required in indent ii is necessary in order to prevent the unethical utilisation of human beings in research that unnecessarily duplicates research or which is otherwise scientifically inadequate. The latest state of scientific knowledge may include the results of any previous relevant studies on human beings or animals, meta-analyses and systematic reviews.

50. Indent iii requires that information on the methods and procedures envisaged be provided to the ethics committee. Chemical substances to be used in a research project are one example of an item of information that could be relevant to the review of the project.

51. Indent iv, which requires the submission of a comprehensive summary of the research project in lay language, underscores the trend in member States to have more and more lay representation in their ethics committees. If the lay representatives are to be able to effectively fulfil their role on the committee, they require sufficient information in a form that is comprehensible to them to enable them to reach an informed opinion. Lay language will also contribute to the transparency concerning the project.

52. Indent v requires the submission of a statement of previous and concurrent submissions of the research project to one or more ethics committees and, if any, the outcome of those

submissions as known at the time of the submission of this project. Nevertheless, if after submission of the research project relevant and important points arise in another ethical review, they should be communicated to the ethics committee. The ethics committee reviewing the research project may then seek further information if any doubts are or have been raised about the ethical acceptability of the research project. This might include concerns that the proponents of the project might be engaging in "forum shopping" (i.e. looking for a venue to accept a research project considered unethical in other jurisdictions). At the same time, the possibility of appeal or a different review should not be discounted entirely, as a previous or concurrent decision might be based on local conditions or culture, or even have been capricious. Such appeals should take place within a previously agreed framework for appeals.

53. Indent vii requires that the ethics committee be informed of the criteria for inclusion or exclusion of any categories of persons and how they are to be selected and recruited. This is both to protect against the inappropriate inclusion of categories of persons in research, such as carrying out research on persons unable to consent which could be carried out on persons able to consent, as well as to protect against the deliberate exclusion of categories of persons from research to whom the research itself or the end product could be beneficial. Examples could be exclusion due to gender or age. Particular care should be taken with respect to persons during the reproductive stage of their lives, and to the possible negative impact on an embryo or foetus.

54. Indent viii asks for the reasons for the use or absence of control groups. This is often essential to ensure the scientific validity of the research project, particularly in most therapeutic research. Treatment is considered to include preventive and diagnostic procedures. As required by Article 23, those in control groups should receive a proven method of prevention, diagnosis or treatment. The use of a placebo is justified if there is no method of proven effectiveness or where withdrawal or withholding of such methods will not expose participants to unacceptable risk or burden.

55. Indent xii refers to timing of the information in the sense of it being essential that the information be provided prior to the consent procedure, as well as to a period of time for reflection that should be given to the potential participant in order to take his/her decision on whether to give consent.

56. Indent xiii specifies that documentation to be used to seek consent or authorisation be submitted. The ethics committee should also be informed of the procedure to be used to obtain consent. This would include information on procedures to seek authorisation in emergency situations in order to ensure protection of persons in such a situation.

57. Indent xv requires researchers to inform the ethics committee of arrangements foreseen for information that might be relevant to the present or future health of potential research participants and their family members. Research may uncover information that would warn participants of a health risk or otherwise be of assistance to them in planning their healthcare or lifestyles. Article 27 of this Protocol sets out the requirement that conclusions of research

of relevance to the current or future health or quality of life of participants must be offered to them. The ethics committee should be informed if foreseen anonymisation of data would prevent the transmission of such relevant information. Individuals have the right not to receive such communications if they so wish. Best practice requires that the wish of the participant to know or not to know should be established prior to commencement of the research. Because proper counselling and other healthcare assistance may be necessary to explain the nature of the results and the options available to the participant, the foreseen provision of such assistance should also be described to the ethics committee.

58. Indent xvi addresses payments and rewards to be made to participants, researchers or institutions in the context of the research project. Such information is important to ethics committees in the interests of transparency and for proper evaluation of the research project. For example, unusually large payments or rewards might influence decisions on the risks that participants are willing to undertake, and could influence the behaviour of researchers in regard to such risks.

59. Indent xviii addresses two sets of issues: further potential uses of research results that are already foreseen by the researchers, and foreseen further uses that may be based on biological materials or personal data from a research intervention being archived after the intervention and then utilised later.

60. Indent xx requires the submission of information on any insurance or indemnity to cover damage arising in the context of the research project. This provision does not require that such arrangements exist but that the ethics committee be informed whether such insurance or indemnity exists or not. Many jurisdictions require the existence of such arrangements while some ethics committees will not approve certain types of research without arrangements for insurance and compensation.

61. The final paragraph of the Appendix makes clear that even if all the other information required by the article has been provided the ethics committee is not precluded from requesting additional information if it regards it as necessary for proper evaluation of the research project.

Article 12. (Undue influence)

62. The first sentence of this article requires the ethics committee assessing the ethical acceptability of a research project to satisfy themselves that no undue influence, including that of a financial nature, will be exerted on persons to encourage participation in research. The usual legal concept of undue influence involves coercion. The coercion need not involve confinement or violence. It may be exerted in particular on a person in a weak or feeble condition, so that very little pressure will overbear the person's will, and make the individual feel that he or she must agree, although it is not the individual's wish to do so. Payments made to research participants are not prohibited by the Protocol but are subject to the scrutiny of the ethics committee.

63. This understanding of undue influence may also be relevant to situations where one party is in a position of trust toward another and may therefore exercise influence on the latter. Such situations may occur where there is a doctor/patient relationship and the doctor is also the researcher. In such cases, having a neutral third person ask for consent or receive the answer regarding participation in the research has been identified as best practice.

64. If any compensation to the research participants, and where appropriate their representatives, is provided, it would not be considered undue influence if it is appropriate to the burden and inconvenience. However, compensation should not be provided at a level that might encourage participants to take risks that they would not otherwise find acceptable. This should be evaluated by the ethics committee. Reimbursement for any expenses or financial loss shall not be regarded as undue influence. While it is permissible to compensate research participants for expenses or lost time, it is not permissible to pay them to accept a higher level of risk than would otherwise be the case. While financial gain is mentioned, the Article does not exclude consideration of other types of undue influence. For example, it would be inappropriate to suggest to potential employees that their promotion prospects or continued employment depended on participating in research; or that the grades a university student might receive could depend on whether or not they participated in research. Other types of undue influence could include limiting or increasing access to medical care.

65. If the ethics committee is not satisfied that undue influence, broadly defined to include inducements such as those mentioned above, is not being exerted on potential participants of a research project then the project should not receive a positive assessment unless changes are made to address the problem.

66. The second sentence lays out the principle that particular attention must be given to dependent persons and vulnerable persons to ensure that they will not be subjected to undue influence.

67. Dependent persons are those whose decision on participation in a research project may be influenced by their reliance on those who may be offering them the possibility of participation in the research. Such persons could be those deprived of their liberty, recipients of health care dependent on their health care provider for continued care, medical or other students, those in military service, health care workers (particularly those in junior positions) or employees to give just a few examples.

68. It can be said that all human beings enrolled in research are vulnerable to harm, since research, by definition, involves uncertainty and the utilisation of human beings in order to further the goal of gathering knowledge. However, some human beings may be more vulnerable than others to the risk of being treated unethically in the context of biomedical research. This can be true even in the case of participants who have given their informed consent to taking part in the research project.

69. Human beings asked to take part in research can be classified as being vulnerable due to cognitive, situational, institutional, deferential, medical, economic, and social factors. Persons with cognitive vulnerability may not have the capacity to come to an informed decision on whether to give consent or not. Such persons might be minors or persons suffering from dementia. Persons with situational vulnerability may have the capacity to make a decision, but are deprived of their ability to exercise their capacity by the situation at hand (for example during an emergency or due to a lack of fluency in the language being used to inform and request the consent). Persons subject to institutional vulnerability could be individuals with full cognitive capacity to consent, but who find themselves subject to the authority of persons or bodies who could have their own, and possibly conflicting, interests in relation to a research project. Examples of those subject to this type of vulnerability could be persons fulfilling their service in the military or other uniformed services, prisoners or medical students. Persons subject to institutional vulnerability could also be described as being dependent. Deferential vulnerability is similar to institutional vulnerability, but in contrast to institutional vulnerability, it is characterised by informal, rather than formal, hierarchies. These hierarchies can be based on social frameworks or on subjective deference to the opinion of a family member. It could also be the deference of a patient to the wishes (perceived or real) of his/her physician. Medical vulnerability affects those suffering from ailments for which there is no satisfactory standard treatment. This type of patient may be vulnerable to exploitation by someone promising him/her a "miracle cure." Economic vulnerability affects those with the cognitive ability to consent to participation but who might easily be induced to take part in research in order to obtain a financial gain or in order not to lose access to some benefits, even if they would not otherwise participate in the research. Social vulnerability arises from the position of certain groups in a given society. Such groups may be stereotyped, may have been historically discriminated against, may have recently arrived in the community, may not speak the language, and may be economically disadvantaged (like the economically vulnerable). Economic, social and educational disadvantage may be more prevalent in some regions or States than in others. In this respect, attention shall be paid to the requirements of Article 29 regarding research in States not party to this Protocol. As the last example shows, membership of these groups can be overlapping.

70. Other examples of undue influence could be in the form of veiled threats to deny access to services to which the person would otherwise be entitled, the insinuation of looking favourably on academic work to be submitted in the future, veiled threats of punishment that the person would otherwise receive or that refusal will diminish the likelihood of career advancement, or the offer of amounts of money large enough to influence the giving or denial of consent.

Chapter IV – Information and consent

Article 13. (Information for research participants)

71. This article states that persons being asked to participate in a research project shall be given adequate information in a comprehensible form on the purpose, the overall plan and the possible risks and benefits. The opinion of the ethics committee shall be included. The

specific information that potential participants in research are to receive where it is relevant is listed in this article. Information on the risks involved in the intervention or in alternative courses of action must cover not only the risks inherent in the type of intervention contemplated, but also any risks related to the individual characteristics of each participant, such as age or the presence of other disorders or conditions. Requests for additional information made by potential participants must be answered as fully as possible. The Article does not require that the information be given to the research participant by a specific person. This should be determined by the nature of the research, the needs of the potential participant, national practice and/or law.

72. Moreover, this information must be sufficiently clear and comprehensible to the person who is to take part in the research. The potential participant must be put in a position, through the use of terms he or she can understand, to reach a valid judgement on the necessity and usefulness of the aim and methods of the research intervention, both in relation to the individual and in relation to others who might benefit, weighing these against any risks or burden it may impose. The information should be provided in a way to make it understandable taking into account the level of knowledge, education and psychological state of the potential participant, be this a patient or a healthy volunteer. Additionally, the information given must be documented, meaning it must be recorded. Whenever possible, the information should be given to the potential participant in its documented form, such as in writing or in the form of a video, a tape, or CD-ROM. Where necessary, the information should be provided in a different language appropriate to a participant/group of participants or in a form appropriate to those with sensory disabilities. It may sometimes be impossible to provide the participant with comprehensible written information because he or she is illiterate. In such cases, the information should be explained to the potential participant and be documented for record keeping purposes and in order to provide it to the potential participant if he/she so wishes. The use of audio tapes and videos can be helpful in imparting information to people who are illiterate. The potential participant should be given sufficient time to review the information, consider his/her participation, and consult with others. Although information listed in the article should be offered to all participants, if the person concerned wishes not to receive detailed information on any area this should be respected so long as he or she has received sufficient information to enable informed consent to be given. The wish of a participant not to receive certain information should be recorded.

73. The second paragraph of the article refers to the "opinion" of the ethics committee. While the conclusion of the ethics committee is referred to as an opinion because it is advisory in many countries, it is considered that this term also includes positive or negative opinions (or decisions) of a binding nature in those countries whose law envisions this. In those States that allow for an appeal of an ethics committee opinion, "opinion" refers to both the initial opinion rendered and the opinion resulting from the appeal.

74. Indent vii requires the researcher to disclose to the potential participant any foreseen commercial use of data, research results or biological materials to be obtained from the potential participant during, or prior to, the research. The requirement in this indent does not reflect any

endorsement or condemnation of research conducted with commercial applications in mind. Rather, it acknowledges the fact that the motivation for participation in biomedical research for many persons may be out of solidarity, and information on foreseen commercial uses of their contribution to the research may be important to them in making a decision on whether to take part or not. Additionally, recital 26 of Directive 98/44/EC of the European Parliament and of the Council of 6 July 1998 on the legal protection of biotechnological inventions states that, "whereas if an invention is based on biological material of human origin or if it uses such material, where a patent application is filed, the person from whose body the material is taken must have had an opportunity of expressing free and informed consent thereto, in accordance with national law."

75. The third paragraph requires that in addition, the persons being asked to participate in a research project shall be informed of the rights and safeguards prescribed by law for their protection, and specifically of their right to refuse consent or to withdraw consent at any time without being subject to any form of discrimination, in particular regarding the right to medical care.

ARTICLE 14. (CONSENT)

76. The Article lays out the requirements for consent to participation in research involving interventions on persons. It affirms at the international level an already well-established rule, which is that no one may, as a matter of principle, be forced to participate in research involving an intervention on him or her without his or her consent. This rule emphasises the autonomy of research participants in their relationship with researchers and health care professionals and states that paternalistic approaches that might ignore their wishes are unacceptable.

77. The person's consent is considered to be free and informed if it is given on the basis of objective information from the responsible researcher or other responsible person as to the nature and potential consequences of the planned intervention or its alternatives, in the absence of pressure from anyone which is of such a degree that the patient is no longer able to make an independent choice. As well as the information that must be provided to the participant about the particular research project, it is also good practice to inform the person of any possible alternatives. The second paragraph states that refusal to participate in research shall not preju-dice the right of the individual to receive medical care. Any downgrading of the medical care offered to an individual because of his/her refusal to participate in research would constitute undue influence on the decision of whether to consent.

78. For their consent to be valid, the persons in question must have been informed about the relevant facts regarding the intervention being contemplated. This information must include the purpose, nature and consequences of the intervention and the possible risks involved. Although the research use of biological materials which have been previously removed in the course of a clinical intervention are beyond the scope of this Protocol, it should be noted that if there is an intention to utilise biological materials or personal data obtained during a medical intervention

for research purposes after the medical intervention, it is good practice for specific consent to be obtained for such research uses not related to the medical intervention.

79. This article requires consent to be informed, free, express, specific and documented. Express consent may be either verbal or written as long as it is documented. Best practice demands that written consent be obtained, except in exceptional circumstances.

80. Freedom of consent implies that consent may be withdrawn at any time and that the decision of the person concerned shall be respected once he or she has been fully informed of the consequences. This principle is laid out in sentence 2 of paragraph 1. Paragraph 2 adds that such a decision shall not lead to any form of discrimination against the person concerned, in particular regarding the right to medical care. The participant cannot be held liable for any consequences of withdrawal, particularly of a financial nature. The participant should not be required to give a reason for withdrawal. Any obligation arising out of the mere fact of withdrawal would be contrary to the right to withdraw consent. This principle does not mean that the withdrawal of a patient's consent must be acted on immediately if, for example, the abrupt discontinuation of a course of therapy could be hazardous to the patient. In such cases, the doctor or other healthcare professional has an obligation to explain to the participant the risks of discontinuing the study concerned, and to seek consent to continue in the study or for treatment as explained in paragraph 38 of the Explanatory Report to the Convention.

81. Paragraph 3 of this article requires arrangements to be put into place to verify whether a potential research participant has the capacity to give informed consent, if the capacity of the person is in doubt. Such persons may be those who have not been declared incapable of giving consent by a legal body, but whose capacity to give consent may be questionable due to an accident or due to a persistent or worsening condition, for instance. The aim of this paragraph is not to set out any particular arrangement for verification, but to require that such procedures exist. The arrangements would not necessarily be in the framework of the courts; they could be developed and implemented through professional standards. In such cases, the researcher is responsible for verifying that the participants from whom he obtains consent have the capacity to give the consent. Information on arrangements for such verification in the context of a specific research project should be submitted to the ethics committee reviewing the project.

Chapter V – Protection of persons not able to consent to research

ARTICLE 15. (PROTECTION OF PERSONS NOT ABLE TO CONSENT TO RESEARCH)

Paragraph 1

82. The Article sets out the requirements governing the participation in research of persons not able to consent. Paragraph 1, indent i establishes a principle with regard to research on a person who is not able to consent: that the research must be potentially beneficial to the health of the person concerned. The benefit must be real and follow from the potential results of the research, and the risk must not be disproportionate to the potential benefit.

83. Moreover, to allow such research, indent ii sets out the principle that there should be no alternative individual with full capacity. It is not sufficient that there should be no volunteers with the capacity to consent. Recourse to research on persons not able to consent must be, scientifically, the sole possibility. This will apply, for instance, to research aimed at improving the understanding of development in children or improving the understanding of diseases affecting these people specifically, such as infant diseases or certain psychiatric disorders such as dementia in adults. Such research can only be carried out, respectively, on children or the adults concerned.

84. Indent iii sets out the requirement that the persons have been informed of their rights and the safeguards prescribed by law for their protection, unless the person is not in a state to receive the information. The indent uses the term "not in a state to receive the information" because there may be cases where a person cannot perceive or comprehend the information because of his/her condition. An example would be the case of someone in a coma.

85. Protection of the person not able to consent is also strengthened by the requirement that the necessary authorisation as provided for under indent iv of this article (and Article 6 of the Convention) be given specifically and in writing. Indent iv further states that previously expressed wishes or objections shall be taken into account. Advance directives are not referred to in the Article, but are recognised as a possible way of clarifying a person's wishes. As specified in Article 6, paragraph 5 of the Convention, such authorisation may be freely withdrawn at any time.

86. Indent v sets out the requirement that the research must not be carried out if the person concerned objects. In the case of infants or very young children, it is necessary to evaluate their attitude taking account of their age and maturity. The rule prohibiting the carrying out of the research against the wish of the person reflects concern, in research, for the autonomy and dignity of the person in all circumstances, even if the person is considered legally incapable of giving consent. Objections may be expressed by non-verbal means. The opinion of the caregiver, when there is one, should be taken into account in interpreting the wishes of those unable to express themselves. This provision is also a means of guaranteeing that the burden of the research is acceptable to the person at all times.

Paragraph 2

87. Paragraph 2 provides exceptionally, under the protective conditions prescribed by domestic law, for the possibility of waiving the direct benefit rule on certain very strict conditions. Were such research to be banned altogether, progress in the battles to maintain and improve health and to combat diseases only afflicting children, mentally disabled persons or persons suffering from senile dementia would become impossible. It is the aim of such research to benefit persons in those groups through a better understanding of the factors which will help to maintain and improve health and well being or through a better understanding of disease processes.

88. As well as the general conditions applicable to research on persons not able to consent, a certain number of supplementary conditions must be fulfilled. In this way the Protocol and Convention enable persons in these categories to enjoy the benefits of science in the fight against disease, while guaranteeing the individual protection of the person who undergoes the research. The required conditions imply that:

– in order to obtain the necessary results for the patient group concerned, there is neither an alternative method of comparable effectiveness to research on humans, nor the possibility of research of comparable effectiveness on individuals capable of giving informed consent;
– the research has the aim of contributing to the ultimate attainment of results capable of conferring a benefit to the person concerned or to other persons in the same age category, or afflicted with the same disease or disorder or having the same condition, through significant improvements in the scientific understanding of the individual's condition, disease or disorder;
– the research entails only minimal risk and minimal burden for the individual concerned (addressed by Article 17 – Interventions with minimal risk and minimal burden);
– the research project not only has scientific merit but is also ethically and legally acceptable and has been given prior approval by the competent bodies;
– the person's representative or an authority or a person or body provided for by law has given authorisation (adequate representation of the interests of the patient);
– the person concerned does not object (the wish of the person concerned prevails and is always decisive);
– authorisation for this research may be withdrawn at any phase of the research.

89. One of the two supplementary conditions is that this research should have the aim of contributing, through significant improvement in the scientific understanding of a person's health condition, disease or disorder, to the ultimate attainment of results capable of conferring benefit to the health of the person undergoing research or the health of persons in the same category. This means, for example, that a minor may participate in research on a condition from which he or she suffers even if the minor would not benefit by the results of the research, provided that the research might be of benefit to other children suffering from the same condition. In the case of healthy minors undergoing research it is obvious that the result of the research might be of benefit only to other children; however such research may well be of ultimate benefit to healthy children taking part in this research. While this article allows research on minors for the benefit of other minors, it would be ethically inappropriate to undertake research on minors who may also be vulnerable for other reasons, if the research could be conducted on those without such additional vulnerabilities.

90. The research on "the individual's condition" might include, with regard to research on children, not only diseases or abnormalities peculiar to childhood or certain aspects of common diseases that are specific to childhood, but also the normal development of the child where knowledge is necessary for the understanding of these diseases or abnormalities.

91. While Article 6 restricts research in general by establishing a criterion of risk/benefit proportionality, this article lays down a more stringent requirement for research without direct benefit to persons incapable of giving consent, namely only minimal risk and minimal burden for the individual concerned. Minimal risk and minimal burden are addressed further in Article 17 of this Protocol.

92. Diagnostic and therapeutic progress for the benefit of sick children depends to a large extent on new knowledge and insight regarding the normal biology of the human organism and calls for research on the age-related functions and development of normal children before it can be applied in the treatment of sick children. Moreover, research on children concerns not only the diagnosis and treatment of serious pathological conditions but also the maintenance and improvement of the state of health of children who are not ill, or who are only slightly ill. In this connection mention should be made of prophylaxis through vaccination or immunisation, dietary measures or preventive treatments whose effectiveness, especially in terms of costs and possible risks, urgently requires evaluation by means of scientifically controlled studies. Any restriction based on the requirement of "potential direct benefit" for the person undergoing the test would make such studies impossible in the future.

93. As examples, the following fields of research can be mentioned, provided all conditions outlined above are met (including the condition that it is impossible to obtain the same results through research carried out on capable persons and the condition of minimal risk and minimal burden):

–   in respect of children: replacing X-ray examinations or invasive diagnostic measures for children by ultrasonic scanning; removal of blood samples from newborn infants without respiratory problems in order to establish the necessary oxygen content for premature infants; discovering the causes and improving treatment of leukaemia in children (for example by taking a blood sample), research on diet and nutrition, immunisation studies;
–   in respect of adults not able to consent: research on patients in intensive care, with Alzheimer's disease and other types of dementia or in a coma to improve the understanding of the causes of coma, Alzheimer's disease and other types of dementia or the treatment in intensive care.

The above-mentioned examples of medical research cannot be described as routine treatment. They are in principle without direct therapeutic benefit for the patient. However, they may be ethically acceptable if the above highly protective conditions are fulfilled.

Paragraph 3

94. The third paragraph requires that objection to participation, refusal to give authorisation or the withdrawal of authorisation to participate in research shall not lead to any form of discrimination against the person concerned, in particular regarding the right to medical care.

ARTICLE 16. (INFORMATION PRIOR TO AUTHORISATION)

95. This article sets out the requirements for the information that must be submitted prior to authorisation being given for participation in research. The information shall be provided to the individual concerned, unless the person is not in a state to receive the information. This information should also be provided to a caregiver or member of the family, when appropriate. In all cases, this is the same information that must be given to those able to consent in Article 13.

ARTICLE 17. (RESEARCH WITH MINIMAL RISK AND MINIMAL BURDEN)

96. The Article defines minimal risk and minimal burden, which is a precondition of Article 15, paragraph 2, for research on persons unable to consent that is not potentially of direct benefit to their health. It is only in respecting this and the other preconditions of Article 15 that such research may be carried out. To act otherwise would be to exploit these persons contrary to their dignity. For example, taking a single blood sample from a child would generally only present a minimal risk, and might therefore be regarded as acceptable. However, it must be noted that minimal risk and minimal burden depend on the current state of knowledge and availability of procedures, and less invasive procedures should be utilised once they become available. Professional bodies, including professional associations in fields such as internal medicine or surgery, may provide guidance on the current state of knowledge in their fields. The risk for such participants cannot be increased beyond minimal even if the research promises a higher level of benefit.

97. The first paragraph defines research bearing minimal risk as that which, in terms of the nature and scale of the intervention(s), would result in an individual case at the most in a very slightly detrimental and temporary impact on the health of the person concerned.

98. The second paragraph defines minimal burden as that for which the expected discomfort, which might be associated with the research, will be at most temporary and very slight for the individual.

99. Furthermore, it states that, where appropriate, a person enjoying the special confidence of the person concerned shall assess the burden. A person enjoying the special confidence of the person could be a family member, a caregiver, partner or close friend.

100. Examples of research with minimal risk and minimal burden may include:

– obtaining bodily fluids without invasive intervention, e.g. taking saliva or urine samples or cheek swab,
– at the time when tissues samples are being taken, for example during a surgical operation, taking small additional tissue samples,
– taking a blood sample from a peripheral vein or taking a sample of capillary blood,

– minor extensions to non-invasive diagnostic measures using technical equipment, such as sonographic examinations, taking an electrocardiogram following rest, one X-ray exposure, carrying out one computer tomographic exposure or one exposure using magnetic resonance imaging without a contrast medium.

However, for certain participants, even these procedures might entail risk or burden which cannot be considered minimal. Assessment on an individual basis must therefore be carried out.

Chapter VI – Specific situations

ARTICLE 18. (RESEARCH DURING PREGNANCY OR BREASTFEEDING)

101. This article covers the woman, foetus, and the embryo in vivo during pregnancy. Further, in its paragraph 2, it covers women breastfeeding during research. The Article does not presuppose that States must permit research with no potential benefit for the woman, the embryo, the foetus, or the child after birth.

102. Paragraph 1 of this article requires that if the results of the research do not have potential direct benefit for the health of the woman, embryo, foetus, or child after birth, there must be no more than minimal risk and minimal burden. The rule is applicable to all those for whom the research may result in risk or burden. Consequently, particular care shall be taken to ensure that the research only entails minimal risk for the woman, the embryo, the foetus, or the child after birth. Minimal risk and minimal burden are addressed in Article 17 and in paragraphs 96 to 100 of this Explanatory Report.

103. Indent i requires that the research be aimed at benefiting other women in relation to reproduction, or other embryos, foetuses or children. The wording "in relation to reproduction" should be understood broadly; for example it would include research relevant to the health of women following pregnancy, or research relevant to women's choice on whether or not to become pregnant. Indent ii requires that research of comparable effectiveness cannot be carried out on women who are not pregnant. Recourse to research on pregnant women, embryos or foetuses must be, scientifically, the sole possibility if it does not produce a significant direct benefit for the participant or her embryo, foetus or child. This provision should not be considered discrimination against the pregnant woman, but protection of her health and that of her embryo, foetus or child. The notion of discrimination has been interpreted consistently by the European Court of Human Rights in its case law regarding Article 14 of the Convention on Human Rights. In particular, this case law has made it clear that not every distinction or difference of treatment amounts to discrimination. As the Court has stated, for example, in the judgement in the case of Abdulaziz, Cabales and Balkandali v. the United Kingdom: "a difference of treatment is discriminatory if it 'has no objective and reasonable justification', that is, if it does not pursue a 'legitimate aim' or if there is not a 'reasonable relationship of proportionality between the means employed and the aim sought to be realised" (judgement of 28 May 1985, Series A, no. 94, paragraph 72).

104. Paragraph 2 of the Article requires that when research is undertaken on a breastfeeding woman, particular care should be taken to avoid any adverse impact on the health of the child.

ARTICLE 19. (RESEARCH ON PERSONS IN EMERGENCY CLINICAL SITUATIONS)

105. The Article addresses research that can only be undertaken in emergency situations and which is intended to improve emergency response or care. A recognised emergency situation is one that is unforeseen and which requires prompt action. Present medical treatment for some conditions giving rise to a clinical emergency situation, for example severe head injury, is still limited, and the risk of death is high. If the person does survive, they may develop serious disability. It is therefore important that research is undertaken both into new treatments for these conditions, and in some cases into the underlying mechanisms that lead to the damage. However, any treatment or research intervention may need to be started rapidly if there is to be any chance of it being effective. Without research, the outcome for patients in a clinical emergency situation, particularly situations in which the risk of death or serious disability is high, is unlikely to improve. There are many examples of research that may be of potential direct benefit to the person that may be covered by this article. They may include new drug treatments, or they may concern the use of devices, such as defibrillators used to restart the heart after a cardiac arrest.

106. Research in which the results do not have the potential to be of direct benefit to the person concerned includes discovering more, for example, about the mechanisms of head injury. Of course, the person will also be receiving standard medical treatment at the same time; but if the research itself, for example performing computed tomography scans, is not of direct benefit to the person concerned it must be of minimal risk and minimal burden. It is for the law of the Parties to determine whether, and under which conditions, this research can take place. Paragraph 1, indent i states that this article is applicable if the person in question is "not in a state to give consent." This takes account of the fact that in some legal systems a distinction may be made between those who are, legally, unable to consent and those who may be de facto unable to consent, but for whom the relevant legal process to declare them unable to consent has not been completed. This article addresses the emergency situation of those who are factually unable to consent as well as those minors or adults who may, according to law, be considered unable to consent. In this respect, paragraph 3 of Article 14 is also relevant because there may be persons who have been involved in an emergency, a car accident for instance, but who are not unconscious. However, because of the shock of the emergency situation, any consent obtained from them would not be acceptable.

107. The reference to "additional" conditions signifies that these conditions are supplementary to the protective conditions of the Protocol otherwise applicable. It was felt that, in addition to the general conditions applicable to other types of research, persons finding themselves in emergency situations should benefit from specific protection. The law must include the conditions that research of comparable effectiveness cannot be carried out on persons in non-emergency situations and that the research project has been approved specifically for emergency situations.

Research without the potential to produce results of direct benefit shall entail only minimal risk and minimal burden. Any relevant previously expressed objections of the person known to the researcher shall be respected. It must be remembered that emergency research must commence very rapidly and a researcher cannot undertake a search of archives, for instance, to establish whether someone has registered an objection. "Known to the researcher" in this context would mean that the potential participant has a card on his person registering such an objection or someone accompanying the potential participant informs the researcher.

108. Paragraph 3 requires that the patient be informed as soon as it becomes possible of his/ her participation in the research. Additionally, if and when the research participant recovers full understanding while still undergoing research, the participant must be asked for consent to continue. If the research participant does not recover full understanding but there is enough time available to obtain the relevant authorisation, such authorisation must be obtained for participation to continue. If the person dies before authorisation or consent is obtained, it is best practice to inform relatives of the research participation.

ARTICLE 20. (RESEARCH ON PERSONS DEPRIVED OF LIBERTY)

109. The Article sets out the additional conditions pertaining to research on persons deprived of their liberty in which the results do not have the potential to produce direct benefit to their health. Those who are deprived of their liberty are in a position of constant dependence on those who provide them with food, health care and the other amenities of life.

110. Persons may be deprived of their liberty for a variety of reasons, for example within the context of the criminal justice system as a consequence of an offence or under mental health legislation. The term "deprived of liberty" comes from Article 5 of the European Convention on Human Rights. In this article, it states that, " No one shall be deprived of his liberty save in the following cases and in accordance with a procedure prescribed by law:

a. the lawful detention of a person after conviction by a competent court;
b. the lawful arrest or detention of a person for non-compliance with the lawful order of a court or in order to secure the fulfilment of any obligation prescribed by law;
c. the lawful arrest or detention of a person effected for the purpose of bringing him before the competent legal authority on reasonable suspicion of having committed an offence or when it is reasonably considered necessary to prevent his committing an offence or fleeing after having done so;
d. the detention of a minor by lawful order for the purpose of educational supervision or his lawful detention for the purpose of bringing him before the competent legal authority;
e. the lawful detention of persons for the prevention of the spreading of infectious diseases, of persons of unsound mind, alcoholics or drug addicts or vagrants;
f. the lawful arrest or detention of a person to prevent his effecting an unauthorised entry into the country or of a person against whom action is being taken with a view to deportation or extradition."

111. Accordingly, deprivation of liberty applies not only to those detained for security reasons but also to those confined for health reasons. The provisions of Article 20 would apply to all persons deprived of liberty irrespective of the lawfulness of their detention. These provisions set out the following conditions.

112. Indent i specifies that it must not be possible for research of comparable effectiveness to be carried out without the participation of persons deprived of liberty. Indent ii specifies that the research must have the aim of contributing to the ultimate attainment of results capable of conferring benefit to persons deprived of liberty. It was agreed that this article should not be interpreted as impeding the possibility, for a Party, to allow participation in research concerning specific situations, such as family genetic studies, if that research could not be carried out without the participation of that specific person, coincidentally deprived of liberty, because of his or her health condition or genetic characteristics. It was considered that, because of its rarity, this exception, noted in the Explanatory Report, did not need to be reflected in the text of the Protocol itself.

113. Indent iii specifies that the research must entail only minimal risk and minimal burden. Any consideration of additional potential benefits of the research shall not be used to justify an increased level of risk or burden above the level of minimal risk and minimal burden.

114. The provisions of Article 20 are additional to the protective conditions of the Protocol otherwise applicable. Particular care must be taken to ensure that the requirements of Article 23 (Non-interference with necessary clinical interventions) addressing the use of placebos in research are fulfilled when persons deprived of liberty are to participate in the research. Good practice requires that particular attention be paid to the fulfilment of the requirement of Article 12 (Undue influence) in regard to persons deprived of their liberty.

Chapter VII – Safety and Supervision

ARTICLE 21. (MINIMISATION OF RISK AND BURDEN)

115. The Article requires that all reasonable measures be taken to ensure safety and to minimise risk and burden for research participants. These must include appropriate arrangements for monitoring the health of participants and promptly recording and assessing adverse events. Article 8 (Scientific quality) also applies here. Best practice recommends, especially in research involving particular risk, the establishment of a safety monitoring board to follow the conduct of a trial. In the course of formulating an opinion on the proposed research project, the ethics committee shall consider the arrangements for monitoring adverse events, including the intention to establish (or not) a safety monitoring board.

116. The second paragraph sets out the requirement that research involving interventions on persons shall be carried out under the supervision of a clinical professional who possesses the necessary qualifications and experience. While acknowledging that students and non-health care professionals may be members of a biomedical research team, the Article requires for

the protection of the research participants that any research involving interventions on persons be under the supervision of such a professional. Such supervision would not be constant in most cases, but the participants must always have access to the professional. The professional should be prepared to respond to their health concerns.

ARTICLE 22. (ASSESSMENT OF HEALTH STATUS)

117. The Article requires that researchers take all necessary steps to assess the state of health of potential research participants if the research involves interventions on persons, to ensure that those at increased risk in relation to a specific project be excluded. The necessary steps may include a clinical examination but this might not always be necessary. For instance, when patients are invited to take part in research by departments caring for them, a formal clinical examination could serve merely as a formality and provide no new information. In other cases when the research involves only an interaction such as an interview, a full clinical examination could also be excessive and not serve to protect the individual in the context of the research.

118. Paragraph 2 requires when research is undertaken on persons in the reproductive stage of their lives that particular consideration be given to the possible adverse impact on a current or future pregnancy and the health of the embryo, foetus or child. However, this protection should not lead to the automatic exclusion of women, or men, in the reproductive stage of their lives from research projects that could be of benefit to them or to others in their position. The necessary conditions for research involving pregnant or breastfeeding women in which the results do not have the potential to produce direct benefit to the woman's health or that of the embryo, foetus or child are found in Article 18 on research during pregnancy or breastfeeding.

ARTICLE 23. (NON-INTERFERENCE WITH NECESSARY CLINICAL INTERVENTIONS)

119. Paragraph 1 of this article lays down the principle that research on human beings shall not delay nor deprive them of medically necessary preventive, diagnostic or therapeutic procedures. "Delay" in this article should be understood as any delay that would be detrimental to the medical care of a patient. The treatment of a patient should not be altered in a detrimental manner in order to facilitate research.

120. Paragraph 2 requires that in research associated with prevention, diagnosis or treatment, participants assigned to control groups be assured of a proven method of prevention, diagnosis, or treatment. It is expected that a proven method of treatment that is available in the country or region concerned be utilised. "Region" may signify several neighbouring countries or an even wider area, to take into account multicentre studies that may cross national boundaries and to recognise the fact that Europeans may often utilise healthcare available in a neighbouring country.

121. The third paragraph permits the use of placebo only where there is no method of proven effectiveness or where withdrawal or withholding of such methods does not present unacceptable risk or burden to the participant. Whether risk or burden is acceptable or not is to be

assessed by the ethics committee and competent body, who should pay particular attention to such projects and assess each specific project individually. If placebo is used in research on persons not able to consent to research, Article 15 also applies.

ARTICLE 24. (NEW DEVELOPMENTS)

122. The Article foresees that scientific developments or events arising in the course of the research may justify the re-examination of the research project. Such scientific developments or events could be, for example, publication of results by other researchers that raise questions concerning the relevance of the research project, or unforeseen complications affecting one or more participants.

123. The Article requires Parties to this Protocol to take measures to ensure that the research project is re-examined if this is justified in the light of scientific developments or events arising in the course of the research. In that regard, national law may provide guidance on the nature of the developments or events that would justify a re-examination. The Article does not set out which person or body shall carry out the re-examination, leaving this to national law or practice. However, if scientific developments or events justify such a re-examination, this may be done by the competent body or ethics committee and where relevant the data and safety monitoring board. Parties may provide further guidance about the nature of the developments or events that should lead to a re-examination, and should clarify the person or body responsible for conducting the re-examination. It is also the duty of the researcher to review the research project him/herself if developments or events seem to undermine its ethical acceptability even if the official bodies have not yet commenced a re-examination.

124. The purpose of the re-examination is to establish whether, in the light of the developments or events, the research needs to be discontinued or if changes to the research project are necessary. Further, its purpose is to establish whether research participants, or if applicable their representatives, need to be informed of the developments or events. Finally, it shall establish whether additional consent or authorisation for participation is required. The consent form presented to future participants may need to be modified in the event of changes to the research project. An example of when it would be appropriate to seek a renewed consent or authorisation for participation would be if the implications for the participants have changed.

125. The third paragraph of the article requires participants, or if applicable their representatives, be made aware of any new information relevant to the person's participation in research. This is in addition to the duty of the researchers to inform the potential participants of foreseeable risks before they consent to participation in the research project.

126. The fourth paragraph of this article addresses permissible premature termination of research. The Article seeks to prevent inappropriate premature termination of the research, for example to prevent an adverse commercial outcome if a statistically significant negative result was reached which would, according to Article 28, need to be made public. Such actions could lead to the research being repeated by other researchers, needlessly involving human

participants and possibly exposing them to risk. The ethics committee must be informed of the reasons for such premature termination and may require that such a termination be justified, but it is not responsible for the termination itself.

127. An example of an acceptable reason for termination of a research project is when it becomes statistically clear that the research treatment is significantly worse than standard treatment, and hence it would be ethically unacceptable to continue the research project. Another example would be the publication of results by other researchers from studies that may either negate the original justification for the study (although it must be remembered that verification is an essential element of the process of validation in science) or that raises questions about the safety of the research in question.

Chapter VIII – Confidentiality and right to information

ARTICLE 25. (CONFIDENTIALITY)

128. Article 25 sets out the principle of confidentiality. The first paragraph establishes the right to privacy of information in the field of biomedical research, thereby reaffirming the principle introduced in Article 8 of the European Convention on Human Rights and reiterated in the Convention for the Protection of Individuals with regard to Automatic Processing of Personal Data. It should be pointed out that, under Article 6 of the latter Convention, personal data concerning health constitute a special category of data and are as such subject to special rules. This principle was also reiterated in Article 10 of the Convention on Human Rights and Biomedicine.

129. The second paragraph states that the law shall protect against inappropriate disclosure of information related to a research project that has been submitted in compliance with the Protocol. Failure to provide such protection could lead researchers to submit information to ethics committees lacking in detail, making it more difficult for the proper evaluation of the research project. Therefore, as the primary goal of this Protocol is to protect research participants, such protection against inappropriate disclosure to competitors or rivals serves also to enable the ethics committees to better protect human beings in research.

ARTICLE 26. (RIGHT TO INFORMATION)

130. This article states that research participants shall be entitled to know any information collected on their health in conformity with Article 10 of the Convention. It adds that all other personal information collected for a research project will be accessible to them in conformity with law on the protection of individuals with regard to processing of personal data.

ARTICLE 27. (DUTY OF CARE)

131. This article sets out the requirement that information arising from research of relevance to the current or future health or quality of life of participants must be made accessible to

those persons. This information could be the conclusions of the research or incidental information collected during the research. In principle, the researcher must evaluate whether such information is of relevance to the current or future health or quality of life of research participants. The researcher may seek the advice of the ethics committee as to the potential relevance of the information in question to research participants. This requirement also applies to anonymised data if it has been coded in such a manner that it can be relinked to the personal identifiers of the participants. The term "offered" was used in order to acknowledge that individuals have the right not to receive such conclusions if they so wish. Best practice requires that the wish of the participant to know or not to know should be established prior to commencement of the research.

132. The second sentence requires, for the protection of these persons, that this information be made accessible within a framework of healthcare or counselling. This is because proper counselling or other healthcare assistance may be necessary to explain the nature of the results and the options available to react to the participant.

133. The third sentence sets out the requirement for due care for the protection of confidentiality and respect for the right not to know in the communication of the conclusions. Patients may have their own reasons for not wishing to know about certain aspects of their health. Participants may only wish to exercise their right to know under certain circumstances and such wishes must also be observed.

134. In some circumstances, the right to know or not to know may be restricted in the patient's own interest or else on the basis of Article 26.1 of the Convention, for example, in order to protect the rights of a third party or one of the specified public interests. Additionally, the last paragraph of Article 10 of the Convention sets out that in exceptional cases domestic law may place restrictions on the right to know or not to know in the interests of the patient's health.

ARTICLE 28. (AVAILABILITY OF RESULTS)

135. Accountability is implicit in the relationship between the researcher and the participant. For this reason, this article requires that the conclusions of the research be made available on request to research participants in a form comprehensible to them.

136. The Article requires researchers to submit a summary or report of the research to the ethics committee or competent body, and to make public the results of their research even if the outcome is negative. Such results must be published or made otherwise available in a manner accessible to other researchers. The aim of the Article is to prevent the needless repetition of research using persons due to the non-publication of previous results, and to prevent the suppression of negative or positive results for commercial or other non-scientific reasons. It is stated that this be done "in reasonable time" so as to not prejudice a patent application or scientific publication. This obligation to publish cannot be restricted by contractual obligations. However, under the terms of Article 26 paragraph 1 of the Convention, the obligation to publish research results would be waived if publication would potentially compromise, for

example, public health or safety or the rights and freedoms of others. An example of such research could be that concerning counter-measures to the use of biological weapons, the publication of which could compromise public safety.

Chapter IX – Research in States not party to this Protocol

ARTICLE 29. (RESEARCH IN STATES NOT PARTY TO THIS PROTOCOL)

137. At present, considerable numbers of research projects are conducted on a multinational basis. Teams of researchers based in different States may participate in a single project. Further, internationally-based organisations may be able to choose the country in which a particular research project that they are conducting or funding is carried out. This has led to concerns being expressed about the possibility of fundamentally different standards of protection for participants being applied in different countries. In particular, concern has been expressed about the possibility of research that might be widely viewed as ethically unacceptable being carried out in another State where systems for the protection of research participants are less well established.

138. The Article sets out the conditions for sponsors and researchers within the territory of a Party to this Protocol who plan to undertake or direct a research project in a State not party to this Protocol. In addition to complying with all the conditions applicable in the State in the territory of which the research is to be undertaken, the principles on which the provisions of this Protocol are based must be complied with. The term "principles" implies that while it may be impracticable to implement all the detailed provisions contained in this Protocol when a research project is carried out in a State that is not party to the Protocol, it is nevertheless mandatory to observe the principles that those provisions develop. For example, there may not be a body capable of undertaking appropriate independent scientific and ethical evaluation of research in the country, but the principle of the research project being submitted to an independent body for review must be observed. Examples of these principles are informed consent, the protection of those unable to consent, confidentiality, the balance between risks and benefits, and ethical review of research projects. This does not imply that a body in the State Party to the Protocol has the authority to approve research in the non-Party State if that State does not approve the research, or to override its regulations. However, researchers from the Party State may be required to observe additional conditions, in accordance with the principles on which the provisions of this Protocol are based, to those applicable in non-Party States. The Article is not intended to discourage otherwise ethical research in less developed countries that might utilise less expensive treatment than that routinely utilised in wealthier countries.

139. The wording "sponsors and researchers within the jurisdiction of a Party to this Protocol" signifies those who fall under the authority of the State concerned. In practice, in conformity with the law of that State, such cases could be those of sponsors having their head office on its territory, or of those established on its territory for the exercise of activities insofar as they plan to undertake or direct the conduct of the research in question; further, such cases could be, in conformity with the law of the Party concerned, of researchers residing on the territory

of the Party, or who are established there professionally, or who are its nationals, insofar as they are involved in directing the conduct of the research in question.

140. It is up to each Party to take appropriate measures with a view to assuring that the research project respect the principles on which the provisions of this Protocol are based. These measures could consist of adoption of norms setting out the obligation, for the relevant sponsors and researchers, of respecting these principles. In the case where the research must be undertaken in States not having well established systems of protection, the provisions could foresee the obligation to submit the research project to an ethics committee of the Party concerned.

Chapter X – Infringement of the provisions of the Protocol

ARTICLE 30. (INFRINGEMENT OF THE RIGHTS OR PRINCIPLES)

141. This article requires the Parties to make available a judicial procedure to prevent or put a stop to an infringement of the principles set forth in the Protocol. It therefore covers not only infringements that have already begun and are ongoing but also the threat of an infringement.

142. The judicial protection requested must be appropriate and proportionate to the infringement or the threats of infringement of the principles. Such is the case, for example, with proceedings initiated by a public prosecutor in cases of infringements affecting several persons unable to defend themselves, in order to put an end to the violation of their rights.

143. Under the Protocol, the appropriate protective mechanisms must be capable of operating rapidly as it has to allow an infringement to be prevented or halted at short notice. This requirement can be explained by the fact that, in many cases, the very integrity of an individual has to be protected and an infringement of this right might have irreversible consequences.

144. The judicial protection provided by the Protocol applies only to unlawful infringements or to threats thereof. The reason for this qualifying adjective is that the Convention, in Article 26.1, permits restrictions to the free exercise of the rights it recognises.

ARTICLE 31. (COMPENSATION FOR DAMAGE)

145. This article sets forth the principle that persons who have suffered damage resulting from their participation in research shall be fairly compensated according to the conditions and procedures prescribed by law. The wording "damage" takes in to account the different contexts in which research is undertaken, ranging from studies on healthy volunteers to research on people suffering a very serious terminal illness. Whether or not compensation was fair would need to take in to account these different contexts, and may need to involve an assessment of the extent to which a given effect can be attributed to the research or may reflect a progression of the patient's existing health condition. On the subject of fair compensation, reference can be made to Article 41 of the European Convention on Human Rights, which allows the Court to afford just satisfaction to the injured party.

146. Compensation conditions and procedures are prescribed by national law. In many cases, this establishes a system of individual liability based either on fault or on the notion of risk. In other cases, the law may provide for a collective system of compensation irrespective of individual liability.

ARTICLE 32. (SANCTIONS)

147. Since the aim of the sanctions provided for in Article 32 is to guarantee compliance with the provisions of the Protocol, they must be in keeping with certain criteria, particularly those of necessity and proportionality. As a result, in order to measure the expediency and determine the nature and scope of the sanction, the domestic law must pay special attention to the content and importance of the provision to be complied with, the seriousness of the offence and the extent of its possible repercussions for the individual and society.

Chapter XI – Relation between this Protocol and other provisions and re-examination of the Protocol

ARTICLE 33. (RELATION BETWEEN THIS PROTOCOL AND THE CONVENTION)

148. As a legal instrument, the Protocol supplements the Convention. Once in force, the Protocol is subsumed into the Convention for those Parties having ratified the Protocol. The provisions of the Convention are therefore to be applied to the Protocol.

149. Thus, Article 36 of the Convention, which sets out the conditions under which a State may make a reservation in respect of any particular provision of the Convention, will also apply to the Protocol. Using this provision States may, under the conditions set out in Article 36 of the Convention, make a reservation in respect of any particular provision of this Protocol.

ARTICLE 34. (WIDER PROTECTION)

150. In pursuance of this article, the Parties may apply rules of a more protective nature than those contained in the Protocol. In other words, the text lays down common standards with which States must comply, while allowing them to provide greater protection of the human being and of human rights with regard to biomedical research.

151. A conflict may arise between the various rights established by the Protocol, for example between a scientist's right of freedom of research and the rights of a person submitting to the research. However, the expression "wider protection" must be interpreted in the light of the purpose of the Protocol, as defined in Article 1, namely the protection of the human being with regard to any research in the field of biomedicine involving interventions on human beings. In the example quoted, any additional statutory protection can only mean greater protection for a person participating in research.

6. International Ethical Guidelines for Biomedical Research Involving Human Subjects

Prepared by the Council for International Organizations of Medical Sciences (CIOMS) in collaboration with the World Health Organization (WHO) CIOMS, Geneva 2002

Preamble

The term "research" refers to a class of activity designed to develop or contribute to generalizable knowledge. Generalizable knowledge consists of theories, principles or relationships, or the accumulation of information on which they are based, that can be corroborated by accepted scientific methods of observation and inference. In the present context "research" includes both medical and behavioural studies pertaining to human health. Usually "research" is modified by the adjective "biomedical" to indicate its relation to health. Progress in medical care and disease prevention depends upon an understanding of physiological and pathological processes or epidemiological findings, and requires at some time research involving human subjects. The collection, analysis and interpretation of information obtained from research involving human beings contribute significantly to the improvement of human health. Research involving human subjects includes:

– studies of a physiological, biochemical or pathological process, or of the response to a specific intervention – whether physical, chemical or psychological – in healthy subjects or patients;
– controlled trials of diagnostic, preventive or therapeutic measures in larger groups of persons, designed to demonstrate a specific generalizable response to these measures against a background of individual biological variation;
– studies designed to determine the consequences for individuals and communities of specific preventive or therapeutic measures; and
– studies concerning human health-related behaviour in a variety of circumstances and environments.

Research involving human subjects may employ either observation or physical, chemical or psychological intervention; it may also either generate records or make use of existing records containing biomedical or other information about individuals who may or maynot be identifiable from the records or information. The use of such records and the protection of the confidentiality of data obtained from those records are discussed in International Guidelines for Ethical Review of Epidemiological Studies (CIOMS, 1991). The research may be concerned with the social environment, manipulating environmental factors in a way that could affect incidentally-exposed individuals. It is defined in broad terms in order to embrace field studies of pathogenic organisms and toxic chemicals under investigation for health-related purposes.

Biomedical research with human subjects is to be distinguished from the practice of medicine, public health and other forms of health care, which is designed to contribute directly to the health of individuals or communities. Prospective subjects may find it confusing when research and practice are to be conducted simultaneously, as when research is designed to obtain new information about the efficacy of a drug or other therapeutic, diagnostic or preventive modality. As stated in Paragraph 32 of the Declaration of Helsinki, "In the treatment of a patient, where proven prophylactic, diagnostic and therapeutic methods do not exist or have been ineffective, the physician, with informed consent from the patient, must be free to use unproven or new prophylactic, diagnostic and therapeutic measures, if in the physician's judgement it offers hope of saving life, re-establishing health or alleviating suffering. Where possible, these measures should be made the object of research, designed to evaluate their safety and efficacy. In all cases, new information should be recorded and, where appropriate, published. The other relevant guidelines of this Declaration should be followed."

Professionals whose roles combine investigation and treatment have a special obligation to protect the rights and welfare of the patient-subjects. An investigator who agrees to act as physician-investigator undertakes some or all of the legal and ethical responsibilities of the subject's primary-care physician. In such a case, if the subject withdraws from the research owing to complications related to the research or in the exercise of the right to withdraw without loss of benefit, the physician has an obligation to continue to provide medical care, or to see that the subject receives the necessary care in the health-care system, or to offer assistance in finding another physician. Research with human subjects should be carried out only by, or strictly supervised by, suitably qualified and experienced investigators and in accordance with a protocol that clearly states: the aim of the research; the reasons for proposing that it involve human subjects; the nature and degree of any known risks to the subjects; the sources from which it is proposed to recruit subjects; and the means proposed for ensuring that subjects' consent will be adequately informed and voluntary. The protocol should be scientifically and ethically appraised by one or more suitably constituted review bodies, independent of the investigators. New vaccines and medicinal drugs, before being approved for general use, must be tested on human subjects in clinical trials; such trials constitute a substantial part of all research involving human subjects.

The Guidelines

Guideline 1: Ethical justification and scientific validity of biomedical research involving human beings

The ethical justification of biomedical research involving human subjects is the prospect of discovering new ways of benefiting people's health. Such research can be ethically justifiable only if it is carried out in ways that respect and protect, and are fair to, the subjects of that research and are morally acceptable within the communities in which the research is carried out. Moreover, because scientifically invalid research is unethical in that it exposes research subjects to risks without possible benefit, investigators and sponsors must ensure that proposed studies involving human subjects conform to generally accepted scientific principles and are based on adequate knowledge of the pertinent scientific literature.

Commentary on Guideline 1

Among the essential features of ethically justified research involving human subjects, including research with identifiable human tissue or data, are that the research offers a means of developing information not otherwise obtainable, that the design of the research is scientifically sound, and that the investigators and other research personnel are competent. The methods to be used should be appropriate to the objectives of the research and the field of study. Investigators and sponsors must also ensure that all who participate in the conduct of the research are qualified by virtue of their education and experience to perform competently in their roles. These considerations should be adequately reflected in the research protocol submitted for review and clearance to scientific and ethical review committees (Appendix I).

Scientific review is discussed further in the Commentaries to Guidelines 2 and 3: Ethical review committees and Ethical review of externally sponsored research. Other ethical aspects of research are discussed in the remaining guidelines and their commentaries. The protocol designed for submission for review and clearance to scientific and ethical review committees should include, when relevant, the items specified in Appendix I, and should be carefully followed in conducting the research.

Guideline 2: Ethical review committees

All proposals to conduct research involving human subjects must be submitted for review of their scientific merit and ethical acceptability to one or more scientific review and ethical review committees. The review committees must be independent of the research team, and any direct financial or other material benefit they may derive from the research should not be contingent on the outcome of their review. The investigator must obtain their approval or clearance before undertaking the research. The ethical review committee should conduct further reviews as necessary in the course of the research, including monitoring of the progress of the study.

Commentary on Guideline 2

Ethical review committees may function at the institutional, local, regional, or national level, and in some cases at the international level. The regulatory or other governmental authorities concerned should promote uniform standards across committees within a country, and, under all systems, sponsors of research and institutions in which the investigators are employed should allocate sufficient resources to the review process. Ethical review committees may receive money for the activity of reviewing protocols, but under no circumstances may payment be offered or accepted for a review committee`s approval or clearance of a protocol.

Scientific review. According to the Declaration of Helsinki (Paragraph 11), medical research involving humans must conform to generally accepted scientific principles, and be based on a thorough knowledge of the scientific literature, other relevant sources of information, and adequate laboratory and, where indicated, animal experimentation. Scientific review must consider, inter alia, the study design, including the provisions for avoiding or minimizing risk and for monitoring safety. Committees competent to review and approve scientific aspects of research proposals must be multidisciplinary.

Ethical review. The ethical review committee is responsible for safeguarding the rights, safety, and well-being of the research subjects. Scientific review and ethical review cannot be separated: scientifically unsound research involving humans as subjects is ipso facto unethical in that it may expose them to risk or inconvenience to no purpose; even if there is no risk of injury, wasting of subjects` and researchers` time in unproductive activities represents loss of a valuable resource. Normally, therefore, an ethical review committee considers both the scientific and the ethical aspects of proposed research. It must either carry out a proper scientific review or verify that a competent expert body has determined that the research is scientifically sound. Also, it considers provisions for monitoring of data and safety. If the ethical review committee finds a research proposal scientifically sound, or verifies that a competent expert body has found it so, it should then consider whether any known or possible risks to the subjects are justified by the expected benefits, direct or indirect, and whether the proposed research methods will minimize harm and maximize benefit. (See Guideline 8: Benefits and risks of study participation.) If the proposal is sound and the balance of risks to anticipated benefits is reasonable, the committee should then determine whether the procedures proposed for obtaining informed consent are satisfactory and those proposed for the selection of subjects are equitable. Ethical review of emergency compassionate use of an investigational therapy. In some countries, drug regulatory authorities require that the so-called compassionate or humanitarian use of an investigational treatment be reviewed by an ethical review committee as though it were research. Exceptionally, a physician may undertake the compassionate use of an investigational therapy before obtaining the approval or clearance of an ethical review committee, provided three criteria are met: a patient needs emergency treatment, there is some evidence of possible effectiveness of the investigational treatment, and there is no other treatment available that is known to be equally effective or superior. Informed consent should be obtained according to the legal requirements and cultural standards of the community in which the intervention is carried out. Within one week the physician must report to the ethical review committee the details of the case and the action taken, and an independent health-care professional must confirm in writing to the ethical review committee the treating physician's judgment that the use of the investigational intervention was justified according to the three specified criteria. (See also Guideline 13 Commentary section: Other vulnerable groups.)

National (centralized) or local review. Ethical review committees may be created under the aegis of national or local health administrations, national (or centralized) medical research councils or other nationally representative bodies. In a highly centralized administration a national, or centralized, review committee may be constituted for both the scientific and the ethical review of research protocols. In countries where medical research is not centrally administered, ethical review is more effectively and conveniently undertaken at a local or regional level. The authority of a local ethical review committee may be confined to a single institution or may extend to all institutions in which biomedical research is carried out within a defined geographical area. The basic responsibilities of ethical review committees are:

- to determine that all proposed interventions, particularly the administration of drugs and vaccines or the use of medical devices or procedures under development, are acceptably safe to be undertaken in humans or to verify that another competent expert body has done so;
- to determine that the proposed research is scientifically sound or to verify that another competent expert body has done so;
- to ensure that all other ethical concerns arising from a protocol are satisfactorily resolved both in principle and in practice;
- to consider the qualifications of the investigators, including education in the principles of research practice, and the conditions of the research site with a view to ensuring the safe conduct of the trial; and
- to keep records of decisions and to take measures to follow up on the conduct of ongoing research projects.

Committee membership. National or local ethical review committees should be so composed as to be able to provide complete and adequate review of the research proposals submitted to them. It is generally presumed that their membership should include physicians, scientists and other professionals such as nurses, lawyers, ethicists and clergy, as well as lay persons qualified to represent the cultural and moral values of the community and to ensure that the rights of the research subjects will be respected. They should include both men and women. When uneducated or illiterate persons form the focus of a study they should also be considered for membership or invited to be represented and have their views expressed.

A number of members should be replaced periodically with the aim of blending the advantages of experience with those of fresh perspectives. A national or local ethical review committee responsible for reviewing and approving proposals for externally sponsored research should have among its members or consultants persons who are thoroughly familiar with the customs and traditions of the population or community concerned and sensitive to issues of human dignity. Committees that often review research proposals directed at specific diseases or impairments, such as HIV/AIDS or paraplegia, should invite or hear the views of individuals or bodies representing patients with such diseases or impairments. Similarly, for research involving such subjects as children, students, elderly persons or employees, committees should invite or hear the views of their representatives or advocates. To maintain the review committee's independence from the investigators and sponsors and to avoid conflict of interest, any member with a special or particular, direct or indirect, interest in a proposal should not take part in its assessment if that interest could subvert the member`s objective judgment. Members of ethical review committees should be held to the same standard of disclosure as scientific and medical research staff with regard to financial or other interests that could be construed as conflicts of interest. A practical way of avoiding such conflict of interest is for the committee to insist on a declaration of possible conflict of interest by any of its members. A member who makes such a declaration should then withdraw, if to do so is clearly the appropriate action to take, either at the member`s own discretion or at the request of the other members. Before withdrawing, the member should be permitted to offer comments on the protocol or to respond to questions of other members.

Multi-centre research. Some research projects are designed to be conducted in a number of centres in different communities or countries. Generally, to ensure that the results will be valid, the study must be conducted in an identical way at each centre. Such studies include clinical trials, research designed for the evaluation of health service programmes, and various kinds of epidemiological research. For such studies, local ethical or scientific review committees are not normally authorized to change doses of drugs, to change inclusion or exclusion criteria, or to make other similar modifications. They should be fully empowered to prevent a study that they believe to be unethical. Moreover, changes that local review committees believe are necessary to protect the research subjects should be documented and reported to the research institution or sponsor responsible for the whole research programme for consideration and due action, to ensure that all other subjects can be protected and that the research will be valid across sites.

To ensure the validity of multi-centre research, any change in the protocol should be made at every collaborating centre or institution, or, failing this, explicit inter-centre comparability procedures must be introduced; changes made at some but not all will defeat the purpose of multi-centre research. For some multi-centre studies, scientific and ethical review may be facilitated by agreement among centres to accept the conclusions of a single review committee; its members could include a representative of the ethical review committee at each of the centres at which the research is to be conducted, as well as individuals competent to conduct scientific review. In other circumstances, a centralized review may be complemented by local review relating to the local participating investigators and institutions. The central committee could review the study from a scientific and ethical standpoint, and the local committees could verify the practicability of the study in their communities, including the infrastructures, the state of training, and ethical considerations of local significance.

In a large multi-centre trial, individual investigators will not have authority to act independently, with regard to data analysis or to preparation and publication of manuscripts, for instance. Such a trial usually has a set of committees which operate under the direction of a steering committee and are responsible for such functions and decisions. The function of the ethical review committee in such cases is to review the relevant plans with the aim of avoiding abuses.

Sanctions. Ethical review committees generally have no authority to impose sanctions on researchers who violate ethical standards in the conduct of research involving humans. They may, however, withdraw ethical approval of a research project if judged necessary. They should be required to monitor the implementation of an approved protocol and its progression, and to report to institutional or governmental authorities any serious or continuing non-compliance with ethical standards as they are reflected in protocols that they have approved or in the conduct of the studies. Failure to submit a protocol to the committee should be considered a clear and serious violation of ethical standards. Sanctions imposed by governmental, institutional, professional or other authorities possessing disciplinary power should be employed as a last resort. Preferred methods of control include cultivation of an atmosphere of mutual trust, and education and support to promote in researchers and in sponsors the capacity for ethical conduct of research. Should sanctions become necessary, they should be directed at the non-compliant researchers or sponsors. They may include fines or suspension of eligibility to receive research funding, to use investigational interventions, or to practise medicine. Unless there are persuasive reasons to do otherwise, editors should refuse to publish the results of research conducted unethically, and retract any articles that are subsequently found to contain falsified or fabricated data or to have been based on unethical research. Drug regulatory authorities should consider refusal to accept unethically obtained data submitted in support of an application for authorization to market a product. Such sanctions, however, may deprive of benefit not only the errant researcher or sponsor but also that segment of society intended to benefit from the research; such possible consequences merit careful consideration. Potential conflicts of interest related to project support. Increasingly, biomedical studies receive funding from commercial firms. Such sponsors have good reasons to support research methods that are ethically and scientifically acceptable, but cases have arisen in which the conditions of funding could have introduced bias. It may happen that investigators have little or no input into trial design, limited access to the raw data, or limited participation in data interpretation, or that the results of a clinical trial may not be published if they are unfavourable to the sponsor's product. This risk of bias may also be associated with other sources of support, such as government or foundations. As the persons directly responsible for their work, investigators should not enter into agreements that interfere unduly with their access to the data or their ability to analyse the data independently, to prepare manuscripts, or to publish them. Investigators must also disclose potential or apparent conflicts of interest on their part to the ethical review committee or to other institutional committees designed to evaluate and manage such conflicts. Ethical review committees should therefore ensure that these conditions are met. See also Multi-centre research, above.

Guideline 3: Ethical review of externally sponsored research

An external sponsoring organization and individual investigators should submit the research protocol for ethical and scientific review in the country of the sponsoring organization, and the ethical standards applied should be no less stringent than they would be for research carried out in that country. The health authorities of the host country, as well as a national or local ethical review committee, should ensure that the proposed research is responsive to the health needs and priorities of the host country and meets the requisite ethical standards.

Commentary on Guideline 3

Definition. The term externally sponsored research refers to research undertaken in a host country but sponsored, financed, and sometimes wholly or partly carried out by an external international or national organization or pharmaceutical company with the collaboration or agreement of the appropriate authorities, institutions and personnel of the host country.

Ethical and scientific review. Committees in both the country of the sponsor and the host country have responsibility for conducting both scientific and ethical review, as well as the authority to withhold approval of research proposals that fail to meet their scientific or ethical standards. As far as possible, there must be assurance that the review is independent and that there is no conflict of interest that might affect the judgement of members of the review committees in relation to any aspect of the research. When the external sponsor is an international organization, its review of the research protocol must be in accordance with its own independent ethical-review procedures and standards.

Committees in the external sponsoring country or international organization have a special responsibility to determine whether the scientific methods are sound and suitable to the aims of the research; whether the drugs, vaccines, devices or procedures to be studied meet adequate standards of safety; whether there is sound justification for conducting the research in the host country rather than in the country of the external sponsor or in another country; and whether the proposed research is in compliance with the ethical standards of the external sponsoring country or international organization. Committees in the host country have a special responsibility to determine whether the objectives of the research are responsive to the health needs and priorities of that country. The ability to judge the ethical acceptability of various aspects of a research proposal requires a thorough understanding of a community's customs and traditions. The ethical review committee in the host country, therefore, must have as either members or consultants persons with such understanding; it will then be in a favourable position to determine the acceptability of the proposed means of obtaining informed consent and otherwise respecting the rights of prospective subjects as well as of the means proposed to protect the welfare of the research subjects. Such persons should be able, for example, to indicate suitable members of the community to serve as intermediaries between investigators and subjects, and to advise on whether material benefits or inducements may be regarded as appropriate in the light of a community's gift-exchange and other customs and traditions.

When a sponsor or investigator in one country proposes to carry out research in another, the ethical review committees in the two countries may, by agreement, undertake to review different aspects of the research protocol. In short, in respect of host countries either with developed capacity for independent ethical review or in which external sponsors and investigators are contributing substantially to such capacity, ethical review in the external, sponsoring country may be limited to ensuring compliance with broadly stated ethical standards. The ethical review committee in the host country can be expected to have greater competence for reviewing the detailed plans for compliance, in view of its better understanding of the cultural and moral values of the population in which it is proposed to conduct the research; it is also likely to be in a better position to monitor compliance in the course of a study. However, in respect of research in host countries with inadequate capacity for independent ethical review, full review by the ethical review committee in the external sponsoring country or international agency is necessary.

Guideline 4: Individual informed consent

For all biomedical research involving humans the investigator must obtain the voluntary informed consent of the prospective subject or, in the case of an individual who is not capable of giving informed consent, the permission of a legally authorized representative in accordance with applicable law. Waiver of informed consent is to be regarded as uncommon and exceptional, and must in all cases be approved by an ethical review committee.

Commentary on Guideline 4

General considerations. Informed consent is a decision to participate in research, taken by a competent individual who has received the necessary information; who has adequately understood the information; and who, after considering the information, has arrived at a decision without having been subjected to coercion, undue influence or inducement, or intimidation.

Informed consent is based on the principle that competent individuals are entitled to choose freely whether to participate in research. Informed consent protects the individual's freedom of choice and respects the individual's autonomy. As an additional safeguard, it must always be complemented by independent ethical review of research proposals. This safeguard of independent review is particularly important as many individuals are limited in their capacity to give adequate informed consent; they include young children, adults with severe mental or behavioural disorders, and persons who are unfamiliar with medical concepts and technology (See Guidelines 13, 14, 15).

Process. Obtaining informed consent is a process that is begun when initial contact is made with a prospective subject and continues throughout the course of the study. By informing the prospective subjects, by repetition and explanation, by answering their questions as they arise, and by ensuring that each individual understands each procedure, investigators elicit their informed consent and in so doing manifest respect for their dignity and autonomy. Each individual must be given as much time as is needed to reach a decision, including time for consultation with family members or others. Adequate time and resources should be set aside for informed-consent procedures.

Language. Informing the individual subject must not be simply a ritual recitation of the contents of a written document. Rather, the investigator must convey the information, whether orally or in writing, in language that suits the individual's level of understanding. The investigator must bear in mind that the prospective subject's ability to understand the information necessary to give informed consent depends on that individual's maturity, intelligence, education and belief system. It depends also on the investigator's ability and willingness to communicate with patience and sensitivity.

Comprehension. The investigator must then ensure that the prospective subject has adequately understood the information. The investigator should give each one full opportunity to ask questions and should answer them honestly, promptly and completely. In some instances the investigator may administer an oral or a written test or otherwise determine whether the information has been adequately understood. Documentation of consent. Consent may be indicated in a number of ways. The subject may imply consent by voluntary actions, express consent orally, or sign a consent form. As a general rule, the subject should sign a consent form, or, in the case of incompetence, a legal guardian or other duly authorized representative should do so. The ethical review committee may approve waiver of the requirement of a signed consent form if the research carries no more than minimal risk – that is, risk that is no more likely and not greater than that attached to routine medical or psychological examination – and if the procedures to be used are only those for which signed consent forms are not customarily required outside the research context. Such waivers may also be approved when existence of a signed consent form would be an unjustified threat to the subject's confidentiality. In some cases, particularly when the information is complicated, it is advisable to give subjects information sheets to retain; these may resemble consent forms in all respects except that subjects are not required to sign them. Their wording should be cleared by the ethical review committee. When consent has been obtained orally, investigators are responsible for providing documentation or proof of consent. Waiver of the consent requirement. Investigators should never initiate research involving human subjects without obtaining each subject's informed consent, unless they have received explicit approval to do so from an ethical review committee. However, when the research design involves no more than minimal risk and a requirement of individual informed consent would make the conduct of the research impracticable (for example, where the research involves only excerpting data from subjects' records), the ethical review committee may waive some or all of the elements of informed consent. Renewing consent. When material changes occur in the conditions or the procedures of a study, and also periodically in long-term studies, the investigator should once again seek informed consent from the subjects. For example, new information may have come to light, either from the study or from other sources, about the risks or benefits of products being tested or about alternatives to them. Subjects should be given such information promptly. In many clinical trials, results are not disclosed to subjects and investigators until the study is concluded. This is ethically acceptable if an ethical review committee has approved their non-disclosure. Cultural considerations. In some cultures an investigator may enter a community to conduct research or approach prospective subjects for their individual consent only after obtaining permission from a community leader, a council of elders, or another designated authority. Such customs must be respected. In no case, however, may the permission of a community leader or other authority substitute for individual informed consent. In some populations the use of a number of local languages may complicate the communication of information to potential subjects and the ability of an investigator to ensure that they truly understand it. Many people in all cultures are unfamiliar with, or do not readily understand, scientific concepts such as those of placebo or randomization. Sponsors and investigators should develop culturally appropriate ways to communicate information that is necessary for adherence to the standard required in the informed consent process. Also, they should describe and justify in the research protocol the procedure they plan to use in communicating information to subjects. For collaborative research in developing countries the research project should, if necessary, include the provision of resources to ensure that informed consent can indeed be obtained legitimately within different linguistic and cultural settings.

Consent to use for research purposes biological materials (including genetic material) from subjects in clinical trials. Consent forms for the research protocol should include a separate section for clinical-trial subjects who are requested to provide their consent for the use of their biological specimens for research. Separate consent may be appropriate in some cases (e.g., if investigators are requesting permission to conduct basic research which is not a necessary part of the clinical trial), but not in others (e.g., the clinical trial requires the use of subjects' biological materials). Use of medical records and biological specimens. Medical records and biological specimens taken in the course of clinical care may be used for research without the consent of the patients/subjects only if an ethical review committee has determined that the research poses minimal risk, that the rights or interests of the patients will not be violated, that their privacy and confidentiality or anonymity are assured, and that the research is designed to answer an important question and would be impracticable if the requirement for informed consent were to be imposed. Patients have a right to know that their records or specimens may be used for research. Refusal or reluctance of individuals to agree to participate would not be evidence of impracticability sufficient to warrant waiving informed consent. Records and specimens of individuals who have specifically rejected such uses in the past may be used only in the case of public health emergencies. (See Guideline 18 Commentary, Confidentiality between physician and patient)

Secondary use of research records or biological specimens. Investigators may want to use records or biological specimens that another investigator has used or collected for use, in another institution in the same or another country. This raises the issue of whether the records or specimens contain personal identifiers, or can be linked to such identifiers, and by whom. (See also Guideline 18: Safeguarding confidentiality) If informed consent or permission was required to authorize the original collection or use of such records or specimens for research purposes, secondary uses are generally constrained by the conditions specified in the original consent. Consequently, it is essential that the original consent process anticipate, to the extent that this is feasible, any foreseeable plans for future use of the records or specimens for research. Thus, in the original process of seeking informed consent a member of the research team should discuss with, and, when indicated, request the permission of, prospective subjects as to: i) whether there will or could be any secondary use and, if so, whether such secondary use will be limited with regard to the type of study that may be performed on such materials; ii) the conditions under which investigators will be required to contact the research subjects for additional authorization for secondary use; iii) the investigators' plans, if any, to destroy or to strip of personal identifiers the records or specimens; and iv) the rights of subjects to request destruction or anonymization of biological specimens or of records or parts of records that they might consider particularly sensitive, such as photographs, videotapes or audiotapes. (See also Guidelines 5: Obtaining informed consent: Essential information for prospective research subjects; 6: Obtaining informed consent: Obligations of sponsors and investigators; and 7: Inducement to participate.)

Guideline 5: Obtaining informed consent: Essential information for prospective research subjects

Before requesting an individual's consent to participate in research, the investigator must provide the following information, in language or another form of communication that the individual can understand: 1. that the individual is invited to participate in research, the reasons for considering the individual suitable for the research, and that participation is voluntary;

2. that the individual is free to refuse to participate and will be free to withdraw from the research at any time without penalty or loss of benefits to which he or she would otherwise be entitled; 3. the purpose of the research, the procedures to be carried out by the investigator and the subject, and an explanation of how the research differs from routine medical care; 4. for controlled trials, an explanation of features of the research design (e.g., randomization, double-blinding), and that the subject will not be told of the assigned treatment until the study has been completed and the blind has been broken; 5. the expected duration of the individual's participation (including number and duration of visits to the research centre and the total time involved) and the possibility of early termination of the trial or of the individual s participation in it; 6. whether money or other forms of material goods will be provided in return for the individual's participation and, if so, the kind and amount; 7. that, after the completion of the study, subjects will be informed of the findings of the research in general, and individual subjects will be informed of any finding that relates to their particular health status;

8. that subjects have the right of access to their data on demand, even if these data lack immediate clinical utility (unless the ethical review committee has approved temporary or permanent non-disclosure of data, in which case the subject should be informed of, and given, the reasons for such nondisclosure); 9. any foreseeable risks, pain or discomfort, or inconvenience to the individual (or others) associated with participation in the research, including risks to the health or well-being of a subject s spouse or partner; 10. the direct benefits, if any, expected to result to subjects from participating in the research 11. the expected benefits of the research to the community or to society at large, or contributions to scientific knowledge; 12. whether, when and how any products or interventions proven by the research to be safe and effective will be made available to subjects after they have completed their participation in the research, and whether they will be expected to pay for them; 13. any currently available alternative interventions or courses of treatment; 14. the provisions that will be made to ensure respect for the privacy of subjects and for the confidentiality of records in which subjects are identified; 15. the limits, legal or other, to the investigators' ability to safeguard confidentiality, and the possible consequences of breaches of confidentiality; 16. policy with regard to the use of results of genetic tests and familial genetic information, and the precautions in place to prevent disclosure of the results of a subject's genetic tests 17. to immediate family relatives or to others (e.g., insurance companies or employers) without the consent of the subject; 18. the sponsors of the research, the institutional affiliation of the investigators, and the nature and sources of funding for the research; 19. the possible research uses, direct or secondary, of the subject's medical records and of biological specimens taken in the course of clinical care (See also Guidelines 4 and 18 Commentaries); 20. whether it is planned that biological specimens collected in the research will be destroyed at its conclusion, and, if not, details about their storage (where, how, for how long, and final disposition) and possible future use, and that subjects have the right to decide about such future use, to refuse storage, and to have the material destroyed (See Guideline 4 Commentary); 21. whether commercial products may be developed from biological specimens, and whether the participant will receive monetary or other benefits from the development of such products; 22. whether the investigator is serving only as an investigator or as both investigator and the subject's physician; 23. the extent of the investigator's responsibility to provide medical services to the participant; 24.

that treatment will be provided free of charge for specified types of research related injury or for complications associated with the research, the nature and duration of such care, the name of the organization or individual that will provide the treatment, and whether there is any uncertainty regarding funding of such treatment. 25. in what way, and by what organization, the subject or the subject's family or dependants will be compensated for disability or death resulting from such injury (or, when indicated, that there are no plans to provide such compensation); 26. whether or not, in the country in which the prospective subject is invited to participate in research, the right to compensation is legally guaranteed; 27. that an ethical review committee has approved or cleared the research protocol.

Guideline 6: Obtaining informed consent: Obligations of sponsors and investigators Sponsors and investigators have a duty to:

- refrain from unjustified deception, undue influence, or intimidation;
- seek consent only after ascertaining that the prospective subject has adequate understanding of the relevant facts and of the consequences of participation and has had sufficient opportunity to consider whether to participate;
- as a general rule, obtain from each prospective subject a signed form as evidence of informed consent – investigators should justify any exceptions to this general rule and obtain the approval of the ethical review committee (See Guideline 4 Commentary, Documentation of consent);
- renew the informed consent of each subject if there are significant changes in the conditions or procedures of the research or if new information becomes available that could affect the willingness of subjects to continue to participate; and,
- renew the informed consent of each subject in long-term studies at predetermined intervals, even if there are no changes in the design or objectives of the research.

Commentary on Guideline 6

The investigator is responsible for ensuring the adequacy of informed consent from each subject. The person obtaining informed consent should be knowledgeable about the research and capable of answering questions from prospective subjects. Investigators in charge of the study must make themselves available to answer questions at the request of subjects. Any restrictions on the subject's opportunity to ask questions and receive answers before or during the research undermines the validity of the informed consent. In some types of research, potential subjects should receive counselling about risks of acquiring a disease unless they take precautions. This is especially true of HIV/AIDS vaccine research (UNAIDS Guidance Document Ethical Considerations in HIV Preventive Vaccine Research, Guidance Point 14). Withholding information and deception. Sometimes, to ensure the validity of research, investigators withhold certain information in the consent process. In biomedical research, this typically takes the form of withholding information about the purpose of specific procedures. For example, subjects in clinical trials are often not told the purpose of tests performed to monitor their compliance with the protocol, since if they knew their compliance was being monitored they might modify their behaviour and hence invalidate results. In most such cases, the prospective subjects are asked to consent to remain uninformed of the purpose of some procedures until the research is completed; after the conclusion of the study they are given the omitted information. In other cases, because a request for permission to withhold some information would jeopardize the validity of the research, subjects are not told that some information has been withheld until the research has been completed. Any such procedure must receive the explicit approval of the ethical review committee. Active deception of subjects is considerably more controversial than simply withholding certain information. Lying to subjects is a tactic not commonly employed in biomedical research. Social and behavioural scientists, however, sometimes deliberately misinform subjects to study their attitudes and behaviour. For example, scientists have pretended to be patients to study the behaviour of health-care professionals and patients in their natural settings.

Some people maintain that active deception is never permissible. Others would permit it in certain circumstances. Deception is not permissible, however, in cases in which the deception itself would disguise the possibility of the subject being exposed to more than minimal risk. When deception is deemed indispensable to the methods of a study the investigators must demonstrate to an ethical review committee that no other research method would suffice; that significant advances could result from the research; and that nothing has been withheld that, if divulged, would cause a reasonable person to refuse to participate. The ethical review committee should determine the consequences for the subject of being deceived, and whether and how deceived subjects should be informed of the deception upon completion of the research. Such informing, commonly called "debriefing", ordinarily entails explaining the reasons for the deception. A subject who disapproves of having been deceived should be offered an opportunity to refuse to allow the investigator to use information thus obtained. Investigators and ethical review committees should be aware that deceiving research subjects may wrong them as well as harm them; subjects may resent not having been informed when they learn that they have participated in a study under false pretences. In some studies there may be justification for deceiving persons other than the subjects by either withholding or disguising elements of information. Such tactics are often proposed, for example, for studies of the abuse of spouses or children. An ethical review committee must review and approve all proposals to deceive persons other than the subjects. Subjects are entitled to prompt and honest answers to their questions; the ethical review committee must determine for each study whether others who are to be deceived are similarly entitled.

Intimidation and undue influence. Intimidation in any form invalidates informed consent. Prospective subjects who are patients often depend for medical care upon the physician/investigator, who consequently has a certain credibility in their eyes, and whose influence over them may be considerable, particularly if the study protocol has a therapeutic component. They may fear, for example, that refusal to participate would damage the therapeutic relationship or result in the withholding of health services. The physician/investigator must assure them that their decision on whether to participate will not affect the therapeutic relationship or other benefits to which they are entitled. In this situation the ethical review committee should consider whether a neutral third party should seek informed consent. The prospective subject must not be exposed to undue influence. The borderline between justifiable persuasion and undue influence is imprecise, however. The researcher should give no unjustifiable assurances about the benefits, risks or inconveniences of the research, for example, or induce a close relative or a community leader to influence a prospective subject's decision. (See also Guideline 4: Individual informed consent.)

Risks. Investigators should be completely objective in discussing the details of the experimental intervention, the pain and discomfort that it may entail, and known risks and possible hazards. In complex research projects it may be neither feasible nor desirable to inform prospective participants fully about every possible risk. They must, however, be informed of all risks that a 'reasonable person' would consider material to making a decision about whether to participate, including risks to a spouse or partner associated with trials of, for example, psychotropic or genital-tract medicaments. (See also Guideline 8 Commentary, Risks to groups of persons.)

Exception to the requirement for informed consent in studies of emergency situations in which the researcher anticipates that many subjects will be unable to consent. Research protocols are sometimes designed to address conditions occurring suddenly and rendering the patients/subjects incapable of giving informed consent. Examples are head trauma, cardiopulmonary arrest and stroke. The investigation cannot be done with patients who can give informed consent in time and there may not be time to locate a person having the authority to give permission. In such circumstances it is often necessary to proceed with the research interventions very soon after the onset of the condition in order to evaluate an investigational treatment or develop the desired knowledge. As this class of emergency exception can be anticipated, the researcher must secure the review and approval of an ethical review committee before initiating the study. If possible, an attempt should be made to identify a population that is likely to develop the condition to be studied. This can be done readily, for example, if the condition is one that recurs periodically in individuals; examples include grand mal seizures and alcohol binges. In such cases, prospective subjects should be contacted while fully capable of informed consent, and invited to consent to their involvement as research subjects during future periods of incapacitation. If they are patients of an independent physician who is also the physician-researcher, the physician should likewise seek their consent while they are fully capable of informed consent. In all cases in which approved research has begun without prior consent of patients/subjects incapable of giving informed consent because of suddenly occurring conditions, they should be given all relevant information as soon as they are in a state to receive it, and their consent to continued participation should be obtained as soon as is reasonably possible. Before proceeding without prior informed consent, the investigator must make reasonable efforts to locate an individual who has the authority to give permission on behalf of an incapacitated patient. If such a person can be located and refuses to give permission, the patient may not be enrolled as a subject. The risks of all interventions and procedures will be justified as required by Guideline 9 (Special limitations on risks when research involves individuals who are not capable of giving consent). The researcher and the ethical review committee should agree to a maximum time of involvement of an individual without obtaining either the individual's informed consent or authorization according to the applicable legal system if the person is not able to give consent. If by that time the researcher has not obtained either consent or permission – owing either to a failure to contact a representative or to a refusal of either the patient or the person or body authorized to give permission – the participation of the patient as a subject must be discontinued. The patient or the person or body providing authorization should be offered an opportunity to forbid the use of data derived from participation of the patient as a subject without consent or permission. Where appropriate, plans to conduct emergency research without prior consent of the subjects should be publicized within the community in which it will be carried out. In the design and conduct of the research, the ethical review committee, the investigators and the sponsors should be responsive to the concerns of the community. If there is cause for concern about the acceptability of the research in the community, there should be a formal consultation with representatives designated by the community. The research should not be carried out if it does not have substantial support in the community concerned. (See Guideline 8 Commentary, Risks to groups of persons.) Exception to the requirement of informed consent for inclusion in clinical trials of persons rendered incapable of informed consent by an acute condition. Certain patients with an acute condition that renders them incapable of giving informed consent may be eligible for inclusion in a clinical trial in which the majority of prospective subjects will be capable of informed consent. Such a trial would relate to a new treatment for an acute condition such as sepsis, stroke or myocardial infarction. The investigational treatment would hold out the prospect of direct benefit and would be justified accordingly, though the investigation might involve certain procedures or interventions that were not of direct benefit but carried no more than minimal risk; an example would be the process of randomization or the collection of additional blood for research purposes. For such cases the initial protocol submitted for approval to the ethical review committee should anticipate that some patients may be incapable of consent, and should propose for such patients a form of proxy consent, such as permission of the responsible relative. When the ethical review committee has approved or cleared such a protocol, an investigator may seek the permission of the responsible relative and enrol such a patient.

Guideline 7: Inducement to participate

Subjects may be reimbursed for lost earnings, travel costs and other expenses incurred in taking part in a study; they may also receive free medical services. Subjects, particularly those who receive no direct benefit from research, may also be paid or otherwise compensated for inconvenience and time spent. The payments should not be so large, however, or the medical services so extensive as to induce prospective subjects to consent to participate in the research against their better judgment ("undue inducement"). All payments, reimbursements and medical services provided to research subjects must have been approved by an ethical review committee.

Commentary on Guideline 7

Acceptable recompense. Research subjects may be reimbursed for their transport and other expenses, including lost earnings, associated with their participation in research. Those who receive no direct benefit from the research may also receive a small sum of money for inconvenience due to their participation in the research. All subjects may receive medical services unrelated to the research and have procedures and tests performed free of charge. Unacceptable recompense. Payments in money or in kind to research subjects should not be so large as to persuade them to take undue risks or volunteer against their better judgment. Payments or rewards that undermine a person's capacity to exercise free choice invalidate consent. It may be difficult to distinguish between suitable recompense and undue influence to participate in research. An unemployed person or a student may view promised recompense differently from an employed person. Someone without access to medical care may or may not be unduly influenced to participate in research simply to receive such care. A prospective subject may be induced to participate in order to obtain a better diagnosis or access to a drug not otherwise available; local ethical review committees may find such inducements acceptable. Monetary and in-kind recompense must, therefore, be evaluated in the light of the traditions of the particular culture and population in which they are offered, to determine whether they constitute undue influence. The ethical review committee will ordinarily be the best judge of what constitutes reasonable material recompense in particular circumstances. When research interventions or procedures that do not hold out the prospect of direct benefit present more than minimal risk, all parties involved in the research – sponsors, investigators and ethical review committees – in both funding and host countries should be careful to avoid undue material inducement. Incompetent persons. Incompetent persons may be vulnerable to exploitation for financial gain by guardians. A guardian asked to give permission on behalf of an incompetent person should be offered no recompense other than a refund of travel and related expenses. Withdrawal from a study. A subject who withdraws from research for reasons related to the study, such as unacceptable side-effects of a study drug, or who is withdrawn on health grounds, should be paid or recompensed as if full participation had taken place. A subject who withdraws for any other reason should be paid in proportion to the amount of participation. An investigator who must remove a subject from the study for willful noncompliance is entitled to withhold part or all of the payment.

Guideline 8: Benefits and risks of study participation

For all biomedical research involving human subjects, the investigator must ensure that potential benefits and risks are reasonably balanced and risks are minimized.

– Interventions or procedures that hold out the prospect of direct diagnostic, therapeutic or preventive benefit for the individual subject must be justified by the expectation that they will be at least as advantageous to the individual subject, in the light of foreseeable risks and benefits, as any available alternative. Risks of such 'beneficial' interventions or procedures must be justified in relation to expected benefits to the individual subject.
– Risks of interventions that do not hold out the prospect of direct diagnostic, therapeutic or preventive benefit for the individual must be justified in relation to the expected benefits to society (generalizable knowledge). The risks presented by such interventions must be reasonable in relation to the importance of the knowledge to be gained.

Commentary on Guideline 8

The Declaration of Helsinki in several paragraphs deals with the well-being of research subjects and the avoidance of risk. Thus, considerations related to the well-being of the human subject should take precedence over the interests of science and society (Paragraph 5); clinical testing must be preceded by adequate laboratory or animal experimentation to demonstrate a reasonable probability of success without undue risk (Paragraph 11); every project should be preceded by careful assessment of predictable risks and burdens in comparison with foreseeable benefits to the subject or to others (Paragraph 16); physician-researchers must be confident that the risks involved have been adequately assessed and can be satisfactorily managed (Paragraph 17); and the risks and burdens to the subject must be minimized, and reasonable in relation to the importance of the objective or the knowledge to be gained (Paragraph 18). Biomedical research often employs a variety of interventions of which some hold out the prospect of direct therapeutic benefit (beneficial interventions) and others are administered solely to answer the research question (non-beneficial interventions). Beneficial interventions are justified as they are in medical practice by the expectation that they will be at least as advantageous to the individuals concerned, in the light of both risks and benefits, as any available alternative. Non-beneficial interventions are assessed differently; they may be justified only by appeal to the knowledge to be gained. In assessing the risks and benefits that a protocol presents to a population, it is appropriate to consider the harm that could result from forgoing the research. Paragraphs 5 and 18 of the Declaration of Helsinki do not preclude well-informed volunteers, capable of fully appreciating risks and benefits of an investigation, from participating in research for altruistic reasons or for modest remuneration. Minimizing risk associated with participation in a randomized controlled trial. In randomized controlled trials subjects risk being allocated to receive the treatment that proves inferior. They are allocated by chance to one of two or more intervention arms and followed to a predetermined end-point. (Interventions are understood to include new or established therapies, diagnostic tests and preventive measures.) An intervention is evaluated by comparing it with another intervention (a control), which is ordinarily the best current method, selected from the safe and effective treatments available globally, unless some other control intervention such as placebo can be justified ethically (See Guideline 11). To minimize risk when the intervention to be tested in a randomized controlled trial is designed to prevent or postpone a lethal or disabling outcome, the investigator must not, for purposes of conducting the trial, withhold therapy that is known to be superior to the intervention being tested, unless the withholding can be justified by the standards set forth in Guideline 11. Also, the investigator must provide in the research protocol for the monitoring of research data by an independent board (Data and Safety Monitoring Board); one function of such a board is to protect the research subjects from previously unknown adverse reactions or unnecessarily prolonged exposure to an inferior therapy. Normally at the outset of a randomized controlled trial, criteria are established for its premature termination (stopping rules or guidelines).

Risks to groups of persons. Research in certain fields, such as epidemiology, genetics or sociology, may present risks to the interests of communities, societies, or racially or ethnically defined groups. Information might be published that could stigmatize a group or expose its members to discrimination. Such information, for example, could indicate, rightly or wrongly, that the group has a higher than average prevalence of alcoholism, mental illness or sexually transmitted disease, or is particularly susceptible to certain genetic disorders. Plans to conduct such research should be sensitive to such considerations, to the need to maintain confidentiality during and after the study, and to the need to publish the resulting data in a manner that is respectful of the interests of all concerned, or in certain circumstances not to publish them. The ethical review committee should ensure that the interests of all concerned are given due consideration; often it will be advisable to have individual consent supplemented by community consultation. [The ethical basis for the justification of risk is elaborated further in Guideline 9] Guideline 9: Special limitations on risk when research involves individuals who are not capable of giving informed consent When there is ethical and scientific justification to conduct research with individuals incapable of giving informed consent, the risk from research interventions that do not hold out the prospect of direct benefit for the individual subject should be no more likely and not greater than the risk attached to routine medical or psychological examination of such persons. Slight or minor increases above such risk may be permitted when there is an overriding scientific or medical rationale for such increases and when an ethical review committee has approved them.

Commentary on Guideline 9

The low-risk standard: Certain individuals or groups may have limited capacity to give informed consent either because, as in the case of prisoners, their autonomy is limited, or because they have limited cognitive capacity. For research involving persons who are unable to consent, or whose capacity to make an informed choice may not fully meet the standard of informed consent, ethical review committees must distinguish between intervention risks that do not exceed those associated with routine medical or psychological examination of such persons and risks in excess of those. When the risks of such interventions do not exceed those associated with routine medical or psychological examination of such persons, there is no requirement for special substantive or procedural protective measures apart from those generally required for all research involving members of the particular class of persons. When the risks are in excess of those, the ethical review committee must find: 1) that the research is designed to be responsive to the disease affecting the prospective subjects or to conditions to which they are particularly susceptible; 2) that the risks of the research interventions are only slightly greater than those associated with routine medical or psychological examination of such persons for the condition or set of clinical circumstances under investigation; 3) that the objective of the research is sufficiently important to justify exposure of the subjects to the increased risk; and 4) that the interventions are reasonably commensurate with the clinical interventions that the subjects have experienced or may be expected to experience in relation to the condition under investigation. If such research subjects, including children, become capable of giving independent informed consent during the research, their consent to continued participation should be obtained. There is no internationally agreed, precise definition of a "slight or minor increase" above the risks associated with routine medical or psychological examination of such persons. Its meaning is inferred from what various ethical review committees have reported as having met the standard. Examples include additional lumbar punctures or bone-marrow aspirations in children with conditions for which such examinations are regularly indicated in clinical practice. The requirement that the objective of the research be relevant to the disease or condition affecting the prospective subjects rules out the use of such interventions in healthy children.

The requirement that the research interventions be reasonably commensurate with clinical interventions that subjects may have experienced or are likely to experience for the condition under investigation is intended to enable them to draw on personal experience as they decide whether to accept or reject additional procedures for research purposes. Their choices will, therefore, be more informed even though they may not fully meet the standard of informed consent. (See also Guidelines 4: Individual informed consent; 13: Research involving vulnerable persons; 14: Research involving children; and 15: Research involving individuals who by reason of mental or behavioural disorders are not capable of giving adequately informed consent.)

Guideline 10: Research in populations and communities with limited resources

Before undertaking research in a population or community with limited resources, the sponsor and the investigator must make every effort to ensure that:

- the research is responsive to the health needs and the priorities of the population or community in which it is to be carried out; and
- any intervention or product developed, or knowledge generated, will be made reasonably available for the benefit of that population or community.

Commentary on Guideline 10

This guideline is concerned with countries or communities in which resources are limited to the extent that they are, or may be, vulnerable to exploitation by sponsors and investigators from the relatively wealthy countries and communities. Responsiveness of research to health needs and priorities. The ethical requirement that research be responsive to the health needs of the population or community in which it is carried out calls for decisions on what is needed to fulfil the requirement. It is not sufficient simply to determine that a disease is prevalent in the population and that new or further research is needed: the ethical requirement of "responsiveness" can be fulfilled only if successful interventions or other kinds of health benefit are made available to the population. This is applicable especially to research conducted in countries where governments lack the resources to make such products or benefits widely available. Even when a product to be tested in a particular country is much cheaper than the standard treatment in some other countries, the government or individuals in that country may still be unable to afford it. If the knowledge gained from the research in such a country is used primarily for the benefit of populations that can afford the tested product, the research may rightly be characterized as exploitative and, therefore, unethical. When an investigational intervention has important potential for health care in the host country, the negotiation that the sponsor should undertake to determine the practical implications of "responsiveness", as well as "reasonable availability", should include representatives of stakeholders in the host country; these include the national government, the health ministry, local health authorities, and concerned scientific and ethics groups, as well as representatives of the communities from which subjects are drawn and non-governmental organizations such as health advocacy groups. The negotiation should cover the health-care infrastructure required for safe and rational use of the intervention, the likelihood of authorization for distribution, and decisions regarding payments, royalties, subsidies, technology and intellectual property, as well as distribution costs, when this economic information is not proprietary. In some cases, satisfactory discussion of the availability and distribution of successful products will necessarily engage international organizations, donor governments and bilateral agencies, international nongovernmental organizations, and the private sector. The development of a health-care infrastructure should be facilitated at the onset so that it can be of use during and beyond the conduct of the research.

Additionally, if an investigational drug has been shown to be beneficial, the sponsor should continue to provide it to the subjects after the conclusion of the study, and pending its approval by a drug regulatory authority. The sponsor is unlikely to be in a position to make a beneficial investigational intervention generally available to the community or population until some time after the conclusion of the study, as it may be in short supply and in any case cannot be made generally available before a drug regulatory authority has approved it. For minor research studies and when the outcome is scientific knowledge rather than a commercial product, such complex planning or negotiation is rarely, if ever, needed. There must be assurance, however, that the scientific knowledge developed will be used for the benefit of the population.

Reasonable availability. The issue of "reasonable availability" is complex and will need to be determined on a case-by-case basis. Relevant considerations include the length of time for which the intervention or product developed, or other agreed benefit, will be made available to research subjects, or to the community or population concerned; the severity of a subject's medical condition; the effect of withdrawing the study drug (e.g., death of a subject); the cost to the subject or health service; and the question of undue inducement if an intervention is provided free of charge. In general, if there is good reason to believe that a product developed or knowledge generated by research is unlikely to be reasonably available to, or applied to the benefit of, the population of a proposed host country or community after the conclusion of the research, it is unethical to conduct the research in that country or community. This should not be construed as precluding studies designed to evaluate novel therapeutic concepts. As a rare exception, for example, research may be designed to obtain preliminary evidence that a drug or a class of drugs has a beneficial effect in the treatment of a disease that occurs only in regions with extremely limited resources, and it could not be carried out reasonably well in more developed communities. Such research may be justified ethically even if there is no plan in place to make a product available to the population of the host country or community at the conclusion of the preliminary phase of its development. If the concept is found to be valid, subsequent phases of the research could result in a product that could be made reasonably available at its conclusion. (See also Guidelines 3: Ethical review of externally sponsored research; 12, Equitable distribution of burdens and benefits; 20: Strengthening capacity for ethical and scientific review and biomedical research; and 21: Ethical obligation of external sponsors to provide health-care services.)

Guideline 11: Choice of control in clinical trials

As a general rule, research subjects in the control group of a trial of a diagnostic, therapeutic, or preventive intervention should receive an established effective intervention. In some circumstances it may be ethically acceptable to use an alternative comparator, such as placebo or "no treatment". Placebo may be used:

– when there is no established effective intervention;
– when withholding an established effective intervention would expose subjects to, at most, temporary discomfort or delay in relief of symptoms;
– when use of an established effective intervention as comparator would not yield scientifically reliable results and use of placebo would not add any risk of serious or irreversible harm to the subjects.

Commentary on Guideline 11

General considerations for controlled clinical trials. The design of trials of investigational diagnostic, therapeutic or preventive interventions raises interrelated scientific and ethical issues for sponsors, investigators and ethical review committees. To obtain reliable results, investigators must compare the effects of an investigational intervention on subjects assigned to the investigational arm (or arms) of a trial with the effects that a control intervention produces in subjects drawn from the same population and assigned to its control arm. Randomization is the preferred method for assigning subjects to the various arms of the clinical trial unless another method, such as historical or literature controls, can be justified scientifically and ethically. Assignment to treatment arms by randomization, in addition to its usual scientific superiority, offers the advantage of tending to render equivalent to all subjects the foreseeable benefits and risks of participation in a trial. A clinical trial cannot be justified ethically unless it is capable of producing scientifically reliable results. When the objective is to establish the effectiveness and safety of an investigational intervention, the use of a placebo control is often much more likely than that of an active control to produce a scientifically reliable result. In many cases the ability of a trial to distinguish effective from ineffective interventions (its assay sensitivity) cannot be assured unless the control is a placebo. If, however, an effect of using a placebo would be to deprive subjects in the control arm of an established effective intervention, and thereby to expose them to serious harm, particularly if it is irreversible, it would obviously be unethical to use a placebo. Placebo control in the absence of a current effective alternative. The use of placebo in the control arm of a clinical trial is ethically acceptable when, as stated in the Declaration of Helsinki (Paragraph 29), "no proven prophylactic, diagnostic or therapeutic method exists." Usually, in this case, a placebo is scientifically preferable to no intervention. In certain circumstances, however, an alternative design may be both scientifically and ethically acceptable, and preferable; an example would be a clinical trial of a surgical intervention, because, for many surgical interventions, either it is not possible or it is ethically unacceptable to devise a suitable placebo; for another example, in certain vaccine trials an investigator might choose to provide for those in the 'control' arm a vaccine that is unrelated to the investigational vaccine. Placebo-controlled trials that entail only minor risks. A placebo-controlled design may be ethically acceptable, and preferable on scientific grounds, when the condition for which patients/subjects are randomly assigned to placebo or active treatment is only a small deviation in physiological measurements, such as slightly raised blood pressure or a modest increase in serum cholesterol; and if delaying or omitting available treatment may cause only temporary discomfort (e.g., common headache) and no serious adverse consequences. The ethical review committee must be fully satisfied that the risks of withholding an established effective intervention are truly minor and short-lived. Placebo control when active control would not yield reliable results. A related but distinct rationale for using a placebo control rather than an established effective intervention is that the documented experience with the established effective intervention is not sufficient to provide a scientifically reliable comparison with the intervention being investigated; it is then difficult, or even impossible, without using a placebo, to design a scientifically reliable study. This is not always, however, an ethically acceptable basis for depriving control subjects of an established effective intervention in clinical trials; only when doing so would not add any risk of serious harm, particularly irreversible harm, to the subjects would it be ethically acceptable to do so. In some cases, the condition at which the intervention is aimed (for example, cancer or HIV/AIDS) will be too serious to deprive control subjects of an established effective intervention. This latter rationale (when active control would not yield reliable results) differs from the former (trials that entail only minor risks) in emphasis. In trials that entail only minor risks the investigative interventions are aimed at relatively trivial conditions, such as the common cold or hair loss; forgoing an established effective intervention for the duration of a trial deprives control subjects of only minor benefits. It is for this reason that it is not unethical to use a placebo-control design. Even if it were possible to design a so-called "non-inferiority", or "equivalency", trial using an active control, it would still not be unethical in these circumstances to use a placebo-control design. In any event, the researcher must satisfy the ethical review committee that the safety and human rights of the subjects will be fully protected, that prospective subjects will be fully informed about alternative treatments, and that the purpose and design of the study are scientifically sound. The ethical acceptability of such placebo-controlled studies increases as the period of placebo use is decreased, and when the study design permits change to active treatment ("escape treatment") if intolerable symptoms occur.

Exceptional use of a comparator other than an established effective intervention. An exception to the general rule is applicable in some studies designed to develop a therapeutic, preventive or diagnostic intervention for use in a country or community in which an established effective intervention is not available and unlikely in the foreseeable future to become available, usually for economic or logistic reasons. The purpose of such a study is to make available to the population of the country or community an effective alternative to an established effective intervention that is locally unavailable. Accordingly, the proposed investigational intervention must be responsive to the health needs of the population from which the research subjects are recruited and there must be assurance that, if it proves to be safe and effective, it will be made reasonably available to that population. Also, the scientific and ethical review committees must be satisfied that the established effective intervention cannot be used as comparator because its use would not yield scientifically reliable results that would be relevant to the health needs of the study population. In these circumstances an ethical review committee can approve a clinical trial in which the comparator is other than an established effective intervention, such as placebo or no treatment or a local remedy. However, some people strongly object to the exceptional use of a comparator other than an established effective intervention because it could result in exploitation of poor and disadvantaged populations. The objection rests on three arguments:

- Placebo control could expose research subjects to risk of serious or irreversible harm when the use of an established effective intervention as comparator could avoid the risk.
- Not all scientific experts agree about conditions under which an established effective intervention used as a comparator would not yield scientifically reliable results.
- An economic reason for the unavailability of an established effective intervention cannot justify a placebo-controlled study in a country of limited resources when it would be unethical to conduct a study with the same design in a population with general access to the effective intervention outside the study. Placebo control when an established effective intervention is not available in the host country. The question addressed here is: when should an exception be allowed to the general rule that subjects in the control arm of a clinical trial should receive an established effective intervention? The usual reason for proposing the exception is that, for economic or logistic reasons, an established effective intervention is not in general use or available in the country in which the study will be conducted, whereas the investigational intervention could be made available, given the finances and infrastructure of the country. Another reason that may be advanced for proposing a placebo-controlled trial is that using an established effective intervention as the control would not produce scientifically reliable data relevant to the country in which the trial is to be conducted. Existing data about the effectiveness and safety of the established effective intervention may have been accumulated under circumstances unlike those of the population in which it is proposed to conduct the trial; this, it may be argued, could make their use in the trial unreliable. One reason could be that the disease or condition manifests itself differently in different populations, or other uncontrolled factors could invalidate the use of existing data for comparative purposes.

The use of placebo control in these circumstances is ethically controversial, for the following reasons:

- Sponsors of research might use poor countries or communities as testing grounds for research that would be difficult or impossible in countries where there is general access to an established effective intervention, and the investigational intervention, if proven safe and effective, is likely to be marketed in countries in which an established effective intervention is already available and it is not likely to be marketed in the host country.
- The research subjects, both active-arm and control-arm, are patients who may have a serious, possibly life-threatening, illness. They do not normally have access to an established effective intervention currently available to similar patients in many other countries. Ac-

cording to the requirements of a scientifically reliable trial, investigators, who may be their attending physicians, would be expected to enrol some of those patients/subjects in the placebo-control arm. This would appear to be a violation of the physician's fiduciary duty of undivided loyalty to the patient, particularly in cases in which known effective therapy could be made available to the patients. An argument for exceptional use of placebo control may be that a health authority in a country where an established effective intervention is not generally available or affordable, and unlikely to become available or affordable in the foreseeable future, seeks to develop an affordable intervention specifically for a health problem affecting its population. There may then be less reason for concern that a placebo design is exploitative, and therefore unethical, as the health authority has responsibility for the population's health, and there are valid health grounds for testing an apparently beneficial intervention. In such circumstances an ethical review committee may determine that the proposed trial is ethically acceptable, provided that the rights and safety of subjects are safeguarded.

Ethical review committees will need to engage in careful analysis of the circumstances to determine whether the use of placebo rather than an established effective intervention is ethically acceptable. They will need to be satisfied that an established effective intervention is truly unlikely to become available and implementable in that country. This may be difficult to determine, however, as it is clear that, with sufficient persistence and ingenuity, ways may be found of accessing previously unattainable medicinal products, and thus avoiding the ethical issue raised by the use of placebo control. When the rationale of proposing a placebo-controlled trial is that the use of an established effective intervention as the control would not yield scientifically reliable data relevant to the proposed host country, the ethical review committee in that country has the option of seeking expert opinion as to whether use of an established effective intervention in the control arm would invalidate the results of the research. An "equivalency trial" as an alternative to a placebo-controlled trial. An alternative to a placebo-control design in these circumstances would be an "equivalency trial", which would compare an investigational intervention with an established effective intervention and produce scientifically reliable data. An equivalency trial in a country in which no established effective intervention is available is not designed to determine whether the investigational intervention is superior to an established effective intervention currently used somewhere in the world; its purpose is, rather, to determine whether the investigational intervention is, in effectiveness and safety, equivalent to, or almost equivalent to, the established effective intervention. It would be hazardous to conclude, however, that an intervention demonstrated to be equivalent, or almost equivalent, to an established effective intervention is better than nothing or superior to whatever intervention is available in the country; there may be substantial differences between the results of superficially identical clinical trials carried out in different countries. If there are such differences, it would be scientifically acceptable and ethically preferable to conduct such 'equivalency' trials in countries in which an established effective intervention is already available. If there are substantial grounds for the ethical review committee to conclude that an established effective intervention will not become available and implementable, the committee should obtain assurances from the parties concerned that plans have been agreed for making the investigational intervention reasonably available in the host country or community once its effectiveness and safety have been established. Moreover, when the study has external sponsorship, approval should usually be dependent on the sponsors and the health authorities of the host country having engaged in a process of negotiation and planning, including justifying the study in regard to local health-care needs.

Means of minimizing harm to placebo-control subjects. Even when placebo controls are justified on one of the bases set forth in the guideline, there are means of minimizing the possibly harmful effect of being in the control arm. First, a placebo-control group need not be untreated. An add-on design may be employed when the investigational therapy and a standard treatment have different mechanisms of action. The treatment to be tested and placebo are each added to a standard treatment. Such studies have a particular place when a standard treatment is known to decrease mortality or irreversible morbidity but a trial with standard treatment as the active control cannot be carried out or would be difficult to interpret [International Conference on Harmonisation (ICH) Guideline: Choice of Control Group and Related Issues in Clinical Trials, 2000]. In testing for improved treatment of life-threatening diseases such as cancer, HIV/AIDS, or heart failure, add-on designs are a particularly useful means of finding improvements in interventions that are not fully effective or may cause intolerable side-effects. They have a place also in respect of treatment for epilepsy, rheumatism and osteoporosis, for example, because withholding of established effective therapy could result in progressive disability, unacceptable discomfort or both.

Second, as indicated in Guideline 8 Commentary, when the intervention to be tested in a randomized controlled trial is designed to prevent or postpone a lethal or disabling outcome, the investigator minimizes harmful effects of placebo-control studies by providing in the research protocol for the monitoring of research data by an independent Data and Safety Monitoring Board (DSMB). One function of such a board is to protect the research subjects from previously unknown adverse reactions; another is to avoid unnecessarily prolonged exposure to an inferior therapy. The board fulfils the latter function by means of interim analyses of the data pertaining to efficacy to ensure that the trial does not continue beyond the point at which an investigational therapy is demonstrated to be effective. Normally, at the outset of a randomized controlled trial, criteria are established for its premature termination (stopping rules or guidelines). In some cases the DSMB is called upon to perform "conditional power calculations", designed to determine the probability that a particular clinical trial could ever show that the investigational therapy is effective. If that probability is very small, the DSMB is expected to recommend termination of the clinical trial, because it would be unethical to continue it beyond that point.

In most cases of research involving human subjects, it is unnecessary to appoint a DSMB. To ensure that research is carefully monitored for the early detection of adverse events, the sponsor or the principal investigator appoints an individual to be responsible for advising on the need to consider changing the system of monitoring for adverse events or the process of informed consent, or even to consider terminating the study.

Guideline 12: Equitable distribution of burdens and benefits in the selection of groups of subjects in research

Groups or communities to be invited to be subjects of research should be selected in such a way that the burdens and benefits of the research will be equitably distributed. The exclusion of groups or communities that might benefit from study participation must be justified.

Commentary on Guideline 12

General considerations: Equity requires that no group or class of persons should bear more than its fair share of the burdens of participation in research. Similarly, no group should be deprived of its fair share of the benefits of research, short-term or long-term; such benefits include the direct benefits of participation as well as the benefits of the new knowledge that the research is designed to yield. When burdens or benefits of research are to be apportioned unequally among individuals or groups of persons, the criteria for unequal distribution should be morally justifiable and not arbitrary. In other words, unequal allocation must not be inequitable. Subjects should be drawn from the qualifying population in the general geographic area of the trial without regard to race, ethnicity, economic status or gender unless there is a sound scientific reason to do otherwise. In the past, groups of persons were excluded from participation in research for what were then considered good reasons. As a consequence of such exclusions, information about the diagnosis, prevention and treatment of diseases in such groups of persons is limited.

This has resulted in a serious class injustice. If information about the management of diseases is considered a benefit that is distributed within a society, it is unjust to deprive groups of persons of that benefit. Such documents as the Declaration of Helsinki and the UNAIDS Guidance Document Ethical Considerations in HIV Preventive Vaccine Research, and the policies of many national governments and professional societies, recognize the need to redress these injustices by encouraging the participation of previously excluded groups in basic and applied biomedical research.

Members of vulnerable groups also have the same entitlement to access to the benefits of investigational interventions that show promise of therapeutic benefit as persons not considered vulnerable, particularly when no superior or equivalent approaches to therapy are available. There has been a perception, sometimes correct and sometimes incorrect, that certain groups of persons have been overused as research subjects. In some cases such overuse has been based on the administrative availability of the populations. Research hospitals are often located in places where members of the lowest socioeconomic classes reside, and this has resulted in an apparent overuse of such persons. Other groups that may have been overused because they were conveniently available to researchers include students in investigators' classes, residents of long-term care facilities and subordinate members of hierarchical institutions. Impoverished groups have been overused because of their willingness to serve as subjects in exchange for relatively small stipends. Prisoners have been considered ideal subjects for Phase I drug studies because of their highly regimented lives and, in many cases, their conditions of economic deprivation. Overuse of certain groups, such as the poor or the administratively available, is unjust for several reasons. It is unjust to selectively recruit impoverished people to serve as research subjects simply because they can be more easily induced to participate in exchange for small payments. In most cases, these people would be called upon to bear the burdens of research so that others who are better off could enjoy the benefits. However, although the burdens of research should not fall disproportionately on socio-economically disadvantaged groups, neither should such groups be categorically excluded from research protocols. It would not be unjust to selectively recruit poor people to serve as subjects in research designed to address problems that are prevalent in their group –malnutrition, for example. Similar considerations apply to institutionalized groups or those whose availability to the investigators is for other reasons administratively convenient.

Not only may certain groups within a society be inappropriately overused as research subjects, but also entire communities or societies may be overused. This has been particularly likely to occur in countries or communities with insufficiently well developed systems for the protection of the rights and welfare of human research subjects. Such overuse is especially questionable when the populations or communities concerned bear the burdens of participation in research but are extremely unlikely ever to enjoy the benefits of new knowledge and products developed as a result of the research. (See Guideline 10: Research in populations and communities with limited resources.)

Guideline 13: Research involving vulnerable persons

Special justification is required for inviting vulnerable individuals to serve as research subjects and, if they are selected, the means of protecting their rights and welfare must be strictly applied.

Commentary on Guideline 13

Vulnerable persons are those who are relatively (or absolutely) incapable of protecting their own interests. More formally, they may have insufficient power, intelligence, education, resources, strength, or other needed attributes to protect their own interests. General considerations. The central problem presented by plans to involve vulnerable persons as research subjects is that such plans may entail an inequitable distribution of the burdens and benefits of research participation. Classes of individuals conventionally considered vulnerable are those with limited capacity or freedom to consent or to decline to consent. They are the subject of specific guidelines in this document (Guidelines 14,15) and include children, and persons who because of mental or behavioural disorders are incapable of giving informed consent. Ethical justification of their involvement usually requires that investigators satisfy ethical review committees that:

– the research could not be carried out equally well with less vulnerable subjects;
– the research is intended to obtain knowledge that will lead to improved diagnosis,

prevention or treatment of diseases or other health problems characteristic of, or unique to, the vulnerable class– either the actual subjects or other similarly situated members of the vulnerable class;
– research subjects and other members of the vulnerable class from which subjects are recruited will ordinarily be assured reasonable access to any diagnostic, preventive or therapeutic products that will become available as a consequence of the research;
– the risks attached to interventions or procedures that do not hold out the prospect of direct health-related benefit will not exceed those associated with routine medical or psychological examination of such persons unless an ethical review committee authorizes a slight increase over this level of risk (Guideline 9); and,
– when the prospective subjects are either incompetent or otherwise substantially unable to give informed consent, their agreement will be supplemented by the permission of their legal guardians or other appropriate representatives.

Other vulnerable groups. The quality of the consent of prospective subjects who are junior or subordinate members of a hierarchical group requires careful consideration, as their agreement to volunteer may be unduly influenced, whether justified or not, by the expectation of preferential treatment if they agree or by fear of disapproval or retaliation if they refuse. Examples of such groups are medical and nursing students, subordinate hospital and laboratory personnel, employees of pharmaceutical companies, and members of the armed forces or police. Because they work in close proximity to investigators, they tend to be called upon more often than others to serve as research subjects, and this could result in inequitable distribution of the burdens and benefits of research. Elderly persons are commonly regarded as vulnerable. With advancing age, people are increasingly likely to acquire attributes that define them as vulnerable. They may, for example, be institutionalized or develop varying degrees of dementia. If and when they acquire such vulnerability-defining attributes, and not before, it is appropriate to consider them vulnerable and to treat them accordingly.

Other groups or classes may also be considered vulnerable. They include residents of nursing homes, people receiving welfare benefits or social assistance and other poor people and the unemployed, patients in emergency rooms, some ethnic and racial minority groups, homeless persons, nomads, refugees or displaced persons, prisoners, patients with incurable disease, individuals who are politically powerless, and members of communities unfamiliar with modern medical concepts. To the extent that these and other classes of people have attributes resembling those of classes identified as vulnerable, the need for special protection of their rights and welfare should be reviewed and applied, where relevant.

Persons who have serious, potentially disabling or life-threatening diseases are highly vulnerable. Physicians sometimes treat such patients with drugs or other therapies not yet licensed for general availability because studies designed to establish their safety and efficacy have not been completed. This is compatible with the Declaration of Helsinki, which states in Paragraph 32: " In the treatment of a patient, where proven therapeutic methods do not exist or have been ineffective, the physician, with informed consent from the patient, must be free to use unproven or new therapeutic measures, if in the physician s judgement it offers hope of saving life, re-establishing health or alleviating suffering". Such treatment, commonly called 'compassionate use', is not properly regarded as research, but it can contribute to ongoing research into the safety and efficacy of the interventions used. Although, on the whole, investigators must study less vulnerable groups before involving more vulnerable groups, some exceptions are justified. In general, children are not suitable for Phase I drug trials or for Phase I or II vaccine trials, but such trials may be permissible after studies in adults have shown some therapeutic or preventive effect. For example, a Phase II vaccine trial seeking evidence of immunogenicity in infants may be justified when a vaccine has shown evidence of preventing or slowing progression of an infectious disease in adults, or Phase I research with children may be appropriate because the disease to be treated does not occur in adults or is manifested differently in children (Appendix 3: The phases of clinical trials of vaccines and drugs).

Guideline 14: Research involving children

Before undertaking research involving children, the investigator must ensure that:

– the research might not equally well be carried out with adults;
– the purpose of the research is to obtain knowledge relevant to the health needs of children;
– a parent or legal representative of each child has given permission;
– the agreement (assent) of each child has been obtained to the extent of the child's capabilities; and,
– a child's refusal to participate or continue in the research will be respected.

Commentary on Guideline 14

Justification of the involvement of children in biomedical research. The participation of children is indispensable for research into diseases of childhood and conditions to which children are particularly susceptible (cf. vaccine trials), as well as for clinical trials of drugs that are designed for children as well as adults. In the past, many new products were not tested for children though they were directed towards diseases also occurring in childhood; thus children either did not benefit from these new drugs or were exposed to them though little was known about their specific effects or safety in children. Now it is widely agreed that, as a general rule, the sponsor of any new therapeutic, diagnostic or preventive product that is likely to be indicated for use in children is obliged to evaluate its safety and efficacy for children before it is released for general distribution. Assent of the child. The willing cooperation of the child should be sought, after the child has been informed to the extent that the child's maturity and intelligence permit. The age at which a child becomes legally competent to give consent differs substantially from one jurisdiction to another; in some countries the "age of consent" established in their different provinces, states or other political subdivisions varies considerably. Often children who have not yet reached the legally established age of consent can understand the implications of informed consent and go through the necessary procedures; they can therefore knowingly agree to serve as research subjects. Such knowing agreement, sometimes referred to as assent, is insufficient to permit participation in research unless it is supplemented by the permission of a parent, a legal guardian or other duly authorized representative. Some children who are too immature to be able to give knowing agreement, or assent, may be able to register a 'deliberate objection', an expression of disapproval or refusal of a proposed procedure. The deliberate objection of an older child, for example, is to be distinguished from the behaviour of an infant, who is likely to cry or withdraw in response to almost any stimulus. Older children, who are more capable of giving assent, should be selected before younger children or infants, unless there are valid scientific reasons related to age for involving younger children first. A deliberate objection by a child to taking part in research should always be respected even if the parents have given permission, unless the child needs treatment that is not available outside the context of research, the investigational intervention shows promise of therapeutic benefit, and there is no acceptable alternative therapy. In such a case, particularly if the child is very young or immature, a parent or guardian may override the child`s objections. If the child is older and more nearly capable of independent informed consent, the investigator should seek the specific approval or clearance of the scientific and ethical review committees for initiating or continuing with the investigational treatment. If child subjects become capable of independent informed consent during the research, their informed consent to continued participation should be sought and their decision respected.

A child with a likely fatal illness may object or refuse assent to continuation of a burdensome or distressing intervention. In such circumstances parents may press an investigator to persist with an investigational intervention against the child`s wishes. The investigator may agree to do so if the intervention shows promise of preserving or prolonging life and there is no acceptable alternative treatment. In such cases, the investigator should seek the specific approval or clearance of the ethical review committee before agreeing to override the wishes of the child. Permission of a parent or guardian. The investigator must obtain the permission of a parent or guardian in accordance with local laws or established procedures. It may be assumed that children over the age of 12 or 13 years are usually capable of understanding what is necessary to give adequately informed consent, but their consent (assent) should normally be complemented by the permission of a parent or guardian, even when local law does not require such permission. Even when the law requires parental permission, however, the assent of the child must be obtained.

In some jurisdictions, some individuals who are below the general age of consent are regarded as "emancipated" or "mature" minors and are authorized to consent without the agreement or even the awareness of their parents or guardians. They may be married or pregnant or be already parents or living independently. Some studies involve investigation of adolescents' beliefs and behaviour regarding sexuality or use of recreational drugs; other research addresses domestic violence or child abuse. For studies on these topics, ethical review committees may waive parental permission if, for example, parental knowledge of the subject matter may place the adolescents at some risk of questioning or even intimidation by their parents.

Because of the issues inherent in obtaining assent from children in institutions, such children should only exceptionally be subjects of research. In the case of institutionalized children without parents, or whose parents are not legally authorized to grant permission, the ethical review committee may require sponsors or investigators to provide it with the opinion of an independent, concerned, expert advocate for institutionalized children as to the propriety of undertaking the research with such children. Observation of research by a parent or guardian. A parent or guardian who gives permission for a child to participate in research should be given the opportunity, to a reasonable extent, to observe the research as it proceeds, so as to be able to withdraw the child if the parent or guardian decides it is in the child's best interests to do so.

Psychological and medical support. Research involving children should be conducted in settings in which the child and the parent can obtain adequate medical and psychological support. As an additional protection for children, an investigator may, when possible, obtain the advice of a child's family physician, paediatrician or other health-care provider on matters concerning the child's participation in the research. (See also Guideline 8: Benefits and risks of study participation; Guideline 9: Special limitations on risks when subjects are not capable of giving consent; and Guideline 13: Research involving vulnerable persons.)

Guideline 15: Research involving individuals who by reason of mental or behavioural disorders are not capable of giving adequately informed consent.

Before undertaking research involving individuals who by reason of mental orbehavioural disorders are not capable of giving adequately informed consent, the investigator must ensure that:

– such persons will not be subjects of research that might equally well be carried out on persons whose capacity to give adequately informed consent is not impaired;
– the purpose of the research is to obtain knowledge relevant to the particular health needs of persons with mental or behavioural disorders;
– the consent of each subject has been obtained to the extent of that person's capabilities, and a prospective subject's refusal to participate in research is always respected, unless, in exceptional circumstances, there is no reasonable medical alternative and local law permits overriding the objection; and,
– in cases where prospective subjects lack capacity to consent, permission is obtained from a responsible family member or a legally authorized representative in accordance with applicable law.

Commentary on Guideline 15

General considerations. Most individuals with mental or behavioural disorders are capable of giving informed consent; this Guideline is concerned only with those who are not capable or who because their condition deteriorates become temporarily incapable. They should never be subjects of research that might equally well be carried out on persons in full possession of their mental faculties, but they are clearly the only subjects suitable for a large part of research into the origins and treatment of certain severe mental or behavioural disorders.

Consent of the individual. The investigator must obtain the approval of an ethical review committee to include in research persons who by reason of mental or behavioural disorders are not capable of giving informed consent. The willing cooperation of such persons should be sought to the extent that their mental state permits, and any objection on their part to taking part in any study that has no components designed to benefit them directly should always be respected. The objection of such an individual to an investigational intervention intended to be of therapeutic benefit should be respected unless there is no reasonable medical alternative and local law permits overriding the objection. The agreement of an immediate family member or other person with a close personal relationship with the individual should be sought, but it should be recognized that these proxies may have their own interests that may call their permission into question. Some relatives may not be primarily concerned with protecting the rights and welfare of the patients. Moreover, a close family member or friend may wish to take advantage of a research study in the hope that it will succeed in "curing" the condition.

Some jurisdictions do not permit third-party permission for subjects lacking capacity to consent. Legal authorization may be necessary to involve in research an individual who has been committed to an institution by a court order. Serious illness in persons who because of mental or behavioural disorders are unable to give adequately informed consent. Persons who because of mental or behavioural disorders are unable to give adequately informed consent and who have, or are at risk of, serious illnesses such as HIV infection, cancer or hepatitis should not be deprived of the possible benefits of investigational drugs, vaccines or devices that show promise of therapeutic or preventive benefit, particularly when no superior or equivalent therapy or prevention is available. Their entitlement to access to such therapy or prevention is justified ethically on the same grounds as is such entitlement for other vulnerable groups. Persons who are unable to give adequately informed consent by reason of mental or behavioural disorders are, in general, not suitable for participation in formal clinical trials except those trials that are designed to be responsive to their particular health needs and can be carried out only with them. (See also Guidelines 8: Benefits and risks of study participation; 9: Special limitations on risks when subjects are not capable of giving consent; and 13: Research involving vulnerable persons.)

Guideline 16: Women as research subjects

Investigators, sponsors or ethical review committees should not exclude women of reproductive age from biomedical research. The potential for becoming pregnant during a study should not, in itself, be used as a reason for precluding or limiting participation. However, a thorough discussion of risks to the pregnant woman and to her fetus is a prerequisite for the woman s ability to make a rational decision to enrol in a clinical study. In this discussion, if participation in the research might be hazardous to a fetus or a woman if she becomes pregnant, the sponsors/ investigators should guarantee the prospective subject a pregnancy test and access to effective contraceptive methods before the research commences. Where such access is not possible, for legal or religious reasons, investigators should not recruit for such possibly hazardous research women who might become pregnant.

Commentary on Guideline 16

Women in most societies have been discriminated against with regard to their involvement in research. Women who are biologically capable of becoming pregnant have been customarily excluded from formal clinical trials of drugs, vaccines and medical devices owing to concern about undetermined risks to the fetus. Consequently, relatively little is known about the safety and efficacy of most drugs, vaccines or devices for such women, and this lack of knowledge can be dangerous.A general policy of excluding from such clinical trials women biologically capable of becoming pregnant is unjust in that it deprives women as a class of persons of the benefits of the new knowledge derived from the trials. Further, it is an affront to their right of self-determination. Nevertheless, although women of childbearing age should be given the opportunity to participate in research, they should be helped to understand that the research could include risks to the fetus if they become pregnant during the research. Although this general presumption favours the inclusion of women in research, it must be acknowledged that in some parts of the world women are vulnerable to neglect or harm in research because of their social conditioning to submit to authority, to ask no questions, and to tolerate pain and suffering. When women in such situations are potential subjects in research, investigators need to exercise special care in the informed consent process to ensure that they have adequate time and a proper environment in which to take decisions on the basis of clearly given information. Individual consent of women: In research involving women of reproductive age, whether pregnant or non-pregnant, only the informed consent of the woman herself is required for her participation. In no case should the permission of a spouse or partner replace the requirement of individual informed consent. If women wish to consult with their husbands or partners or seek voluntarily to obtain their permission before deciding to enrol in research, that is not only ethically permissible but in some contexts highly desirable. A strict requirement of authorization of spouse or partner, however, violates the substantive principle of respect for persons.

A thorough discussion of risks to the pregnant woman and to her fetus is a prerequisite for the woman's ability to make a rational decision to enrol in a clinical study. For women who are not pregnant at the outset of a study but who might become pregnant while they are still subjects, the consent discussion should include information about the alternative of voluntarily withdrawing from the study and, where legally permissible, terminating the pregnancy. Also, if the pregnancy is not terminated, they should be guaranteed a medical follow-up.

Guideline 17: Pregnant women as research participants

Pregnant women should be presumed to be eligible for participation in biomedical research. Investigators and ethical review committees should ensure that prospective subjects who are pregnant are adequately informed about the risks and benefits to themselves, their pregnancies, the fetus and their subsequent offspring, and to their fertility. Research in this population should be performed only if it is relevant to the particular health needs of a pregnant woman or her fetus, or to the health needs of pregnant women in general, and, when appropriate, if it is supported by reliable evidence from animal experiments, particularly as to risks of teratogenicity and mutagenicity .

Commentary on Guideline 17

The justification of research involving pregnant women is complicated by the fact that it may present risks and potential benefits to two beings – the woman and the fetus – as well as to the person the fetus is destined to become. Though the decision about acceptability of risk should be made by the mother as part of the informed consent process, it is desirable in research directed at the health of the fetus to obtain the father´s opinion also, when possible. Even when evidence concerning risks is unknown or ambiguous, the decision about acceptability of risk to the fetus should be made by the woman as part of the informed consent process. Especially in communities or societies in which cultural beliefs accord more importance to the fetus than to the woman's life or health, women may feel constrained to participate, or not to participate, in research. Special safeguards should be established to prevent undue inducement to pregnant women to participate in research in which interventions hold out the prospect of direct benefit to the fetus. Where fetal abnormality is not recognized as an indication for abortion, pregnant women should not be recruited for research in which there is a realistic basis for concern that fetal abnormality may occur as a consequence of participation as a subject in research. Investigators should include in protocols on research on pregnant women a plan for monitoring the outcome of the pregnancy with regard to both the health of the woman and the short-term and long-term health of the child.

Guideline 18: Safeguarding confidentiality

The investigator must establish secure safeguards of the confidentiality of subjects research data. Subjects should be told the limits, legal or other, to the investigators' ability to safeguard confidentiality and the possible consequences of breaches of confidentiality.

Commentary on Guideline 18

Confidentiality between investigator and subject. Research relating to individuals and groups may involve the collection and storage of information that, if disclosed to third parties, could cause harm or distress. Investigators should arrange to protect the confidentiality of such information by, for example, omitting information that might lead to the identification of individual subjects, limiting access to the information, anonymizing data, or other means. During the process of obtaining informed consent the investigator should inform the prospective subjects about the precautions that will be taken to protect confidentiality.

Prospective subjects should be informed of limits to the ability of investigators to ensure strict confidentiality and of the foreseeable adverse social consequences of breaches of confidentiality. Some jurisdictions require the reporting to appropriate agencies of, for instance, certain communicable diseases or evidence of child abuse or neglect. Drug regulatory authorities have the right to inspect clinical-trial records, and a sponsor`s clinical-compliance audit staff may require and obtain access to confidential data. These and similar limits to the ability to maintain confidentiality should be anticipated and disclosed to prospective subjects.

Participation in HIV/AIDS drug and vaccine trials may impose upon the research subjects significant associated risks of social discrimination or harm; such risks merit consideration equal to that given to adverse medical consequences of the drugs and vaccines. Efforts must be made to reduce their likelihood and severity. For example, subjects in vaccine trials must be enabled to demonstrate that their HIV seropositivity is due to their having been vaccinated rather than to natural infection. This may be accomplished by providing them with documents attesting to their participation in vaccine trials, or by maintaining a confidential register of trial subjects, from which information can be made available to outside agencies at a subject's request.

Confidentiality between physician and patient. Patients have the right to expect that their physicians and other health-care professionals will hold all information about them in strict confidence and disclose it only to those who need, or have a legal right to, the information, such as other attending physicians, nurses, or other health-care workers who perform tasks related to the diagnosis and treatment of patients. A treating physician should not disclose any identifying information about patients to an investigator unless each patient has given consent to such disclosure and unless an ethical review committee has approved such disclosure.

Physicians and other health care professionals record the details of their observations and interventions in medical and other records. Epidemiological studies often make use of such records. For such studies it is usually impracticable to obtain the informed consent of each identifiable patient; an ethical review committee may waive the requirement for informed consent when this is consistent with the requirements of applicable law and provided that there are secure safeguards of confidentiality. (See also Guideline 4 Commentary: Waiver of the consent requirement.) In institutions in which records may be used for research purposes without the informed consent of patients, it is advisable to notify patients generally of such practices; notification is usually by means of a statement in patient-information brochures. For research limited to patients' medical records, access must be approved or cleared by an ethical review committee and must be supervised by a person who is fully aware of the confidentiality requirements. Issues of confidentiality in genetic research. An investigator who proposes to perform genetic tests of known clinical or predictive value on biological samples that can be linked to an identifiable individual must obtain the informed consent of the individual or, when indicated, the permission of a legally authorized representative. Conversely, before performing a genetic test that is of known predictive value or gives reliable information about a known heritable condition, and individual consent or permission has not been obtained, investigators must see that biological samples are fully anonymized and unlinked; this ensures that no information about specific individuals can be derived from such research or passed back to them. When biological samples are not fully anonymized and when it is anticipated that there may be valid clinical or research reasons for linking the results of genetic tests to research subjects, the investigator in seeking informed consent should assure prospective subjects that their identity will be protected by secure coding of their samples (encryption) and by restricted access to the database, and explain to them this process. When it is clear that for medical or possibly research reasons the results of genetic tests will be reported to the subject or to the subject's physician, the subject should be informed that such disclosure will occur and that the samples to be tested will be clearly labelled. Investigators should not disclose results of diagnostic genetic tests to relatives of subjects without the subjects` consent. In places where immediate family relatives would usually expect to be informed of such results, the research protocol, as approved or cleared by the ethical review committee, should indicate the precautions in place to prevent such disclosure of results without the subjects` consent; such plans should be clearly explained during the process of obtaining informed consent.

Guideline 19: Right of injured subjects to treatment and compensation.

Investigators should ensure that research subjects who suffer injury as a result of their participation are entitled to free medical treatment for such injury and to such financial or other assistance as would compensate them equitably for any resultant impairment, disability or handicap. In the case of death as a result of their participation, their dependants are entitled to compensation. Subjects must not be asked to waive the right to compensation.

Commentary on Guideline 19

Guideline 19 is concerned with two distinct but closely related entitlements. The first is the uncontroversial entitlement to free medical treatment and compensation for accidental injury inflicted by procedures or interventions performed exclusively to accomplish the purposes of research (non-therapeutic procedures). The second is the entitlement of dependants to material compensation for death or disability occurring as a direct result of study participation. Implementing a compensation system for research-related injuries or death is likely to be complex, however. Equitable compensation and free medical treatment. Compensation is owed to research subjects who are disabled as a consequence of injury from procedures performed solely to accomplish the purposes of research. Compensation and free medical treatment are generally not owed to research subjects who suffer expected or foreseen adverse reactions to investigational therapeutic, diagnostic or preventive interventions when such reactions are not different in kind from those known to be associated with established interventions in standard medical practice. In the early stages of drug testing (Phase I and early Phase II), it is generally unreasonable to assume that an investigational drug holds out the prospect of direct benefit for the individual subject; accordingly, compensation is usually owed to individuals who become disabled as a result of serving as subjects in such studies. The ethical review committee should determine in advance: i) the injuries for which subjects will receive free treatment and, in case of impairment, disability or handicap resulting from such injuries, be compensated; and ii) the injuries for which they will not be compensated. Prospective subjects should be informed of the committee's decisions, as part of the process of informed consent. As an ethical review committee cannot make such advance determination in respect of unexpected or unforeseen adverse reactions, such reactions must be presumed compensable and should be reported to the committee for prompt review as they occur. Subjects must not be asked to waive their rights to compensation or required to show negligence or lack of a reasonable degree of skill on the part of the investigator in order to claim free medical treatment or compensation. The informed consent process or form should contain no words that would absolve an investigator from responsibility in the case of accidental injury, or that would imply that subjects would waive their right to seek compensation for impairment, disability or handicap. Prospective subjects should be informed that they will not need to take legal action to secure the free medical treatment or compensation for injury to which they may be entitled. They should also be told what medical service or organization or individual will provide the medical treatment and what organization will be responsible for providing compensation.

Obligation of the sponsor with regard to compensation. Before the research begins, the sponsor, whether a pharmaceutical company or other organization or institution, or a government (where government insurance is not precluded by law), should agree to provide compensation for any physical injury for which subjects are entitled to compensation, or come to an agreement with the investigator concerning the circumstances in which the investigator must rely on his or her own insurance coverage (for example, for negligence or failure of the investigator to follow the protocol, or where government insurance coverage is limited to negligence). In certain circumstances it may be advisable to follow both courses. Sponsors should seek adequate insurance against risks to cover compensation, independent of proof of fault.

Guideline 20: Strengthening capacity for ethical and scientific review and biomedical research

Many countries lack the capacity to assess or ensure the scientific quality or ethical acceptability of biomedical research proposed or carried out in their jurisdictions. In externally sponsored collaborative research, sponsors and investigators have an ethical obligation to ensure that biomedical research projects for which they are responsible in such countries contribute effectively to national or local capacity to design and conduct biomedical research, and to provide scientific and ethical review and monitoring of such research. Capacity-building may include, but is not limited to, the following activities:

– establishing and strengthening independent and competent ethical review processes/ committees
– strengthening research capacity
– developing technologies appropriate to health-care and biomedical research
– training of research and health-care staff
– educating the community from which research subjects will be drawn

Commentary on Guideline 20

External sponsors and investigators have an ethical obligation to contribute to a host country's sustainable capacity for independent scientific and ethical review and biomedical research. Before undertaking research in a host country with little or no such capacity, external sponsors and investigators should include in the research protocol a plan that specifies the contribution they will make. The amount of capacity building reasonably expected should be proportional to the magnitude of the research project. A brief epidemiological study involving only review of medical records, for example, would entail relatively little, if any, such development, whereas a considerable contribution is to be expected of an external sponsor of, for instance, a large-scale vaccine field-trial expected to last two or three years. The specific capacity-building objectives should be determined and achieved through dialogue and negotiation between external sponsors and host-country authorities. External sponsors would be expected to employ and, if necessary, train local individuals to function as investigators, research assistants or data managers, for example, and to provide, as necessary, reasonable amounts of financial, educational and other assistance for capacity-building. To avoid conflict of interest and safeguard the independence of review committees, financial assistance should not be provided directly to them; rather, funds should be made available to appropriate authorities in the host-country government or to the host research institution. (See also Guideline 10: Research in populations and communities with limited resources)

Guideline 21: Ethical obligation of external sponsors to provide health-care services

External sponsors are ethically obliged to ensure the availability of:

- health-care services that are essential to the safe conduct of the research;
- treatment for subjects who suffer injury as a consequence of research interventions; and,
- services that are a necessary part of the commitment of a sponsor to make a beneficial intervention or product developed as a result of the research reasonably available to the population or community concerned.

Commentary on Guideline 21

Obligations of external sponsors to provide health-care services will vary with the circumstances of particular studies and the needs of host countries. The sponsors' obligations in particular studies should be clarified before the research is begun. The research protocol should specify what health-care services will be made available, during and after the research, to the subjects themselves, to the community from which the subjects are drawn, or to the host country, and for how long. The details of these arrangements should be agreed by the sponsor, officials of the host country, other interested parties, and, when appropriate, the community from which subjects are to be drawn. The agreed arrangements should be specified in the consent process and document. Although sponsors are, in general, not obliged to provide health-care services beyond that which is necessary for the conduct of the research, it is morally praiseworthy to do so. Such services typically include treatment for diseases contracted in the course of the study. It might, for example, be agreed to treat cases of an infectious disease contracted during a trial of a vaccine designed to provide immunity to that disease, or to provide treatment of incidental conditions unrelated to the study. The obligation to ensure that subjects who suffer injury as a consequence of research interventions obtain medical treatment free of charge, and that compensation be provided for death or disability occurring as a consequence of such injury, is the subject of Guideline 19, on the scope and limits of such obligations. When prospective or actual subjects are found to have diseases unrelated to the research, or cannot be enrolled in a study because they do not meet the health criteria, investigators should, as appropriate, advise them to obtain, or refer them for, medical care. In general, also, in the course of a study, sponsors should disclose to the proper health authorities information of public health concern arising from the research. The obligation of the sponsor to make reasonably available for the benefit of the population or community concerned any intervention or product developed, or knowledge generate d, as a result of the research is considered in Guideline 10: Research in populations and communities with limited resources.

7. Directive 2001/20/EC of the European Parliament and of the Council L 121/34 Official Journal of the European Communities 1.5.2001 of 4 April 2001 relating to the implementation of good clinical practice in the conduct of clinical trials on medicinal products for human use

...

(2) The accepted basis for the conduct of clinical trials in humans is founded in the protection of human rights and the dignity of the human being with regard to the application of biology and medicine, as for instance reflected in the 1996 version of the Helsinki Declaration. The clinical trial subject's protection is safeguarded through risk assessment based on the results of toxicological experiments prior to any clinical trial, screening by ethics committees and Member States' competent authorities, and rules on the protection of personal data.

(3) Persons who are incapable of giving legal consent to clinical trials should be given special protection. It is incumbent on the Member States to lay down rules to this effect. Such persons may not be included in clinical trials if the same results can be obtained using persons capable of giving consent. Normally these persons should be included in clinical trials only when there are grounds for expecting that the administering of the medicinal product would be of direct benefit to the patient, thereby outweighing the risks. However, there is a need for clinical trials involving children to improve the treatment available to them. Children represent a vulnerable population with developmental, physiological and psychological differences from adults, which make age- and development- related research important for their benefit. Medicinal products, including vaccines, for children need to be tested scientifically before widespread use. This can only be achieved by ensuring that medicinal products which are likely to be of significant clinical value for children are fully studied. The clinical trials required for this purpose should be carried out under conditions affording the best possible protection for the subjects. Criteria for the protection of children in clinical trials therefore need to be laid down.

(4) In the case of other persons incapable of giving their consent, such as persons with dementia, psychiatric patients, etc., inclusion in clinical trials in such cases should be on an even more restrictive basis. Medicinal products for trial may be administered to all such individuals only when there are grounds for assuming that the direct benefit to the patient outweighs the risks. Moreover, in such cases the written consent of the patient's legal representative, given in co-operation with the treating doctor, is necessary before participation in any such clinical trial.

...

(6) In order to achieve optimum protection of health, obsolete or repetitive tests will not be carried out, whether within the Community or in third countries. The harmonization of technical requirements for the development erefore be pursued through the appropriate fora, in particular the International Conference on Harmonisation.

(7) For medicinal products falling within the scope of Part A of the Annex to Council Regulation (EEC) No 2309/93 of 22 July 1993 laying down Community procedures for the authorisation and supervision of medicinal products for human and veterinary use and establishing a European Agency for the Evaluation of Medicinal Products (1), which include products intended for gene therapy or cell therapy, prior scientific evaluation by the European Agency for the Evaluation of Medicinal Products (hereinafter referred to as the 'Agency'), assisted by the Committee for Proprietary Medicinal Products, is mandatory before the Commission grants marketing authorisation. In the course of this evaluation, the said Committee may request full details of the results of the clinical trials on which the application for marketing authorisation is based and, consequently, on the manner in which these trials were conducted and the same Committee may go so far as to require the applicant for such authorisation to conduct further clinical trials. Provision must therefore be made to allow the Agency to have full information on the conduct of any clinical trial for such medicinal products.

(9) Information on the content, commencement and termination of a clinical trial should be available to the Member States where the trial takes place and all the other Member States should have access to the same information. A European database bringing together this information should therefore be set up, with due regard for the rules of confidentiality.

(10) Clinical trials are a complex operation, generally lasting one or more years, usually involving numerous participants and several trial sites, often in different Member States. Member States' current practices diverge considerably on the rules on commencement and conduct of the clinical trials and the requirements for carrying them out vary widely. This therefore results in delays and complications detrimental to effective conduct of such trials in the Community. It is therefore necessary to simplify and harmonise the administrative provisions governing such trials by establishing a clear, transparent procedure and creating conditions conducive to effective coordination of such clinical trials in the Community by the authorities concerned.

(11) As a rule, authorisation should be implicit, i.e. if there has been a vote in favour by the Ethics Committee and the competent authority has not objected within a given period, it should be possible to begin the clinical trials. In exceptional cases raising especially complex problems, explicit written authorisation should, however, be required.

....

(16) The person participating in a trial must consent to the scrutiny of personal information during inspection by competent authorities and properly authorised persons, provided that such personal information is treated as strictly confidential and is not made publicly available.

....

Have adopted this Directive:

ARTICLE 1. SCOPE

1. This Directive establishes specific provisions regarding the conduct of clinical trials, including multi-centre trials, on human subjects involving medicinal products as defined in Article 1 of Directive 65/65/EEC, in particular relating to the implementation of good clinical practice. This Directive does not apply to non-interventional trials.

2. Good clinical practice is a set of internationally recognized ethical and scientific quality requirements which must be observed for designing, conducting, recording and reporting clinical trials that involve the participation of human subjects. Compliance with this good practice provides assurance that the rights, safety and well-being of trial subjects are protected, and that the results of the clinical trials are credible.

3. The principles of good clinical practice and detailed guidelines in line with those principles shall be adopted and, if necessary, revised to take account of technical and scientific progress in accordance with the procedure referred to in Article 21(2). These detailed guidelines shall be published by the Commission.

4. All clinical trials, including bioavailability and bioequivalence studies, shall be designed, conducted and reported in accordance with the principles of good clinical practice.

ARTICLE 2. DEFINITIONS

For the purposes of this Directive the following definitions shall apply:

(a) 'clinical trial': any investigation in human subjects intended to discover or verify the clinical, pharmacological and/or other pharmacodynamic effects of one or more investigational medicinal product(s), and/or to identify any adverse reactions to one or more investigational medicinal product(s) and/or to study absorption, distribution, metabolism and excretion of one or more investigational medicinal product(s) with the object of ascertaining its (their) safety and/or efficacy; This includes clinical trials carried out in either one site or multiple sites, whether in one or more than one Member State;
(b) 'multi-centre clinical trial': a clinical trial conducted according to a single protocol but at more than one site, and therefore by more than one investigator, in which the trial sites may be located in a single Member State, in a number of Member States and/or in Member States and third countries;
(c) 'non-interventional trial': a study where the medicinal product(s) is (are) prescribed in the usual manner inaccordance with the terms of the marketing authorisation. The assignment of the patient to a particular therapeutic strategy is not decided in advance by a trial protocol but falls within current practice and the prescription of the medicine is clearly separated from the decision to include the patient in the study. No additional diagnostic or monitoring

procedures shall be applied to the patients and epidemiological methods shall be used for the analysis of collected data;

(d) 'investigational medicinal product': a pharmaceutical form of an active substance or placebo being tested or used as a reference in a clinical trial, including products already with a marketing authorisation but used or assembled (formulated or packaged) in a way different from the authorized form, or when used for an unauthorised indication, or when used to gain further information about the authorized form;

(e) 'sponsor': an individual, company, institution or organization which takes responsibility for the initiation, management and/or financing of a clinical trial;

(f) 'investigator': a doctor or a person following a profession agreed in the Member State for investigations because of the scientific background and the experience in patient care it requires. The investigator is responsible for the conduct of a clinical trial at a trial site. If a trial is conducted by a team of individuals at a trial site, the investigator is the leader responsible for the team and may be called the principal investigator;

(g) 'investigator's brochure': a compilation of the clinical and non-clinical data on the investigational medicinal product or products which are relevant to the study of the product or products in human subjects;

(h) 'protocol': a document that describes the objective(s), design, methodology, statistical considerations and organization of a trial. The term protocol refers to the protocol, successive versions of the protocol and protocol amendments;

(i) 'subject': an individual who participates in a clinical trial as either a recipient of the investigational medicinal product

(j) 'informed consent': decision, which must be written, dated and signed, to take part in a clinical trial, taken freely after being duly informed of its nature, significance, implications and risks and appropriately documented, by any person capable of giving consent or, where the person is not capable of giving consent, by his or her legal representative; if the person concerned is unable to write, oral consent in the presence of at least one witness may be given in exceptional cases, as provided for in national legislation.

(k) 'ethics committee': an independent body in a Member State, consisting of healthcare professionals and nonmedical members, whose responsibility it is to protect the rights, safety and wellbeing of human subjects involved in a trial and to provide public assurance of that protection, by, among other things, expressing an opinion on the trial protocol, the suitability of the investigators and the adequacy of facilities, and on the methods and documents to be used to inform trial subjects and obtain their informed consent;

(l) 'inspection': the act by a competent authority of conducting an official review of documents, facilities, records, quality assurance arrangements, and any other resources that are deemed by the competent authority to be related to the clinical trial and that may be located at the site of the trial, at the sponsor's and/or contract research organisation's facilities, or at other establishments which the competent authority sees fit to inspect;

(m) 'adverse event': any untoward medical occurrence in a patient or clinical trial subject administered a medicinal product and which does not necessarily have a causalrelationship with this treatment;

(n) 'adverse reaction': all untoward and unintended responses to an investigational medicinal product related to any dose administered;

(o) 'serious adverse event or serious adverse reaction': any untoward medical occurrence or effect that at any dose results in death, is life-threatening, requires hospitalization or prolongation of existing hospitalisation, results in persistent or significant disability or incapacity, or is a congenital anomaly or birth defect;

(p) 'unexpected adverse reaction': an adverse reaction, the nature or severity of which is not consistent with the applicable product information (e.g. investigator's brochure for an unauthorised investigational product or summary of product characteristics for an authorized product).

ARTICLE 3. PROTECTION OF CLINICAL TRIAL SUBJECTS

1. This Directive shall apply without prejudice to the national provisions on the protection of clinical trial subjects if they are more comprehensive than the provisions of this Directive and consistent with the procedures and time-scales specified therein. Member States shall, insofar as they have not already done so, adopt detailed rules to protect from abuse individuals who are incapable of giving their informed consent.

2. A clinical trial may be undertaken only if, in particular:

(a) the foreseeable risks and inconveniences have been weighed against the anticipated benefit for the individual trial subject and other present and future patients. A clinical trial may be initiated only if the Ethics Committee and/or the competent authority comes to the conclusion that the anticipated therapeutic and public health benefits justify the risks and may be continued only if compliance with this requirement is permanently monitored;

(b) the trial subject or, when the person is not able to give informed consent, his legal representative has had the opportunity, in a prior interview with the investigator or a member of the investigating team, to understand the objectives, risks and inconveniences of the trial, and the conditions under which it is to be conducted and has also been informed of his right to withdraw from the trial at any time;

(c) the rights of the subject to physical and mental integrity, to privacy and to the protection of the data concerning him in accordance with Directive 95/46/EC are safeguarded;

(d) the trial subject or, when the person is not able to give informed consent, his legal representative has given his written consent after being informed of the nature, significance, implications and risks of the clinical trial; if the individual is unable to write, oral consent in the presence of at least one witness may be given in exceptional cases, as provided for in national legislation;

(e) the subject may without any resulting detriment withdraw from the clinical trial at any time by revoking his informed consent;

(f) provision has been made for insurance or indemnity to cover the liability of the investigator and sponsor.

3. The medical care given to, and medical decisions made on behalf of, subjects shall be the responsibility of an appropriately qualified doctor or, where appropriate, of a qualified dentist.

4. The subject shall be provided with a contact point where he may obtain further information.

ARTICLE 4. CLINICAL TRIALS ON MINORS

In addition to any other relevant restriction, a clinical trial on minors may be undertaken only if:

(a) the informed consent of the parents or legal representative has been obtained; consent must represent the minor's presumed will and may be revoked at any time, without detriment to the minor;
(b) the minor has received information according to its capacity of understanding, from staff with experience with minors, regarding the trial, the risks and the benefits;
(c) the explicit wish of a minor who is capable of forming an opinion and assessing this information to refuse participation or to be withdrawn from the clinical trial at any time is considered by the investigator or where appropriate the principal investigator;
(d) no incentives or financial inducements are given except compensation;
(e) some direct benefit for the group of patients is obtained from the clinical trial and only where such research is essential to validate data obtained in clinical trials on persons able to give informed consent or by other research methods; additionally, such research should either relate directly to a clinical condition from which the minor concerned suffers or be of such a nature that it can only be carried out on minors;
(f) the corresponding scientific guidelines of the Agency have been followed;
(g) clinical trials have been designed to minimise pain, discomfort, fear and any other foreseeable risk in relation to the disease and developmental stage; both the risk threshold and the degree of distress have to be specially defined and constantly monitored;
(h) the Ethics Committee, with paediatric expertise or after taking advice in clinical, ethical and psychosocial problems in the field of paediatrics, has endorsed the protocol; and the interests of the patient always prevail over those of science and society.

ARTICLE 5. CLINICAL TRIALS ON INCAPACITATED ADULTS NOT ABLE TO GIVE INFORMED LEGAL CONSENT

In the case of other persons incapable of giving informed legal consent, all relevant requirements listed for persons capable of giving such consent shall apply. In addition to these requirements, inclusion in clinical trials of incapacitated adults who have not given or not refused informed consent before the onset of their incapacity shall be allowed only if:

(a) the informed consent of the legal representative has been obtained; consent must represent the subject's presumed will and may be revoked at any time, without detriment to the subject;
(b) the person not able to give informed legal consent has received information according to his/her capacity of understanding regarding the trial, the risks and the benefits;

(c) the explicit wish of a subject who is capable of forming an opinion and assessing this information to refuse participation in, or to be withdrawn from, the clinical trial at any time is considered by the investigator or where appropriate the principal investigator;

(d) no incentives or financial inducements are given except compensation;

(e) such research is essential to validate data obtained in clinical trials on persons able to give informed consent or by other research methods and relates directly to a life-threatening or debilitating clinical condition from which the incapacitated adult concerned suffers;

(f) clinical trials have been designed to minimise pain, discomfort, fear and any other foreseeable risk in relation to the disease and developmental stage; both the risk threshold and the degree of distress shall be specially defined and constantly monitored;

(g) the Ethics Committee, with expertise in the relevant disease and the patient population concerned or after taking advice in clinical, ethical and psychosocial questions in the field of the relevant disease and patient population concerned, has endorsed the protocol;

(h) the interests of the patient always prevail over those of science and society; and

(i) there are grounds for expecting that administering the medicinal product to be tested will produce a benefit to the patient outweighing the risks or produce no risk at all.

ARTICLE 6 ETHICS COMMITTEE

1. For the purposes of implementation of the clinical trials, Member States shall take the measures necessary for establishment and operation of Ethics Committees.

2. The Ethics Committee shall give its opinion, before a clinical trial commences, on any issue requested.

3. In preparing its opinion, the Ethics Committee shall consider, in particular:

(a) the relevance of the clinical trial and the trial design;

(b) whether the evaluation of the anticipated benefits and risks as required under Article 3(2) (a) is satisfactory and whether the conclusions are justified;

(c) the protocol;

(d) the suitability of the investigator and supporting staff;

(e) the investigator's brochure;

(f) the quality of the facilities;

(g) the adequacy and completeness of the written information to be given and the procedure to be followed for the purpose of obtaining informed consent and the justification for the research on persons incapable of giving informed consent as regards the specific restrictions laid down in Article 3;

(h) provision for indemnity or compensation in the event of injury or death attributable to a clinical trial;

(i) any insurance or indemnity to cover the liability of the investigator and sponsor;

(j) the amounts and, where appropriate, the arrangements for rewarding or compensating investigators and trial subjects and the relevant aspects of any agreement between the sponsor and the site;

(k) the arrangements for the recruitment of subjects. 4. Notwithstanding the provisions of this Article, a Member State may decide that the competent authority it has designated for the purpose of Article 9 shall be responsible for the consideration of, and the giving of an opinion on, the matters referred to in paragraph 3(h), (i) and (j) of this Article. When a Member State avails itself of this provision, it shall notify the Commission, the other Member States and the Agency.

5. The Ethics Committee shall have a maximum of 60 days from the date of receipt of a valid application to give its reasoned opinion to the applicant and the competent authority in the Member State concerned.

6. Within the period of examination of the application for an opinion, the Ethics Committee may send a single request for information supplementary to that already supplied by the applicant. The period laid down in paragraph 5 shall be suspended until receipt of the supplementary information.

7. No extension to the 60-day period referred to in paragraph 5 shall be permissible except in the case of trials involving medicinal products for gene therapy or somatic cell therapy or medicinal products containing genetically modified organisms. In this case, an extension of a maximum of 30 days shall be permitted. For these products, this 90-day period may be extended by a further 90 days in the event of consultation of a group or a committee in accordance with the regulations and procedures of the Member States concerned. In the case of xenogenic cell therapy, there shall be no time limit to the authorisation period.

ARTICLE 7. SINGLE OPINION

For multi-centre clinical trials limited to the territory of a single Member State, Member States shall establish a procedure providing, notwithstanding the number of Ethics Committees, for the adoption of a single opinion for that Member State. In the case of multi-centre clinical trials carried out in more than one Member State simultaneously, a single opinion shall be given for each Member State concerned by the clinical trial.

ARTICLE 8. DETAILED GUIDANCE

The Commission, in consultation with Member States and interested parties, shall draw up and publish detailed guidance on the application format and documentation to be submitted in an application for an ethics committee opinion, in particular regarding the information that is given to subjects, and on the appropriate safeguards for the protection of personal data.

ARTICLE 9. COMMENCEMENT OF A CLINICAL TRIAL

1. Member States shall take the measures necessary to ensure that the procedure described in this Article is followed for commencement of a clinical trial. The sponsor may not start a clinical trial until the Ethics Committee has issued a favourable opinion and inasmuch as

the competent authority of the Member State concerned has not informed the sponsor of any grounds for non-acceptance. The procedures to reach these decisions can be run in parallel or not, depending on the sponsor.

2. Before commencing any clinical trial, the sponsor shall be required to submit a valid request for authorisation to the competent authority of the Member State in which the sponsor plans to conduct the clinical trial.

3. If the competent authority of the Member State notifies the sponsor of grounds for non-acceptance, the sponsor may, on one occasion only, amend the content of the request referred to in paragraph 2 in order to take due account of the grounds given. If the sponsor fails to amend the request accordingly, the request shall be considered rejected and the clinical trial may not commence.

4. Consideration of a valid request for authorisation by the competent authority as stated in paragraph 2 shall be carried out as rapidly as possible and may not exceed 60 days. The Member States may lay down a shorter period than 60 days within their area of responsibility if that is in compliance with current practice. The competent authority can nevertheless notify the sponsor before the end of this period that it has no grounds for non-acceptance. No further extensions to the period referred to in the first subparagraph shall be permissible except in the case of trials involving the medicinal products listed in paragraph 6, for which an extension of a maximum of 30 days shall be permitted. For these products, this 90-day period may be extended by a further 90 days in the event of consultation of a group or a committee in accordance with the regulations and procedures of the Member States concerned. In the case of xenogenic cell therapy there shall be no time limit to the authorisation period.

5. Without prejudice to paragraph 6, written authorization may be required before the commencement of clinical trials for such trials on medicinal products which do not have a marketing authorisation within the meaning of Directive 65/ 65/EEC and are referred to in Part A of the Annex to Regulation (EEC) No 2309/93, and other medicinal products with special characteristics, such as medicinal products the active ingredient or active ingredients of which is or are a biological product or biological products of human or animal origin, or contains biological components of human or animal origin, or the manufacturing of which requires such components.

6. Written authorisation shall be required before commencing clinical trials involving medicinal products for gene therapy, somatic cell therapy including xenogenic cell therapy and all medicinal products containing genetically modified organisms. No gene therapy trials may be carried out which result in modifications to the subject's germ line genetic identity.

7. This authorisation shall be issued without prejudice to the application of Council Directives 90/219/EEC of 23 April 1990 on the contained use of genetically modified micro-organisms

8. In consultation with Member States, the Commission shall draw up and publish detailed guidance on:

(a) the format and contents of the request referred to in paragraph 2 as well as the documentation to be submitted to support that request, on the quality and manufacture of the investigational medicinal product, any toxicological and pharmacological tests, the protocol and clinical information on the investigational medicinal product including the investigator's brochure;
(b) the presentation and content of the proposed amendment referred to in point (a) of Article 10 on substantial amendments made to the protocol;
(c) the declaration of the end of the clinical trial.

ARTICLE 10. CONDUCT OF A CLINICAL TRIAL

Amendments may be made to the conduct of a clinical trial following the procedure described hereinafter:

(a) after the commencement of the clinical trial, the sponsor may make amendments to the protocol. If those amendments are substantial and are likely to have an impact on the safety of the trial subjects or to change the interpretation of the scientific documents in support of the conduct of the trial, or if they are otherwise significant, the sponsor shall notify the competent authorities of the Member State or Member States concerned of the reasons for, and content of, these amendments and shall inform the ethics committee or committees concerned in accordance with Articles 6 and 9. On the basis of the details referred to in Article 6(3) and in accordance with Article 7, the Ethics Committee shall give an opinion within a maximum of 35 days of the date of receipt of the proposed amendment in good and due form. If this opinion is unfavourable, the sponsor may not implement the amendment to the protocol. If the opinion of the Ethics Committee is favourable and the competent authorities of the Member States have raised no grounds for non-acceptance of the abovementioned substantial amendments, the sponsor shall proceed to conduct the clinical trial following the amended protocol. Should this not be the case, the sponsor shall either take account of the grounds for non-acceptance and adapt the proposed amendment to the protocol accordingly or withdraw the proposed amendment;
(b) without prejudice to point (a), in the light of the circumstances, notably the occurrence of any new event relating to the conduct of the trial or the development of the investigational medicinal product where that new event is likely to affect the safety of the subjects, the sponsor and the investigator shall take appropriate urgent safety measures to protect the subjects against any immediate hazard. The sponsor shall forthwith inform the competent authorities of those new events and the measures taken and shall ensure that the Ethics Committee is notified at the same time;
(c) within 90 days of the end of a clinical trial the sponsor shall notify the competent authorities of the Member State or Member States concerned and the Ethics Committee that the clinical trial has ended. If the trial has to be terminated early, this period shall be reduced to 15 days and the reasons clearly explained.

ARTICLE 11. EXCHANGE OF INFORMATION

1. Member States in whose territory the clinical trial takes place shall enter in a European database, accessible only to the competent authorities of the Member States, the Agency and the Commission:

(a) extracts from the request for authorisation referred to in Article 9(2);
(b) any amendments made to the request, as provided for in Article 9(3);
(c) any amendments made to the protocol, as provided for in point a of Article 10;
(d) the favourable opinion of the Ethics Committee;
(e) the declaration of the end of the clinical trial; and (f) a reference to the inspections carried out on conformity with good clinical practice.

2. At the substantiated request of any Member State, the Agency or the Commission, the competent authority to which the request for authorisation was submitted shall supply all further information concerning the clinical trial in question other than the data already in the European database.

3. In consultation with the Member States, the Commission shall draw up and publish detailed guidance on the relevant data to be included in this European database, which it operates with the assistance of the Agency, as well as the methods for electronic communication of the data. The detailed guidance thus drawn up shall ensure that the confidentiality of the data is strictly observed.

ARTICLE 12. SUSPENSION OF THE TRIAL OR INFRINGEMENTS

1. Where a Member State has objective grounds for considering that the conditions in the request for authorization referred to in Article 9(2) are no longer met or has information raising doubts about the safety or scientific validity of the clinical trial, it may suspend or prohibit the clinical trial and shall notify the sponsor thereof. Before the Member State reaches its decision it shall, except where there is imminent risk, ask the sponsor and/or the investigator for their opinion, to be delivered within one week. In this case, the competent authority concerned shall forthwith inform the other competent authorities, the Ethics Committee concerned, the Agency and the Commission of its decision to suspend or prohibit the trial and of the reasons for the decision.

2. Where a competent authority has objective grounds for considering that the sponsor or the investigator or any other person involved in the conduct of the trial no longer meets the obligations laid down, it shall forthwith inform him thereof, indicating the course of action which he must take to remedy this state of affairs. The competent authority concerned shall forthwith inform the Ethics Committee, the other competent authorities and the Commission of this course of action.

ARTICLE 13. MANUFACTURE AND IMPORT OF INVESTIGATIONAL MEDICINAL PRODUCTS

1. Member States shall take all appropriate measures to ensure that the manufacture or impor-tation of investigational medicinal products is subject to the holding of authorisation. In order to obtain the authorisation, the applicant and, subsequently, the holder of the authorisation, shall meet at least the requirements defined in accordance with the procedure referred to in Article 21(2).

2. Member States shall take all appropriate measures to ensure that the holder of the authorisa-tion referred to in paragraph 1 has permanently and continuously at his disposal the services of at least one qualified person who, in accordance with the conditions laid down in Article 23 of the second Council Directive 75/319/EEC of 20 May 1975 on the approximation of provi-sions laid down by law, regulation or administrative action relating to proprietary medicinal products (1), is responsible in particular for carrying out the duties specified in paragraph 3 of this Article.

3. Member States shall take all appropriate measures to ensure that the qualified person re-ferred to in Article 21 of Directive 75/319/EEC, without prejudice to his relationship with the manufacturer or importer, is responsible, in the context of the procedures referred to in Article 25 of the said Directive, for ensuring:

(a) in the case of investigational medicinal products manufactured in the Member State con-cerned, that each batch of medicinal products has been manufactured and checked in compli-ance with the requirements of Commission Directive 91/356/EEC of 13 June 1991 laying down the principles and guidelines of good manufacturing practice for medicinal products for human use (2), the product specification file and the information notified pursuant to Article 9(2) of this Directive;
(b) in the case of investigational medicinal products manufactured in a third country, that each production batch has been manufactured and checked in accordance with standards of good manufacturing practice at least equivalent to those laid down in Commission Directive 91/356/EEC, in accordance with the product specification file, and that each production batch has been checked in accordance with the information notified pursuant to Article 9(2) of this Directive;
(c) in the case of an investigational medicinal product which is a comparator product from a third country, and which has a marketing authorisation, where the documentation certifying that each production batch has been manufactured in conditions at least equivalent to the standards of good manufacturing practice referred to above cannot be obtained, that each production batch has undergone all relevant analyses, tests or checks necessary to confirm its quality in accordance with the information notified pursuant to Article 9(2) of this Directive. Detailed guidance on the elements to be taken into account when evaluating products with the object of releasing batches within the Community shall be drawn up pursuant to the good manufacturing practice guidelines, and in particular Annex 13 to the said guidelines. Such guidelines will be adopted in accordance with the procedure referred to in Article 21(2) of this Directive and published in accordance with Article 19a of Directive 75/319/EEC. Insofar as the provisions

laid down in (a), (b) or (c) are complied with, investigational medicinal products shall not have to undergo any further checks if they are imported into another Member State together with batch release certification signed by the qualified person.

4. In all cases, the qualified person must certify in a register or equivalent document that each production batch satisfies the provisions of this Article. The said register or equivalent document shall be kept up to date as operations are carried out and shall remain at the disposal of the agents of the competent authority for the period specified in the provisions of the Member States concerned. This period shall in any event be not less than five years.

5. Any person engaging in activities as the qualified person referred to in Article 21 of Directive 75/319/EEC as regards investigational medicinal products at the time when this Directive is applied in the Member State where that person is, but without complying with the conditions laid down in Articles 23 and 24 of that Directive, shall be authorised to continue those activities in the Member State concerned.

Article 14. Labelling

The particulars to appear in at least the official language(s) of the Member State on the outer packaging of investigational medicinal products or, where there is no outer packaging, on the immediate packaging, shall be published by the Commission in the good manufacturing practice guidelines on investigational medicinal products adopted in accordance with Article 19a of Directive 75/319/EEC. In addition, these guidelines shall lay down adapted provisions relating to labelling for investigational medicinal products intended for clinical trials with the following characteristics:

- the planning of the trial does not require particular manufacturing or packaging processes;
- the trial is conducted with medicinal products with, in the Member States concerned by the study, a marketing authorization within the meaning of Directive 65/65/EEC, manufactured or imported in accordance with the provisions of Directive 75/319/EEC;
- the patients participating in the trial have the same characteristics as those covered by the indication specified in the abovementioned authorisation.

Article 15. Verification of compliance of investigational medicinal products with good clinical and manufacturing practice

1. To verify compliance with the provisions on good clinical and manufacturing practice, Member States shall appoint inspectors to inspect the sites concerned by any clinical trial conducted, particularly the trial site or sites, the manufacturing site of the investigational medicinal product, any laboratory used for analyses in the clinical trial and/or the sponsor's premises. The inspections shall be conducted by the competent authority of the Member State concerned, which shall inform the Agency; they shall be carried out on behalf of the Community and the results shall be recognised by all the other Member States. These inspections

shall be coordinated by the Agency, within the framework of its powers as provided for in Regulation (EEC) No 2309/93. A Member State may request assistance from another Member State in this matter.

2. Following inspection, an inspection report shall be prepared. It must be made available to the sponsor while safeguarding confidential aspects. It may be made available to the other Member States, to the Ethics Committee and to the Agency, at their reasoned request.

3. At the request of the Agency, within the framework of its powers as provided for in Regulation (EEC) No 2309/93, or of one of the Member States concerned, and following consultation with the Member States concerned, the Commission may request a new inspection should verification of compliance with this Directive reveal differences between Member States.

4. Subject to any arrangements which may have been concluded between the Community and third countries, the Commission, upon receipt of a reasoned request from a Member State or on its own initiative, or a Member State may propose that the trial site and/or the sponsor's premises and/or the manufacturer established in a third country undergo an inspection. The inspection shall be carried out by duly qualified Community inspectors.

5. The detailed guidelines on the documentation relating to the clinical trial, which shall constitute the master file on the trial, archiving, qualifications of inspectors and inspection procedures to verify compliance of the clinical trial in question with this Directive shall be adopted and revised in accordance with the procedure referred to in Article 21(2).

ARTICLE 16. NOTIFICATION OF ADVERSE EVENTS

1. The investigator shall report all serious adverse events immediately to the sponsor except for those that the protocol or investigator's brochure identifies as not requiring immediate reporting. The immediate report shall be followed by detailed, written reports. The immediate and follow-up reports shall identify subjects by unique code numbers assigned to the latter.

2. Adverse events and/or laboratory abnormalities identified in the protocol as critical to safety evaluations shall be reported to the sponsor according to the reporting requirements and within the time periods specified in the protocol.

3. For reported deaths of a subject, the investigator shall supply the sponsor and the Ethics Committee with any additional information requested.

4. The sponsor shall keep detailed records of all adverse events which are reported to him by the investigator or investigators. These records shall be submitted to the Member States in whose territory the clinical trial is being conducted, if they so request.

Article 17. Notification of serious adverse reactions

1. (a) The sponsor shall ensure that all relevant information about suspected serious unexpected adverse reactions that are fatal or life-threatening is recorded and reported as soon as possible to the competent authorities in all the Member States concerned, and to the Ethics Committee, and in any case no later than seven days after knowledge by the sponsor of such a case, and that relevant follow-up information is subsequently communicated within an additional eight days.

(b) All other suspected serious unexpected adverse reactions shall be reported to the competent authorities concerned and to the Ethics Committee concerned as soon as possible but within a maximum of fifteen days of first knowledge by the sponsor.

(c) Each Member State shall ensure that all suspected unexpected serious adverse reactions to an investigational medicinal product which are brought to its attention are recorded.

(d) The sponsor shall also inform all investigators.

2. Once a year throughout the clinical trial, the sponsor shall provide the Member States in whose territory the clinical trial is being conducted and the Ethics Committee with a listing of all suspected serious adverse reactions which have occurred over this period and a report of the subjects' safety.

3. (a) Each Member State shall see to it that all suspected unexpected serious adverse reactions to an investigational medicinal product which are brought to its attention are immediately entered in a European database to which, in accordance with Article 11(1), only the competent authorities of the Member States, the Agency and the Commission shall have access.

(b) The Agency shall make the information notified by the sponsor available to the competent authorities of the Member States.

Article 19. General provisions

This Directive is without prejudice to the civil and criminal liability of the sponsor or the investigator. To this end, the sponsor or a legal representative of the sponsor must be established in the Community. Unless Member States have established precise conditions for exceptional circumstances, investigational medicinal products and, as the case may be, the devices used for their administration shall be made available free of charge by the sponsor. The Member States shall inform the Commission of such conditions.

8. World Medical Association Declaration of Helsinki

Ethical Principles for Medical Research Involving Human Subjects Adopted by the 18th WMA General Assembly, Helsinki, Finland, June 1964, and amended by the: 29th WMA General Assembly, Tokyo, Japan, October 1975 35th WMA General Assembly, Venice, Italy, October 1983 41st WMA General Assembly, Hong Kong, September 1989 48th WMA General Assembly, Somerset West, Republic of South Africa, October 1996 52nd WMA General Assembly, Edinburgh, Scotland, October 2000 53th WMA General Assembly, Washington 2002 (Note of Clarification on paragraph 29 added) 55th WMA General Assembly, Tokyo 2004 (Note of Clarification on Paragraph 30 added) 59th WMA General Assembly, Seoul, October 2008

A. Introduction

1. The World Medical Association (WMA) has developed the Declaration of Helsinki as a statement of ethical principles for medical research involving human subjects, including research on identifiable human material and data. The Declaration is intended to be read as a whole and each of its constituent paragraphs should not be applied without consideration of all other relevant paragraphs.

2. Although the Declaration is addressed primarily to physicians, the WMA encourages other participants in medical research involving human subjects to adopt these principles.

3. It is the duty of the physician to promote and safeguard the health of patients, including those who are involved in medical research. The physician's knowledge and conscience are dedicated to the fulfilment of this duty.

4. The Declaration of Geneva of the WMA binds the physician with the words, "The health of my patient will be my first consideration," and the International Code of Medical Ethics declares that, "A physician shall act in the patient's best interest when providing medical care."

5. Medical progress is based on research that ultimately must include studies involving human subjects. Populations that are underrepresented in medical research should be provided appropriate access to participation in research.

6. In medical research involving human subjects, the well-being of the individual research subject must take precedence over all other interests.

7. The primary purpose of medical research involving human subjects is to understand the causes, development and effects of diseases and improve preventive, diagnostic and therapeutic interventions (methods, procedures and treatments). Even the best current interventions must be evaluated continually through research for their safety, effectiveness, efficiency, accessibility and quality.

8. In medical practice and in medical research, most interventions involve risks and burdens.

9. Medical research is subject to ethical standards that promote respect for all human subjects and protect their health and rights. Some research populations are particularly vulnerable and need special protection. These include those who cannot give or refuse consent for themselves and those who may be vulnerable to coercion or undue influence.

10. Physicians should consider the ethical, legal and regulatory norms and standards for research involving human subjects in their own countries as well as applicable international norms and standards. No national or international ethical, legal or regulatory requirement should reduce or eliminate any of the protections for research subjects set forth in this Declaration.

B. Principles for all Medical Research

11. It is the duty of physicians who participate in medical research to protect the life, health, dignity, integrity, right to self-determination, privacy, and confidentiality of personal information of research subjects.

12. Medical research involving human subjects must conform to generally accepted scientific principles, be based on a thorough knowledge of the scientific literature, other relevant sources of information, and adequate laboratory and, as appropriate, animal experimentation. The welfare of animals used for research must be respected.

13. Appropriate caution must be exercised in the conduct of medical research that may harm the environment.

14. The design and performance of each research study involving human subjects must be clearly described in a research protocol. The protocol should contain a statement of the ethical considerations involved and should indicate how the principles in this Declaration have been addressed. The protocol should include information regarding funding, sponsors, institutional affiliations, other potential conflicts of interest, incentives for subjects and provisions for treating and/or compensating subjects who are harmed as a consequence of participation in the research study. The protocol should describe arrangements for post-study access by study subjects to interventions identified as beneficial in the study or access to other appropriate care or benefits.

15. The research protocol must be submitted for consideration, comment, guidance and approval to a research ethics committee before the study begins. This committee must be independent of the researcher, the sponsor and any other undue influence. It must take into consideration the laws and regulations of the country or countries in which the research is to be performed as well as applicable international norms and standards but these must not be allowed to reduce or eliminate any of the protections for research subjects set forth in this Declaration. The committee must have the right to monitor ongoing studies. The researcher must provide

monitoring information to the committee, especially information about any serious adverse events. No change to the protocol may be made without consideration and approval by the committee.

16. Medical research involving human subjects must be conducted only by individuals with the appropriate scientific training and qualifications. Research on patients or healthy volunteers requires the supervision of a competent and appropriately qualified physician or other health care professional. The responsibility for the protection of research subjects must always rest with the physician or other health care professional and never the research subjects, even though they have given consent.

17. Medical research involving a disadvantaged or vulnerable population or community is only justified if the research is responsive to the health needs and priorities of this population or community and if there is a reasonable likelihood that this population or community stands to benefit from the results of the research.

18. Every medical research study involving human subjects must be preceded by careful assessment of predictable risks and burdens to the individuals and communities involved in the research in comparison with foreseeable benefits to them and to other individuals or communities affected by the condition under investigation.

19. Every clinical trial must be registered in a publicly accessible database before recruitment of the first subject.

20. Physicians may not participate in a research study involving human subjects unless they are confident that the risks involved have been adequately assessed and can be satisfactorily managed. Physicians must immediately stop a study when the risks are found to outweigh the potential benefits or when there is conclusive proof of positive and beneficial results.

21. Medical research involving human subjects may only be conducted if the importance of the objective outweighs the inherent risks and burdens to the research subjects.

22. Participation by competent individuals as subjects in medical research must be voluntary. Although it may be appropriate to consult family members or community leaders, no competent individual may be enrolled in a research study unless he or she freely agrees.

23. Every precaution must be taken to protect the privacy of research subjects and the confidentiality of their personal information and to minimize the impact of the study on their physical, mental and social integrity.

24. In medical research involving competent human subjects, each potential subject must be adequately informed of the aims, methods, sources of funding, any possible conflicts of interest, institutional affiliations of the researcher, the anticipated benefits and potential risks of the study and the discomfort it may entail, and any other relevant aspects of the study. The potential

subject must be informed of the right to refuse to participate in the study or to withdraw consent to participate at any time without reprisal. Special attention should be given to the specific information needs of individual potential subjects as well as to the methods used to deliver the information. After ensuring that the potential subject has understood the information, the physician or another appropriately qualified individual must then seek the potential subject's freely-given informed consent, preferably in writing. If the consent cannot be expressed in writing, the non-written consent must be formally documented and witnessed.

25. For medical research using identifiable human material or data, physicians must normally seek consent for the collection, analysis, storage and/or reuse. There may be situations where consent would be impossible or impractical to obtain for such research or would pose a threat to the validity of the research. In such situations the research may be done only after consideration and approval of a research ethics committee.

26. When seeking informed consent for participation in a research study the physician should be particularly cautious if the potential subject is in a dependent relationship with the physician or may consent under duress. In such situations the informed consent should be sought by an appropriately qualified individual who is completely independent of this relationship.

27. For a potential research subject who is incompetent, the physician must seek informed consent from the legally authorized representative. These individuals must not be included in a research study that has no likelihood of benefit for them unless it is intended to promote the health of the population represented by the potential subject, the research cannot instead be performed with competent persons, and the research entails only minimal risk and minimal burden.

28. When a potential research subject who is deemed incompetent is able to give assent to decisions about participation in research, the physician must seek that assent in addition to the consent of the legally authorized representative. The potential subject's dissent should be respected.

29. Research involving subjects who are physically or mentally incapable of giving consent, for example, unconscious patients, may be done only if the physical or mental condition that prevents giving informed consent is a necessary characteristic of the research population. In such circumstances the physician should seek informed consent from the legally authorized representative. If no such representative is available and if the research cannot be delayed, the study may proceed without informed consent provided that the specific reasons for involving subjects with a condition that renders them unable to give informed consent have been stated in the research protocol and the study has been approved by a research ethics committee. Consent to remain in the research should be obtained as soon as possible from the subject or a legally authorized representative.

30. Authors, editors and publishers all have ethical obligations with regard to the publication of the results of research. Authors have a duty to make publicly available the results of their

research on human subjects and are accountable for the completeness and accuracy of their reports. They should adhere to accepted guidelines for ethical reporting. Negative and inconclusive as well as positive results should be published or otherwise made publicly available. Sources of funding, institutional affiliations and conflicts of interest should be declared in the publication. Reports of research not in accordance with the principles of this Declaration should not be accepted for publication.

C. Additional Principles for Medical Research Combined with Medical Care

31. The physician may combine medical research with medical care only to the extent that the research is justified by its potential preventive, diagnostic or therapeutic value and if the physician has good reason to believe that participation in the research study will not adversely affect the health of the patients who serve as research subjects.

32. The benefits, risks, burdens and effectiveness of a new intervention must be tested against those of the best current proven intervention, except in the following circumstances:

- The use of placebo, or no treatment, is acceptable in studies where no current proven intervention exists; or
- Where for compelling and scientifically sound methodological reasons the use of placebo is necessary to determine the efficacy or safety of an intervention and the patients who receive placebo or no treatment will not be subject to any risk of serious or irreversible harm. Extreme care must be taken to avoid abuse of this option.

33. At the conclusion of the study, patients entered into the study are entitled to be informed about the outcome of the study and to share any benefits that result from it, or example, access to interventions identified as beneficial in the study or to other appropriate care or benefits.

34. The physician must fully inform the patient which aspects of the care are related to the research. The refusal of a patient to participate in a study or the patient's decision to withdraw from the study must never interfere with the patient-physician relationship.

35. In the treatment of a patient, where proven interventions do not exist or have been ineffective, the physician, after seeking expert advice, with informed consent from the patient or a legally authorized representative, may use an unproven intervention if in the physician's judgement it offers hope of saving life, re-establishing health or alleviating suffering. Where possible, this intervention should be made the object of research, designed to evaluate its safety and efficacy. In all cases, new information should be recorded and, where appropriate, made publicly available.

Organ Transplantation

PART IV

1. Additional Protocol to the Convention on Human Rights and Biomedicine, on Transplantation of Organs and Tissues of Human Origin, ETS No. 186

Preamble

The member States of the Council of Europe, the other States and the European Community signatories to this Additional Protocol to the Convention for the Protection of Human Rights and Dignity of the Human Being with regard to the Application of Biology and Medicine (hereinafter referred to as "Convention on Human Rights and Biomedicine"), Considering that the aim of the Council of Europe is the achievement of greater unity between its members and that one of the methods by which this aim is pursued is the maintenance and further realisation of human rights and fundamental freedoms; Considering that the aim of the Convention on Human Rights and Biomedicine, as defined in Article 1, is to protect the dignity and identity of all human beings and guarantee everyone, without discrimination, respect for their integrity and other rights and fundamental freedoms with regard to the application of biology and medicine; Considering that progress in medical science, in particular in the field of organ and tissue transplantation, contributes to saving lives or greatly improving their quality; Considering that transplantation of organs and tissues is an established part of the health services offered to the population; Considering that, in view of the shortage of organs and tissues, appropriate action should be taken to increase organ and tissue donation, in particular by informing the public of the importance of organ and tissue transplantation and by promoting European co-operation in this field; Considering moreover the ethical, psychological and socio-cultural problems inherent in the transplantation of organs and tissues; Considering that the misuse of organ and tissue transplantation may lead to acts endangering human life, well being or dignity; Considering that organ and tissue transplantation should take place under conditions protecting the rights and freedoms of donors, potential donors and recipients of organs and tissues and that institutions must be instrumental in ensuring such conditions; Recognising that, in facilitating the transplantation of organs and tissues in the interest of patients in Europe, there is a need to protect individual rights and freedoms and to prevent the commercialisation of parts of the human body involved in organ and tissue procurement, exchange and allocation activities; Taking into account previous work of the Committee of Ministers and the Parliamentary Assembly of the Council of Europe in this field; Resolving to take such measures as are necessary to safeguard human dignity and the rights and fundamental freedoms of the individual with regard to organ and tissue transplantation,

Have agreed as follows:

Chapter I – Object and scope

ARTICLE 1. OBJECT

Parties to this Protocol shall protect the dignity and identity of everyone and guarantee, without discrimination, respect for his or her integrity and other rights and fundamental freedoms with regard to transplantation of organs and tissues of human origin.

ARTICLE 2. SCOPE AND DEFINITIONS

1. This Protocol applies to the transplantation of organs and tissues of human origin carried out for therapeutic purposes.

2. The provisions of this Protocol applicable to tissues shall apply also to cells, including haematopoietic stem cells.

3. The Protocol does not apply:

a. to reproductive organs and tissue;
b. to embryonic or foetal organs and tissues;
c. to blood and blood derivatives.

4. For the purposes of this Protocol:

– the term "transplantation" covers the complete process of removal of an organ or tissue from one person and implantation of that organ or tissue into another person, including all procedures for preparation, preservation and storage;
– subject to the provisions of Article 20, the term "removal" refers to removal for the purposes of implantation.

Chapter II – General provisions

ARTICLE 3. TRANSPLANTATION SYSTEM

Parties shall guarantee that a system exists to provide equitable access to transplantation services for patients. Subject to the provisions of Chapter III, organs and, where appropriate, tissues shall be allocated only among patients on an official waiting list, in conformity with transparent, objective and duly justified rules according to medical criteria. The persons or bodies responsible for the allocation decision shall be designated within this framework. In case of international organ exchange arrangements, the procedures must also ensure justified, effective distribution across the participating countries in a manner that takes into account the solidarity principle within each country. The transplantation system shall ensure the collection and recording of the information required to ensure traceability of organs and tissues.

ARTICLE 4. PROFESSIONAL STANDARDS

Any intervention in the field of organ or tissue transplantation must be carried out in accordance with relevant professional obligations and standards.

ARTICLE 5. INFORMATION FOR THE RECIPIENT

The recipient and, where appropriate, the person or body providing authorisation for the implantation shall beforehand be given appropriate information as to the purpose and nature of the implantation, its consequences and risks, as well as on the alternatives to the intervention.

ARTICLE 6. HEALTH AND SAFETY

All professionals involved in organ or tissue transplantation shall take all reasonable measures to minimise the risks of transmission of any disease to the recipient and to avoid any action which might affect the suitability of an organ or tissue for implantation.

ARTICLE 7. MEDICAL FOLLOW-UP

Appropriate medical follow-up shall be offered to living donors and recipients after transplantation.

ARTICLE 8. INFORMATION FOR HEALTH PROFESSIONALS AND THE PUBLIC

Parties shall provide information for health professionals and for the public in general on the need for organs and tissues. They shall also provide information on the conditions relating to removal and implantation of organs and tissues, including matters relating to consent or authorisation, in particular with regard to removal from deceased persons.

Chapter III – Organ and tissue removal from living persons

ARTICLE 9. GENERAL RULE

Removal of organs or tissue from a living person may be carried out solely for the therapeutic benefit of the recipient and where there is no suitable organ or tissue available from a deceased person and no other alternative therapeutic method of comparable effectiveness.

ARTICLE 10. POTENTIAL ORGAN DONORS

Organ removal from a living donor may be carried out for the benefit of a recipient with whom the donor has a close personal relationship as defined by law, or, in the absence of such relationship, only under the conditions defined by law and with the approval of an appropriate independent body.

ARTICLE 11. EVALUATION OF RISKS FOR THE DONOR

Before organ or tissue removal, appropriate medical investigations and interventions shall be carried out to evaluate and reduce physical and psychological risks to the health of the donor. The removal may not be carried out if there is a serious risk to the life or health of the donor.

Article 12. Information for the donor

The donor and, where appropriate, the person or body providing authorisation according to Article 14, paragraph 2, of this Protocol, shall beforehand be given appropriate information as to the purpose and nature of the removal as well as on its consequences and risks. They shall also be informed of the rights and the safeguards prescribed by law for the protection of the donor. In particular, they shall be informed of the right to have access to independent advice about such risks by a health professional having appropriate experience and who is not involved in the organ or tissue removal or subsequent transplantation procedures.

Article 13. Consent of the living donor

Subject to Articles 14 and 15 of this Protocol, an organ or tissue may be removed from a living donor only after the person concerned has given free, informed and specific consent to it either in written form or before an official body. The person concerned may freely withdraw consent at any time.

Article 14. Protection of persons not able to consent to organ or tissue removal

1. No organ or tissue removal may be carried out on a person who does not have the capacity to consent under Article 13 of this Protocol.

2. Exceptionally, and under the protective conditions prescribed by law, the removal of regenerative tissue from a person who does not have the capacity to consent may be authorised provided the following conditions are met:

i   there is no compatible donor available who has the capacity to consent;
ii   the recipient is a brother or sister of the donor;
iii   the donation has the potential to be life-saving for the recipient;
iv   the authorisation of his or her representative or an authority or a person or body provided for by law has been given specifically and in writing and with the approval of the competent body;
v   the potential donor concerned does not object.

Article 15. Cell removal from a living donor

The law may provide that the provisions of Article 14, paragraph 2, indents ii and iii, shall not apply to cells insofar as it is established that their removal only implies minimal risk and minimal burden for the donor.

Chapter IV – Organ and tissue removal from deceased persons

ARTICLE 16. CERTIFICATION OF DEATH

Organs or tissues shall not be removed from the body of a deceased person unless that person has been certified dead in accordance with the law. The doctors certifying the death of a person shall not be the same doctors who participate directly in removal of organs or tissues from the deceased person, or subsequent transplantation procedures, or having responsibilities for the care of potential organ or tissue recipients.

ARTICLE 17. CONSENT AND AUTHORISATION

Organs or tissues shall not be removed from the body of a deceased person unless consent or authorisation required by law has been obtained. The removal shall not be carried out if the deceased person had objected to it.

ARTICLE 18. RESPECT FOR THE HUMAN BODY

During removal the human body must be treated with respect and all reasonable measures shall be taken to restore the appearance of the corpse.

ARTICLE 19. PROMOTION OF DONATION

Parties shall take all appropriate measures to promote the donation of organs and tissues.

Chapter V – Implantation of an organ or tissue removed for a purpose other than donation for implantation

ARTICLE 20. IMPLANTATION OF AN ORGAN OR TISSUE REMOVED FOR A PURPOSE OTHER THAN DONATION FOR IMPLANTATION

1. When an organ or tissue is removed from a person for a purpose other than donation for implantation, it may only be implanted if the consequences and possible risks have been explained to that person and his/her informed consent, or appropriate authorisation in the case of a person not able to consent, has been obtained .

2. All the provisions of this Protocol apply to the situations referred to in paragraph 1, except for those in Chapter III and IV.

Chapter VI – Prohibition of financial gain

ARTICLE 21. PROHIBITION OF FINANCIAL GAIN

1. The human body and its parts shall not, as such, give rise to financial gain or comparable advantage. The aforementioned provision shall not prevent payments which do not constitute a financial gain or a comparable advantage, in particular:

– compensation of living donors for loss of earnings and any other justifiable expenses caused by the removal or by the related medical examinations;
– payment of a justifiable fee for legitimate medical or related technical services rendered in connection with transplantation;
– compensation in case of undue damage resulting from the removal of organs or tissues from living persons.

2. Advertising the need for, or availability of, organs or tissues, with a view to offering or seeking financial gain or comparable advantage, shall be prohibited.

ARTICLE 22. PROHIBITION OF ORGAN AND TISSUE TRAFFICKING

Organ and tissue trafficking shall be prohibited.

Chapter VII – Confidentiality

ARTICLE 23. CONFIDENTIALITY

1. All personal data relating to the person from whom organs or tissues have been removed and those relating to the recipient shall be considered to be confidential. Such data may only be collected, processed and communicated according to the rules relating to professional confidentiality and personal data protection.

2. The provisions of paragraph 1 shall be interpreted without prejudice to the provisions making possible, subject to appropriate safeguards, the collection, processing and communication of the necessary information about the person from whom organs or tissues have been removed or the recipient(s) of organs and tissues in so far as this is required for medical purposes, including traceability, as provided for in Article 3 of this Protocol.

Chapter VIII – Infringements of the provisions of the Protocol

ARTICLE 24. INFRINGEMENTS OF RIGHTS OR PRINCIPLES

Parties shall provide appropriate judicial protection to prevent or to put a stop to an unlawful infringement of the rights and principles set forth in this Protocol at short notice.

ARTICLE 25. COMPENSATION FOR UNDUE DAMAGE

The person who has suffered undue damage resulting from transplantation procedures is entitled to fair compensation according to the conditions and procedures prescribed by law.

ARTICLE 26. SANCTIONS

Parties shall provide for appropriate sanctions to be applied in the event of infringement of the provisions contained in this Protocol.

Chapter IX – Co-operation between Parties

ARTICLE 27. CO-OPERATION BETWEEN PARTIES

Parties shall take appropriate measures to ensure that there is efficient co-operation between them on organ and tissue transplantation, inter alia through information exchange. In particular, they shall undertake appropriate measures to facilitate the rapid and safe transportation of organs and tissues to and from their territory.

Chapter X – Relation between this Protocol and the Convention, and re-examination of the Protocol

ARTICLE 28. RELATION BETWEEN THIS PROTOCOL AND THE CONVENTION

As between the Parties, the provisions of Articles 1 to 27 of this Protocol shall be regarded as additional articles to the Convention on Human Rights and Biomedicine, and all the provisions of that Convention shall apply accordingly.

ARTICLE 29. RE-EXAMINATION OF THE PROTOCOL

In order to monitor scientific developments, the present Protocol shall be examined within the Committee referred to in Article 32 of the Convention on Human Rights and Biomedicine no later than five years from the entry into force of this Protocol and thereafter at such intervals as the Committee may determine.

Chapter XI – Final clauses

…

ARTICLE 32. ACCESSION

1. After the entry into force of this Protocol, any State which has acceded to the Convention may also accede to this Protocol.

2. Accession shall be effected by the deposit with the Secretary General of the Council of Europe of an instrument of accession which shall take effect on the first day of the month following the expiration of a period of three months after the date of its deposit.

2. Additional Protocol to the Convention on Human Rights and Biomedicine concerning Transplantation of Organs and Tissues of Human Origin, (ETS No. 186)

EXPLANATORY REPORT

I. This Explanatory Report to the Additional Protocol to the Convention on Human Rights and biomedicine, concerning transplantation of organs and tissues of human origin, was drawn up under the responsibility of the Secretary General of the Council of Europe, on the basis of a draft prepared, at the request of the Working Party, by Dr Peter DOYLE (United Kingdom), member of the Working Party.

II. The Committee of Ministers has authorised the publication of this Explanatory Report on 8 November 2001.

III. The Explanatory Report is not an authoritative interpretation of the Protocol. Nevertheless it covers the main issues of the preparatory work and provides information to clarify the object and purpose of the Protocol and to better understand the scope of its provisions.

Introduction

1. This Additional Protocol to the Convention on Human Rights and Biomedicine on the Transplantation of Organs and Tissues of Human Origin amplifies the principles embodied in the Convention, with a view to ensuring protection of people in the specific field of transplantation of organs and tissues of human origin.

2. The purpose of the Protocol is to define and safeguard the rights of organ and tissue donors, whether living or deceased, and those of persons receiving implants of organs and tissues of human origin.

Drafting of the Protocol

3. In 1991 in its Recommendation 1160, the Council of Europe Parliamentary Assembly recommended that the Committee of Ministers "envisage a framework convention comprising a main text with general principles and additional protocols on specific aspects". The same year, the Committee of Ministers instructed the CAHBI (ad hoc Committee of Experts on Bioethics), re-designated the CDBI (Steering Committee on Bioethics) "to prepare, ... Protocols to this Convention, relating to, in a preliminary phase: organ transplants and the use of substances of human origin; medical research on human beings".

...

7. This Protocol extends the provisions of the Convention on Human Rights and Biomedicine in the field of transplantation of organs, tissues and cells of human origin. The provisions of

the Convention are to be applied to the Protocol. For ease of consultation by its users, the Protocol has been drafted in such a way that they need not keep referring to the Convention in order to understand the scope of the Protocol's provisions. However, the Convention contains principles which the Protocol is intended to develop. Accordingly, systematic examination of both texts may prove helpful and sometimes indispensable.

...

Comments on the provisions of the Protocol

Title

11. The title identifies this instrument as the "Additional Protocol to the Convention for the Protection of Human Rights and Dignity of the Human Being with regard to the Application of Biology and Medicine, concerning Transplantation of Organs and Tissues of Human Origin".

12. The expression "of human origin" underlines the exclusion of xenotransplantation from the scope of the Protocol.

Preamble

13. The Preamble highlights the fact that Article 1 of the Convention on Human Rights and Biomedicine protecting the dignity and the identity of all human beings and guaranteeing everyone respect for their integrity, forms a suitable basis on which to formulate additional standards for safeguarding the rights and freedoms of donors, potential donors and recipients of organs and tissues.

14. In November 1987 the Third Conference of European Health Ministers convened in Paris dealt with organ transplantation, and a number of guidelines on the subject were adopted as a result. This Preamble echoes the main introductory paragraphs of their Final Declaration: while the transplantation of organs and tissues is an established part of the health services offered to the population, helping to save lives or improve their quality, emphasis is placed on the need to take specific measures to promote organ and tissue donation but also to prevent misuse of transplantation and the risk of commercialisation.

15. In addition, the Preamble stresses that it is important to take into account previous work of the Committee of Ministers and the Parliamentary Assembly of the Council of Europe on transplantation of organs and tissues, in particular Committee of Ministers Resolution (78) 29 on harmonisation of legislation of member States relating to removal, grafting and transplantation of human substances and on the management of organ transplant waiting lists and waiting times, Recommendation no. REC (2001)5.

Chapter I – Object and scope

ARTICLE 1. OBJECT

16. This article specifies that the object of the Protocol is to protect the dignity and identity of everyone and guarantee, without discrimination, respect for his or her integrity and other rights and fundamental freedoms with regard to transplantation of organs and tissues of human origin.

17. The term "everyone" is used in Article 1 because it is seen as the most concordant with the exclusion of embryonic and foetal organs or tissues from the scope of the Protocol as stated in Article 2 (see paragraph 24 below). The Protocol solely concerns removal of organs and tissues from someone who has been born, whether now living or dead, and the implantation of organs and tissues of human origin into someone else who has likewise been born.

ARTICLE 2. SCOPE AND DEFINITIONS

18. This article sets out the scope of the Protocol and defines the main terms used.

Scope

19. The Protocol applies solely to the transplantation of organs, tissues and cells of human origin (see paragraph 22 below). Organs, tissues and cells used for implantation are normally obtained from any one of the following three sets of circumstances:

a. a living person may, under certain conditions, consent to the removal of an organ or tissue for the purpose of implantation into another person; Chapter III was therefore drafted with the aim of protecting living donors from the psychological and physical risks and the consequences of implantation, particularly with regard to confidentiality and burdens arising from the requirements of traceability;
b. organs or tissues may be removed from a deceased person and implanted into another person; Chapter IV was designed to regulate the various stages of removal from deceased persons and to guarantee in particular that no removal is carried out if the deceased person had objected to it;
c. a person who is undergoing a procedure for his/her own medical benefit may consent to any removed organ or tissue being implanted into another person; Chapter V was designed to specify the conditions under which such organs or tissues may be implanted, in particular by stipulating that specific information must be provided and informed consent or appropriate authorisation obtained.

20. The second paragraph of Article 2 states that the provisions of this Protocol applicable to tissues shall also apply to cells. Indeed Chapter VI of the Convention enunciates the fundamental principles with regard to removal of organs and tissues from living donors for the purpose of transplantation, but none of these provisions mention the term "cells". However, in many

respects, transplantation of cells poses problems, particularly the consequences of testing and traceability, which are the same as those relating to the transplantation of tissues. Therefore, subject to Article 15, the Protocol applies the same regulations to the transplantation of cells as it does to the transplantation of tissues. In particular, the provisions concerning informed consent or authorisation by or on behalf of the donor, confidentiality, health and safety, and the prohibition of profit apply as for tissues.

21. The transplantation of haematopoietic stem cells, whatever their origin, comes within the scope of the Protocol, as does the transplantation of any kind of cells other than those that have been specifically excluded (see paragraphs 23 to 25 below). It should be emphasised that Recommendation No. R (98) 2 of the Committee of Ministers to member States on provision of haematopoietic progenitor cells is also relevant.

22. This Protocol does not apply to organs or tissues, whether genetically modified or not, removed from animals. These types of treatment are largely theoretical or at best experimental in the present state of scientific knowledge, and raise particular ethical problems. One should note that it is moreover foreseen that the issue of xenotransplantation will be addressed in another instrument presently under preparation. Thus it was agreed to place xenotransplantation outside the Protocol's scope.

23. Reproductive organs and tissues (comprising ova, sperm and their precursors) are excluded from the scope of the Protocol because organ and tissue transplantation is deemed to have different implications from those of medically assisted procreation and therefore should not be governed by the same rules. Therefore ovaries and testes are excluded but the uterus is not.

24. Transplantation of embryonic and foetal organs and tissue, including embryonic stem cells are also excluded from the scope of this Protocol. It is foreseen that these subjects will be addressed in another Protocol now being prepared on protection of the human embryo and foetus.

25. Blood and its derivatives covers blood and the products derived from blood for use in transfusion medicine. Blood and such products are thus subject to specific regulations, or specific standards, such as Recommendation R(95) 15 on the Preparation, use and quality assurance of blood components. Blood and its derivatives are therefore excluded from the scope of the Protocol. However, haematopoietic stem cells, whatever their origin, are within the scope of this Protocol as noted in paragraphs 21 and 109.

26. Implantation, in its traditional sense, does not include utilisation of tissues of human origin in the form of medical devices or pharmaceuticals; nevertheless, it was agreed that professional standards imply that the principles contained in this Protocol regarding namely safety, traceability, information and consent for such uses should be applicable mutatis mutandis.

Definitions

27. It is not a simple matter to decide what terms to use to signify the grafting or implantation of organs and tissues. In normal usage organs are "grafted" and tissues "implanted", or we refer to the "implantation of a graft". For the purposes of this Protocol it was agreed that in English "implantation" best described the surgical procedures involved.

28. There is also difficulty in agreeing on a scientifically precise definition of "organ" and "tissue". Traditionally an "organ" has been described as part of a human body consisting of a structured arrangement of tissues which, if wholly removed, cannot be replicated by the body. In 1994 the Committee of Ministers adopted a definition of tissues as being "All constituent parts of the human body, including surgical residues, but excluding organs, blood, blood products as well as reproductive tissue such as sperm, eggs and embryos. Hair, nails, placentas and body waste products also excluded" (Recommendation No. R (94) 1 of the Committee of Ministers to member States on human tissue banks). These were useful definitions in the early days of transplantation when only a few solid organs were transplanted e.g. kidney, heart and liver. However, developments in transplantation have given rise to difficulties of definition. For example, only a part of an adult liver may be removed and transplanted into a child and the residual liver will re-grow and the transplant will grow to adult size. This is a liver transplant but is clearly not an "organ" transplant according to the traditional definitions. Conversely, if a whole bone is removed and transplanted, the body cannot replicate the bone, but bone is normally considered to be a tissue not an organ.

29. The Protocol sets out to overcome this difficulty by using the terms "organs" and "tissues" throughout the text, except in Article 10 (see paragraphs 30 to 32 below), so that all provisions apply to all parts of the body. The distinction between the removal of "tissues" and "cells" is also difficult. In effect, more than one cell may be considered to be a tissue. Similarly, the Protocol sets out to overcome this difficulty by stating that the provisions applicable to tissues shall also apply to cells. In the same way, unless specifically stated, explanations relating to tissues in this explanatory report also apply to cells.

30. It is nevertheless possible to distinguish between vascularised grafts that is organs or parts of organs which need re-connection of their blood supply, e.g. heart, lungs, liver, kidney, pancreas, bowel, from non vascularised tissue grafts and cells. The former, once removed from the body, normally only remain viable for relatively short periods and need to be transplanted within a few hours. Thus they cannot currently be processed and stored as can most tissues and cells. For this reason the rules relating to transplantation of vascularised "organs" may differ from those applying to tissues and cells.

31. Live organ donation is currently confined primarily to kidneys, lobes of either liver or lung, and isolated sections of small bowel. Their removal is a major procedure which carries a high risk. On the other hand, removal of tissues from a living donor generally carries a low risk of harm, and removal of cells might in certain cases involve an even smaller risk (see paragraph 90 below). These differences justify different rules; for this reason Article 10 deals

with the specific case of organ removal from a living person and Article 15 with the case of cell removal from a living person.

32. For the purposes of this Protocol, the term "organ" is accordingly applied to vascularised organs or parts of organs which require a major surgical procedure for removal and which need to be transplanted rapidly. The terms "tissues" and "cells" cover all other parts of the body except those specifically excluded.

33. Transplantation is defined as the whole process starting with removal of an organ or tissue from one person and ending with implantation of that organ or tissue into a different person. The person from whom the material is removed is generally designated by the word donor and the person into whom the material is implanted by the word recipient. Furthermore tissues such as bone may be processed and the resulting products implanted into more than one recipient. Similarly, cells may be cultured to supply more than one recipient. Increasingly livers removed from a deceased person are split so that even in the case of organ transplantation there may be more than one recipient. The safeguards in the Protocol apply to all possible steps in the transplant process and to all possible recipients. Moreover, they apply to the entire process of each step in transplantation; for example the word "removal" refers to all the medical interventions necessary for the removal, including investigation and preparation of the donor.

34. The provisions of this Protocol concerning removal apply if its purpose is transplantation. Removal of tissue carried out for any other purpose is not covered by the Protocol. Nevertheless, as stated in Article 20, when in the course of an intervention an organ or tissue is removed for a purpose other than donation for implantation, it may be suitable for implantation but may only be so used if the consequences and possible risks have been explained to that person and informed consent or, in the case of a person who is not able to consent, appropriate authorisation, has been obtained (see paragraphs 108 to 111 below). Besides, the protection afforded to recipients by this Protocol applies to all transplanted human material irrespective of why it was removed.

Chapter II – General provisions

ARTICLE 3. TRANSPLANTATION SYSTEM

35. Parties to the Protocol undertake to ensure that a transplant system exists in their State within which transplant services operate. The nature or organisation of the system is not defined in this Protocol; it rests with individual States to decide whether to use local, regional, national or international organisations to meet the requirements of this article. As indicated in the 9th paragraph of the Preamble, institutions must be instrumental in ensuring that conditions protecting the rights and freedoms of donors, potential donors and recipients are observed.

36. The requirements of this article are that access to a transplant service is equitable – that is, all people, whatever their condition or background, must be equally able to be assessed by whatever transplant services are available. The concern is to ensure that there is no unjustified

discrimination against any person within the jurisdiction of the Party who might benefit from a transplant. It has to be emphasised that there is a severe shortage of most organs and some of the tissues which can be transplanted. Scarce organs and tissues should be allocated so as to maximise the benefit of transplantation. The State-recognised system will be responsible for ensuring equitable access to assessment for transplantation and to transplant waiting lists.

37. The criteria by which organs and tissues are allocated should be determined in advance but be capable of amendment, be evaluated regularly and modified if or when circumstances change. The system governing transplantation may lay down different criteria according to the type of graft because of the particular characteristics and availability of the different organs and tissues. Organs and tissues should be allocated according to medical criteria. This notion should be understood in its broadest sense, in the light of the relevant professional standards and obligations, extending to any circumstance capable of influencing the state of the patient's health, the quality of the transplanted material or the outcome of the transplant. Examples would be the compatibility of the organ or tissue with the recipient, medical urgency, the transportation time for the organ, the time spent on the waiting list, particular difficulty in finding an appropriate organ for certain patients (e.g. patients with a high degree of immunisation or rare tissue characteristics) and the expected transplantation result. It should be noted that the transplantation of organs removed from a living donor takes place generally between persons having a close personal relationship; for this reason, the general provision in Article 3 is subject to the specific provisions contained in Chapter III, Articles 10 (Potential organ donors) and 14, paragraph 2, subparagraph ii (Protection of persons not able to consent to organ or tissue removal). Organs removed from deceased persons should only be allocated to patients registered on an official waiting list. As to the tissues, there may be or there may not be an official waiting list. Patients may be registered only on one official transplant list, be it regional, national or international so as not to prejudice the chances of others. However this principle does not preclude a system where a patient is registered on a local waiting which is part of a national waiting list (see Recommendation Rec (2001) 5 of the Committee of Ministers to Member States on the management of organ transplant waiting lists and waiting times). The most important factor is to maximise equality of opportunity for patients and to do so by taking into account objective medical criteria. The allocation system should be as far as possible patient-oriented. In case of international organ exchange arrangement, the procedures for distribution across participating countries should take into account the principle of solidarity within each country.

38. In order to ensure the allocation rules are transparent and well founded, they should state clearly who, within the system recognised by the member State, has the responsibility for the determination and the application of these rules. The person(s) or body(ies) responsible for organ and tissue allocation should be accountable for their decisions. Parties should bear in mind the provisions of Recommendation Rec (2001)5 on the management of organ transplant waiting lists and waiting times.

39. Traceability means being able to track all organs or tissues from donor to recipient and vice versa. It is required because it is impossible to eliminate entirely the risks of transmission of

disease from donor to recipient and contamination of preserved material. Furthermore, new diseases or disease risks may emerge. Therefore for both public health reasons and the need to inform donors or recipients of potential problems that come to light following transplantation, it is important that any transplant material can be traced forward to recipients and back to the donor. For example, bone may be processed and turned into a variety of products with a long storage life available to treat multiple recipients. If a transmissible disease had been detected not at the outset but later in a recipient, donors would have to be traced to identify the one who transmitted the disease and unused products withdrawn. When seeking consent, both donors and recipients should be warned of such long-term consequences of transplantation and the possible need for prolonged surveillance. In addition, it may be necessary to analyse how organs and tissues were used to detect illegal or unethical use of such material, prevent organ and tissue trafficking and to validate allocation systems. For these reasons the transplant system must ensure a comprehensive system to enable all transplant material to be traced, without prejudice to the provisions on confidentiality set out in Article 23 (see paragraphs 122 and 123).

40. The question of methods for verifying the effectiveness with which the Parties implement systems for applying the various principles set out in article 3 is related to the general issue of Parties' honouring of the obligations in the Convention on Human Rights and Biomedicine, or any of its Protocols. In this context, reference should be made to i) the second paragraph of Article 1 of the Convention, which stipulates that "Each Party shall take in its internal law the necessary measures to give effect to the provisions of this Convention", ii) Article 28 of this Protocol, according to which Articles 1 to 27 are regarded as additional articles to the Convention, and iii) Article 30 of the Convention, which empowers the Secretary General to request any Party to "furnish an explanation of the manner in which its internal law ensures the effective implementation of any of the provisions of the Convention".

ARTICLE 4. PROFESSIONAL STANDARDS

41. The provisions here use the wording of Article 4 of the Convention and apply to all health care professionals whether involved in the decision-making process or in performing a transplant. The text of the explanatory report of the Convention also applies in general, but some further explanation is required for the purposes of this Protocol.

42. The term "intervention" must be understood here in a broad sense. It covers all medical acts performed in connection with transplantation of organs or tissue for purposes of treating a patient. An intervention carried out in connection with experimental transplantation must furthermore comply with the rules governing research.

43. The relevant professional obligations and standards in accordance with which all interventions must be performed, are those laws, specific or general and any codes of practice or rules of conduct in force in the member State. Such codes or rules may take various forms such as health legislation, a code of professional practice or accepted medical ethical principles. Specifically, transplants should only be performed in accordance with the agreed allocation

criteria. The rules and criteria may differ somewhat between countries but the fundamental principles of medical practice apply in all countries.

44. The competence of a doctor or other health care worker to take part in a transplant procedure must be determined in relation to the scientific knowledge and clinical experience appropriate to transplantation of organs or tissue at a given time. However, it is accepted that medical knowledge is rarely absolute and while acting according to the highest professional standards more than one therapeutic option may be perfectly justified. Recognised medical practice may therefore allow several alternative forms of intervention leaving some justified clinical freedom in the choice of methods or techniques. However, the choice of technique may affect the risk of inducing disease in the recipient, e.g. lymphoma or graft versus host disease, and such considerations should also be taken into account and the safest transplantation technique used.

45. Professional standards also require that organ and tissue implantation is only performed in accordance with a clear and specific medical indication for the recipient and not for any other reason such as a perceived social benefit. The recipient must have a defined medical problem which should be improved by a successful transplant before a transplant can be performed. The potential benefit of the procedure to the recipient must outweigh any risk. At all times, a decision to transplant must be taken only in the best interests of the patient.

46. Professional standards related to live transplantation require that, even if there is only one transplant team, different clinicians take responsibility for the care of the donor and the recipient, to ensure that the clinical needs of each party are properly and independently managed. In addition, it may be advisable to offer donors systematic long-term follow-up.

Article 5. Information for the recipient

47. This article sets forth the recipient's right to be properly informed prior to implantation. Even though a transplant is intended to improve the health or even save the life of the recipient, the fact remains that the recipient shall be informed beforehand of the purpose and nature of the implantation, its consequences and risks, as well as on the alternatives to the intervention. This information must be as exact as possible and couched in terms which the recipient can understand. Information should be provided in a format appropriate to the needs of the recipient. In addition to proper discussion, written information which the recipient can study when there is adequate time may be particularly helpful. When the recipient is too ill to be able to give informed consent, in particular in emergency cases, the information shall also be given to the person or body providing the authorisation to the implantation, as foreseen by Article 6 of the Convention of Human Rights and Biomedicine.

Article 6. Health and safety

48. This article deals with the health and safety aspects of the transplant process. It places an obligation on all those involved in the transplant process of organ and tissue to do everything

that can be reasonably expected of them to ensure that organs and tissues are healthy and undamaged, that they are handled, transported and where appropriate preserved and stored by means that maximise their viability and minimise the risk of contamination. These measures will ensure that when grafted into a recipient, the risk to the health of the recipient has been minimised. However, it recognises that the risk of transmission of disease cannot be entirely eliminated. Exceptionally, circumstances may arise when some risk of transmission of disease to the recipient, or of failure of the organ or tissue graft, is acceptable if the consequence of not grafting is more serious, in particular, if the alternative is certain death. An assessment of the risks and benefits should be made on a case-by-case basis.

49. The expression "transmission of any disease" covers also the transmission of a pathology to the recipient which may or may not later develop into the disease (for instance, in the case of hepatitis C virus, the recipient might be infected but never develop overt disease).

50. The ultimate responsibility for deciding whether to use a particular graft lies with the recipient's implant team. However, it is essential that, in deciding whether to proceed with a graft, the practitioner has access to all the relevant information pertaining to the likely viability of the graft and the risk of transmission of disease. It is the responsibility of everyone involved to ensure that accurate information about the donor and the graft are collected, recorded and accompany the graft. The practitioners responsible for the removal of an organ or tissue have a duty to ensure that the donor is properly screened for transmissible diseases, both infectious and malignant. They are responsible for ensuring that a proper medical history has been obtained and that appropriate tests have either been performed or the necessary samples collected for testing.

51. However, organ transplantation sometimes has to be carried out in difficult circumstances as a matter of extreme urgency without having all the necessary information or knowing whether there is a risk for the recipient. In such circumstances, the doctor in charge should balance the risks and benefits and consequently, the implant should only be performed if the benefits to the recipient outweigh the risks and consent or authorisation has been given after information appropriate to the circumstances has been provided.

52. Moreover, because of the shortage of organs and some tissues, even when a disease risk is detected, it may not be appropriate to reject the donor without first checking whether there is a suitable recipient. The more urgent the type of transplant, the more essential it is to assess the risk and check whether there is any recipient who could benefit. For example in fulminant liver failure, the patient may only have a few hours to live and even a high risk organ may be considered preferable to almost certain death. In the case of tissue transplants which, except for bone marrow, are rarely if ever life saving, donor screening and testing should be more rigorous and disease transmission as far as possible prevented. Consequently, it may still be reasonable to bank tissues, i.e. keep them in quarantine, awaiting the outcome of further investigations such as a post mortem or retesting of a living donor.

53. It is the responsibility of the persons involved in the removal of organs and tissues to use the highest standards of removal, preservation and, where appropriate, storage. They shall also take reasonable steps to ensure the continued quality and safety of the organs and tissues to minimise the risk of damage to the graft and to maximise its viability. In the case of organs this also means ensuring transport is available to minimise delays.

54. Those involved in the transport, preservation and storage of grafts are also responsible for ensuring that all relevant information has been obtained, checked, and accompanies the graft to the recipient, albeit nothing in this provision overrides the obligation of confidentiality as stated in Article 23.

55. Parties should also take account of other relevant national or international instruments in the field of health and safety, for example, guidance on the avoidance of transmission of infectious or malignant diseases during transplantation produced under the auspices of the European Health Committee (3).

ARTICLE 7. MEDICAL FOLLOW-UP

56. Article 7 of the Protocol states that a medical follow-up must be offered to living donors and recipients after transplantation. This is also a further specification of a principle of professional standards. The nature and duration of such follow-up should depend on the nature of the intervention and its potential impact on the individual's health. Short term follow up is essential to ensure recovery from the procedure. Life long follow up is essential for recipients requiring immunosupressive therapy. Such follow-up is also desirable for living organ donors to enable any long term effects of the donation to be identified. However, living donors and even recipients cannot be forced to accept long term follow up.

ARTICLE 8. INFORMATION FOR HEALTH PROFESSIONALS AND THE PUBLIC

57. It is for Parties to the Protocol to ensure that appropriate information about organ and tissue transplantation is made available to health professionals and to the general public. The information should cover all the relevant medical, legal, social, ethical and other issues concerned, particularly sensitive issues such as the means of certifying death. In view of the organ shortage it is seen as advisable to inform all health care workers about the success and benefits of transplantation because of their ability to inform the general public. Parties should also use every opportunity to inform the general public directly of those same benefits and successes. Informing the general public is important in promoting organ and tissue donation but it is also important that people make up their minds on the issues in full knowledge of the facts. Information for the public should be available on donation both from the living and the deceased (however, the provision of this general information should be without prejudice to that which is given to living donors in accordance with Article 12). The information should include the consequences and risks of organs or tissues being implanted into another person. Testing may reveal unrecognised diseases which may have implications for any living donor and possibly for the relatives of deceased persons from whom organs and tissues are removed.

The need to ensure traceability should also be explained as the consequences may not be realised until some time in the future. It is particularly important that such information is made available for people who may opt to become organ donors.

58. There is a very specific duty for the Parties, that is to ensure that the rules on consent and/or authorisation for organ or tissue retrieval and transplantation are well known and acceptable to the society. It is important to establish a relationship of trust between potential donors and the transplantation system. Transplant issues are constantly changing so the provision of information is an ongoing responsibility, not just an occasional one.

Chapter III – Organ and tissue removal from living persons

ARTICLE 9. GENERAL RULE

59. According to the first principle set out in the text, organs or tissues should be removed from deceased persons rather than from living donors whenever possible. Removing organs or tissues from living donors for implantation purposes always has consequences and may carry some risk for that donor. This implies that organs and tissues from living persons should not be used where an appropriate organ or tissue from a deceased person is available.

60. The second condition in the case of living donors is that there exists no alternative therapeutic method of comparable effectiveness. In view of the risk involved in any organ and tissue removal, there is indeed no justification for resorting to this if there is another way of bringing the same benefit to the recipient, such as the use of artificial skin for instance. The transplant must therefore be necessary in the sense that there is no other treatment that would produce similar results. In this respect dialysis treatment is not considered to provide results in terms of the patient's quality of life comparable with those obtained by a kidney transplant.

61. However, if the results of a living donor transplantation are expected to be significantly better than those expected utilising a graft removed from a deceased person, live donation may be the preferred therapeutic option for a particular recipient.

ARTICLE 10. POTENTIAL ORGAN DONORS

62. This article is specific to the removal of organs as defined in Article 2. It does not apply to the removal of tissues or cells. It defines the conditions under which, in addition of those of Article 9, living donation of an organ may be performed.

63. Those conditions would normally require that a close personal relationship, based on the principle of mutual aid, exists between the donor and recipient. The exact nature of the relationship is a matter for national law to determine and may depend on cultural or other local factors. Those with a close personal relationship with the recipient may include for instance members of the recipient's immediate family, parents, brothers, sisters, spouses or long-standing partners, godparents or close personal friends. Most countries have laws defining the nature

of the relationship which is required to exist between donor and recipient and which makes live donation acceptable. The intention of such laws and this Article is to prevent undue pressure to donate being brought to bear on people without a strong emotional relationship with the recipient.

64. However, not all national laws define close personal relationship, and where relationships are defined, the question of donation by a person not in such a relationship may be proposed. As there is some evidence that, despite the risks incurred, there may be perceptible long-term psychological benefit to organ donors who, even if not closely related, have helped improve the health or even save the life of a recipient, this Article allows such circumstances to be taken into account. But they may only be considered when the national law sets out the conditions under which such circumstances may be considered. Those conditions include the provision of an appropriate independent body, for example an ethics committee, to consider each case. The body is responsible for ensuring that the other conditions required by law have been met, and that, for example, no coercion or inducement is involved. These provisions are thus an important safeguard against potential organ trafficking or the use of inducements.

65. The independent body required under this Article is not the same as the official body identified in Article 13 before which the living donor can give his/her consent. However, the law may provide for the independent body provided for by Article 10 to be the same as the competent body identified in Article 14, even if their responsibilities are different (see paragraph 87 below).

66. The reason for excluding tissues from this Article is that the therapeutic interests of a recipient who may not be known at the time of removal have to be taken into account. Here, the principles of Recommendation No. R (94) 1 of the Committee of Ministers to member States on human tissue banks are relevant.

ARTICLE 11. EVALUATION OF RISKS FOR THE DONOR

67. This article deals with evaluation of risk to the donor, which must be kept to a minimum. The health care professional's role here is twofold: to carry out whatever investigations may be required to evaluate the donor's state of health and therefore the potential risk of donation and, second, to take all reasonable measures to limit the risks to the donor without compromising the quality or viability of the organ or tissue removed for transplantation. The principal risks for the donor are the physical risks arising for the surgical procedure. However, there are also short and long-term psychological risks that also need to be fully assessed.

68. Whereas the word "investigation" covers all the examinations or tests to be performed, the word "intervention" is to be understood in a broad sense as covering all relevant medical acts.

69. The article places a ban on removal from a living donor where there is serious risk to the donor's life or health. This raises questions as to what a serious risk to the donor is and who

judges the risk to be a serious one. Essentially there are three possible parties who may deem it a serious risk, the donor, the recipient or the medical team. For the purposes of this article, the decision about the risk is a matter for the transplant medical team looking after the donor or the body authorising the donation. The medical team should not propose a removal which they think presents an unacceptable risk even if the donor (for example, because he/she is a relative of the recipient) is ready to consent. In judging the risks involved, the donor's interests must take precedence, although in some circumstances the balance of risk to the donor compared to potential benefit to the recipient may be taken into consideration. The donation being acceptable or not depends not just on the physical risk associated with the procedure but must include psychological factors. Thus, the donor's emotional status should be independently assessed. An example of psychological harm is if the donor develops an undue sense of ownership towards the recipient or the recipient feels unduly obligated to the donor. If, following full assessment, the medical team looking after the donor judge there to be a significant risk of death or long term severe disability to the donor, the donation procedure should not go ahead.

ARTICLE 12. INFORMATION FOR THE DONOR

70. This article sets out the donor's right to be given appropriate information. In the case of donation of regenerative tissue, the most common instance is bone marrow transplantation between brothers and sisters, where the donor may be a minor. It is specifically to cater for this type of donation that the article requires the supply of information also to the representative, authority, person or body providing authorisation according to Article 14.2 of this Protocol.

71. There are two main requirements in the first part of the article. The information should be appropriate to explain the purpose and nature of the proposed removal as well as its consequences and risks, and the need for appropriate testing prior to the removal. It must be given prior to consent or authorisation and removal. Thus the information has to be as accurate as possible and given in terms the donor can understand, e.g. comparing the risks of a complication with other risks encountered in everyday life. In particular, in cases where the donor is a very young child, the content and form of the information presented must be adapted to his or her age and capacity for understanding. The donor must be given adequate time to fully consider the information provided and discuss it with friends and/or relatives. In addition to proper discussion, written information which the donor can study when there is adequate time may be particularly helpful. If the donation requires an authorising party under Article 14.2 those discussions will normally include the potential donor.

72. The second paragraph defines a more specific right for the donor in that it requires all concerned to inform the potential donor of his/her rights and safeguards under domestic and international law. In particular, it states that the donor shall be informed of the right to have access to a source of independent advice about the risks of the removal procedure. This source of information, who may be a doctor or other suitably qualified health care worker, must be independent of the team or teams involved in the transplant. However, that person must have appropriate experience of the risks associated with donation and transplantation to be able to

give proper advice. This advice can be requested by the donor if he/she wishes. An authorising party under Article 14.2 should have the same access to independent advice.

ARTICLE 13. CONSENT OF THE LIVING DONOR

73. This article is based on Article 5 of the Convention and requires that interventions in the field of organ and tissue transplantation can only be performed after a person has given free and informed consent which can be freely withdrawn at any time. In order to avoid undue pressure on the donor, he/she should be assured that he/she can refuse to donate or withdraw his/her consent at any time in complete confidence. To that end, the donor should be interviewed in private and helped to cope with the consequences of his/her decision.

74. In seeking the consent of the donor it is essential to discuss what should happen if for any reason the proposed recipient cannot accept the donation. Any possible alternative use for the donated organ or tissue should be considered prior to the donation.

75. This article does not apply to persons who do not have capacity to consent to the removal of an organ, such persons being protected by the provisions of Article 14 and 15 of this Protocol.

76. The first paragraph of this article is more stringent than Article 5 of the Convention in that, for organ or tissue removal, the donor's consent must also be specific and given in written form or before an official body, a court, a judge or an official notary for example. The responsibility of this body is to ensure that consent is adequate and informed.

77. The second paragraph provides the freedom to withdraw consent to the removal at any time. There is no requirement for withdrawal of consent to be in writing or to follow any particular form. The donor need simply say no to the removal at any time, even if a procedure performed under local anaesthetic has commenced. Article 14 affords the same protection to donors of regenerative tissue lacking capacity to consent to their removal. However, professional standards and obligations may require that the team continue with the procedure if not to do so would seriously endanger the health of the donor.

78. This article concerning consent of the living donor is included in Chapter III "Organ and tissue removal from living persons". The consent, as well as withdrawal of consent, therefore only applies to the removal process. If, exceptionally, the donor seeks to withdraw consent to the agreed implantation after removal, national law or professional standards should provide a means of resolving such problems.

ARTICLE 14. PROTECTION OF PERSONS NOT ABLE TO CONSENT TO ORGAN OR TISSUE REMOVAL

79. Provisions relating to consent to organ or tissue removal for implantation apply in the case of live donors having the capacity to consent. Those relating to authorisation apply where a potential donor cannot formally give consent on account of incapacity.

80. Article 14 deals specifically with the question of the removal of organs or tissues from a living person not having the capacity to give consent. The principle is that this practice is prohibited. Article 14 follows the wording of Article 20 of the Convention.

81. Only in very exceptional circumstances may derogations be made to this rule and only for the removal of regenerative tissues. Within the meaning of this article, regenerative tissue is that capable of reconstituting its tissue mass and function after partial removal. These exceptions are justified by the fact that regenerative tissue, in particular bone marrow, can only be transplanted between genetically compatible persons, often brothers and sisters. Furthermore, Article 15 provides that Article 14, paragraph 2, indents ii. and iii. might not be applied, only in cases in which cell removal implies minimal risk and minimal burden for the donor.

82. If at the present time bone marrow transplants among brothers and sisters is the most important situation which meets the condition of this article, the formula "regenerative tissue" takes into account future developments in medicine.

83. Paragraph 2 therefore permits removal of bone marrow from a minor for the benefit of his or her brother or sister. The principle of mutual aid between very close members of a family and the possibility for psychological benefits to the donor arising from donation can justify, subject to certain conditions, an exception to the prohibition of removal which is intended to protect the persons who are not able to give their consent. This exception to the general rule is qualified by a number of conditions designed to protect the person who is incapable of giving consent, and these may be supplemented by national law. The conditions stated in the general rule of Article 9 also apply.

84. The first condition is the absence, within reasonable limits, of a compatible donor who is able to consent.

85. It is also required that the beneficiary be a brother or sister. This restriction is intended to avoid both family and doctors going to extreme lengths to find a donor at any price, even if kinship is distant and the chances for a successful transplant are not very likely because of tissue incompatibility.

86. Moreover, removal is only authorised on the condition that, in the absence of the donation, the life of the recipient is in danger. It goes without saying that the risks to the donor should be acceptable; the professional standards of Article 4 naturally apply, in particular as regards the balance between risk and benefit.

87. Furthermore, in keeping with Article 6 of the Convention, the authorisation of the representative of the person not able to consent or the authorisation of the authority or person or body provided for by law is needed before the removal can be carried out.

88. The agreement of the competent body is also required. The intervention of such a body (which might be a court, a professionally qualified body, an ethics committee, etc.) aims to

guarantee that the decision to be taken is impartial. When the donor is an adopted person, it is for this body to verify that there has not been any misuse of the adoption process to enable a removal which would otherwise be forbidden. In this respect, it is important to note the important guarantees established in Article 14 for the protection of incapable persons and reinstated in the above paragraphs 80 to 86.

89. Finally, the removal may not be carried out if the potential donor objects in any way. This opposition, in whatever form, is decisive and must always be observed.

Article 15. Cell removal from a living donor

90. Although transplantation procedures for cells generally pose problems similar to those related to the transplantation of tissues, there may however be a significant difference with regard to the risks arising from the removal of cells in comparison with removal of tissues. In certain cases such as obtaining a limited number of cells from the skin, the procedure itself may not involve more than minimal risk and minimal burden for the donor. In such cases, and only in such cases, it is foreseen that the Parties to the Protocol can choose not to apply the provisions of Article 14, paragraph 2, indents ii. and iii. The purpose of those provisions is to protect the donor from physical risks and from instrumentalisation contrary to their dignity, but where the risks and burdens are minimal it may not be appropriate to prohibit, for example, a minor donating cells to a family member other than a sibling.

91. One should also emphasise that the requirements of Article 14, paragraph 2, indents i., iv. and v. remain applicable. If compatibility is not medically required, it will always be possible to obtain a donor with capacity to consent. It is therefore not envisaged that cell removal be carried out on persons not able to consent outside of the immediate family circle.

92. This provision is an option for States, not an obligation; States can make use of this option at the time of ratification of the Protocol or at a later stage, depending on scientific and technical developments. Moreover, having in mind that technical developments in the future could permit the reconstitution of tissue in the laboratory from a limited number of cells, the inclusion of this option in the Protocol alleviates the potential need to amend it later if these foreseeable developments become reality.

93. Moreover, in recognition of the need to monitor the appropriate use of this provision, it was decided during the adoption of the draft Protocol by the CDBI that the States utilising this option would be requested to inform the other Parties by a notification addressed to the Secretary General.

Chapter IV – Organ and tissue removal from deceased persons

ARTICLE 16. CERTIFICATION OF DEATH

94. According to the first paragraph, a person's death must have been established before organs or tissues may be removed "in accordance with the law". It is the responsibility of the States to legally define the specific procedure for the declaration of death while the essential functions are still artificially maintained. In this respect, it can be noted that in most countries, the law defines the concept and the conditions of brain death.

95. The death is confirmed by doctors following an agreed procedure and only this form of death certification can permit the transplantation to go ahead. The retrieval team must satisfy themselves that the required procedure has been completed before any retrieval operation is started. In some States, this procedure for certification of death is separate from the formal issuance of the death certificate.

96. The second paragraph of Article 16 provides an important safeguard for the deceased person by ensuring the impartiality of the certification of death, by requiring that the medical team which certifies death should not be the same one that is involved in any stage of the transplant process. It is important that the interests of any such deceased person and the subsequent certification of death are, and are seen to be, the responsibility of a medical team entirely separate from those involved in transplantation. Failure to keep the two functions separate would jeopardise the public's trust in the transplantation system and might have an adverse effect on donation.

97. For the purposes of this Protocol, neonates including anencephalic neonates receive the same protection as any person and the rules on certification of death are applicable to them.

ARTICLE 17. CONSENT AND AUTHORISATION

98. Article 17 bars the removal of any organ or tissue unless the consent or authorisation required by national law has been obtained by the person proposing to remove the organ or tissue. This requires member States to have a legally recognised system specifying the conditions under which removal of organs or tissues is authorised. Furthermore, by virtue of Article 8, the Parties should take appropriate measures to inform the public, namely about matters relating to consent or authorisation with regard to removal from deceased persons (see paragraph 58 above).

99. If a person has made known their wishes for giving or denying consent during their lifetime, these wishes should be respected after his/her death. If there is an official facility for recording these wishes and a person has registered consent to donation, such consent should prevail: removal should go ahead if it is possible. By the same token, it may not proceed if the person is known to have objected. Nonetheless, consultation of an official register of last wishes is

valid only in respect of the persons entered in it. Nor may it be considered the only way of ascertaining the deceased person's wishes unless their registration is compulsory.

100. The removal of organs or tissues can be carried out on a deceased person who has not had, during his/her life, the capacity to consent if all the authorisations required by law have been obtained. The authorisation may equally be required to carry out a removal on a deceased person who, during his/her life, was capable of giving consent but did not make known his wishes regarding an eventual removal post-mortem.

101. Without anticipating the system to be introduced, the Article accordingly provides that if the deceased person's wishes are at all in doubt, it must be possible to rely on national law for guidance as to the appropriate procedure. In some States the law permits that if there is no explicit or implicit objection to donation, removal can be carried out. In that case, the law provides means of expressing intention, such as drawing up a register of objections. In other countries, the law does not prejudge the wishes of those concerned and prescribes enquiries among relatives and friends to establish whether or not the deceased person was in favour of organ donation.

102. Whatever the system, if the wishes of the deceased are not sufficiently established, the team in charge of the removal of organs must beforehand endeavour to obtain testimony from relatives of the deceased. Unless national law otherwise provides, such authorisation should not depend on the preferences of the close relatives themselves for or against organ and tissue donation. Close relatives should be asked only about the deceased persons expressed or presumed wishes. It is the expressed views of the potential donor which are paramount in deciding whether organs or tissue may be retrieved. Parties should make clear whether organ or tissue retrieval can take place if a deceased person's wishes are not known and cannot be ascertained from relatives or friends.

103. When a person dies in a country in which he/she is not normally resident, the retrieval team shall take all reasonable measures to ascertain the wishes of the deceased. In case of doubt, the retrieval team should respect the relevant applicable laws in the country in which the deceased is normally resident or, by default, the law of the country of which the deceased person is a national.

ARTICLE 18. RESPECT FOR THE HUMAN BODY

104. A dead body is not legally regarded as a person, but nonetheless should be treated with respect. This article accordingly provides that during removal the human body must be treated with respect and after removal the body should be restored as far as possible to its original appearance.

105. Because of the shortage of available organs, this article makes a provision for Parties to take all appropriate measures to promote the donation of organs and tissues.

106. The "appropriate" measures are not defined but will include the provisions on information to be provided to health professionals and to the public (Article 8), the need to set up a transplant system (Article 3) and to have recognised means of giving consent or authorisation (Article 17).

107. It is also appropriate to remember that organ and tissue removal from deceased persons has to be given priority if living donation is to be minimised, in conformity with Article 9. However, organ and tissue removal from deceased persons must itself carry safeguards and these are set out in Chapter IV.

Chapter V – Implantation of an organ or tissue

removed for a purpose other than donation for implantation

Article 20. Implantation of an organ or tissue

removed for a purpose other than donation for implantation

108. In principle, this Protocol applies to the removal of organs or tissues for transplantation purposes. There are particular circumstances, however, in which those organs or tissues are removed for another purpose than donation for implantation but will nevertheless be donated at a later stage. The classic situation is the so-called "domino" transplant. When for instance a person needs a heart, or more often a lung transplant, it may be technically easier to remove their heart and lungs en bloc and replace them with a donor heart/lung block. Depending on the reason for the transplant, it is possible that the explanted heart, or at least the heart valves, will be in good condition and suitable for transplantation into another recipient. In this way the first recipient becomes a live donor for the second recipient. In the case of a "domino" heart transplant, the heart valves might be harvested from the second recipient's heart and be transplanted into a third person.

109. This article is also applicable where, in the course of a medical intervention, tissues are removed then processed and re-implanted into someone else, even if they are regarded as discarded tissues at the time of the intervention. In this respect, one could mention the following examples: the use of bone from femoral heads removed during hip replacement; the implant of a kidney removed for medical reasons; the use of vessels obtained from placentae or haematopoietic stem cells from cord blood.

110. The first paragraph of the article stresses the need to inform a person from whom organ or tissue have been removed for a purpose other than donation for implantation of the conse-

quences associated with implantation of the organ or tissue into another person, namely the need for appropriate testing and recording of information which ensures the traceability of the organs or tissues; the information must include potential risks, for instance any modification, even minor, of the surgical procedure needed to retrieve the organ or tissue in the best possible condition for implantation. The first paragraph also stresses the need to obtain the informed consent of the person from whom organ or tissue have been removed or appropriate authorisation for the use of the organ or tissue for implantation. The first recipient of a heart can for instance be a child. In turn his/her heart or the valves which are removed can be implanted in another child, if the persons providing authorisation have agreed after being duly informed.

111. As indicated in Article 2, the second paragraph of Article 20 provides that all the provisions of this Protocol, except for those in Chapters III and IV, which concern issues relating to removal for implantation purposes, apply to the situations referred to in paragraph 1. Indeed, the general provisions of the Protocol that guarantee fundamental rights (with regard namely to safety, confidentiality, non-commercialisation) will apply to the cases referred to in this article.

Chapter VI – Prohibition of financial gain

Article 21. Prohibition of financial gain

112. This article applies the principle of human dignity as laid down in Article 1 of this Protocol.

113. It states in particular that the human body and its parts must not, as such, give rise to financial gain or comparable advantage. Under this provision, organs and tissues should not be bought or sold or give rise to direct financial gain for the person from whom they have been removed for a third party. Nor should the person from whom they have been removed, or a third party, gain any other advantage whatsoever comparable to a financial gain such as benefits in kind or promotion for example. A third party involved in the transplant process such as a health professional or a tissue bank may not make a profit from organs or tissues or any products developed from them (but see paragraph 115 below).

114. However, Article 21 states that certain payments that a donor may receive are not to be treated as financial gain within the meaning of this article. Essentially, apart from the last indent, these provide examples of expenses that may be incurred during or as a result of donation or other parts of the transplant process. This paragraph does not make exceptions to the principle laid down but gives examples of compensation to avoid possible financial disadvantage which may otherwise occur. In the case of the donor it allows for compensation for loss of earnings and other justifiable expenses.

115. The second indent of the first paragraph refers to payment of a justifiable fee for medical or technical services performed as part of the transplant process. Such acts might include the

cost of retrieval, transport, preparation, preservation and storage of organs or tissues, which may legitimately give rise to reasonable remuneration.

116. The third indent allows donors to receive compensation for undue damage resulting from the removal. By undue damage is meant any harm whose occurrence is not a normal consequence of a transplant procedure. This provision refers to the compensation provided for in Article 25.

117. The second paragraph of this article makes it clear that any attempt to advertise anything to do with organ or tissue transplantation with a view to financial or equivalent gain for any party is prohibited.

118. This article refers solely to organs and tissues covered by the Protocol. The provision does not refer to such products as hair and nails for example, which are discarded tissues, and the sale of which is not an affront to human dignity.

Article 22. Prohibition of organ and tissue trafficking

119. As stated by Article 21 of the Convention, the human body and its parts shall not, as such, give rise to financial gain. Any trade in organs and tissues for direct or indirect financial gain, as defined by Article 21 of this Protocol is prohibited. Organ trafficking and tissue trafficking are important examples of such illegal trading and of direct financial gain. Organ or tissue traffickers may also use coercion either in addition to or as an alternative to offering inducements. Such practices cause particular concern because they exploit vulnerable people and may undermine people's faith in the transplant system. This is why the prohibition of trafficking in organs and tissues is specifically referred to in Article 22.

120. This does not in any way reduce either the seriousness of infringements of other rights and principles enshrined in the Protocol, or the force of the prohibition of infringements of these rights and principles, as laid down in Articles 24 and 26.

121. In conformity with Article 26 of this Protocol, Parties shall provide for appropriate sanctions to deter organ and tissue trafficking or any attempt at commercial trade in organs or tissues.

Chapter VII – Confidentiality

Article 23. Confidentiality

122. Article 23 lays down the principle of confidentiality. Preserving the anonymity of the person from whom organs or tissues have been removed may be impossible in certain circumstances, for example because of the requirement of an appropriate relation between the latter and the recipient in the case of living organ donation. However, personal data concerning persons from whom organs or tissues have been removed and recipients must nonetheless be treated as

confidential and handled in accordance with the rules on professional confidentiality (4) and personal data protection. Here, the principles laid down in the Convention for the Protection of Individuals with regard to Automatic Processing of Personal Data of 28 January 1981 (ETS 108) must be observed. In particular, Article 5.b of Convention 108 provides that personal data are "stored for specified and legitimate purposes and not used in a way incompatible with those purposes". Parties should take account of other national or international instruments, such as Recommendation (97) 5 of the Committee of Ministers to the member States on the protection of medical data and, where applicable, Directive 95/46/EC of the European Parliament and of the Council of 24 October 1995 on the protection of individuals with regard to the processing of personal data and on free movement of such data.

123. In transplantation, it is nevertheless essential that the principle of confidentiality should not prevent the medical team involved in any transplant process from obtaining the necessary information on the person from whom organs or tissues have been removed and the recipient, and keeping track of the exchange of organs or tissues between them, subject to appropriate safeguards to ensure adequate data protection. One such person may in fact supply several organs or tissues to be implanted in more than one recipient. If a disease is subsequently detected in that person, the recipients must be traceable. Equally, if a recipient of a transplant develops a disease which may have been transmitted, the person from whom organs or tissues had been removed must be identified, again to trace any other recipients. The rules applicable to traceability of organs and tissues are as set out in Article 3 paragraph 3 of this Protocol.

Chapter VIII – Infringements of the provisions of the Protocol

ARTICLE 24. INFRINGEMENTS OF RIGHTS OR PRINCIPLES

124. This article requires the Parties to make available a judicial procedure to prevent or put a stop to an infringement of the principles set forth in the Protocol. It therefore covers not only infringements which have already begun and are ongoing but also the threat of an infringement.

125. The requisite judicial protection must be appropriate and proportionate to the infringement or the threats of infringement of the principles. Such is the case, for example, with proceedings initiated by a public prosecutor in cases of infringements affecting several persons unable to defend themselves, in order to put an end to the violation of their rights.

126. Under the Protocol, the appropriate protective machinery must be capable of operating rapidly as it must ensure that an infringement is prevented or halted at short notice. This requirement can be explained by the fact that, in many cases, the very integrity of an individual has to be protected and an infringement of this right might have irreversible consequences.

127. The judicial protection thus provided by the Protocol applies only to unlawful infringements or to threats thereof.

ARTICLE 25. COMPENSATION FOR UNDUE DAMAGE

128. This article sets forth the principle that the person who has suffered undue damage resulting from a transplantation is entitled to fair compensation. Like the Convention, the Protocol uses the expression "undue damage" because there can be damage which is inherent in the transplantation itself.

129. The due or undue nature of the damage will have to be determined in the light of the circumstances of each case. The cause of the damage must be either an act or an omission during the transplantation procedure. In order to give entitlement to compensation, the damage must result from the transplantation. Potential donors might be wronged during investigations to determine their suitability, as might recipients. In view of the altruistic nature of live organ donation, particular attention should be paid to the rights of donors and potential donors to an adequate compensation for damage resulting from transplantation.

130. Compensation conditions and procedures are not prescribed in this Article. In many cases, the national law establishes a system of individual liability based either on fault or on the notion of risk or strict liability. In other cases, the law may provide for a collective system of compensation irrespective of individual liability.

131. On the subject of fair compensation, reference can be made to Article 41 of the European Convention on Human Rights, which allows the Court to afford just satisfaction to the injured party.

132. Article 21 of this Protocol makes reference to the aforementioned compensation in such terms as to exclude it from any payments constituting a financial gain or a comparable advantage.

ARTICLE 26. SANCTIONS

133. Since the aim of the sanctions provided for in Article 26 is to guarantee compliance with the provisions of the Protocol, they must be in keeping with certain criteria, particularly those of necessity and proportionality. As a result, in order to measure the expediency and determine the nature and scope of the sanction, domestic law must pay special attention to the content and importance of the provision to be complied with, the seriousness of the offence and the extent of its possible repercussions for the individual and for society.

Chapter IX – Co-operation between Parties

ARTICLE 27. CO-OPERATION BETWEEN PARTIES

134. International co-operation in transplantation matters is important for two main reasons. The first is that information about the organisation and effectiveness of services, successful methods of e.g. informing and educating the public or procuring organs, success rates and

new developments should all be freely exchanged to help all States achieve the most effective transplant services possible within the resources available.

135. Secondly, difficulties of tissue matching or the urgency of the clinical condition may require access to a large or very large population if the transplant is to be successful. For example, matching for unrelated bone marrow transplants requires a very large pool of donors. People with fulminant liver failure may need a suitable organ within a few hours if they are to survive. If an organ becomes available in a country which has no suitable patient on its waiting list, there must be arrangements in place to allow that organ to be offered rapidly to patients on other transplant waiting lists if the organ is not to be wasted. States Party to this Protocol are expected to set up transborder links so as to facilitate the exchange of information and the transportation of organs and tissues between States but without prejudice to public safety as specified in Article 6 and the need for confidentiality as specified in Article 23.

Chapter X – Relation between this Protocol and the Convention, and re-examination of the Protocol

ARTICLE 28. RELATION BETWEEN THIS PROTOCOL AND THE CONVENTION

136. As a legal instrument, the Protocol supplements the Convention. Once in force, the Protocol is subsumed into the Convention vis-à-vis Parties having ratified the Protocol. The provisions of the Convention are therefore to be applied to the Protocol.

137. Thus, Article 36 of the Convention, which sets out the conditions under which a State may make a reservation in respect of any particular provision of the Convention, will also apply to the Protocol. Using this provision States may, under the conditions set out in Article 36 of the Convention, make a reservation in respect of any particular provision of this Protocol.

ARTICLE 29. RE-EXAMINATION OF THE PROTOCOL

138. This article provides that the Protocol shall be re-examined no later than five years from its entry into force and thereafter at such intervals as the Committee in charge of the re-examination may determine. Article 32 of the Convention identifies this Committee as the Steering Committee on Bioethics (CDBI), or any other Committee so designated by the Committee of Ministers. The provisions of the Protocol to be re-examined would especially concern aspects of transplantation where scientific developments would give rise to particular ethical or legal issues; for example, it is conceivable that the question of removing cells from a living person will need to be reconsidered after a few years.

Chapter XI – Final clauses

Article 30. Signature and ratification

139. Only States which have signed or ratified the Convention may sign this Protocol. Ratification of the Protocol is subject to prior or simultaneous ratification of the Convention. Under the provisions of Article 31 of the Convention, a State which has signed or ratified the Convention is not obliged to sign the Protocol or, if applicable, to ratify it.

3. World Medical Association Statement on Human Organ Donation and Transplantation

Adopted by the 52nd WMA General Assembly in Edinburgh, Scotland during October 2000 and revised by the WMA General Assembly, Pilanesberg, South Africa, October 2006

A. Introduction

Advances in medical sciences, especially surgical techniques, tissue typing and immuno-suppressive drugs, have made possible a significant increase in the rates of successful transplantation of organs. In the light of these developments, there is a need for renewed reflection on ethical issues concerning organ donation and transplantation and on principles relevant to the resolution of these issues. Therefore, the World Medical Association has undertaken a review of issues and principles concerning transplantation and has developed this policy to provide guidance to medical associations, physicians and other health care providers as well as to those who develop policy and protocols bearing on these issues.

This policy is based on principles of general and medical ethics. In matters of ethics, conflicts of values and principles are unavoidable; for example, there is a tension between a desire to procure organs for the purpose of providing important medical treatments on the one hand and the preservation of choice and personal liberty on the other. Applicable principles are referenced throughout this policy where they may help to clarify and make explicit the reasoning behind a given statement.

B. Professional Obligations of Physicians

The primary obligation of physicians is to their individual patients, whether they are potential donors or recipients of transplanted organs. In conjunction with this obligation physicians may also have responsibilities to the family members and close friends of their patients, for example, to seek and consider their views on organ retrieval from their deceased relative or friend. The obligation to the patient has primacy over any obligations that may exist in relationship to family members. Nevertheless, this obligation is not absolute; for example, the physician's responsibility for the well-being of a patient who needs a transplant does not justify unethical or illegal procurement of organs.

Physicians have responsibilities to society, which include promoting the fair use of resources, preventing harm and promoting health benefit for all; this may include promoting donation of organs.

Transplant surgeons should attempt to ensure that the organs they transplant have been obtained in accordance with the provisions of this policy and shall refrain from transplanting organs that they know or suspect have not been procured in a legal and ethical manner.

C. Organ Procurement: Social Aspects

The WMA encourages its members to support the development of comprehensive, coordinated national strategies concerning organ procurement in consultation and cooperation with all relevant stakeholders. In developing strategy, due consideration should be given to human rights, ethical principles and medical ethics. Ethical, cultural and societal issues arising in connection with such a strategy, and with the subject of donation and transplantation in general, should be resolved, wherever possible, in an open process involving public dialogue and debate informed by sound evidence.

Some types of organ transplantation have become established and important health care services. To the extent that the lack of organs is a barrier to the provision of needed treatment, the medical profession has an obligation to promote policies and protocols to procure organs for needed treatment consistent with societal values.

It is important that individuals become aware of the option of donation and have the opportunity to choose whether or not to donate (e.g. facilitated choice). Awareness and choice should be facilitated in a coordinated multi-faceted approach by a variety of stakeholders and means, including media awareness and public campaigns. Physicians should provide their patients with the opportunity to make a choice with respect to organ donation, ideally in the context of an ongoing relationship with the patient and in advance of any crisis giving urgency to the choice.

The WMA supports informed donor choice. National Medical Associations in countries that have adopted or are considering a policy of "presumed consent", whereby there is a presumption that consent has been given unless there is evidence to the contrary, or "mandated choice", whereby all persons would be required to declare whether they wish to donate, should make every effort to ensure that these policies do not diminish informed donor choice, including the patient's right to refuse to donate.

Consideration should be given to the establishment of national donor registries to collect and maintain a list of country citizens who have chosen either to donate or not to donate their organs. Any such registry must protect individual privacy and the individual's ability to control the collection, use, disclosure of and access to his or her health information for purposes other than registration. Provisions must be in place to ensure that the decision is adequately informed and that registrants can withdraw from the registry without penalty.

D. Organ Procurement at the Institutional and Individual Levels

Organ donation can be enhanced by local policies and protocols. The WMA recommends that organ procurement programmes, hospitals and other institutions in which procurement occurs should:

Develop policies and protocols encouraging the procurement of organs consistent with the statements in this policy. Such policies should be consistent with physicians' professional obligations and societal values, including free and informed decision making, privacy, and equitable access to needed medical care.

Make these policies and protocols known to transplant coordinators, physicians and other health care providers in the institution.

Ensure that adequate resources are available to support proper implementation of the policies and protocols.

E. Donation after death

Physicians have an obligation to ensure that interactions at the bedside, including those discussions related to organ donation, are sensitive and consistent with ethical principles and with their fiduciary obligations to their patients. This is particularly so given that conditions at the bedside of dying patients are not ideal for the process of free and informed decision making. Protocols should specify that whoever approaches the patient, family members or other designated decision maker about the donation of organs should possess the appropriate combination of knowledge, skill and sensitivity for engaging in such discussions. Medical students and practising physicians should seek the necessary training for this task, and the appropriate authorities should provide the resources necessary to secure that training. It is mandatory that the person who approaches the patient or family about the donation decision not be a member of the transplant team.

F. Free and Informed Decision Making About Organ Donation

The WMA considers that the potential donor's wishes are paramount. In the event that the potential donor's wishes about donation are unknown and the potential donor has died without expressing a clear wish about donation, the family or a specified other person may serve as a substitute decision-maker and may be entitled to give or refuse permission for donation unless there are previously expressed wishes to the contrary.

Evidence of the free and informed decision of the potential donor, or, where legally relevant, of the appropriate substitute decision-maker, must be ascertained before organ procurement can begin. In countries where presumed consent is the legal norm, the organ procurement process should include reasonable steps to discover whether the potential donor has opted out of donation.

Success in procuring organs for transplant should not be construed as a criterion for measuring the quality of the process of free and informed decision-making. The quality of this process depends on whether the choice was adequately informed and free of coercion and not on whether the outcome is a decision to donate.

Free and informed decision making is a process requiring the exchange and understanding of information and the absence of coercion. Because prisoners and other individuals in custody are not in a position to give consent freely and can be subject to coercion, their organs must not be used for transplantation except for members of their immediate family.

In order for the choice to donate organs to be duly informed, prospective donors or their substitute decision makers should, if they desire, be provided with meaningful and relevant information. Normally, this will include information about:

– in the case of living donors, the benefits and risks of transplantation,
– in the case of deceased donors, procedures and definitions involved in the determination of death,
– testing of organs to determine their suitability for transplantation, which may reveal unsuspected health risks in the prospective donors and their families,
– in the case of deceased donors measures that may be required to preserve organ function until death is determined and transplantation can occur,
– in the case of deceased donors what will happen to the body once death has been declared, what organs they are agreeing to donate, the protocol that will be followed concerning the family in the event that the family objects to donation, and
– in the case of living donors, the implications of living without the donated organ.

Prospective donors should be informed that families sometimes object to donation; donors should be encouraged to discuss their choice with their family to prevent conflict.

Prospective donors or their substitute decision makers should be given the opportunity to ask questions about donation and should have their questions answered sensitively and intelligibly.

Where the wishes of the patient are known and there is no reason to believe that the choice to donate has been coerced, has not been adequately informed, or has changed, these wishes should be carried out. This should be clarified in law, policy and protocols. Under these circumstances, families should be encouraged to respect the patient's clearly expressed wishes.

Where the wishes of the patient are unknown or there is uncertainty about the patient's wishes, national law should prevail.

Protocols for free and informed decision making should also be followed in the case of recipients of organs. Normally, this should include information about:

– the risks of the procedure,
– the likely short, medium and long-term survival, morbidity, and quality-of-life prospects,
– alternatives to transplantation, and
– how organs are obtained.

In the case of living donors, special efforts should be made to ensure that the choice about donation is free of coercion. Financial incentives for providing or obtaining organs for transplantation can be coercive and should be prohibited. Individuals who are incapable of making informed decisions, for example minors or mentally incompetent persons, should not be considered as potential living donors except in extraordinary circumstances and in accordance with ethics committee review or established protocols. In order to avoid a conflict of interest, the physician who obtains informed consent from the living donor should not be part of the transplant team for the recipient.

G. Determination of Death

The WMA considers that the determination of death is a clinical matter that should be made according to widely accepted guidelines established by expert medical groups, and as outlined in The World Medical Association's Declaration of Sydney on the Determination of Death and the Recovery of Organs.

Protocols and procedures should be developed to educate patients and families about procedures for diagnosing death and the opportunities for donation after death.

In order to avoid a conflict of interest, the physician who determines and/or certifies the death of a potential organ donor should not be involved in the organ removal or in subsequent transplantation procedures or responsible for the care of potential recipients of these organs.

H. Justice in Access to Organs

The WMA considers there should be explicit policies open to public scrutiny governing all aspects of organ donation and transplantation, including the management of waiting lists for organs to ensure fair and appropriate access.

Policies governing the management of waiting lists should ensure efficiency and fairness. Criteria that should be considered in allocating organs include severity of medical need, length of time on the waiting list, and medical probability of success measured by such factors as type of disease, other complications, and histocompatibility. There should be no discrimination based on social status, lifestyle or behaviour.

Special appeals for organs for a specific recipient require further study and ethical examination to evaluate the potential impact on the fairness of allocation.

Payment for organs for donation and transplantation must be prohibited. A financial incentive compromises the voluntariness of the choice and the altruistic basis for organ donation. Furthermore, access to needed medical treatment based on ability to pay is inconsistent with the principles of justice. Organs suspected to have been obtained through commercial transaction must not be accepted for transplantation. In addition, the advertisement of organs in exchange for money should be prohibited. However, reasonable reimbursement of expenses such as those incurred in procurement, transport, processing, preservation, and implantation is permissible.

Physicians who are asked to transplant an organ that has been obtained through a commercial transaction should refuse to do so and should explain to the patient why such a medical act would be unethical: because the person who provided the organ risked his or her future health for financial rather than altruistic motives, and because such transactions are contrary to the principle of justice in the allocation of organs for transplantation.

I. Experimental and Newly Developing Transplantation Procedures

The WMA considers that, although many transplantation procedures have become standard medical care for a range of medical conditions, others are experimental and/or morally controversial and require further research, safeguards, guidelines, and public debate.

Experimental procedures require protocols, including ethics review, that are different and more rigorous than those for standard medical procedures.

Xenotransplantation raises special issues, particularly in light of the risk of unwitting cross-species transmission of viruses and other pathogens. There is an urgent need for extensive public debate about xenotransplantation to ensure that developments in this field are consistent with societal values. International guidelines to govern these practices should be developed.

Transplantation of organs developed using cell nuclear replacement technologies requires scientific review, public debate and appropriate guidelines before becoming accepted.

4. Proposal for a Directive of the European Parliament and of the Council on standards of quality and safety of human organs intended for transplantation COM(2008) 819

Brussels, 8.12.2008

Explanatory memorandum

Introduction

1. Organ transplantation is the therapeutic use of human organs involving the substitution of a non-functional organ by an organ from a donor. Organ transplantation is now the most cost-effective treatment for end-stage renal failure, and for end-stage failure of organs such the liver, lung and heart, it is the only available treatment.

2. The use of organs in therapy poses a risk of transmission of diseases to the recipient; infectious or cancerous diseases could be transmitted. While most Member States have adopted legislation on the ethical aspects of organ transplantation, many have yet to agree on rules covering quality and safety. In 2003, the Commission carried out a survey of legal requirements relating to organ transplantation in the EU which showed discrepancies in quality and safety requirements between Member States.

3. The exchange of organs between Member States in an effort to achieve better quality in the allocation process is already common practice. There are, however, large differences between the number of organs exchanged across borders between Member States that have set up bodies and laid down rules for the international exchange of organs such as Eurotransplant and Scandiatransplant and the other Member States.

4. The shortage of organs is a major factor affecting transplantation programmes. Nearly 56.000 patients are now on waiting lists. Mortality rates while waiting for a heart, liver or lung transplant usually range from 15 to 30%. Donation rates and availability of organs varies considerably across Europe with achievable good practice delivering far greater benefits in some Member States than in others.

5. One of the potential consequences of the scarcity of organs is the trafficking of human organs by organised criminal groups. Trafficking in human organs can be linked with trafficking in human beings for the purpose of the removal of organs which constitutes a serious violation of fundamental rights and, in particular, of human dignity and physical integrity. It is recognised that the best way of fighting organ trafficking is increasing the number of available organs and securing their quality and safety. This Directive, although having as its first objective the safety and quality of organs, will indirectly contribute to combating organ trafficking through the establishment of competent authorities, the authorisation of transplantation centres, the establishment of conditions of procurement and systems of traceability.

6. Since 1999, Article 152 of the EC Treaty, as introduced by the Treaty of Amsterdam, has enabled the European Parliament and the Council to adopt health measures setting high standards of quality and safety of organs and substances of human origin, blood and blood derivatives. The Community has already adopted directives, on quality and safety standards for blood in 2003 and for Tissues and Cells in 2004.

7. There are important differences between organ transplantation and the use of other human substances such as blood, tissues and cells. Given the current shortage of organs, two factors have to be balanced: the need for organs' transplantation that is usually a matter of life and death with the need to ensure high standards of quality and safety.

8. The Venice Conference on Safety and Quality in Organ Donation and Transplantation in the European Union was held on 17-18 September 2003 under the Italian presidency. The conclusions of the expert conference organised by the Italian government during its Presidency of the EU Council listed the shortage of organs as the main priority in this area and stressed the importance of addressing the quality and safety aspects given the current situation regarding the supply and demand for organs.

9. When adopting the Tissues and cells Directive on 31 March 2004, the Commission committed itself to conducting a thorough scientific review of the situation regarding organ transplantation. On 31 May 2007, the Commission adopted a Communication on organ donation and transplantation based on that analysis. This Communication proposes what activities the EU should undertake in the field of organ transplantation. The Communication concludes that a flexible European legal framework establishing quality and safety standards would be the right Community response to meeting the mandate provided in Article 152 (4) (a) of the Treaty.

10. On 6 December 2007, the Council adopted conclusions on organ donation and transplantation. The Council recognises the importance of having high standards with respect to the quality and safety of organs for transplantation, so as to ensure a high level of protection for patients throughout Europe and called on the Commission to consult the Member States, and continue its examination of the need for an EU framework on quality and safety for human organs.

11. The European Parliament resolution adopted on 22 April 2008 recognised that it is vitally important to improve the quality and safety of organ donation and transplantation to reduce transplant risks. Hence, the resolution looks forward to the Commission's proposal for a directive stipulating requirements to ensure the quality and safety of organ donation across the EU.

Scope and Objectives

12. This proposal for a Directive covers human organs, that are used for transplantation, during all the phases of the process – donation, procurement, testing, preservation, transport and use – and aims to ensure their quality and safety and hence a high level of health protection.

13. The proposal excludes blood and blood components, human tissues and cells and organs or tissues and cells of animal origin. Blood and blood products are currently covered by Directives 2002/98/EC, 2004/33/EC, 2005/61/EC and 2005/62/EC, whereas Human Tissues and Cells are regulated by Directive 2004/23/EC, 2006/17/EC and 2006/86/EC.

14. This Directive does not intend to cover research using human organs, for purposes other than transplantation. However, organs that are transplanted into the human body in clinical trials should comply with the quality and safety standards laid down in this Directive.

15. This proposal aims to ensure that human organs used for transplantation in the EU comply with the same quality and safety requirements. In this way, the Directive will facilitate their exchange between Member States.

The Added Value of the Directive

Ensuring quality and safety for patients at EU level

16. There are significant risks to using organs in therapy, but these can be effectively offset through the application of quality and safety procedures. A well-regulated donation and transplantation system is essential if organs are to be delivered on time, with accurate information and without any unnecessary risk of transmitting disease to the recipient.

17. This Directive sets out the basic quality and safety requirements needed in every transplant system. A sound infrastructure and responsible institutions for organ procurement and transplantation have been identified as the main features of a successful transplantation system. The proposed Directive provides for the creation or designation of a competent national authority in each Member State. These Competent authorities will ensure compliance with the requirements of the Directive. The Directive also establishes a system for the authorisation of programmes of organ procurement and transplantation based on common quality and safety criteria. This system would provide a complete list of authorised centres throughout the European Union, accessible to the public and professionals alike.

18. Procurement, evaluation and selection of the donor are the first and decisive steps in the transplantation chain. The proposed Directive will establish common quality and safety standards for the processes of evaluating donors and human organs, thus ensuring the health of recipients.

19. Of equal importance is to ensure the quality of the processes performed by the various organisations in the field. To improve these processes, the Directive proposes the introduction of national quality programmes to ensure continuous monitoring of performance and improvement and learning. Specific standards for the procurement and transport of human organs and training of professionals will be part of the national quality programmes.

20. Establishment of a system to ensure that all organs can be traced from donation to reception and vice versa is a key factor to ensure safety but also in order to prevent remuneration, trade and trafficking in organs. The proposed Directive will ensure that Member States put in place organ traceability systems. The Commission will adopt procedures for guaranteeing full traceability of organs exchanged between Member States. Traceability does not mean that the organ receiver will learn the names and further details of the donor, or vice versa. Traceability therefore aims at safeguarding the health of donors and recipients and serves no other purpose than guaranteeing the quality and safety of the organs. The anonymity of both the donor and the recipient remains a cornerstone for their protection. But the relevant competent authorities should keep the necessary documentation and records, e.g. where the organ originated from, who supplied it and under which circumstances.

21. As organ donors are often also tissue and cell donors, it is additionally important that information about adverse events and infections can be quickly traced to a donation and immediately relayed to the tissue vigilance system provided for by the Tissue and Cell Directive 2004/23/EC. Currently such a system does not exist.

22. In addition, the proposal includes measures to capture serious adverse events related to the procurement, testing and transport of organs, as well as any serious adverse reactions observed during or after transplantation which may be connected to the procurement, testing and transport of the organ in the European Union. The Commission will adopt procedures for ensuring interoperability between the reporting systems on adverse events and reactions.

Ensuring the protection of donors

23. The use of human organs should be under conditions protecting the rights and health of donors. As a matter of principle, organ transplantation programmes should be based on the principle of voluntary and unpaid donation, altruism of the donor and solidarity between donor and recipient while ensuring anonymity of the deceased donor, the living donor (when relevant) and the recipient(s) and the protection of personal data. They should comply with the Charter of Fundamental Rights of the European Union, and take the principles of the Convention of Human Rights and Biomedicine of the Council of Europe fully into account.

24. Consent for procurement is as a general rule regulated by Member States in very different ways; ranging from presumed consent systems to systems where the consent of relatives is required. The Commission believes that this is a very sensitive field and that it raises a number of ethical concerns that falls within the competence of the Member States and should not be dealt with in this Directive.

25. The use of living donors is an increasing alternative given the failure to meet the growing need for organs with cadaver donation. The increase in living organ donation can be attributed to multiple factors, including pressure created by the shortage of deceased donors, surgical advances, and strong evidence of favourable transplant outcome and low donor risk.

26. The proposed Directive contains a number of measures to protect living donors. These include correct evaluation of the health of the donor and comprehensive information about the risks prior to donation, the introduction of registers for living donors to follow up their health and measures to ensure the altruistic and voluntary donation of organs by living donors.

Facilitating cooperation between Member States and cross-border exchanges

27. The current proposal seeks to ensure a high level of quality and safety throughout the 'organ transplantation chain' in all Member States, bearing in mind the freedom of movement of citizens and the need to enhance the cross-border exchange of organs within the European Union. The establishment of quality and safety standards will help to reassure the public that human organs derived from donation in another Member State carry nonetheless the same guarantees as those in their own country.

28. The cross-border exchange of organs has clear benefits. Given that donor and recipient have to be matched, a large donor pool is important to cover the needs of all the patients on the waiting lists. If there is no exchange of organs between Member States, recipients in need of a rare match will have very low prospects of finding an organ, while at the same time donors will not be considered because there are no compatible recipients on the waiting lists. This holds particularly true for difficult to treat patients (paediatric, urgent or hypersensitised patients that require very specific matching) and small Member States.

29. The Directive will put in place the quality and safety conditions needed to facilitate cross-border exchanges. It will standardise the collection of the relevant information on the characteristics of the organ needed to make a proper risk assessment. It will also establish a mechanism for transmission of the information. Transplant teams in all Member States will be reassured that they will receive the appropriate and complete information required regardless of the country of origin of the organ. This will minimise the risks to the recipient and optimise the allocation of the organs across the EU level.

30. In addition the Directive will provide for the necessary mechanisms to be put in place for cross-border exchanges of organs to ensure traceability of the organ and pre-empt serious adverse reporting.

31. The establishment of competent authorities in all Member States and the organisation of regular meetings between them will help to promote European cooperation in this field as shown in the cases of blood and tissues and cells. Coordination between these authorities would make for a more efficient allocation of organs (especially helpful for smaller Member States and for urgent and difficult–to-treat patients). As more people move across borders information will need to move with them to optimise donation and transplantation while maintaining citizens' confidence in the system in the country they are visiting.

Proposal for a

DIRECTIVE OF THE EUROPEAN PARLIAMENT AND OF THE COUNCIL

on standards of quality and safety of human organs intended for transplantation

THE EUROPEAN PARLIAMENT AND THE COUNCIL OF THE EUROPEAN UNION,

Having regard to the Treaty establishing the European Community, and in particular Article 152 (4) (a) thereof,

...

Whereas:

(1) Over the past 50 years organ transplantation has become an established worldwide practice, bringing immense benefits to hundreds of thousands of patients. The use of human organs for transplantation has steadily increased during the last two decades. Organ transplantation is now the most cost-effective treatment for end-stage renal failure, while for end-stage failure of organs such as the liver, lung and heart it is the only available treatment.

(2) Risks however are associated with the use of organs in transplantation. The extensive therapeutic use of human organs for transplantation demands that their quality and safety should be such as to minimise any risks associated with the transmission of diseases.

(3) In addition the availability of organs of human origin used for therapeutic purposes is dependent on Community citizens being prepared to donate them. In order to safeguard public health and to prevent the transmission of diseases by these organs, precautionary measures should be taken during their procurement, transport and use.

(4) Every year organs are exchanged between Member States. The exchange of organs is an important way of expanding the pool of organs available and ensuring a better match between donor and recipient and therefore improving the quality of the transplant. This is particularly important for the optimum treatment of specific patients such as patients requiring urgent treatments, hypersensitised patients or paediatric patients. Available organs should be able to cross borders without unnecessary problems and delays.

(5) However, the transplantation process is carried out by hospitals or professionals falling under different jurisdictions and there are significant differences in quality and safety requirements between Member States.

(6) There is therefore a need for common quality and safety standards for the procurement, transport and use of human organs at Community level. These standards would facilitate exchanges of organs to the benefit of thousands of European patients in need of this type of therapy each year. Community legislation should ensure that human organs comply with ac-

ceptable standards of quality and safety. Therefore such standards will help to reassure the public that human organs procured in another Member State nonetheless carry the same basic quality and safety guarantees as those obtained in their own country.

(7) In order to reduce the risks and maximise the benefits of the transplantation process. Member States need to operate an effective national quality programme. This programme should be implemented and maintained throughout the entire chain from donation to transplantation or disposal, and should cover the personnel and organisation, premises, equipment, materials, documentation and record-keeping involved. The national quality programme should include auditing where necessary. Member States should be able to delegate, through written agreements, the responsibility for parts of this programme to European organ exchange organisations.

(8) The conditions of procurement should be supervised by the Competent Authorities through the authorisation of identified procurement organisations. The authorisation should assume that proper organisation, qualified staff and adequate facilities and material are in place.

(9) The risk-benefit ratio is a fundamental approach to organ transplantation. Owing to the shortage of organs and the inherent life threatening nature of organ transplants, the overall benefits of organ transplantation are high and more risks are accepted than with blood or most tissues and cell-based treatments. The clinician plays an important role in this context by deciding whether or not organs are suitable for transplantation; therefore this Directive stipulates the information required to make this assessment.

(10) Pre-transplant evaluation of potential donors is an essential part of organ transplantation. This evaluation must provide enough information for the transplant centre to undertake a proper risk-benefit analysis. The risks and characteristics of the organ must be identified and documented to allow allocation to a suitable recipient. Information should be collected for complete characterisation of the organ and the donor.

(11) Effective rules for the transportation of organs should be provided which minimises ischemic times and prevents organ damage. While maintaining medical confidentiality, the organ container should be clearly labelled and contain the necessary documentation.

(12) The transplant system must ensure traceability of organs from donation to reception. The system must have the capacity to raise the alert if there is any unexpected complication. A system should therefore be put in place to detect and investigate serious adverse events or reactions, for the protection of vital interest of the individuals concerned.

(13) An organ donor is also very often a tissue donor. Quality and safety requirements for organs should complement and be linked with the existing Community system for tissues and cells laid down in Directive 2004/23/EC of the European Parliament and of the Council of 31 March 2004 on setting standards of quality and safety for the donation, procurement, testing, processing, preservation, storage and distribution of human tissues and cells [10]. An

unexpected adverse reaction in an organ donor or recipient should be traced by the competent authority and reported in the tissue vigilance system as provided for in that Directive.

(14) Personnel directly involved in the donation, procurement, testing, preservation, transport and transplantation of human organs should be suitable qualified and trained.

(15) As a general principle, exchange of organs from/to third countries should be supervised by the Competent Authority. Authorisation should be granted only if standards equivalent to those provided for in this Directive are met. However, the important role played by existing European organ exchange organisations in the exchange of organs between the Member States and third countries participating in such organisations should be taken into account.

(16) This Directive should respect the fundamental rights and observe the principles recognised in particular by the Charter of Fundamental Rights of the European Union. In line with that charter and to take account of, as appropriate the Convention on human rights and biomedicine, organ transplantation programmes should be founded on the principles of voluntary and unpaid donation, altruism of the donor and solidarity between donor and recipient while ensuring anonymity of the deceased donor and the recipient(s).

(17) Article 8 of Directive 95/46/EC of the European Parliament and of the Council of 24 October 1995 on the protection of individuals with regard to the processing of personal data and on the free movement of such data prohibits in principle the processing of data concerning health. Limited exemptions to this prohibition principle are laid down. Directive 95/46/EC also requires the controller to implement appropriate technical and organisational measures to protect personal data against accidental or unlawful destruction or accidental loss, alteration, unauthorised disclosure or access and against all other unlawful forms of processing.

(18) Living donor should undertake an adequate evaluation to determine their suitability for donation in order to minimise the risk of transmission of diseases to the recipient. In addition living donors of organs face risks linked both to testing to ascertain their suitability as a donor and to the procedure to obtain the organ. Complications may be medical, surgical, social, financial or psychological. The level of risk very much depends on the type of organ to be donated. Therefore, living donations needs to be performed in a manner that minimizes the physical, psychological and social risk to the individual donor and the recipient and does not jeopardise the public's trust in the healthcare community. The potential living donor must be able to take an independent decision on the basis of all the relevant information and should be informed in advance as to the purpose and nature of the donation, the consequences and risks, as established in the additional protocol to the Convention on Human Rights and Biomedicine, on Transplantation of Organs and Tissues of Human Origin of the Council of Europe. This will contribute to assess the exclusion of persons whose donation could present a health risk to others, such as the possibility of transmitting diseases, or a serious risk to themselves.

(19) The competent authorities of the Member States should have a key role to play in ensuring the quality and safety of organs during the entire chain from donation to transplantation.

As emphasised by the Recommendation of the Committee of Ministers to Member States on the background, functions and responsibilities of a National Transplant Organisation (NTO) of the Council of Europe, it is preferable to have a single body which is officially recognised and non-profit making with overall responsibility for donation, allocation, traceability and accountability. However, depending especially on the repartition of competences within the Member States, a combination of local, regional, national and/or international bodies may work together to co-ordinate donation, allocation and/or transplantation, provided that the framework in place ensures accountability, co-operation and efficiency.

(20) The Member States should lay down rules on penalties applicable to infringements of the provisions of this Directive and ensure that these penalties are implemented. Those penalties must be effective, proportionate and dissuasive.

(21) The measures needed to implement this Directive should be adopted in accordance with Council Decision 1999/468/EC of 28 June 1999 laying down the procedures for the exercise of implementing powers conferred on the Commission.

(22) In particular, power should be conferred on the Commission to lay down, where the organs concerned are to be exchanged between Member States, the procedures for the transmission to transplantation centres of the information on the characteristics of the organs, the procedures needed to ensure the traceability of the organs, including labelling requirements, and the procedures for the reporting of serious adverse events or reactions. Since these measures are of general scope and are designed to amend non-essential elements of this Directive, or to supplement this Directive with new non-essential elements, they must be adopted in accordance with the regulatory procedure with scrutiny provided for in Article 5a of Decision 1999/468/EC.

(23) Since the objectives of this Directive, namely laying down quality and safety standards for human organs intended for transplantation, cannot be sufficiently achieved by the Member States and can therefore, by reason of the scale of the action, be better achieved at Community level, the Community may adopt measures, in accordance with the principle of subsidiarity as set out in Article 5 of the Treaty. In accordance with the principle of proportionality, as set out in that Article, this Directive does not go beyond what is necessary in order to achieve those objectives.

HAVE ADOPTED THIS DIRECTIVE:

CHAPTER I. Subject matter, scope and definitions

Article 1 – Subject Matter

This Directive lays down rules to ensure high standards of quality and safety for organs of human origin intended for transplantation to the human body, in order to ensure a high level of human health protection.

ARTICLE 2 – SCOPE

1. This Directive applies to the donation, procurement, testing, characterisation, preservation, transport and transplantation of organs of human origin intended for transplantation.

2. However, where such organs are used for research purposes, this Directive only applies where they are intended for transplantation into the human body.

ARTICLE 3 – DEFINITIONS

For the purposes of this Directive, the following definitions apply:

(a) 'authorisation' means authorisation, accreditation, designation or licensing, depending of the concepts used in each Member State;

(b) 'disposal' means the final placement of an organ when it is not used for transplantation;

(c) 'donor' means every human source of organs, whether living or deceased ;

(d) 'donation' means donating human organs for transplantation;

(e) 'donor characterisation' means the collection of the relevant information on the characteristics of the donor needed to undertake a proper risk assessment in order to minimise the risks for the recipient and to optimise organ allocation;

(f) 'European organ exchange organisation' means a non-profit organisation, whether public or private, dedicated especially to cross-border organ exchange; the countries members of such an organisation are in their majority Member States of the Community;

(g) 'organ' means a differentiated and vital part of the human body, formed by different tissues, that maintains its structure, vascularisation, and capacity to develop physiological functions with an important level of autonomy;

(h) 'organ characterisation' means the collection of the relevant information on the characteristics of the organ needed to undertake a proper risk assessment in order to minimise the risks for the recipient and to optimise organ allocation;

(i) 'procurement' means a process by which the donated organs become available;

(j) "procurement organisation" means a health care establishment, a team or a unit of a hospital or another body which is authorised by the competent authority to undertakes procurement of human organs;

(k) 'preservation' means the use of chemical agents, alterations in environmental conditions or other means during processing to prevent or retard biological or physical deterioration of human organs from the procurement until the transplantation;

(l) 'recipient': means a person who receives a transplant of an organ;

(m) 'serious adverse event' means any unexpected occurrence associated with any stage of the chain from donation to transplantation that might lead to the transmission of a communicable disease, to death or life-threatening, disabling, or incapacitating conditions for patients or which results in, or prolongs, hospitalisation or morbidity;

(n) 'serious adverse reaction' means an unintended response, including a communicable disease, in the donor or in the recipient associated with any stage of the chain from donation to transplantation that is fatal, life-threatening, disabling, incapacitating, or which results in, or prolongs, hospitalisation or morbidity;

(o) 'standard operating procedures' means written instructions describing the steps in a specific process, including the materials and methods to be used and the expected end product;

(p) 'transplantation' means the process of restoring certain functions of the human body by transferring equivalent organs to a recipient.;

(q) 'transplantation centre' means a health care establishment, a team or a unit of a hospital or any other body which is authorised by the competent authority to undertake transplantation of human organs;

(r) 'traceability' means the ability for a competent authority to locate and identify the organ at each stage in the chain from donation to transplantation or disposal, which under specified circumstances in this Directive is authorised to :

– identify the donor and the procurement organisation
– identify the recipient(s) at the transplantation centre(s)
– locate and identify all relevant non-personal information relating to products and materials coming into contact with that organ;

CHAPTER II. The quality and safety of organs

ARTICLE 4

National quality programmes

1. Member States shall ensure that a national quality programme is established to cover all stages of the chain from donation to transplantation or disposal, in order to ensure compliance with the rules laid down in this Directive.

2. The national quality programmes shall provide for the adoption and implementation of:

(a) standard operating procedures for the verification of donor identity;

(b) standard operating procedures for the verification of the details of donor or donor family consent or authorisation in accordance with national rules;

(c) standard operating procedures for the verification of the completion of the organ and donor characterisation in accordance with Article 7 and with the model set out in the Annex;

(d) procedures for the procurement, preservation packaging and labelling of organs, in accordance with Article 5, 6 and 8 ;

(e) rules for the transportation of human organs in accordance with Article 8.

3. The national quality programmes shall

(a) lay down rules to ensure the traceability of organs at all stages of the chain from donation to transplantation or disposal, in accordance with Article 10, including

– the standard operating procedures under which the traceability of organs is ensured at national level,
– the data necessary to ensure traceability and how the legal requirements on the protection of personal data and confidentiality are complied with,
– the responsibilities of procurement organisations and transplantation centres with regard to traceability.

(b) establish the standard operating procedures for:

– the accurate, rapid and verifiable reporting of serious adverse events and reactions in accordance with Article 11(1),
– the recall of organs as referred in Article 11(2),
– the responsibilities of procurement organisations and transplantation centres in the process of reporting.

(c) establish the qualifications required by the personnel involved at all stages of the chain from donation to transplantation or disposal, and develop specific training programmes for personnel in accordance with recognised international standards.

Article 5 – Procurement organisations

1. Member States shall ensure that the procurement takes place in procurement organisations that comply with the rules laid down in this Directive.

2. The organisational structure and operational procedures of procurement organisations shall include:

(a) an organisational chart which clearly defines job descriptions, accountability and reporting relationships;

(b) standard operating procedures as specified in national quality programmes .

3. Member States shall, upon the request of the Commission or another Member State, provide information on the national requirements for the authorisation of procurement organisations.

Article 6 – Organ procurement

1. Member States shall ensure that medical activities in procurement organisations, such as donor selection, are performed under the advice and the supervision of a medical doctor as defined in Directive 2005/36/EC.

2. Member States shall ensure that procurement takes place in dedicated facilities, which are designed, constructed, maintained and operated so as to comply with the requirements laid down in this Directive and which allow minimising bacterial or other contamination of procured human organs in accordance with best medical practices.

Those facilities shall comply with normal standard for operating theatres, including:

(a) Restricted access;

(b) personnel that are appropriately dressed for sterile operations, wearing sterile gloves, hats and facemasks.

3. Member States shall ensure that procurement material and equipment are managed in accordance with relevant national and international regulation, standards and guidelines covering the sterilisation of medicines and medical devices. Qualified, sterile instruments and procurement devices shall be used for procurement.

Article 7 – Organ and donor characterisation

1. Member States shall ensure that all procured organs and donors thereof are characterised before transplantation through the collection of the information and data listed in the organ characterisation form in the Annex. The tests required for organ characterisation shall be carried out by a qualified laboratory.

2. Member States shall ensure that organisations, bodies and qualified laboratories involved in organ and donor characterisation have appropriate standard operating procedures in place to ensure that the information on organ and donor characterisation reaches the transplantation centre in time.

Article 8 – Transport of organs

1. Member States shall ensure that the following requirements are met:

(a) the organisations, bodies or companies involved in the transportation of organs have appropriate standard operating procedures in place to ensure the integrity of the organ during transport and that transport time is minimised.

(b) the shipping containers used for transporting organs are labelled with the following information:

– identification of the procurement organisation, including its address and telephone number;
– identification of the transplantation centre of destination, including address and telephone number;
– a statement that the package contains a human organ and marked HANDLE WITH CARE;
– recommended transport conditions, including instructions for keeping the container at a certain temperature and in a certain position
– safety instructions and method of cooling (when applicable).

However point (b) shall not apply where the transportation is carried out within the same establishment

Article 9 – Transplantation centres

1. Member States shall ensure that transplantation takes place in transplantation centres that comply with the rules laid down in this Directive.

2. The Competent authority shall indicate in the accreditation, designation, authorisation or licence which activities the transplantation centre concerned may undertake.

3. Transplantation centres shall verify before proceeding to transplantation that:

a) the organ and donor characterisation is completed in accordance with the model set out in the Annex and that records are kept of the information contained in that form;

b) the indicated storage temperature and other conditions of transport of shipped human organs have been maintained.

4. Member States shall, upon the request of the Commission or another Member State, provide information on the national requirements for the authorisation of transplantation centres.

Article 10 – Traceability

1. Member States shall ensure that all organs procured and allocated on their territory can be traced from the donor to the recipient and vice versa in order to safeguard the health of donors and recipients.

2. Member States shall ensure the implementation of a donor identification system that can identify each donation and each of the organs associated with it. Member States shall ensure that this donor identification system are designed and selected in accordance with the aim of collecting, processing or using no personal data or as little personal data as possible. In particular, use is to be made of the possibilities for pseudonymisation or rendering individuals anonymous.

3. Member States shall ensure that:

a) The Competent authority or other bodies involved in the chain from donation to transplantation or disposal keep the data needed to ensure traceability at all stages of the chain from donation to transplantation or disposal in accordance with the national quality programmes.

b) Data required for full traceability is kept for a minimum of 30 years after donation. Such data storage may be stored in electronic form.

Article 11

Reporting systems for serious adverse events and reactions

1. Member States shall ensure that there is a reporting system in place to report, investigate, register and transmit relevant and necessary information concerning serious adverse events and reactions that may influence the quality and safety of human organs and which may be attributed to the procurement, testing, and transport of organs, as well as any serious adverse reaction observed during or after transplantation which may be connected to those activities.

2. Member States shall ensure that a procedure is in place to enable the rapid recall of any organ which may be related to a serious adverse event or reaction as specified in the national quality programme.

3. Member States shall ensure the interconnection between the reporting system referred to in paragraph 1 of this Article and the reporting system established in accordance with Article 11 of Directive 2004/23/EC.

ARTICLE 12 – PERSONNEL

Member States shall ensure that personnel directly involved in the chain from donation to the transplantation or disposal of organs are qualified to perform their tasks and are provided with the relevant training, as specified in the national quality programmes.

CHAPTER III. Donor and recipient protection

ARTICLE 13 – PRINCIPLES GOVERNING ORGAN DONATION

1. Member States shall ensure that donations of human organs from deceased and living donors are voluntary and unpaid.

2. Member States shall prohibit advertising the need for or, availability of, human organs where such advertising has a view to offering or seeking financial gain or comparable advantage.

3. Member States shall ensure that the procurement of organs is carried out on a non-profit basis.

ARTICLE 14 – CONSENT AND AUTHORISATION REQUIREMENTS PRIOR TO PROCUREMENT

Procurement shall only be carried out only after compliance with all mandatory consent or authorisation requirements in force in the Member State concerned.

ARTICLE 15 – PROTECTION OF THE LIVING DONOR

1. Member States shall take all necessary measures to ensure that potential living donors are provided with all the information necessary, as to the purpose and nature of the donation, the consequences and risks, and on alternative therapies for the potential recipient to enable them to make an informed decision. The information shall be supplied in advance of the donation.

2. Member States shall ensure that living donors are selected on the basis of their health and medical history, including a psychological evaluation if deemed necessary, by qualified and trained professionals. Such assessments may provide for the exclusion of persons whose donation could present a health risk to others, such as the possibility of transmitting diseases, or a serious risk to themselves.

3. Member States shall ensure that the competent authority keeps a register of the living donors after the donation, in line with provisions on the protection of the personal data and statistical confidentiality, and collects information on their follow up and, and specifically, on complications related to their donation that might appear in the short, mid and long term.

ARTICLE 16 – PROTECTION OF PERSONAL DATA, CONFIDENTIALITY AND SECURITY OF PROCESSING.

Member States shall ensure that the fundamental right to protection of personal data is fully and effectively protected in all organ transplantation activities, in conformity with Community provisions on the protection of personal data, such as Directive 95/46/EC, and in particular Articles 8 (3), 16, 17 and 28 (2) of that Directive.

Article 17 – Anonymisation of donors and recipients

Member States shall take all necessary measures to ensure that all personal data of donors and recipients processed within the scope of this Directive are rendered anonymous so that neither donors nor recipients remain identifiable.

CHAPTER IV. Obligations of the competent authorities and exchanges of information

Article 18 – Designation and tasks of competent authorities

Member States shall designate the competent authority, or authorities (hereafter competent authority), responsible for implementing the requirements of this Directive.

The competent authorities shall, in particular, take the following measures:

(a) put in place and keep updated a national quality programme in accordance with Article 4;

(b) ensure that procurement organisations and transplantations centres are controlled and audited on a regular basis to ascertain compliance with the requirements of this Directive;

(c) grant, suspend, or withdraw, as appropriate, the authorisations of procurement organisations or transplantation centres if control measures demonstrate that such organisations or centres do not comply with the requirements of this Directive;

(d) put in place a reporting system and a system for the recall of organs as provided for in Article 11(1) and (2);

(e) issue appropriate guidance to health care establishments, professionals and other parties involved in all stages of the chain from donation to transplantation or disposal;

(f) participate in the Community network referred to in Article 20 and coordinate at national level input to the activities of the network;

(g) supervise the exchanges of organs with other Member States and with third countries;

(f) ensure, in cooperation with the supervisory authority established in compliance with Article 28 of Directive 95/46/EC, that the fundamental right to protection of personal data is fully and effectively protected in all organ transplantation activities, in conformity with Community provisions on the protection of personal data, in particular Directive 95/46/EC.

Article 19 – Registers and reports concerning procurement organisations and transplantation centres

1. Member States shall ensure that the competent authority:

(a) keeps a record of the activities of procurement organisations and transplantation centres, includeing aggregated and anonymised numbers of living and deceased donors, and the types

and quantities of organs procured and transplanted, or otherwise disposed of in line with provisions on the protection of personal data and statistical confidentiality;
(b) draws up and makes publicly accessible an annual report on those activities;
(c) establishes and maintains a register of procurement organisations and transplantation centres.

2. Member States shall, upon the request of the Commission or another Member State, provide information on the register of procurement organisations and transplantation centres.

ARTICLE 20 – EXCHANGE OF INFORMATION

1. The Commission shall set up a network of the competent authorities with a view to exchanging information on the experience acquired with regard to the implementation of this Directive.

2. Where appropriate, experts on organ transplantation, representatives from European organ exchange organisations, as well as data protection supervisory authorities and other relevant parties may be associated to this network.

CHAPTER V. Exchanges of organs with third countries and european organ exchange organisations

ARTICLE 21 – EXCHANGE OF ORGANS WITH THIRD COUNTRIES

1. Member States shall ensure that all exchanges of organs from or to third countries, are authorised by the competent authority.

2. Authorisations for exchanges of organs, as referred to in paragraph 1, shall only be granted if the organs:
(a) can be traced from the donor to the recipient and vice versa;
(b) meet quality and safety requirements equivalent to the ones laid down in this Directive.

ARTICLE 22. EUROPEAN ORGAN EXCHANGE ORGANISATIONS

Member States may establish written agreements with European organ exchange organisations, provided that such organisations ensure compliance with the requirements laid down in this Directive, delegating to them:

(a) the performance of activities provided for under the national quality programmes;
(b) the granting of authorisation and specific tasks in relation to the exchanges of organs to and from Member States and third countries.

…

ANNEX

…

Genetics

PART V

1   Council for International Organizations of Medical Sciences. The Declaration of Inuyama, 1990

Human Genome Mapping, Genetic Screening and Gene Therapy

In addition to biomedical scientists and physicians, the participants represented a wide range of disciplines including sociology, psychology, epidemiology, law, social policy, philosophy and theology, and brought with them experience in hospital and public health medicine, universities and private industry, and the executive and legislative branches of government. Through presentations and discussions in plenary sessions and working groups, they reached broad agreement on a number of central issues. At its final session the Conference agreed on the following Declaration.

I. Discussion of human genetics is dominated today by the efforts now under way on an international basis to map and sequence the human genome. Such attention is warranted by the scale of the undertaking and its expected contribution to knowledge about human biology and disease. At the same time, the nature of the undertaking, concerned as it is with the basic elements of life, and the potential for abuse of the new knowledge which the project will generate, are giving rise to anxiety. The Conference agrees that efforts to map the human genome present no inherent ethical problems but are eminently worthwhile, especially as the knowledge revealed will be universally applicable to benefit human health. In terms of ethics and human values, what must be assured are that the manner in which gene mapping efforts are implemented adheres to ethical standards of research and that the knowledge gained will be used appropriately, particularly in genetic screening and gene therapy.

II. Public concern about the growth of genetic knowledge stems in part from the misconception that while the knowledge reveals an essential aspect of humanness it also diminishes human beings by reducing them to mere base pairs of deoxyribonucleic acid (DNA). This misconception can be corrected by education of the public and open discussion, which should reassure the public that plans for the medical use of genetic findings and techniques will be made openly and responsibly.

III. Some types of genetic testing or treatment not yet in prospect could raise novel issues – for example, whether limits should be placed on DNA alterations in human germ cells, because such changes would affect future generations, whose consent cannot be obtained and whose best interests would be difficult to calculate. The Conference concludes, however, that for the most part present genetic research and services do not raise unique or even novel issues, although their connection to private matters such as reproduction and personal health and life prospects, and the rapidity of advances in genetic knowledge and technology, accentuate the need for ethical sensitivity in policy-making.

IV. It is primarily in regard to genetic testing that the human genome project gives rise to concern about ethics and human values. The identification, cloning and sequencing of new genes without first needing to know their protein products greatly expand the possible scope for screening and diagnostic tests. The central objective of genetic screening and diagnosis should always be to safeguard the welfare of the person tested: test results must always be protected against unconsented disclosure, confidentiality must be ensured at all costs, and adequate counselling must be provided. Physicians and others who counsel should endeavour to ensure that all those concerned understand the difference between being the carrier of a defective gene and having the corresponding genetic disease. In autosomal recessive conditions, the health of carriers (heterozygotes) is usually not affected by their having a single copy of the disease gene; in dominant disorders, what is of concern is the manifestation of the disease, not the mere presence of the defective gene, especially when years may elapse between the results of a genetic test and the manifestation of the disease.

V. The genome project will produce knowledge of relevance to human gene therapy, which will very soon be clinically applicable to a few rare but very burdensome recessive disorders. Alterations in somatic cells, which will affect only the DNA of the treated individual, should be evaluated like other innovative therapies. Particular attention by independent ethical review committees is necessary, especially when gene therapy involves children, as it will for many of the disorders in question. Interventions should be limited to conditions that cause significant disability and not employed merely to enhance or suppress cosmetic, behavioural or cognitive characteristics unrelated to any recognized human disease.

VI. The modification of human germ cells for therapeutic or preventive purposes would be technically much more difficult than that of somatic cells and is not at present in prospect. Such therapy might, however, be the only means of treating certain conditions, so continued discussion of both its technical and its ethical aspects is essential. Before germ-line therapy is undertaken, its safety must be very well established, for changes in germ cells would affect the descendants of patients.

VII. Genetic researchers and therapists have a strong responsibility to ensure that the techniques they develop are used ethically. By insisting on truly voluntary programmes designed to benefit directly those involved, they can ensure that no precedents are set for eugenic programmes or other misuse of the techniques by the State or by private parties. One means of ensuring the setting and observance of ethical standards is continuous multidisciplinary and transcultural dialogue.

VIII. The needs of developing countries should receive special attention, to ensure that they obtain their due share of the benefits that ensue from the human genome project. In particular, methods and techniques of testing and therapy that are affordable and easily accessible to the populations of such countries should be developed and disseminated whenever possible.

2. International Declaration on Human Genetic Data, 16 October 2003

The General Conference, Recalling the Universal Declaration of Human Rights of 10 December 1948, the two United Nations International Covenants on Economic, Social and Cultural Rights and on Civil and Political Rights of 16 December 1966, the United Nations International Convention on the Elimination of All Forms of Racial Discrimination of 21 December 1965, the United Nations Convention on the Elimination of All Forms of Discrimination against Women of 18 December 1979, the United Nations Convention on the Rights of the Child of 20 November 1989, the United Nations Economic and Social Council resolutions 2001/39 on Genetic Privacy and Non-Discrimination of 26 July 2001 and 2003/232 on Genetic Privacy and Non-Discrimination of 22 July 2003, the ILO Convention (No. 111) concerning Discrimination in Respect of Employment and Occupation of 25 June 1958, the UNESCO Universal Declaration on Cultural Diversity of 2 November 2001, the Trade Related Aspects of Intellectual Property Rights Agreement (TRIPS) annexed to the Agreement establishing the World Trade Organization, which entered into force on 1 January 1995, the Doha Declaration on the TRIPS Agreement and Public Health of 14 November 2001 and the other international human rights instruments adopted by the United Nations and the specialized agencies of the United Nations system, Recalling more particularly the Universal Declaration on the Human Genome and Human Rights which it adopted, unanimously and by acclamation, on 11 November 1997 and which was endorsed by the United Nations General Assembly on 9 December 1998 and the Guidelines for the implementation of the Universal Declaration on the Human Genome and Human Rights which it endorsed on 16 November 1999 by 30 C/Resolution 23, Welcoming the broad public interest worldwide in the Universal Declaration on the Human Genome and Human Rights, the firm support it has received from the international community and its impact in Member States drawing upon it for their legislation, regulations, norms and standards, and ethical codes of conduct and guidelines, Bearing in mind the international and regional instruments, national laws, regulations and ethical texts relating to the protection of human rights and fundamental freedoms and to respect for human dignity as regards the collection, processing, use and storage of scientific data, as well as of medical data and personal data, Recognizing that genetic information is part of the overall spectrum of medical data and that the information content of any medical data, including genetic data and proteomic data, is highly contextual and dependent on the particular circumstances, Also recognizing that human genetic data have a special status on account of their sensitive nature since they can be predictive of genetic predispositions concerning individuals and that the power of predictability can be stronger than assessed at the time of deriving the data; they may have a significant impact on the family, including offspring, extending over generations, and in some instances on the whole group; they may contain information the significance of which is not necessarily known at the time of the collection of biological samples; and they may have cultural significance for persons or groups, Emphasizing that all medical data, including genetic data and proteomic data, regardless of their apparent information content, should be treated with the same high standards of confidentiality, Noting the increasing importance of human genetic data for economic and commercial purposes, Having regard to the special needs and vulnerabilities of developing countries and the need to reinforce international cooperation in the field of human genetics, Considering that the collection, processing, use and storage of human genetic data are of paramount importance for the progress of life sciences and medicine, for their applications and for the use of such data for non-medical purposes, Also considering that the growing amount of personal data collected makes genuine irretrievability increasingly difficult, Aware that the collection, processing, use and storage of human genetic data have potential risks for the exercise and observance of human rights and fundamental freedoms and respect for human dignity, Noting that the interests and welfare of the individual should have priority over the rights and interests of society and research, Reaffirming the principles established in the Universal Declaration on the Human Genome and Human Rights and the principles of equality, justice, solidarity and responsibility as well as respect for human dignity, human rights and fundamental freedoms, particularly freedom of thought and expression, including freedom of research, and privacy and security of the person, which must underlie the collection, processing, use and storage of human genetic data, Proclaims the principles that follow and adopts the present Declaration.

A. General provisions

ARTICLE 1. AIMS AND SCOPE

(a) The aims of this Declaration are: to ensure the respect of human dignity and protection of human rights and fundamental freedoms in the collection, processing, use and storage of human genetic data, human proteomic data and of the biological samples from which they are derived, referred to hereinafter as "biological samples", in keeping with the requirements of equality, justice and solidarity, while giving due consideration to freedom of thought and expression, including freedom of research; to set out the principles which should guide States in the formulation of their legislation and their policies on these issues; and to form the basis for guidelines of good practices in these areas for the institutions and individuals concerned.

(b) Any collection, processing, use and storage of human genetic data, human proteomic data and biological samples shall be consistent with the international law of human rights.

(c) The provisions of this Declaration apply to the collection, processing, use and storage of human genetic data, human proteomic data and biological samples, except in the investigation, detection and prosecution of criminal offences and in parentage testing that are subject to domestic law that is consistent with the international law of human rights.

ARTICLE 2. USE OF TERMS

For the purposes of this Declaration, the terms used have the following meanings:

(i)   Human genetic data: Information about heritable characteristics of individuals obtained by analysis of nucleic acids or by other scientific analysis;
(ii)   Human proteomic data: Information pertaining to an individual's proteins including their expression, modification and interaction;

(iii) Consent: Any freely given specific, informed and express agreement of an individual to his or her genetic data being collected, processed, used and stored;

(iv) Biological samples: Any sample of biological material (for example blood, skin and bone cells or blood plasma) in which nucleic acids are present and which contains the characteristic genetic make-up of an individual;

(v) Population-based genetic study: A study which aims at understanding the nature and extent of genetic variation among a population or individuals within a group or between individuals across different groups;

(vi) Behavioural genetic study: A study that aims at establishing possible connections between genetic characteristics and behaviour;

(vii) Invasive procedure: Biological sampling using a method involving intrusion into the human body, such as obtaining a blood sample by using a needle and syringe;

(viii) Non-invasive procedure: Biological sampling using a method which does not involve intrusion into the human body, such as oral smears;

(ix) Data linked to an identifiable person: Data that contain information, such as name, birth date and address, by which the person from whom the data were derived can be identified;

(x) Data unlinked to an identifiable person: Data that are not linked to an identifiable person, through the replacement of, or separation from, all identifying information about that person by use of a code;

(xi) Data irretrievably unlinked to an identifiable person: Data that cannot be linked to an identifiable person, through destruction of the link to any identifying information about the person who provided the sample;

(xii) Genetic testing: A procedure to detect the presence or absence of, or change in, a particular gene or chromosome, including an indirect test for a gene product or other specific metabolite that is primarily indicative of a specific genetic change;

(xiii) Genetic screening: Large-scale systematic genetic testing offered in a programme to a population or subsection thereof intended to detect genetic characteristics in asymptomatic people;

(xiv) Genetic counseling: A procedure to explain the possible implications of the findings of genetic testing or screening, its advantages and risks and where applicable to assist the individual in the long-term handling of the consequences; It takes place before and after genetic testing and screening;

(xv) Cross-matching: Matching of information about an individual or a group contained in various data files set up for different purposes.

ARTICLE 3. PERSON'S IDENTITY

Each individual has a characteristic genetic make-up. Nevertheless, a person's identity should not be reduced to genetic characteristics, since it involves complex educational, environmental and personal factors and emotional, social, spiritual and cultural bonds with others and implies a dimension of freedom.

ARTICLE 4. SPECIAL STATUS

(a) Human genetic data have a special status because:

(i)   they can be predictive of genetic predispositions concerning individuals;
(ii)   they may have a significant impact on the family, including offspring, extending over generations, and in some instances on the whole group to which the person concerned belongs;
(iii)   they may contain information the significance of which is not necessarily known at the time of the collection of the biological samples;
(iv)   they may have cultural significance for persons or groups.

(b) Due consideration should be given to the sensitivity of human genetic data and an appropriate level of protection for these data and biological samples should be established.

ARTICLE 5. PURPOSES

Human genetic data and human proteomic data may be collected, processed, used and stored only for the purposes of:

(i)   diagnosis and health care, including screening and predictive testing;
(ii)   medical and other scientific research, including epidemiological, especially population-based genetic studies, as well as anthropological or archaeological studies, collectively referred to hereinafter as "medical and scientific research";
(iii)   forensic medicine and civil, criminal and other legal proceedings, taking into account the provisions of Article 1(c);
(iv)   or any other purpose consistent with the Universal Declaration on the Human Genome and Human Rights and the international law of human rights.

ARTICLE 6. PROCEDURES

(a) It is ethically imperative that human genetic data and human proteomic data be collected, processed, used and stored on the basis of transparent and ethically acceptable procedures. States should endeavour to involve society at large in the decision-making process concerning broad policies for the collection, processing, use and storage of human genetic data and human proteomic data and the evaluation of their management, in particular in the case of population-based genetic studies. This decision-making process, which may benefit from international experience, should ensure the free expression of various viewpoints.

(b) Independent, multidisciplinary and pluralist ethics committees should be promoted and established at national, regional, local or institutional levels, in accordance with the provisions of Article 16 of the Universal Declaration on the Human Genome and Human Rights. Where appropriate, ethics committees at national level should be consulted with regard to the establishment of standards, regulations and guidelines for the collection, processing, use and storage of human genetic data, human proteomic data and biological samples. They should also be consulted concerning matters where there is no domestic law. Ethics committees at institutional or local levels should be consulted with regard to their application to specific research projects.

(c) When the collection, processing, use and storage of human genetic data, human proteomic data or biological samples are carried out in two or more States, the ethics committees in the States concerned, where appropriate, should be consulted and the review of these questions at the appropriate level should be based on the principles set out in this Declaration and on the ethical and legal standards adopted by the States concerned.

(d) It is ethically imperative that clear, balanced, adequate and appropriate information shall be provided to the person whose prior, free, informed and express consent is sought. Such information shall, alongside with providing other necessary details, specify the purpose for which human genetic data and human proteomic data are being derived from biological samples, and are used and stored. This information should indicate, if necessary, risks and consequences. This information should also indicate that the person concerned can withdraw his or her consent, without coercion, and this should entail neither a disadvantage nor a penalty for the person concerned.

ARTICLE 7. NON-DISCRIMINATION AND NON-STIGMATIZATION

(a) Every effort should be made to ensure that human genetic data and human proteomic data are not used for purposes that discriminate in a way that is intended to infringe, or has the effect of infringing human rights, fundamental freedoms or human dignity of an individual or for purposes that lead to the stigmatization of an individual, a family, a group or communities.

(b) In this regard, appropriate attention should be paid to the findings of population-based genetic studies and behavioural genetic studies and their interpretations.

B. Collection

ARTICLE 8. CONSENT

(a) Prior, free, informed and express consent, without inducement by financial or other personal gain, should be obtained for the collection of human genetic data, human proteomic data or biological samples, whether through invasive or non-invasive procedures, and for their subsequent processing, use and storage, whether carried out by public or private institutions. Limitations on this principle of consent should only be prescribed for compelling reasons by domestic law consistent with the international law of human rights.

(b) When, in accordance with domestic law, a person is incapable of giving informed consent, authorization should be obtained from the legal representative, in accordance with domestic law. The legal representative should have regard to the best interest of the person concerned.

(c) An adult not able to consent should as far as possible take part in the authorization procedure. The opinion of a minor should be taken into consideration as an increasingly determining factor in proportion to age and degree of maturity.

(d) In diagnosis and health care, genetic screening and testing of minors and adults not able to consent will normally only be ethically acceptable when they have important implications for the health of the person and have regard to his or her best interest.

ARTICLE 9. WITHDRAWAL OF CONSENT

(a) When human genetic data, human proteomic data or biological samples are collected for medical and scientific research purposes, consent may be withdrawn by the person concerned unless such data are irretrievably unlinked to an identifiable person. In accordance with the provisions of Article 6(d), withdrawal of consent should entail neither a disadvantage nor a penalty for the person concerned.

(b) When a person withdraws consent, the person's genetic data, proteomic data and biological samples should no longer be used unless they are irretrievably unlinked to the person concerned.

(c) If not irretrievably unlinked, the data and biological samples should be dealt with in accordance with the wishes of the person. If the person's wishes cannot be determined or are not feasible or are unsafe, the data and biological samples should either be irretrievably unlinked or destroyed.

ARTICLE 10. THE RIGHT TO DECIDE WHETHER OR NOT TO BE INFORMED ABOUT RESEARCH RESULTS

When human genetic data, human proteomic data or biological samples are collected for medical and scientific research purposes, the information provided at the time of consent should indicate that the person concerned has the right to decide whether or not to be informed of the results. This does not apply to research on data irretrievably unlinked to identifiable persons or to data that do not lead to individual findings concerning the persons who have participated in such a research. Where appropriate, the right not to be informed should be extended to identified relatives who may be affected by the results.

ARTICLE 11. GENETIC COUNSELLING

It is ethically imperative that when genetic testing that may have significant implications for a person's health is being considered, genetic counselling should be made available in an appropriate manner. Genetic counselling should be non-directive, culturally adapted and consistent with the best interest of the person concerned.

ARTICLE 12. COLLECTION OF BIOLOGICAL SAMPLES FOR FORENSIC MEDICINE OR IN CIVIL, CRIMINAL AND OTHER LEGAL PROCEEDINGS

When human genetic data or human proteomic data are collected for the purposes of forensic medicine or in civil, criminal and other legal proceedings, including parentage testing, the collection of biological samples, in vivo or post-mortem, should be made only in accordance with domestic law consistent with the international law of human rights.

C. Processing

ARTICLE 13. ACCESS

No one should be denied access to his or her own genetic data or proteomic data unless such data are irretrievably unlinked to that person as the identifiable source or unless domestic law limits such access in the interest of public health, public order or national security.

ARTICLE 14. PRIVACY AND CONFIDENTIALITY

(a) States should endeavour to protect the privacy of individuals and the confidentiality of human genetic data linked to an identifiable person, family or, where appropriate, group, in accordance with domestic law consistent with the international law of human rights.

(b) Human genetic data, human proteomic data and biological samples linked to an identifiable person should not be disclosed or made accessible to third parties, in particular, employers, insurance companies, educational institutions and the family, except for an important public interest reason in cases restrictively provided for by domestic law consistent with the international law of human rights or where the prior, free, informed and express consent of the person concerned has been obtained provided that such consent is in accordance with domestic law and the international law of human rights. The privacy of an individual participating in a study using human genetic data, human proteomic data or biological samples should be protected and the data should be treated as confidential.

(c) Human genetic data, human proteomic data and biological samples collected for the purposes of scientific research should not normally be linked to an identifiable person. Even when such data or biological samples are unlinked to an identifiable person, the necessary precautions should be taken to ensure the security of the data or biological samples.

(d) Human genetic data, human proteomic data and biological samples collected for medical and scientific research purposes can remain linked to an identifiable person, only if necessary to carry out the research and provided that the privacy of the individual and the confidentiality of the data or biological samples concerned are protected in accordance with domestic law.

(e) Human genetic data and human proteomic data should not be kept in a form which allows the data subject to be identified for any longer than is necessary for achieving the purposes for which they were collected or subsequently processed.

Article 15. Accuracy, reliability, quality and security

The persons and entities responsible for the processing of human genetic data, human proteomic data and biological samples should take the necessary measures to ensure the accuracy, reliability, quality and security of these data and the processing of biological samples. They should exercise rigour, caution, honesty and integrity in the processing and interpretation of human genetic data, human proteomic data or biological samples, in view of their ethical, legal and social implications.

D. Use

Article 16. Change of purpose

(a) Human genetic data, human proteomic data and the biological samples collected for one of the purposes set out in Article 5 should not be used for a different purpose that is incompatible with the original consent, unless the prior, free, informed and express consent of the person concerned is obtained according to the provisions of Article 8(a) or unless the proposed use, decided by domestic law, corresponds to an important public interest reason and is consistent with the international law of human rights. If the person concerned lacks the capacity to consent, the provisions of Article 8(b) and (c) should apply mutatis mutandis.

(b) When prior, free, informed and express consent cannot be obtained or in the case of data irretrievably unlinked to an identifiable person, human genetic data may be used in accordance with domestic law or following the consultation procedures set out in Article 6(b).

Article 17. Stored biological samples

(a) Stored biological samples collected for purposes other than set out in Article 5 may be used to produce human genetic data or human proteomic data with the prior, free, informed and express consent of the person concerned. However, domestic law may provide that if such data have significance for medical and scientific research purposes e.g. epidemiological studies, or public health purposes, they may be used for those purposes, following the consultation procedures set out in Article 6(b).

(b) The provisions of Article 12 should apply mutatis mutandis to stored biological samples used to produce human genetic data for forensic medicine.

Article 18. Circulation and international cooperation

(a) States should regulate, in accordance with their domestic law and international agreements, the cross-border flow of human genetic data, human proteomic data and biological samples so as to foster international medical and scientific cooperation and ensure fair access to these data. Such a system should seek to ensure that the receiving party provides adequate protection in accordance with the principles set out in this Declaration.

(b) States should make every effort, with due and appropriate regard for the principles set out in this Declaration, to continue fostering the international dissemination of scientific knowledge concerning human genetic data and human proteomic data and, in that regard, to foster scientific and cultural cooperation, particularly between industrialized and developing countries.

(c) Researchers should endeavour to establish cooperative relationships, based on mutual respect with regard to scientific and ethical matters and, subject to the provisions of Article 14, should encourage the free circulation of human genetic data and human proteomic data in order to foster the sharing of scientific knowledge, provided that the principles set out in this Declaration are observed by the parties concerned. To this end, they should also endeavour to publish in due course the results of their research.

Article 19. Sharing of benefits

(a) In accordance with domestic law or policy and international agreements, benefits resulting from the use of human genetic data, human proteomic data or biological samples collected for medical and scientific research should be shared with the society as a whole and the international community. In giving effect to this principle, benefits may take any of the following forms:

(i)   special assistance to the persons and groups that have taken part in the research;
(ii)   access to medical care;
(iii)   provision of new diagnostics, facilities for new treatments or drugs stemming from the research;
(iv)   support for health services;
(v)   capacity-building facilities for research purposes;
(vi)   development and strengthening of the capacity of developing countries to collect and process human genetic data, taking into consideration their specific problems;
(vii)   any other form consistent with the principles set out in this Declaration.

(b) Limitations in this respect could be provided by domestic law and international agreements.

E. Storage

ARTICLE 20. MONITORING AND MANAGEMENT FRAMEWORK

States may consider establishing a framework for the monitoring and management of human genetic data, human proteomic data and biological samples based on the principles of independence, multidisciplinarity, pluralism and transparency as well as the principles set out in this Declaration. This framework could also deal with the nature and purposes of the storage of these data.

ARTICLE 21. DESTRUCTION

(a) The provisions of Article 9 apply mutatis mutandis in the case of stored human genetic data, human proteomic data and biological samples.

(b) Human genetic data, human proteomic data and the biological samples collected from a suspect in the course of a criminal investigation should be destroyed when they are no longer necessary, unless otherwise provided for by domestic law consistent with the international law of human rights.

(c) Human genetic data, human proteomic data and biological samples should be available for forensic purposes and civil proceedings only for as long as they are necessary for those proceedings, unless otherwise provided for by domestic law consistent with the international law of human rights.

ARTICLE 22. CROSS-MATCHING

Consent should be essential for the cross-matching of human genetic data, human proteomic data or biological samples stored for diagnostic and health care purposes and for medical and other scientific research purposes, unless otherwise provided for by domestic law for compelling reasons and consistent with the international law of human rights.

F. Promotion and implementation

ARTICLE 23. IMPLEMENTATION

(a) States should take all appropriate measures, whether of a legislative, administrative or other character, to give effect to the principles set out in this Declaration, in accordance with the international law of human rights. Such measures should be supported by action in the sphere of education, training and public information.

(b) In the framework of international cooperation, States should endeavour to enter into bilateral and multilateral agreements enabling developing countries to build up their capacity to participate in generating and sharing scientific knowledge concerning human genetic data and the related know-how.

Article 24. Ethics education, training and information

In order to promote the principles set out in this Declaration, States should endeavour to foster all forms of ethics education and training at all levels as well as to encourage information and knowledge dissemination programmes about human genetic data. These measures should aim at specific audiences, in particular researchers and members of ethics committees, or be addressed to the public at large. In this regard, States should encourage the participation of international and regional intergovernmental organizations and international, regional and national non-governmental organizations in this endeavour.

Article 25. Roles of the International Bioethics Committee (IBC) and the Intergovernmental Bioethics Committee (IGBC)

The International Bioethics Committee (IBC) and the Intergovernmental Bioethics Committee (IGBC) shall contribute to the implementation of this Declaration and the dissemination of the principles set out therein. On a collaborative basis, the two Committees should be responsible for its monitoring and for the evaluation of its implementation, inter alia, on the basis of reports provided by States. The two Committees should be responsible in particular for the formulation of any opinion or proposal likely to further the effectiveness of this Declaration. They should make recommendations in accordance with UNESCO's statutory procedures, addressed to the General Conference.

Article 26. Follow-up action by UNESCO

UNESCO shall take appropriate action to follow up this Declaration so as to foster progress of the life sciences and their applications through technologies, based on respect for human dignity and the exercise and observance of human rights and fundamental freedoms.

Article 27. Denial of acts contrary to human rights, fundamental freedoms and human dignity

Nothing in this Declaration may be interpreted as implying for any State, group or person any claim to engage in any activity or to perform any act contrary to human rights, fundamental freedoms and human dignity, including, in particular, the principles set out in this Declaration.

3. Additional Protocol to the Convention on Human Rights and Biomedicine concerning Genetic Testing for Health Purposes, ETS No 203

Preamble

The member States of the Council of Europe, the other States and the European Community, signatories to this Additional Protocol to the Convention for the Protection of Human Rights and Dignity of the Human Being with regard to the Application of Biology and Medicine (hereinafter referred to as "the Convention on Human Rights and Biomedicine", ETS No. 164), Considering that the aim of the Council of Europe is the achievement of greater unity between its members and that one of the methods by which this aim is pursued is the maintenance and further realisation of human rights and fundamental freedoms; Considering that the aim of the Convention on Human Rights and Biomedicine, as defined in Article 1, is to protect the dignity and identity of all human beings and guarantee everyone, without discrimination, respect for their integrity and other rights and fundamental freedoms with regard to the application of biology and medicine; Bearing in mind the Convention for the Protection of Individuals with regard to Automatic Processing of Personal Data (ETS No. 108) of 28 January 1981; Bearing in mind the work carried out by other intergovernmental organisations, in particular the Universal Declaration on the Human Genome and Human Rights, endorsed by the General Assembly of the United Nations on 9 December 1998; Recalling that the human genome is shared by all human beings, thereby forming a mutual bond between them while slight variations contribute to the individuality of each human being; Stressing the particular bond that exists between members of the same family; Considering that progress in medical science can contribute to saving lives and improving their quality; Acknowledging the benefit of genetics, in particular genetic testing, in the field of health; Considering that genetic services in the field of health form an integral part of the health services offered to the population and recalling the importance of taking appropriate measures, taking into account health needs and available resources, with a view to providing equitable access to genetic services of appropriate quality; Aware also of the concerns that exist regarding possible improper use of genetic testing, in particular of the information generated thereby; Reaffirming the fundamental principle of respect for human dignity and the prohibition of all forms of discrimination, in particular those based on genetic characteristics; Taking into account national and international professional standards in the field of genetic services and the previous work of the Committee of Ministers and the Parliamentary Assembly of the Council of Europe in this field; Resolving to take such measures as are necessary to safeguard human dignity and the fundamental rights and freedoms of the individual with regard to genetic testing for health purposes, Have agreed as follows:

Chapter I – Object and scope

ARTICLE 1. OBJECT AND PURPOSE

Parties to this Protocol shall protect the dignity and identity of all human beings and guarantee everyone, without discrimination, respect for their integrity and other rights and fundamental freedoms with regard to the tests to which this Protocol applies in accordance with Article 2.

ARTICLE 2. SCOPE

1. This Protocol applies to tests, which are carried out for health purposes, involving analysis of biological samples of human origin and aiming specifically to identify the genetic characteristics of a person which are inherited or acquired during early prenatal development (hereinafter referred to as "genetic tests").

2. This Protocol does not apply:

a. to genetic tests carried out on the human embryo or foetus;
b. to genetic tests carried out for research purposes.

3. For the purposes of paragraph 1:

a. "analysis" refers to:
    i   chromosomal analysis,
    ii   DNA or RNA analysis,
    iii analysis of any other element enabling information to be obtained which is equivalent to that obtained with the methods referred to in sub-paragraphs a.i. and a.ii.;
b. "biological samples" refers to:
    i   biological materials removed for the purpose of the test concerned,
    ii   biological materials previously removed for another purpose.

Chapter II – General provisions

ARTICLE 3. PRIMACY OF THE HUMAN BEING

The interests and welfare of the human being concerned by genetic tests covered by this Protocol shall prevail over the sole interest of society or science.

ARTICLE 4. NON-DISCRIMINATION AND NON-STIGMATISATION

1. Any form of discrimination against a person, either as an individual or as a member of a group on grounds of his or her genetic heritage is prohibited.

2. Appropriate measures shall be taken in order to prevent stigmatisation of persons or groups in relation to genetic characteristics.

Chapter III – Genetic services

ARTICLE 5. QUALITY OF GENETIC SERVICES

Parties shall take the necessary measures to ensure that genetic services are of appropriate quality. In particular, they shall see to it that:

a. genetic tests meet generally accepted criteria of scientific validity and clinical validity;
b. a quality assurance programme is implemented in each laboratory and that laboratories are subject to regular monitoring;
c. persons providing genetic services have appropriate qualifications to enable them to perform their role in accordance with professional obligations and standards.

ARTICLE 6. CLINICAL UTILITY

Clinical utility of a genetic test shall be an essential criterion for deciding to offer this test to a person or a group of persons.

ARTICLE 7. INDIVIDUALISED SUPERVISION

1. A genetic test for health purposes may only be performed under individualised medical supervision.

2. Exceptions to the general rule referred to in paragraph 1 may be allowed by a Party, subject to appropriate measures being provided, taking into account the way the test will be carried out, to give effect to the other provisions of this Protocol.

However, such an exception may not be made with regard to genetic tests with important implications for the health of the persons concerned or members of their family or with important implications concerning procreation choices.

Chapter IV – Information, genetic counselling and consent

ARTICLE 8. INFORMATION AND GENETIC COUNSELLING

1. When a genetic test is envisaged, the person concerned shall be provided with prior appropriate information in particular on the purpose and the nature of the test, as well as the implications of its results.

2. For predictive genetic tests as referred to in Article 12 of the Convention on Human Rights and Biomedicine, appropriate genetic counselling shall also be available for the person concerned.

The tests concerned are:

– tests predictive of a monogenic disease,
– tests serving to detect a genetic predisposition or genetic susceptibility to a disease,
– tests serving to identify the subject as a healthy carrier of a gene responsible for a disease.

The form and extent of this genetic counselling shall be defined according to the implications of the results of the test and their significance for the person or the members of his or her family, including possible implications concerning procreation choices.

Genetic counselling shall be given in a non-directive manner.

ARTICLE 9. CONSENT

1. A genetic test may only be carried out after the person concerned has given free and informed consent to it. Consent to tests referred to in Article 8, paragraph 2, shall be documented.

2. The person concerned may freely withdraw consent at any time.

Chapter V – Persons not able to consent

ARTICLE 10. PROTECTION OF PERSONS NOT ABLE TO CONSENT

Subject to Article 13 of this Protocol, a genetic test on a person who does not have the capacity to consent may only be carried out for his or her direct benefit.

Where, according to law, a minor does not have the capacity to consent, a genetic test on this person shall be deferred until attainment of such capacity unless that delay would be detrimental to his or her health or well-being.

ARTICLE 11. INFORMATION PRIOR TO AUTHORISATION, GENETIC COUNSELLING AND SUPPORT

1. When a genetic test is envisaged in respect of a person not able to consent, the person, authority or body whose authorisation is required shall be provided with prior appropriate information in particular with regard to the purpose and the nature of the test, as well as the implications of its results.

Appropriate prior information shall also be provided to the person not able to consent in respect of whom the test is envisaged, to the extent of his or her capacity to understand.

A qualified person shall be available to answer possible questions by the person, authority or body whose authorisation is required, and, if appropriate, the person in respect of whom the test is envisaged.

2. The provisions of Article 8, paragraph 2, shall apply in the case of persons not able to consent to the extent of their capacity to understand.

Where relevant, appropriate support shall be available for the person whose authorisation is required.

ARTICLE 12. AUTHORISATION

1. Where, according to law, a minor does not have the capacity to consent to a genetic test, that test may only be carried out with the authorisation of his or her representative or an authority or a person or body provided for by law.

The opinion of the minor shall be taken into consideration as an increasingly determining factor in proportion to his or her age and degree of maturity.

2. Where, according to law, an adult does not have the capacity to consent to a genetic test because of a mental disability, a disease or for similar reasons, that test may only be carried out with the authorisation of his or her representative or an authority or a person or body provided for by law.

Wishes relating to a genetic test expressed previously by an adult at a time where he or she had capacity to consent shall be taken into account.

The individual concerned shall, to the extent of his or her capacity to understand, take part in the authorisation procedure.

3. Authorisation to tests referred to in Article 8, paragraph 2, shall be documented.

4. The authorisation referred to in paragraphs 1 and 2 above may be withdrawn at any time in the best interests of the person concerned.

Chapter VI – Tests for the benefit of family members

ARTICLE 13. TESTS ON PERSONS NOT ABLE TO CONSENT

Exceptionally, and by derogation from the provisions of Article 6, paragraph 1, of the Convention on Human Rights and Biomedicine and of Article 10 of this Protocol, the law may allow a genetic test to be carried out, for the benefit of family members, on a person who does not have the capacity to consent, if the following conditions are met:

a. the purpose of the test is to allow the family member(s) concerned to obtain a preventive, diagnostic or therapeutic benefit that has been independently evaluated as important for their health, or to allow them to make an informed choice with respect to procreation;
b. the benefit envisaged cannot be obtained without carrying out this test;

c. the risk and burden of the intervention are minimal for the person who is undergoing the test;

d. the expected benefit has been independently evaluated as substantially outweighing the risk for private life that may arise from the collection, processing or communication of the results of the test;

e. the authorisation of the representative of the person not able to consent, or an authority or a person or body provided for by law has been given;

f. the person not able to consent shall, in proportion to his or her capacity to understand and degree of maturity, take part in the authorisation procedure. The test shall not be carried out if this person objects to it.

ARTICLE 14. TESTS ON BIOLOGICAL MATERIALS WHEN IT IS NOT POSSIBLE TO CONTACT THE PERSON CONCERNED

When it is not possible, with reasonable efforts, to contact a person for a genetic test for the benefit of his or her family member(s) on his or her biological material previously removed for another purpose, the law may allow the test to be carried out in accordance with the principle of proportionality, where the expected benefit cannot be otherwise obtained and where the test cannot be deferred.

Provisions shall be made, in accordance with Article 22 of the Convention on Human Rights and Biomedicine, for the case where the person concerned has expressly opposed such test.

ARTICLE 15. TESTS ON DECEASED PERSONS

A genetic test for the benefit of other family members may be carried out on biological samples:

– removed from the body of a deceased person, or
– removed, when he or she was alive, from a person now deceased,

only if the consent or authorisation required by law has been obtained.

Chapter VII – Private life and right to information

ARTICLE 16. RESPECT FOR PRIVATE LIFE AND RIGHT TO INFORMATION

1. Everyone has the right to respect for his or her private life, in particular to protection of his or her personal data derived from a genetic test.

2. Everyone undergoing a genetic test is entitled to know any information collected about his or her health derived from this test.

The conclusions drawn from the test shall be accessible to the person concerned in a comprehensible form.

3. The wish of a person not to be informed shall be respected.

4. In exceptional cases, restrictions may be placed by law on the exercise of the rights contained in paragraphs 2 and 3 above in the interests of the person concerned.

ARTICLE 17. BIOLOGICAL SAMPLES

Biological samples referred to in Article 2 shall only be used and stored in such conditions as to ensure their security and the confidentiality of the information which can be obtained therefrom.

ARTICLE 18. INFORMATION RELEVANT TO FAMILY MEMBERS

Where the results of a genetic test undertaken on a person can be relevant to the health of other family members, the person tested shall be informed.

Chapter VIII – Genetic screening programmes for health purposes

ARTICLE 19. GENETIC SCREENING PROGRAMMES FOR HEALTH PURPOSES

A health screening programme involving the use of genetic tests may only be implemented if it has been approved by the competent body. This approval may only be given after independent evaluation of its ethical acceptability and fulfilment of the following specific conditions:

a. the programme is recognised for its health relevance for the whole population or section of population concerned;
b. the scientific validity and effectiveness of the programme have been established;
c. appropriate preventive or treatment measures in respect of the disease or disorder which is the subject of the screening, are available to the persons concerned;
d. appropriate measures are provided to ensure equitable access to the programme;
e. the programme provides measures to adequately inform the population or section of population concerned of the existence, purposes and means of accessing the screening programme as well as the voluntary nature of participation in it.

Chapter IX – Public information

ARTICLE 20. PUBLIC INFORMATION

Parties shall take appropriate measures to facilitate access for the public to objective general information on genetic tests, including their nature and the potential implications of their results.

Chapter X – Relation between this Protocol and other provisions and re-examination of the Protocol

ARTICLE 21. RELATION BETWEEN THIS PROTOCOL AND THE CONVENTION

As between the Parties, the provisions of Articles 1 to 20 of this Protocol shall be regarded as additional articles to the Convention on Human Rights and Biomedicine, and all the provisions of the Convention shall apply accordingly.

ARTICLE 22. WIDER PROTECTION

None of the provisions of this Protocol shall be interpreted as limiting or otherwise affecting the possibility for a Party to grant persons concerned by genetic testing for health purposes a wider measure of protection than is stipulated in this Protocol.

...

4. Additional Protocol to the Convention on Human Rights and Biomedicine, concerning Genetic Testing for Health Purposes (CETS No. 203)

Explanatory Report

I. This Explanatory Report to the Additional Protocol to the Convention on Human Rights and Biomedicine, concerning Genetic Testing for Health Purposes was drawn up under the responsibility of the Secretary General of the Council of Europe.

II. The Explanatory Report takes into account the discussions held in the Steering Committee on Bioethics (CDBI) and its Working Party entrusted with the drafting of the Protocol; it also takes into account the remarks and proposals made by delegations. The Committee of Ministers has authorised its publication on 7 May 2008.

The Explanatory Report is not an authoritative interpretation of the Protocol. Nevertheless, it covers the main issues of the preparatory work and provides information to clarify the object and purposes of the Protocol and to better understand the scope of its provisions.

Introduction

1. Remarkable progress has been made in the field of human health thanks to research in biology and medicine. In that respect, genetics is one of the sciences seen as most promising. Knowledge on the human genome has been the source of considerable advances, in particular the development of genetic tests involving analysis enabling the identification of genetic characteristics responsible for a disease (monogenic diseases), or involved in its development (multifactorial diseases the development of which is also influenced by other factors). These tests make it possible to diagnose or to confirm the diagnosis in a person already presenting symptoms. But they also make possible the identification of genetic mutations responsible for a disease which only develops later in life, or of a predisposition to a disease before symptoms appear.

2. Early identification of genetic characteristics by a test can present a health benefit, if it makes it possible to take preventive measures or to limit the risks by modifying the behaviour, life style or environment of the person concerned. However, for most genetic diseases, such possibilities are still very limited. Furthermore, the results of genetic analysis are often complex and a proper understanding of their implications is, in many cases, difficult to understand for the persons concerned.

3. Finally, genetic tests are to become more and more an integral part of medical practice, but at the same time a direct commercial offer for genetic tests outside any health system is developing.

4. This Additional Protocol to the Convention on Human Rights and Biomedicine concerning genetic testing for health purposes builds on the principles embodied in the Convention

with a view to ensuring protection of people in the specific field of genetic testing for health purposes.

5. The purpose of the Protocol is to define and safeguard fundamental rights of the persons concerned by genetic testing for health purposes.

Drafting of the Protocol

6. In 1991, in its Recommendation 1160, the Council of Europe Parliamentary Assembly recommended that the Committee of Ministers "envisage a framework convention comprising a main text with general principles and additional protocols on specific aspects."

7. The Convention on Human Rights and Biomedicine was adopted by the Committee of Ministers on 19 November 1996. The same year, the Committee of Ministers instructed the Steering Committee on Bioethics (CDBI) "to draw up a Protocol to the Convention on Human Rights and Biomedicine concerning the problems relating to human genetics..." and accordingly invited the CDBI "...to start work on it as soon as possible, taking also into account questions relating to the use and protection of the results of predictive genetic tests for purposes other than health or scientific research linked to health."

...

Title

16. The title identifies this instrument as the "Additional Protocol to the Convention for the Protection of Human Rights and Dignity of the Human Being with regard to the Applications of Biology and Medicine (Convention on Human Rights and Biomedicine), concerning Genetic Testing for Health Purposes."

Preamble

17. Protection and guarantees in the fields of biology and medicine, including human genetics, are provided by the Convention for the Protection of Human Rights and Dignity of the Human Being with regard to the Application of Biology and Medicine (Convention on Human Rights and Biomedicine) hereafter the "Convention".

18. After the Protocol on the prohibition of cloning human beings, the Protocol concerning transplantation of organs and tissues of human origin, and the Protocol concerning biomedical research, the Additional Protocol on genetic testing for health purposes supplements further the provisions of the Convention. The Protocols are designed to address ethical and legal issues raised by present or future scientific advances through the further development, in specific fields such as genetic testing, of the principles of the Convention.

19. The Preamble of this Protocol reaffirms the aims of the Council of Europe, and of the Convention. It refers to the Convention for the Protection of Individuals with regard to Automatic Processing of Personal Data of 28 January 1981. It also recalls the work carried out by other intergovernmental organisations, and in particular the Universal Declaration on the Human Genome and Human Rights, endorsed by the General Assembly of the United Nations on 9 December 1998.

20. It recalls the particular bond existing between the members of the same family, which is due to the genetic characteristics that they share.

21. It underlines the role of progress in biomedical sciences in reducing morbidity and mortality and in improving the quality of life, and notes the potential benefit of genetics in the field of health. However, it also acknowledges the concerns raised regarding possible improper uses of the information generated by genetic testing.

22. Furthermore, it takes in due consideration the previous work of the Committee of Ministers and the Parliamentary Assembly concerning genetic services, which was taken into account in the elaboration of this Additional Protocol.

23. The preamble reaffirms the commitment of the Parties to take, with regard to genetic testing for health purposes, all necessary measures to safeguard human dignity and the fundamental rights and freedoms of the person. It highlights some of the fundamental principles that underline this commitment:

– the prohibition of any discrimination, in particular based on genetic characteristics;
– equitable access to genetic services of appropriate quality.

Chapter I – Object and scope

ARTICLE 1 – OBJECT AND PURPOSE

24. This article is based on the wording of Article 1 of the Convention on Human Rights and Biomedicine. It specifies that the object of the Protocol is to protect the dignity and identity of all human beings, and guarantee everyone, without discrimination, respect for their integrity and other rights and fundamental freedoms with regard to such tests as specified in this Protocol.

ARTICLE 2 – SCOPE

25. This article specifies the scope of the Protocol and defines the main terms it employs.

26. Paragraph 1 states that the Protocol applies to tests, carried out for health purposes, which involve analysis of biological samples of human origin, and specifically aim to iden-

tify genetic characteristics of a person which are inherited or acquired during early prenatal development.

27. Therefore, not covered by the Protocol are the genetic tests carried out for identification purposes, such as those carried out within the framework of a medico-legal expertise or in view of establishing parentage, except if this research is carried out for medical purposes.

28. Furthermore, the requirement that the test involves the analysis of a biological sample excludes as such the collection of genetic information through family history.

29. The notion of "genetic test" is based here on two elements: the method used and the purpose of the test. It is to be understood as a procedure including removal of biological material of human origin, where relevant, as well as the analysis of the personal information obtained there from. This procedure aims specifically to identify genetic characteristics of a person which are inherited or acquired during early prenatal development. These genetic characteristics cover those already present in the gametes of the parents and therefore transmitted by the latter, as well as those which appear during the early stage of prenatal development before the differentiation of the germ line. It is sometimes referred to the genetic characteristics inherited or acquired during early prenatal development as "genetic characteristics transmissible to descendants". The genetic modifications acquired during lifetime by only certain somatic cells due for example to external factors in the environment, are therefore not covered.

30. The Protocol covers any genetic test carried out for health purposes on a person whether living or dead (in the interests of the latter's family members), or on biological material of human origin. This includes diagnostic, predictive or healthy carrier tests as well as pharmacogenetic tests. Genetic tests offered in the framework of a genetic screening programme are also covered by the Protocol.

31. The Protocol excludes from its scope genetic tests on the human embryo and foetus. Therefore, preimplantation (PGD) and prenatal genetic diagnosis (PND) are not covered, including tests on polar bodies (small haploid cells containing a single set of chromosomes – produced by the ovocyte during meiosis – the process whereby reproductive cells divide to produce gametes), as well as tests on components of embryonic or foetal origin (such as DNA or cells) present in the mother's blood to obtain information about the foetus or embryo.

32. Genetic tests carried out for research purposes are also excluded from the scope of the Protocol. It should, however, be noted that Article 12 of the Convention also applies to predictive tests for health research purposes, and states that such tests may only be carried out subject to appropriate genetic counselling.

33. It has to be noted that some genetic tests, even at an experimental stage, may reveal personal information relevant to the health of the person concerned. The Additional Protocol to the Convention on Human Rights and Biomedicine, concerning biomedical research, provides in Article 13, paragraph 2.v. on information for research participants that these persons must be

given specific information on arrangements for access in particular to "information relevant to the participant arising from the research". Furthermore, the Appendix to that same Protocol provides in paragraph xv that the ethics committee must be informed of the "arrangements foreseen for information which may be generated and be relevant to the present or future health of those persons who would participate in research and their family members". This applies precisely to genetic tests. As the Explanatory Report comments under this provision (paragraph 57), "… Because proper counselling and other health care assistance may be necessary to explain the nature of the results and the options available to the participant, …". It is therefore good practice to provide this information and, where appropriate, to offer genetic counselling, according to the principles set out in Chapter IV of this Protocol.

34. More often than not the analysis of biological samples are analysis of chromosomes, or analysis concerning DNA or RNA. However, tests using analysis of any other element enabling information to be obtained which is equivalent to that obtained by the methods referred to above for the determination of genetic characteristics which are inherited or acquired during early prenatal development are also considered to be covered by the Protocol.

35. The term "equivalent information" must be understood as referring to information directly linked to the genetic characteristics sought. The analyses in question enable direct information to be obtained on the genetic heritage of the person on whom the test is carried out. This is the case in particular with analysis of gene expression products such as proteins. A distinction must be drawn between analysis providing information of that kind and analysis simply providing indications on genetic characteristics without enabling a direct link with them to be established. These indications alone do not provide a sufficient basis for confirming or otherwise the presence of a genetic modification, but they may call for further investigations. This distinction may be illustrated, for example, by the case of a genetic modification leading to hypercholesterolemia in which the gene involved is the MTP (Microsomal Triglyceride Transfer Protein) gene and its expression product: the MTP protein. The action of this protein results in a change in the cholesterol level in the blood. However, blood analysis of the cholesterol level will only give an indication on the genetic characteristics of the person concerned, since the cause of the hypercholesterolemia may be unconnected with the MTP gene and be due to another factor. Consequently, this analysis does not provide "information equivalent" to that provided by DNA, RNA or even the MTP protein, the MTP gene's expression product. Generally speaking, the definition of the types of analysis specified in paragraph 3a. does not include analysis of elements that are not directly linked to the genetic characteristics sought.

36. "Biological sample" refers to biological material removed for the purpose of the genetic test considered, but also any biological material originally removed for another purpose, on which the test is performed.

Chapter II – General provisions

Article 3 – Primacy of the human being

37. This article affirms the primacy of the human being concerned by genetic tests covered by the Protocol, over the sole interest of society or science. Priority is given to the former, which must in principle take precedence over the latter in the event of conflict between them.

38. The whole additional Protocol, the aim of which is to protect human rights and dignity, is inspired by the principle of the primacy of the human being, and all its articles must be interpreted in this light.

Article 4 - Non-discrimination and non-stigmatisation

39. Paragraph 1 repeats the wording of Article 11 of the Convention on Human Rights and Biomedicine. Non-discrimination is an individual right enshrined in Article 14 of the Convention for the Protection of Human Rights and Fundamental Freedoms. Under Article 14 of this Convention, the enjoyment of the rights and freedoms set forth in the Convention must be secured without discrimination on any ground such as sex, race, colour, language, religion, political or other opinion, national or social origin, association with a national minority, property, birth or other status. The provisions of Article 11 of the Convention on Human Rights and Biomedicine, repeated in Article 4, paragraph 1 of this Protocol, add the person's genetic heritage to this list.

40. The concept of discrimination therefore relates to a difference in the treatment of the person concerned. Yet not all differences in treatment necessarily amount to discrimination. In particular, positive measures that may be implemented with the aim of re-establishing a certain balance in favour of persons at a disadvantage because of their genetic heritage are not regarded as discrimination. The criteria for assessment, according to the case-law of the European Court of Human Rights on Article 14 of the Convention, are the relevance and legitimacy of the aim pursued and the reasonable relationship of proportionality between that aim and the means used.

41. The Article also requires, in its paragraph 2, that appropriate measures be taken to prevent stigmatisation of individuals or groups in relation to genetic characteristics.

42. A distinction can be drawn between stigmatisation and discrimination, in that stigmatisation is not necessarily relevant to the exercise of an individual right. The concept of "stigmatisation" rather relates to the way in which a person or group is perceived on the basis, in this case, of their genetic characteristics, whether these exist or are thought to exist. It takes, in particular, the form of words or acts that negatively label a person or group of persons on account of their known or supposed characteristics.

43. Possible measures to prevent stigmatisation include general information campaigns on the human genome and its characteristics and on advances in our knowledge of human genetics, aimed at the general public as well as incorporated into education and training curricula. Parties should encourage such initiatives.

44. The provision of more targeted and more specific information can also be included by the competent authorities concerned in the setting up of a screening programme. Problems of stigmatisation may indeed arise with regard to those taking part in such a screening programme, or other members of the population or sub-group offered the screening. Screening programmes of this type are aimed at detecting or excluding, by means of a genetic test, the presence of certain genetic characteristics linked to a disease. The perception of the disease in question and the interpretation that could be made of the purpose of the screening could result in the individuals concerned being stigmatised. Particular attention should therefore be paid to the information and communication aspects of such programmes in order to limit the risk of these individuals being stigmatised.

Chapter III – Genetic services

ARTICLE 5 - QUALITY OF GENETIC SERVICES

45. This article defines an aim and imposes an obligation on States to take measures to achieve it. The aim is to ensure an appropriate quality of genetic services. The purpose of these services, be they public or private, is to respond to the needs of individuals and families wishing to know whether they are at risk of developing or transmitting a disease or disorder with a genetic component, or who are faced with such a disease or disorder. This includes in particular providing information and, where appropriate, genetic counselling, carrying out genetic tests and interpreting their results, ensuring care for the persons concerned and their families, including preventive care, as well as training the persons involved in providing genetic services.

46. This article defines specific requirements at three different levels: the genetic test, the laboratory and the persons providing genetic services.

47. Paragraph a. requires Parties to take measures to ensure that genetic tests meet generally accepted criteria of scientific validity and clinical validity.

48. "Scientific validity", also called "analytical validity", refers to the way in which the test measures the characteristic it is designed to identify. In particular, this concept includes the capacity that the test will be positive if the genetic characteristic is present (analytical sensitivity), and negative if it is absent (analytical specificity).

49. The notion of "clinical validity" of a test is to be understood as corresponding to a measurement of the accuracy with which the test identifies or predicts a clinical condition. It is defined in terms of clinical specificity, sensitivity and predictive value.

50. "Generally accepted criteria" means those criteria which are widely recognised at international level.

51. According to this provision, it is the responsibility of the State to ensure the existence of a system (e.g. an approval system), which guarantees the reliability of a genetic test in respect of a determined disease, i.e. that its results with regard to the identification of particular genetic characteristics related to this disease are accurate and can be reproduced.

52. The "quality assurance programme" referred to in paragraph b concerns general quality controls on laboratory procedures rather than specific genetic tests. This requirement also applies to procedures undertaken in the framework of screening programmes. An accreditation system constitutes, for example, a generally effective measure to satisfy quality assurance requirements in particular for laboratories carrying out complex cytogenetic or molecular genetic analyses. By accreditation is meant, a procedure formally establishing the competence of the laboratory to carry out genetic tests.

53. Laboratories shall be monitored regularly, preferably by means of an external structure, to make sure they are complying with the established rules. This monitoring aims to ensure in particular respect of the confidentiality of data and security of the biological samples, the quality of the procedures and the specific scientific and technical skills of the staff involved.

54. In this context, it can be useful to refer to the guidelines elaborated in this field by intergovernmental bodies.

55. In paragraph c, the term "persons providing genetic services" includes medical doctors, nurses and other health care professionals as well as non-medical staff such as biologists and technicians working in the analysis laboratories. It is required that they have "appropriate qualifications", which shall be understood as taking into account possible qualification systems in place at national level and including in-service training. As genetic tests are destined to become an increasingly regular part of ordinary medical practice, medical genetics, including what concerns counselling, should in particular be part of the education and training programme of all health care professionals.

ARTICLE 6 – CLINICAL UTILITY

56. This article emphasises the importance of taking into account the clinical utility of a genetic test as an essential criterion for deciding to offer this test to a person or a group of persons.

57. "Clinical utility" is to be understood by the value of the test results in guiding the person concerned in his or her choices regarding prevention or therapeutic strategies. It is therefore a particularly important factor in deciding whether or not it is appropriate to offer a genetic test.

58. Criteria generally considered for determining the clinical utility of a test may be grouped in two large categories:

- Criteria concerning the test:
- the "service rendered" by the latter (in particular the value of the test results to determine the possible medical measures in terms of prevention or treatment);
- the circumstances in which the test is offered (quality and accessibility of the genetic services available, including genetic counselling, etc);
- Criteria relating to the situation of the individual to whom the test is offered.

59. The measure of the clinical utility of a test may vary from one individual to another, depending on that individual's situation, with social and cultural aspects also being taken into account. For example, awareness of relevant information for the health of his or her family members, or information on the risk of developing the disease, even in the absence of a prevention or treatment strategy, could, for a particular individual, be beneficial, including in terms of well-being; this will play a part in determining the clinical utility of the test in question for that individual.

60. Taking account of the clinical utility of a test can be regarded as an integral part of good medical practice with regard to any decision to carry out the test under individualised medical supervision.

61. The provision of this article is of special importance for tests proposed without such medical supervision, and for the planning of screening programmes.

62. Existing evidence on a genetic test's clinical utility have thus to be available, in particular, to the health professionals and the persons concerned by that test. Such evidence should be obtainable from the laboratories carrying out the test.

Article 7 – Individualised supervision

63. Paragraph 1 establishes the general rule according to which a genetic test may only be carried out under individualised medical supervision. The concept of "medical supervision" shall be understood as referring to a process within which the genetic test will take place.

64. This provision is driven by the concern, in particular, to enable the person concerned to have suitable preliminary information with a view to an informed decision regarding the carrying out of this test and, if appropriate, to have access to an appropriate genetic counselling. A precise evaluation of the situation of the person concerned, involving direct contact with him or her, is a determining element in that respect. A mere telephone conversation with a medical doctor, for example, does not allow for such an evaluation.

65. The conduct of a genetic test for health purposes must be in response to a specific request made on the basis of a precise evaluation of the situation of the person concerned, carried out by a medical doctor.

66. Paragraph 2 provides for exceptions to the general rule laid down in paragraph 1, on condition that appropriate measures, taking into account the way the test will be carried out, are provided to give effect to the other provisions of this Protocol. The main purpose is to ensure, in particular, compliance with the provisions concerning the nature and quality of the prior information, free and informed consent and genetic counselling.

67. The exceptions under consideration do not concern the performance of a test on a particular individual but rather readily identifiable test device for which the genetic characteristics it is meant to identify would be specified. The genetic tests concerned may be carried out by a laboratory after the biological material has been removed by a professional or by the person concerned him or herself who then sends it to the laboratory. They may also be tests entirely carried out by the person concerned with a kit enabling him or her to remove the biological sample as well as to carry out the analysis.

68. The objective is the protection of the person concerned. It is left to each State to determine how to implement this provision effectively. The same applies to the procedure to be followed and to the authorities or bodies involved in the decision to authorise a test complying with the legal requirements for marketing it, to be carried out without individualised medical supervision. Particular attention must be paid in this process to the importance of the potential implications of the test considered for the persons on whom it would be carried out or for the members of their family, the ease of interpretation of the results and, if appropriate, the treatment possibilities for the disease or disorder concerned. The envisaged measures to give effect to the provisions of this Protocol could be different depending on whether the test considered is fully carried out by the person concerned by means of a kit or whether the analysis is carried out by a laboratory.

69. The performance without individualised medical supervision of genetic tests on persons not able to consent, raises special concerns. States should bear these in mind when authorising, or not, direct access to such tests.

70. The correct interpretation of results and the guarantee of appropriate genetic counselling to understand their implications remain the main concern. It is considered, in this respect, that these requirements envisaged by the present Protocol cannot be satisfied outside of individualised medical supervision in the case of genetic tests with important implications for the health of the person concerned or of members of his or her family, or for choices concerning procreation. The test results may be particularly complex to interpret and require, for example, additional medical information or information concerning family history to be taken into account. With many predictive tests, even if they reveal a strong likelihood of developing a particularly serious disease, the time of onset, if at all, and the severity of the symptoms will often remain uncertain. Finally, understanding the nature and implications of the test, including

for family members, the possible psychological impact of the results on the person concerned and the often important decisions he or she is faced with requires such tests to be performed under individualised medical supervision.

Chapter IV – Information, genetic counselling and consent

ARTICLE 8 – INFORMATION AND GENETIC COUNSELLING

71. In accordance with Article 5 of the Convention on Human Rights and Biomedicine, Article 8 of this Protocol stipulates in its paragraph 1 that any person on whom a genetic test is envisaged shall be provided with prior appropriate information. This preliminary information shall include in particular the purpose and nature of the test considered as well as the implications of its results for the person concerned. Where appropriate, especially in the case of a predictive test, information on the implications for members of his or her family must also be included. These requirements relate to all the genetic tests covered by this Protocol, including those covered by the provisions of Article 7 paragraph 2, envisaged outside of the individualised medical supervision.

72. The "implications" of the test results are to be understood, in particular, as covering the benefits and the risks, including at psychological level. Possible preventive or therapeutic measures and the constraints they entailed shall also be specified. The person shall also be informed of the consequences of not carrying out the test and, where appropriate, of the possible alternatives. To health consequences shall also be added, where applicable, those concerning future procreation choices, both for the person concerned and possibly for the members of his or her family. The possibilities open to the person shall also be explained to him or her, in particular, in accordance with the provisions of Article 16 of this Protocol, his or her right not to be informed of the results of the test. Also, the information must include the forms of support available to the person, in particular genetic counselling.

73. Those elements listed above are not meant to be exhaustive; it merely explains the essential tenor of the information to be provided. However, this information must be adapted to the test envisaged, as well as to the person concerned. The implications of test results for a person already showing symptoms of a disease or disorder (diagnostic test), for example, will be different from those of a predictive genetic test which will provide information about the person's future health. Furthermore, the person's individual characteristics – such as his or her age – must also be taken into account, for example when considering the possible consequences in terms of procreation choices. Moreover, at the request of the person concerned, additional information, clarification or precision must be provided in order to enable an informed decision.

74. The content of the information but also the form in which it is transmitted are paramount in guaranteeing a free and informed decision by the person concerned. The information must be sufficiently clear and comprehensible for the person, bearing in mind his or her level of knowledge, his or her education and psychological condition. Furthermore, like all information

prior to a medical act, it must be conveyed in a fair and neutral manner, to enable the person concerned to reach a free and informed decision.

75. For genetic tests referred to in paragraph 2 of this article, oral communication of information is essential. In particular it makes it easier to facilitate and ensure proper understanding by the person concerned by answering his or her possible questions and supplying clarifications if necessary.

76. Information could also be provided concerning any possible subsequent use of the biological material removed which is foreseen. It would be preferable for this information not to be disclosed at the same time as that concerning the proposed test, in order to avoid confusion. It should be made clear that any subsequent use would require further consent distinct from that required for the genetic test.

77. Paragraph 2 refers to tests covered by Article 12 of the Convention on Human Rights and Biomedicine. These are tests predictive of a monogenic genetic disease or serving to detect a genetic predisposition or susceptibility to a disease. They also include tests which make it possible to identify the person tested as the healthy carrier of a gene responsible for a disease. That gene's presence will not affect the health of the person concerned, but may have implications for the health of his or her descendants.

78. The tests referred to here all relate to diseases, and do not therefore include pharmaco-genetic tests.

79. The predictive nature of the information obtained with tests covered, the emotional impact for the person concerned of knowing about a genetic risk, the possible implications for family members and the often important decisions with which the person concerned may be faced, including where appropriate in relation to procreation choices, explain the importance of an appropriate genetic counselling for those tests.

80. Some diagnostic tests may also have important implications for decisions on procreation choices. Indeed they may provide information about the origin, possibly genetic, of the disease, the symptoms of which are observed in the person tested, which may, where appropriate, affect his or her descendants. For such tests, it is good practice that the person concerned also has access to appropriate genetic counselling.

81. The notion of "genetic counselling" is to be understood here as a communication and support process aiming to enable individuals and, where appropriate, families to make informed choices with regard to a genetic test and its implications.

82. It includes the provision of information prior to consent as required in paragraph 1. It also includes an offer of support before and, if appropriate, after the test, to the person concerned, to help him or her to deal with the implications of the test and its results, including, where

appropriate, communication to family members of information relevant to their health, or procreation choices.

83. Genetic counselling is an individualised process taking into account, in particular, the psychological and family context of the person concerned and involving an exchange between him or her and the person providing the counselling. This support process may therefore vary in form and extent depending on the test considered but also on the particular significance of the information that the test is likely to provide for the person concerned or for members of his or her family. In certain cases, the person concerned would also benefit from psychological support provided by persons with appropriate competencies.

84. When the results of a test carried out on a person may have important health implications for members of his or her family, one must refer to Article 18 (Information relevant to family members) of this Protocol and to paragraphs 138 to 141 of this Explanatory Report.

85. At all events, genetic counselling shall not be delivered in a directive manner. However it can be difficult for the person providing the genetic counselling to avoid influencing the subject to some extent, because, among other things, of the counsellor's status, knowledge and experience and the subject's perception of them. At all events the person providing the genetic counselling must explain the different options open to the subject in such a way as not to influence unduly the subject's decision, which must be freely taken.

ARTICLE 9 – CONSENT

86. Paragraph 1 follows the wording of Article 5 of the Convention on Human Rights and Biomedicine, in requiring the free and informed consent of the person concerned before any genetic test is carried out. The test may be performed on a biological sample removed for that purpose, or on biological material originally taken from the person concerned for another purpose.

87. Because of the predictive nature of the results of the tests referred to in paragraph 2 of Article 8 and their potential implications for the person concerned and/or for the members of his or her family, the article provides for the consent to be documented. This is generally achieved through a signature by the person concerned. However, this does not necessarily rule out the possibility of using other forms of registration of the expression of consent as long as it attests the authenticity of the consent and permits to keep a permanent record of it. It should also be noted that if the elements of capacity to consent, appropriate prior information and voluntariness have not been satisfied, a signature on a form will not make the consent valid.

88. Freedom of consent implies that consent may be withdrawn at any time. The person must be informed of the possible consequences of withdrawing the concent. His or her decision must be respected. There is no requirement for withdrawal of consent to be made in writing or in any other specific form.

Chapter V – Persons not able to consent

Article 10 – Protection of persons not able to consent

89. The article establishes the rule that, subject to Article 13 of this Protocol, in cases where a person has been recognised as not having the capacity to consent, be he or she a minor or an adult, a genetic test may be carried out on that person only for his or her direct benefit.

90. The second paragraph provides some clarifications concerning minors. In such case, a genetic test shall be deferred until the person has attained the capacity to consent. However there is provision for making an exception to this if carrying out the test without delay is in the minor's best interests. In particular this covers cases where delaying the test might harm the subject's health by depriving him or her from a health benefit. For example, when the information which the genetic test would provide would allow appropriate therapeutic measures to be taken for a disease or disorder from which the subject is suffering.

91. The exception also applies to some situations where the genetic test would provide predictive information allowing timely preventive measures to be taken. In particular this applies to tests for diseases which might develop before the subject has attained legal capacity.

92. In addition to the consequences on the subject's health of deferring the test, regard is also had to the subject's well-being in deciding whether to perform a test without delay. The word "well-being" refers both to physical and mental well-being. For example, a predictive test performed without delay and producing a negative result might spare the subject highly invasive regular examinations as in the case of adenomatous polyposis.

93. For adults not able to consent, where the clinical situation of the person makes it possible, it is good practice to defer genetic tests until recovery of capacity to consent.

Article 11 – Information prior to authorisation, genetic counselling and support

94. Article 10 of this Protocol provides that subject to Article 13, a genetic test may only be carried out on a person who does not have the capacity to consent, for his or her direct benefit. Compliance with this requirement is therefore an essential precondition for envisaging a genetic test on a person who does not have the capacity to consent.

95. In accordance with Article 6 paragraph 4 of the Convention, Article 11 provides in its paragraph 1 that the person, authority or body whose authorisation is required for a genetic test on a person not able to consent, must be given appropriate information beforehand. This information is the same, in both content and form, as that which must be given in the case of persons able to give consent, under Article 8.

96. The article also requires that appropriate prior information is provided, to the extent of his or her capacity to understand, to the person not able to consent on whom a test is envis-

aged. Capacity to understand must be construed in a relatively broad sense as taking in both discernment and reasoning. In the case of a minor such capacity will depend, in particular, on the subject's age and degree of maturity.

97. The person, authority or body whose authorisation is required and, where appropriate, the person concerned by the envisaged test, may wish certain information concerning the test to be further clarified. In the case of a person being able to consent, these clarifications can be obtained by the person him or herself, within the framework of his or her dialogue with the doctor, in view of an informed decision. Such is not the case for the person, the authority or body whose authorization is required for a test on a person not having the capacity to consent. It is important that a suitably trained person with the necessary knowledge of clinical genetics be available to answer these possible questions. The aim is to facilitate and ensure understanding of the information provided.

98. The provisions of Article 8 paragraph 2 concerning genetic counselling also apply to persons not able to consent when their capacity to understand permits this. For predictive tests referred to in Article 12 of the Convention, the person concerned shall therefore, where possible, have access to appropriate genetic counselling.

99. The last sub-paragraph provides that, where appropriate, appropriate follow-up be available for the person whose authorisation is required, in order to allow him or her to deal with the implications of the test and its results. Such requirement is explained in particular by the predictive nature of information obtained by the envisaged test and the implications for the person on whom the test is being considered and, where appropriate, for the members of his or her family.

ARTICLE 12 – AUTHORISATION

100. In accordance with paragraphs 2 and 3 of Article 6 of the Convention, this article lays down the principle that genetic tests may not be carried out on persons not able to consent, whether minors (paragraph 1) or adults (paragraph 2), without authorisation from their representative, or authority, person or body provided for by law. However, to preserve their autonomy to the maximum extent possible:

– minors' opinions must be taken into consideration as an increasingly determining factor, in proportion to their age and degree of maturity;
– whenever their capacity to understand permits this, adults must be involved in the authorisation process.

101. The second sub-paragraph in paragraph 2 applies to adults who have foreseen the possibility of becoming not able to give consent, and have indicated their wishes concerning a genetic test in advance. In accordance with Article 9 of the Convention, those wishes shall be taken into account.

102. Because of the predictive nature of the results of the tests referred to in paragraph 2 of Article 8 and their potential implications for the person concerned and/or the members of his or her family, paragraph 3 provides for the authorisation to be documented. As a general rule, the authorisation will be given in writing and will bear the signature of its author. This does not rule out the possibility of using, in certain cases, other forms of registration of authorisation as long as it permits to identify without ambiguity the person on whom the test is envisaged and the person, authority or body giving the authorisation.

103. Paragraph 4 provides that the person, authority or body who gave the authorisation may withdraw it at any time provided that this is in the best interests of the person not able to consent. In this regard, as for the authorisation process, the latter's opinion shall be taken into consideration, in the case of a minor as an increasingly determining factor in proportion to his or her age and degree of maturity and, in the case of an adult, depending on his or her capacity to understand.

Chapter VI – Tests for the benefit of family members

ARTICLE 13 – TESTS ON PERSON NOT ABLE TO CONSENT

104. This article lays down the conditions to be met so that exceptionally and by derogation from the provisions of Article 6 of the Convention on Human Rights and Biomedicine and Article 10 of this Protocol, a test may be carried out on a person not able to consent without direct benefit for him or her.

105. The purpose of the test must be to enable family members, with whom the person concerned has a biological link, to obtain a preventive, diagnostic or therapeutic benefit that has been independently evaluated as important for their health, or to allow them to make an informed choice with respect to procreation.

106. The situation in question can be illustrated by three examples. The first corresponds to the case of a person not able to consent and suffering from cancer, which is considered to have a genetic basis. The performance of a genetic test identifying the involved genetic mutation may not modify the way in which the cancer of this person will be treated. But, the test could provide information which could be used for the analysis of the genetic characteristics of the other members of the family in order to determine if they are likely to develop the same cancer. If the same mutation is found in some of the family members, they could be subject to more frequent controls in order to allow cancer detection at an early stage of the emergence of the disease.

107. Another example is that of a child who was diagnosed, on the basis of clinical signs and symptoms and biochemical tests, with cystic fibrosis. This disease can be related to many different genetic mutations. For possible future procreation choices, it can be important to identify the existing mutation in the affected child. This will make it possible to look for the mutation in the child's parents in order to determine if it is them who transmitted it or if it is a mutation

newly appeared in the child having developed the disease. In the latter case, there would be no particular reason to fear for the health of a future child of the couple concerned.

108. A last example is the case of diseases, especially rare ones, for which the genetic mutation involved has not been identified. In such case, the transmission of the mutation can be traced by studying genetic linkage. In order to determine a genetic risk in a family in which a genetic disease with an unidentified genetic mutation has manifested itself, it is possible that genetic tests on affected but also unaffected children would be necessary, so as to obtain an acceptable degree of diagnostic certainty – for example, for other members of the family, whether of child-bearing age or not.

109. This evaluation of the benefit for the family members must not be made by the medical doctor of the family members for the benefit of whom the test is envisaged. However, it is not required to set up a special structure, and the choice of entrusting for example another medical doctor or a body (e.g. committee, tribunal, etc.) with the task of carrying out the evaluation is left to the State.

110. The second condition is that the benefit envisaged can only be obtained by performing the test. The term "benefit envisaged" refers here both to the nature of the benefit and to the time it takes to materialise. The benefit envisaged must be necessary now for the health of a (the) family member(s) and, in particular, cannot wait, when the test is to be carried out on a minor, for the minor to reach legal capacity. This provision would also be considered to cover the case where the information sought for the benefit of a (the) family member(s) could be obtained without carrying out a test on the person not able to consent but only at the cost of highly complex and laborious analyses.

111. Paragraph c lays down another condition: the risks and burdens associated with the intervention shall be minimal for the person undergoing the test. This means that the intervention would only result at the most in a very slightly detrimental and temporary impact on the health of the person on whom the test is carried out. Furthermore, the expected discomfort, which might be associated with the intervention, shall be at most temporary and very slight for this person. Thus taking blood samples from peripheral vessels will be considered as acceptable.

112. Paragraph d. requires that the expected benefits of the test be independently evaluated as substantially outweighing risks for private life that may be associated with collection, processing or communication of the data it produces. These data are the main concern.

113. In accordance with Article 16 of this Protocol, personal data resulting from a genetic test are considered confidential. Their collection, processing and communication must meet the requirements of the legislation governing the protection of individuals with regard to the processing of personal data. In the cases covered by this article, the genetic test is carried out on one person but in the context of an analysis involving one or more members of his or her family, who are informed of the test and will benefit from its results. Even if such cases are very rare, provision must be made for these particular situations where the exchanges of

information within the family concerned can be made easier. Paragraph d takes into account the risks, arising in particular from the very special situations involved, to the private life of the person on whom the test is being considered. It requires that the expected benefits have been independently evaluated as substantially outweighing those risks. The clarification concerning "independent evaluation" in paragraph a are also relevant here.

114. Authorisation by the representative of the person, on whom the test is to be carried out, or by an authority, person or body provided for by law, is also required. In the specific case of this type of test, as the representative of the person not able to consent is often a member of his or her family, he or she may also be a beneficiary of the test envisaged. The law should make proper provision for such situations.

115. Finally, with a view to respecting, as far as possible, the autonomy of person on whom the test is to be carried out, he or she must be associated with the authorisation procedure, as far as his or her capacities to understand and degree of maturity permit.

116. In any case, if he or she objects, the test must not be carried out. This last provision reiterates the requirement already stated in the specific field of biomedical research and trans-plantation of organs and tissues, in Articles 17 and 20 of the Convention and the additional corresponding Protocols. The concept of objection implies from the person concern a certain capacity to understand and that he or she expresses a will. A difference must be made between a simple gesture of fear or dissatisfaction by a young child, gesture which is not to be termed legally as an objection, and the will expressed by an older child capable of discernment. How-ever, even with a young child with no capacity of discernment, attention shall be paid to the requirement that the medical intervention does not entail more than minimum burden.

ARTICLE 14 – TESTS ON BIOLOGICAL MATERIALS WHEN IT IS NOT POSSIBLE TO CONTACT THE PERSON CONCERNED

117. This article concerns genetic tests envisaged on biological material of a person for the benefit of his or her family members. Under Article 9 of this Protocol, the consent of the person concerned must be obtained for all genetic tests. This also applies to tests carried out on biological material originally removed from that person for another purpose. Reasonable efforts, in terms of both means and time, must therefore be made to re-contact the person on the biological material of whom the test is considered.

118. However, in spite of such reasonable efforts, in some rare cases, it may prove impossible to get in contact with the person. Whereas in some cases, failure to carry out the envisaged genetic test may have serious consequences for the health of those family members whom it was intended to benefit. This applies, for example, to families in which there have been several cases of ovarian cancer, and the genetic mutation involved has not been identified. The genetic test envisaged might help to carry out a family study with a view to identify that mutation, making it unnecessary to remove the ovaries of female family members in whom it would not be identified. In such cases, it may be considered that the benefit for the family members

concerned is particularly important and substantially outweigh any risks to the person whose biological material would be used – in particular for his or her private life – if the test were carried out without his or her consent.

119. In the case when it is not possible to get in touch with the person concerned, this article provides that the law can, in accordance with the principle of proportionality, allow the test to be carried out under condition that the expected benefit cannot be otherwise obtained and that the test cannot be deferred.

120. The objective of the test must be to allow family members to obtain an important benefit for their health in terms of prevention, diagnosis or treatment, or enable them to take informed decisions in relation to procreation choices.

121. In accordance with the principle of necessity, the expected benefit cannot be obtained without the test being carried out and the test cannot be deferred. Furthermore, in accordance with the principle of proportionality, the expected benefit must be significantly greater than the risks to the individual's private life that may arise from the collection, use or communication of the test results.

122. Finally, the article requires that provisions be made, in agreement with Article 22 of the Convention, for the cases where the person concerned has expressly objected to such a test. Article 22 of the Convention enacts the general rule according to which the parts of the body removed with a given purpose can only be stored and used for other purposes if done in conformity with appropriate information and consent procedures. In this respect, the Explanatory Report to the Convention specifies that information and consent arrangements may vary according to circumstances. In respect of these principles it is the responsibility of each state to put in place the necessary provisions to address the situations where an objection would have been expressly made by the person concerned.

ARTICLE 15 – TESTS ON DECEASED PERSONS

123. The possibility of carrying out a genetic test on biological material removed from the body of a deceased person, or removed, when he or she was alive, from a person now deceased, can prove to be important from a medical point of view, for the members of his or her family. However, a legal framework for such a possibility must be defined.

124. The article requires that the consent or authorisation required by law be obtained before carrying out any genetic test on biological samples removed from the body of a person after his or her death for the benefit of family members of this person. The same requirement applies to test performed on biological material removed, from a person, when he or she was alive and is now deceased.

125. It is left to national law to determine the rules governing consent (e.g. express or presumed) or authorisation applicable to genetic tests hence implemented.

126. It is also left to national law to specify the conditions for the evaluation of "the benefit of other family members". For the evaluation of such a concept, the principles of necessity and proportionality must be taken into account.

127. In the field of genetics, because of the biological links with the deceased person, descendants or other family members may have specific interests. Even though, according to law, the decision is not for them to take, they should be consulted, taking into account in this context the risk of conflict of interest regarding the benefit envisaged.

Chapter VII – Private life and right to information

ARTICLE 16 – RESPECT FOR PRIVATE LIFE AND RIGHT TO INFORMATION

128. In accordance with Article 10 of the Convention on Human Rights and Biomedicine, Article 16 recognises the right to respect for private life, when it comes in particular to personal data derived from a genetic test. It thus reaffirms the principle laid down in Article 8 of the Convention for the Protection of Human Rights and Fundamental Freedoms, and re-stated in the Convention for the Protection of Individuals with regard to Automatic Processing of Personal Data.

129. The genetic tests covered by this Protocol aim at providing information concerning health. It should be pointed out that, under Article 6 of the Convention for the Protection of Individuals with regard to Automatic Processing of Personal Data, personal data concerning health constitute a special category of data regarded as particularly sensitive, and require thus appropriate guarantee.

130. However, a genetic test performed for health purposes may incidentally provide personal information not relating to health which could have important consequences for the person concerned or members of his or her family. For example it might bring to light the default of an expected biological link or an unexpected presence of a biological link.

131. The conditions of form and substance for making such unexpected information available to the person concerned are a matter for national law. In this connection, regard should be had, in particular, to any wishes expressed by the person concerned about having access to such information, and regard should likewise be had to any damage which such information might bring to this person or other members of his or her family.

132. Paragraph 2 gives everyone the right to know all information collected on his or her health by a genetic test. The individual in question must therefore have in principle access to all the data that concerns him or her, contained in particular in his or her medical file.

133. On the other hand, with regard to the conclusions of medical nature drawn from the test, the article lays down a further requirement: the person concerned must have access to these in a form that is comprehensible. Where necessary, this could require the conclusions to be

reworded in more simple terms so that they can be understood by the individual in question, in the light of his or her level of knowledge, education and psychological state. In certain cases, like those of the tests covered by the exceptions envisaged in Article 7 paragraph 2, the dialogue with the medical doctor will not be possible; other arrangements will have to be envisaged in order to fulfil the requirements of paragraph 2.

134. The right to know goes hand in hand with the right not to know as recognised in paragraph 3. The person may have his or her own reasons for not wishing to know about certain aspects of his or her health. This may apply, for example, to a test aiming at identifying the presence of a gene responsible for a particularly serious disease, for which there is currently no treatment. The person concerned may agree to the test – the results of which could be useful for procreation choices or for the health of members of his or her family – without wanting to know whether he/she carries that gene. This wish must be observed.

135. Both the right to know and the right not to know may, in specific circumstances, be subject to certain restrictions in the interests of the person concerned. Information on the health of a person who has expressed a wish not to know is sometimes particularly important for him or her. For example, knowing that he or she has a predisposition to a disease might be the only way to enable him or her to take measures to prevent that disease or delay its development. In such cases, the doctor's duty to provide care, stated in Article 4 of the Convention on Human Rights and Biomedicine, might conflict with the patient's right not to know. It is up to national law to indicate whether, having regard to the circumstances of the particular case, the doctor may make an exception to the right not to know.

ARTICLE 17 – BIOLOGICAL SAMPLES

136. The biological samples on which genetic tests referred to in Article 2 of this Protocol are carried out, shall only be used and stored in such conditions as to ensure their security. Appropriate measures shall thus be taken in particular, against accidental or unauthorised deterioration, destruction as well as unauthorised access or use.

137. Biological samples may, moreover, be a source of information on the persons from whom they have been removed. Samples must therefore be used and stored under such conditions as to ensure the confidential nature of the information which might be obtained from them.

ARTICLE 18 – INFORMATION RELEVANT TO FAMILY MEMBERS

138. The results of certain genetic tests may be relevant for the health of other family members. The person concerned must have been informed of this before the test is carried out, in accordance with the provisions of Article 8 of this Protocol.

139. When analysis of the test results confirms the relevance for the health of his or her family members, the person on whom the test has been carried out must be informed and made aware of the importance of access to this information for his or her family members. The person

should be made aware of this at an appropriate time, depending, amongst other things, on his or her clinical situation and any decisions on his or her health that could be taken in the light of the test results.

140. For the communication of this information to the family members, appropriate provisions should be made, bearing in mind the rules on confidentiality and the protection of the private life of the various persons concerned (person on whom the test is performed and members of his or her family). The choice of procedure(s) is left to the States. If the person tested is unable or unwilling to contact his or her family members directly he or she may be given appropriate material or letters to pass on to the family member(s). Consideration could be given to setting up a mediating body responsible for contacting family members of the person concerned if the latter has asked for them to be informed without him or herself being identifiable as the source of the information. Another example, would be the possibility to provide for a decision by a competent body, following comparative assessment of the respective interests of the persons concerned, on whether or not the information in question must be communicated to the members of the family.

141. The persons informed of the importance for their health of the results of a test performed on a member of their family should be invited to consult a medical doctor and, where a genetic test referred to in Article 8 paragraph 2 is envisaged, appropriate genetic counselling shall also be available for them.

Chapter VIII – Genetic screening programmes for health purposes

Article 19 – Genetic screening programmes for health purposes

142. Article 19 states the conditions to be fulfilled before implementing a genetic screening programme. "Screening programme" refers to the general offer of a genetic test to an entire population or to a section of population, with a view to enable early identification or exclusion of:

– a genetic disease,
– a genetic predisposition to a disease, or
– another genetic characteristic relevant for the health of the members of this population or section of population or for their descendants (e.g. a gene involved in resistance to a disease).

143. Genetic tests proposed as part of a screening programme are motivated by a public health concern. Their relevance for each member of the population or section of population concerned is not based on individual or family data. It differs in this respect from the relevance of a test carried out in the context of medical supervision, which is based on individual indications. The purpose of proposing a genetic test as part of a screening programme for health purposes is to allow the members of the population or section of population concerned to make ap-

propriate personal choices concerning their health or in relation to procreation, on the basis of the results of the proposed test.

144. The approval by a competent body is required before the implementation of a screening programme for health purposes. The term "competent body" means a body recognised by the State to perform a certain task.

145. The approval by this body may only be given subject to the fulfilment of specific conditions, which must be independently evaluated.

146. The specific conditions listed in sub-paragraphs a. to d. of this article supplement those defined in the other chapters of this Protocol which apply at individual level, in particular the general provisions (Chapter II) as well as those concerning the quality of genetic services and the clinical utility of genetic tests (Chapter III), information, genetic counselling and consent (Chapter IV) and private life and right to information (Chapter VII).

147. The programme must be recognised for its health relevance for all the members of the population or section of population concerned. The disease targeted by the screening must represent a significant health problem for the population concerned because of its severity or the number of people affected. The programme will enable the members of the population concerned to take appropriate decisions, in particular concerning the prevention or treatment of the disease.

148. The scientific validity of the screening programme and its effectiveness must have been established. This scientific validity must be determined in respect of the purpose of the screening and on the basis of the sensitivity, specificity and reliability of the proposed test which must fulfil the requirements of paragraph a. of Article 5 of this Protocol. A reduction in mortality or morbidity is generally considered an essential criterion of the effectiveness of a screening programme.

149. To that end, appropriate preventive or treatment measures must be available to the persons concerned. The notion of prevention is to be understood here in a broad sense, including in particular close health monitoring, for example through regular examinations (e.g. for a predisposition to breast cancer). This may include measures (as in the case of cystic fibrosis or Duchenne's muscular dystrophy, for example), that limit or delay the development of the disease symptoms and that significantly improve the well-being or living conditions of the person concerned. Finally, a choice concerning procreation – a field which is relevant to health – may, in certain cases, in particular when there is a risk of transmission of a particularly severe disease very difficult to treat, be considered as an appropriate measure.

150. Carrying out a pilot study on a small section of the target population before implementing the programme will make it possible to evaluate all the negative and positive implications of the proposed programme at every level: technical, organisational, scientific, clinical and even psychological and social.

151. Appropriate measures shall be provided to ensure equitable access to the screening programme to the members of the population or section of the population concerned. This provision reiterates the principle established in Article 3 of the Convention applied here to screening. Equity in this context primarily means the absence of discrimination. Subsequently, not being synonymous with absolute equality, the equitable access indicates a satisfactory degree in access to screening.

152. Lastly, the programme shall provide for measures to allow the population or section of the population concerned to benefit from adequate information concerning the screening programme. The information shall enable the persons concerned to know the existence of the screening programme and its purpose, as well as the voluntary nature of participation in it. It shall also specify the way to access to the programme and where to obtain more detailed information, in particular on the screening process, benefits and possible negative effects (for example, anxiety regarding the test results) and possible implications for family members, so as to enable them to decide whether or not to accept the test proposed.

Chapter IX – Public information

ARTICLE 20 – PUBLIC INFORMATION

153. The purpose of the article is to prompt the States to take appropriate measures to facilitate access for the public to objective general information about genetic tests. Genetics is increasingly going to become an integral part of health care. However it is still a relatively new and complex field. Outside a medical context the possibilities of access to objective general information about genetic tests are still often very limited. To enable better understanding of this area of genetics, the progress it opens up for health and its limitations, it is important for the general public to have access to such information in a comprehensible form about the different types of test available (diagnostic tests, tests predictive of monogenic diseases and those permitting to detect a predisposition to a disease, healthy carrier tests). They must also relate to the applications of these tests in the medical field and in particular to the extent and, if necessary, the limit of the significance of the information resulting from such tests. Such information is also contributing to the prevention of stigmatisation based on genetic characteristics.

154. The choice of appropriate measures is left to the individual State; and will depend in particular on the quality of the information already accessible for the public. Information campaigns or creation of Internet sites are examples of how to meet the object of informing the general public. Education and training syllabuses could also be added to for that purpose. Promoting and supporting such initiatives are examples of measures which States can take to satisfy the requirements of this provision.

155. Such general information could, when appropriate, be supplemented by other more specific information on particular tests, in particular tests available outside individualised medical supervision. The companies marketing such tests often advertise them extensively, and may not always provide the information which the persons concerned need for making

an informed choice. In this context, availability of objective information about such tests is particularly important and would help to protect the public against incomplete, wrong or in some cases deliberately misleading information.

Chapter X 150; Relation between this Protocol and other provisions and re-examination of the Protocol

ARTICLE 21 - RELATION BETWEEN THIS PROTOCOL AND THE CONVENTION

156. As a legal instrument, the Protocol supplements the Convention. Once in force, the Protocol is subsumed into the Convention for those Parties having ratified the Protocol. The provisions of the Convention are therefore to be applied to the Protocol.

157. Thus, Article 36 of the Convention, which sets out the conditions under which a State may make a reservation in respect of any particular provision of the Convention, will also apply to the Protocol. Using this provision States may, under the conditions set out in Article 36 of the Convention, make a reservation in respect of any particular provision of this Protocol.

ARTICLE 22 – WIDER PROTECTION

158. In pursuance of this article, the Parties may apply rules of a more protective nature than those contained in the Protocol. In other words, the text lays down common standards with which States must comply, while allowing them to provide greater protection of the human being and of human rights with regard to genetic testing for health purposes.

ARTICLE 23 – RE-EXAMINATION OF THE PROTOCOL

159. This article provides that the Protocol shall be re-examined no later than five years from its entry into force and thereafter at such intervals as the designated Committee may determine. Article 32 of the Convention identifies this Committee as the Steering Committee on Bioethics (CDBI), or any other Committee so designated by the Committee of Ministers.

Chapter XI – Final clauses

ARTICLE 24 – SIGNATURE AND RATIFICATION

160. Under the provisions of Article 31 of the Convention, only States that have signed or ratified the Convention may sign this Protocol. Ratification of the Protocol is subject to prior or simultaneous ratification of the Convention. A State which has signed or ratified the Convention is not obliged to sign the Protocol or, if applicable, to ratify it.

Public Health

PART VI

Chapter 1. General

1.1. International Health Regulations (2005)

Adopted by the World Health Assembly on 23 May 2005,
the IHR (2005) entered into force on 15 June 2007

Part I – Definitions, Purpose and Scope, Principles and Responsible Authorities

ARTICLE 1. DEFINITIONS

1. For the purposes of the International Health Regulations (hereinafter "the IHR" or "Regulations"):

– "affected" means persons, baggage, cargo, containers, conveyances, goods, postal parcels or human remains that are infected or contaminated, or carry sources of infection or contamination, so as to constitute a public health risk;
– "affected area" means a geographical location specifically for which health measures have been recommended by WHO under these Regulations;
– "aircraft" means an aircraft making an international voyage;
– "airport" means any airport where international flights arrive or depart;
– "arrival" of a conveyance means:

(a) in the case of a seagoing vessel, arrival or anchoring in the defined area of a port;
(b) in the case of an aircraft, arrival at an airport;
(c) in the case of an inland navigation vessel on an international voyage, arrival at a point of entry;
(d) in the case of a train or road vehicle, arrival at a point of entry;

– "baggage" means the personal effects of a traveller;
– "cargo" means goods carried on a conveyance or in a container;
– "competent authority" means an authority responsible for the implementation and application of health measures under these Regulations;
– "container" means an article of transport equipment:

(a) of a permanent character and accordingly strong enough to be suitable for repeated use;
(b) specially designed to facilitate the carriage of goods by one or more modes of transport, without intermediate reloading;

(c) fitted with devices permitting its ready handling, particularly its transfer from one mode of transport to another; and

(d) specially designed as to be easy to fill and empty;

- "container loading area" means a place or facility set aside for containers used in international traffic;
- "contamination" means the presence of an infectious or toxic agent or matter on a human or animal body surface, in or on a product prepared for consumption or on other inanimate objects, including conveyances, that may constitute a public health risk;
- "conveyance" means an aircraft, ship, train, road vehicle or other means of transport on an international voyage;
- "conveyance operator" means a natural or legal person in charge of a conveyance or their agent;
- "crew" means persons on board a conveyance who are not passengers;
- "decontamination" means a procedure whereby health measures are taken to eliminate an infectious or toxic agent or matter on a human or animal body surface, in or on a product prepared for consumption or on other inanimate objects, including conveyances, that may constitute a public health risk;
- "departure" means, for persons, baggage, cargo, conveyances or goods, the act of leaving a territory;
- "deratting" means the procedure whereby health measures are taken to control or kill rodent vectors of human disease present in baggage, cargo, containers, conveyances, facilities, goods and postal parcels at the point of entry;
- "Director-General" means the Director-General of the World Health Organization;
- "disease" means an illness or medical condition, irrespective of origin or source, that presents or could present significant harm to humans;
- "disinfection" means the procedure whereby health measures are taken to control or kill infectious agents on a human or animal body surface or in or on baggage, cargo, containers, conveyances, goods and postal parcels by direct exposure to chemical or physical agents;
- "disinsection" means the procedure whereby health measures are taken to control or kill the insect vectors of human diseases present in baggage, cargo, containers, conveyances, goods and postal parcels;
- "event" means a manifestation of disease or an occurrence that creates a potential for disease;
- "*free pratique*" means permission for a ship to enter a port, embark or disembark, discharge or load cargo or stores; permission for an aircraft, after landing, to embark or disembark, discharge or load cargo or stores; and permission for a ground transport vehicle, upon arrival, to embark or disembark, discharge or load cargo or stores;
- "goods" mean tangible products, including animals and plants, transported on an international voyage, including for utilization on board a conveyance;
- "ground crossing" means a point of land entry in a State Party, including one utilized by road vehicles and trains;
- "ground transport vehicle" means a motorized conveyance for overland transport on an international voyage, including trains, coaches, lorries and automobiles;

- "health measure" means procedures applied to prevent the spread of disease or contamination; a health measure does not include law enforcement or security measures;
- "ill person" means an individual suffering from or affected with a physical ailment that may pose a public health risk;
- "infection" means the entry and development or multiplication of an infectious agent in the body of humans and animals that may constitute a public health risk;
- "inspection" means the examination, by the competent authority or under its supervision, of areas, baggage, containers, conveyances, facilities, goods or postal parcels, including relevant data and documentation, to determine if a public health risk exists;
- "international traffic" means the movement of persons, baggage, cargo, containers, conveyances, goods or postal parcels across an international border, including international trade;
- "international voyage" means:

  (a) in the case of a conveyance, a voyage between points of entry in the territories of more than one State, or a voyage between points of entry in the territory or territories of the same State if the conveyance has contacts with the territory of any other State on its voyage but only as regards those contacts;
  (b) in the case of a traveller, a voyage involving entry into the territory of a State other than the territory of the State in which that traveller commences the voyage;

- "intrusive" means possibly provoking discomfort through close or intimate contact or questioning;
- "invasive" means the puncture or incision of the skin or insertion of an instrument or foreign material into the body or the examination of a body cavity. For the purposes of these Regulations, medical examination of the ear, nose and mouth, temperature assessment using an ear, oral or cutaneous thermometer, or thermal imaging; medical inspection; auscultation; external palpation; retinoscopy; external collection of urine, faeces or saliva samples; external measurement of blood pressure; and electrocardiography shall be considered to be non-invasive;
- "isolation" means separation of ill or contaminated persons or affected baggage, containers, conveyances, goods or postal parcels from others in such a manner as to prevent the spread of infection or contamination;
- "medical examination" means the preliminary assessment of a person by an authorized health worker or by a person under the direct supervision of the competent authority, to determine the person's health status and potential public health risk to others, and may include the scrutiny of health documents, and a physical examination when justified by the circumstances of the individual case;
- "National IHR Focal Point" means the national centre, designated by each State Party, which shall be accessible at all times for communications with WHO IHR Contact Points under these Regulations;
- "Organization" or "WHO" means the World Health Organization;
  "permanent residence" has the meaning as determined in the national law of the State Party concerned;

- "personal data" means any information relating to an identified or identifiable natural person;
- "point of entry" means a passage for international entry or exit of travellers, baggage, cargo, containers, conveyances, goods and postal parcels as well as agencies and areas providing services to them on entry or exit;
- "port" means a seaport or a port on an inland body of water where ships on an international voyage arrive or depart;
- "postal parcel" means an addressed article or package carried internationally by postal or courier services;
- "public health emergency of international concern" means an extraordinary event which is determined, as provided in these Regulations:

  (i) to constitute a public health risk to other States through the international spread of disease and
  (ii) to potentially require a coordinated international response;

- "public health observation" means the monitoring of the health status of a traveller over time for the purpose of determining the risk of disease transmission;
- "public health risk" means a likelihood of an event that may affect adversely the health of human populations, with an emphasis on one which may spread internationally or may present a serious and direct danger;
- "quarantine" means the restriction of activities and/or separation from others of suspect persons who are not ill or of suspect baggage, containers, conveyances or goods in such a manner as to preventthe possible spread of infection or contamination;
- "recommendation" and "recommended" refer to temporary or standing recommendations issued under these Regulations;
- "reservoir" means an animal, plant or substance in which an infectious agent normally lives and whose presence may constitute a public health risk;
- "road vehicle" means a ground transport vehicle other than a train;
- "scientific evidence" means information furnishing a level of proof based on the established and accepted methods of science;
- "scientific principles" means the accepted fundamental laws and facts of nature known through the methods of science;
- "ship" means a seagoing or inland navigation vessel on an international voyage;
- "standing recommendation" means non-binding advice issued by WHO for specific ongoing public health risks pursuant to Article 16 regarding appropriate health measures for routine or periodic application needed to prevent or reduce the international spread of disease and minimize interferencewith international traffic;
- "surveillance" means the systematic ongoing collection, collation and analysis of data for public health purposes and the timely dissemination of public health information for assessment and public health response as necessary;
- "suspect" means those persons, baggage, cargo, containers, conveyances, goods or postal parcels considered by a State Party as having been exposed, or possibly exposed, to a public health risk and that could be a possible source of spread of disease;

- "temporary recommendation" means non-binding advice issued by WHO pursuant to Article 15 for application on a time-limited, risk-specific basis, in response to a public health emergency of international concern, so as to prevent or reduce the international spread of disease and minimize interference with international traffic;
- "temporary residence" has the meaning as determined in the national law of the State Party concerned;
- "traveller" means a natural person undertaking an international voyage;
- "vector" means an insect or other animal which normally transports an infectious agent that constitutes a public health risk;
- "verification" means the provision of information by a State Party to WHO confirming the status of an event within the territory or territories of that State Party;
- "WHO IHR Contact Point" means the unit within WHO which shall be accessible at all times for communications with the National IHR Focal Point. Unless otherwise specified or determined by the context, reference to these Regulations includes the annexes thereto.

ARTICLE 2. PURPOSE AND SCOPE

The purpose and scope of these Regulations are to prevent, protect against, control and provide a public health response to the international spread of disease in ways that are commensurate with and restricted to public health risks, and which avoid unnecessary interference with international traffic and trade.

ARTICLE 3. PRINCIPLES

1. The implementation of these Regulations shall be with full respect for the dignity, human rights and fundamental freedoms of persons.

2. The implementation of these Regulations shall be guided by the Charter of the United Nations and the Constitution of the World Health Organization.

3. The implementation of these Regulations shall be guided by the goal of their universal application for the protection of all people of the world from the international spread of disease.

4. States have, in accordance with the Charter of the United Nations and the principles of international law, the sovereign right to legislate and to implement legislation in pursuance of their health policies. In doing so they should uphold the purpose of these Regulations.

ARTICLE 4. RESPONSIBLE AUTHORITIES

1. Each State Party shall designate or establish a National IHR Focal Point and the authorities responsible within its respective jurisdiction for the implementation of health measures under these Regulations.

2. National IHR Focal Points shall be accessible at all times for communications with the WHO IHR Contact Points provided for in paragraph 3 of this Article. The functions of National IHR Focal Points shall include:

(a) sending to WHO IHR Contact Points, on behalf of the State Party concerned, urgent communications concerning the implementation of these Regulations, in particular under Articles 6 to 12; and

(b) disseminating information to, and consolidating input from, relevant sectors of the administration of the State Party concerned, including those responsible for surveillance and reporting, points of entry, public health services, clinics and hospitals and other government departments.

3. WHO shall designate IHR Contact Points, which shall be accessible at all times for communications with National IHR Focal Points. WHO IHR Contact Points shall send urgent communications concerning the implementation of these Regulations, in particular under Articles 6 to 12, to the National IHR Focal Point of the States Parties concerned. WHO IHR Contact Points may be designated by WHO at the headquarters or at the regional level of the Organization.

4. States Parties shall provide WHO with contact details of their National IHR Focal Point and WHO shall provide States Parties with contact details of WHO IHR Contact Points. These contact details shall be continuously updated and annually confirmed. WHO shall make available to all States Parties the contact details of National IHR Focal Points it receives pursuant to this Article.

Part II – Information and Public Health Response

Article 5. Surveillance

1. Each State Party shall develop, strengthen and maintain, as soon as possible but no later than five years from the entry into force of these Regulations for that State Party, the capacity to detect, assess, notify and report events in accordance with these Regulations, as specified in Annex 1.

2. Following the assessment referred to in paragraph 2, Part A of Annex 1, a State Party may report to WHO on the basis of a justified need and an implementation plan and, in so doing, obtain an extension of two years in which to fulfil the obligation in paragraph 1 of this Article. In exceptional circumstances, and supported by a new implementation plan, the State Party may request a further extension not exceeding two years from the Director-General, who shall make the decision, taking into account the technical advice of the Committee established under Article 50 (hereinafter the "Review Committee"). After the period mentioned in paragraph 1 of this Article, the State Party that has obtained an extension shall report annually to WHO on progress made towards the full implementation.

3. WHO shall assist States Parties, upon request, to develop, strengthen and maintain the capacities referred to in paragraph 1 of this Article.

4. WHO shall collect information regarding events through its surveillance activities and assess their potential to cause international disease spread and possible interference with international traffic. Information received by WHO under this paragraph shall be handled in accordance with Articles 11 and 45 where appropriate.

ARTICLE 6. NOTIFICATION

1. Each State Party shall assess events occurring within its territory by using the decision instrument in Annex 2. Each State Party shall notify WHO, by the most efficient means of communication available, by way of the National IHR Focal Point, and within 24 hours of assessment of public health information, of all events which may constitute a public health emergency of international concern within its territory in accordance with the decision instrument, as well as any health measure implemented in response to those events. If the notification received by WHO involves the competency of the International Atomic Energy Agency (IAEA), WHO shall immediately notify the IAEA.

2. Following a notification, a State Party shall continue to communicate to WHO timely, accurate and sufficiently detailed public health information available to it on the notified event, where possible including case definitions, laboratory results, source and type of the risk, number of cases and deaths, conditions affecting the spread of the disease and the health measures employed; and report, when necessary, the difficulties faced and support needed in responding to the potential public health emergency of international concern.

ARTICLE 7. INFORMATION-SHARING DURING UNEXPECTED OR UNUSUAL PUBLIC HEALTH EVENTS

If a State Party has evidence of an unexpected or unusual public health event within its territory, irrespective of origin or source, which may constitute a public health emergency of international concern, it shall provide to WHO all relevant public health information. In such a case, the provisions of Article 6 shall apply in full.

ARTICLE 8. CONSULTATION

In the case of events occurring within its territory not requiring notification as provided in Article 6, in particular those events for which there is insufficient information available to complete the decision instrument, a State Party may nevertheless keep WHO advised thereof through the National IHR Focal Point and consult with WHO on appropriate health measures. Such communications shall be treated in accordance with paragraphs 2 to 4 of Article 11. The State Party in whose territory the event has occurred may request WHO assistance to assess any epidemiological evidence obtained by that State Party.

ARTICLE 9. OTHER REPORTS

1. WHO may take into account reports from sources other than notifications or consultations and shall assess these reports according to established epidemiological principles and then communicate information on the event to the State Party in whose territory the event is allegedly occurring. Before taking any action based on such reports, WHO shall consult with and attempt to obtain verification from the State Party in whose territory the event is allegedly occurring in accordance with the procedure set forth in Article 10. To this end, WHO shall make the information received available to the States Parties and only where it is duly justified may WHO maintain the confidentiality of the source. This information will be used in accordance with the procedure set forth in Article 11.

2. States Parties shall, as far as practicable, inform WHO within 24 hours of receipt of evidence of a public health risk identified outside their territory that may cause international disease spread, as manifested by exported or imported:

(a) human cases;
(b) vectors which carry infection or contamination; or
(c) goods that are contaminated.

ARTICLE 10. VERIFICATION

1. WHO shall request, in accordance with Article 9, verification from a State Party of reports from sources other than notifications or consultations of events which may constitute a public health emergency of international concern allegedly occurring in the State's territory. In such cases, WHO shall inform the State Party concerned regarding the reports it is seeking to verify.

2. Pursuant to the foregoing paragraph and to Article 9, each State Party, when requested by WHO, shall verify and provide:

(a) within 24 hours, an initial reply to, or acknowledgement of, the request from WHO;
(b) within 24 hours, available public health information on the status of events referred to in WHO's request; and
(c) information to WHO in the context of an assessment under Article 6, including relevant information as described in that Article.

3. When WHO receives information of an event that may constitute a public health emergency of international concern, it shall offer to collaborate with the State Party concerned in assessing the potential for international disease spread, possible interference with international traffic and the adequacy of control measures. Such activities may include collaboration with other standard-setting organizations and the offer to mobilize international assistance in order to support the national authorities in conducting and coordinating on-site assessments. When requested by the State Party,

WHO shall provide information supporting such an offer.

4. If the State Party does not accept the offer of collaboration, WHO may, when justified by the magnitude of the public health risk, share with other States Parties the information available to it, whilst encouraging the State Party to accept the offer of collaboration by WHO, taking into account the views of the State Party concerned.

ARTICLE 11. PROVISION OF INFORMATION BY WHO

1. Subject to paragraph 2 of this Article, WHO shall send to all States Parties and, as appropriate, to relevant intergovernmental organizations, as soon as possible and by the most efficient means available, in confidence, such public health information which it has received under Articles 5 to 10 inclusive and which is necessary to enable States Parties to respond to a public health risk. WHO should communicate information to other States Parties that might help them in preventing the occurrence of similar incidents.

2. WHO shall use information received under Articles 6 and 8 and paragraph 2 of Article 9 for verification, assessment and assistance purposes under these Regulations and, unless otherwise agreed with the States Parties referred to in those provisions, shall not make this information generally available to other States Parties, until such time as:

(a) the event is determined to constitute a public health emergency of international concern in accordance with Article 12; or
(b) information evidencing the international spread of the infection or contamination has been confirmed by WHO in accordance with established epidemiological principles; or
(c) there is evidence that:

(i) control measures against the international spread are unlikely to succeed because of the nature of the contamination, disease agent, vector or reservoir; or
(ii) the State Party lacks sufficient operational capacity to carry out necessary measures to prevent further spread of disease; or

(d) the nature and scope of the international movement of travellers, baggage, cargo, containers, conveyances, goods or postal parcels that may be affected by the infection or contamination requires the immediate application of international control measures.

3. WHO shall consult with the State Party in whose territory the event is occurring as to its intent to make information available under this Article.

4. When information received by WHO under paragraph 2 of this Article is made available to States Parties in accordance with these Regulations, WHO may also make it available to the public if other information about the same event has already become publicly available and there is a need for the dissemination of authoritative and independent information.

Article 12. Determination of a public health emergency of international concern

1. The Director-General shall determine, on the basis of the information received, in particular from the State Party within whose territory an event is occurring, whether an event constitutes a public health emergency of international concern in accordance with the criteria and the procedure set out in these Regulations.

2. If the Director-General considers, based on an assessment under these Regulations, that a public health emergency of international concern is occurring, the Director-General shall consult with the State Party in whose territory the event arises regarding this preliminary determination. If the Director-General and the State Party are in agreement regarding this determination, the Director-General shall, in accordance with the procedure set forth in Article 49, seek the views of the Committee established under Article 48 (hereinafter the "Emergency Committee") on appropriate temporary recommendations.

3. If, following the consultation in paragraph 2 above, the Director-General and the State Party in whose territory the event arises do not come to a consensus within 48 hours on whether the event constitutes a public health emergency of international concern, a determination shall be made in accordance with the procedure set forth in Article 49.

4. In determining whether an event constitutes a public health emergency of international concern, the Director-General shall consider:

(a) information provided by the State Party;
(b) the decision instrument contained in Annex 2;
(c) the advice of the Emergency Committee;
(d) scientific principles as well as the available scientific evidence and other relevant information; and
(e) an assessment of the risk to human health, of the risk of international spread of disease and of the risk of interference with international traffic.

5. If the Director-General, following consultations with the State Party within whose territory the public health emergency of international concern has occurred, considers that a public health emergency of international concern has ended, the Director-General shall take a decision in accordance with the procedure set out in Article 49.

Article 13. Public health response

1. Each State Party shall develop, strengthen and maintain, as soon as possible but no later than five years from the entry into force of these Regulations for that State Party, the capacity to respond promptly and effectively to public health risks and public health emergencies of international concern as set out in Annex 1. WHO shall publish, in consultation with Member States, guidelines to support States Parties in the development of public health response capacities.

2. Following the assessment referred to in paragraph 2, Part A of Annex 1, a State Party may report to WHO on the basis of a justified need and an implementation plan and, in so doing, obtain an extension of two years in which to fulfil the obligation in paragraph 1 of this Article. In exceptional circumstances and supported by a new implementation plan, the State Party may request a further extension not exceeding two years from the Director-General, who shall make the decision, taking into account the technical advice of the Review Committee. After the period mentioned in paragraph 1 of this Article, the State Party that has obtained an extension shall report annually to WHO on progress made towards the full implementation.

3. At the request of a State Party, WHO shall collaborate in the response to public health risks and other events by providing technical guidance and assistance and by assessing the effectiveness of the control measures in place, including the mobilization of international teams of experts for on-site assistance, when necessary.

4. If WHO, in consultation with the States Parties concerned as provided in Article 12, determines that a public health emergency of international concern is occurring, it may offer, in addition to the support indicated in paragraph 3 of this Article, further assistance to the State Party, including an assessment of the severity of the international risk and the adequacy of control measures. Such collaboration may include the offer to mobilize international assistance in order to support the national authorities in conducting and coordinating on-site assessments. When requested by the State Party, WHO shall provide information supporting such an offer.

5. When requested by WHO, States Parties should provide, to the extent possible, support to WHO-coordinated response activities.

6. When requested, WHO shall provide appropriate guidance and assistance to other States Parties affected or threatened by the public health emergency of international concern.

ARTICLE 14. COOPERATION OF WHO WITH INTERGOVERNMENTAL ORGANIZATIONS AND INTERNATIONAL BODIES

1. WHO shall cooperate and coordinate its activities, as appropriate, with other competent intergovernmental organizations or international bodies in the implementation of these Regulations, including through the conclusion of agreements and other similar arrangements.

2. In cases in which notification or verification of, or response to, an event is primarily within the competence of other intergovernmental organizations or international bodies, WHO shall coordinate its activities with such organizations or bodies in order to ensure the application of adequate measures for the protection of public health.

3. Notwithstanding the foregoing, nothing in these Regulations shall preclude or limit the provision by WHO of advice, support, or technical or other assistance for public health purposes.

Part III – Recommendations

ARTICLE 15. TEMPORARY RECOMMENDATIONS

1. If it has been determined in accordance with Article 12 that a public health emergency of international concern is occurring, the Director-General shall issue temporary recommendations in accordance with the procedure set out in Article 49. Such temporary recommendations may be modified or extended as appropriate, including after it has been determined that a public health emergency of international concern has ended, at which time other temporary recommendations may be issued as necessary for the purpose of preventing or promptly detecting its recurrence.

2. Temporary recommendations may include health measures to be implemented by the State Party experiencing the public health emergency of international concern, or by other States Parties, regarding persons, baggage, cargo, containers, conveyances, goods and/or postal parcels to prevent or reduce the international spread of disease and avoid unnecessary interference with international traffic.

3. Temporary recommendations may be terminated in accordance with the procedure set out in Article 49 at any time and shall automatically expire three months after their issuance. They may be modified or extended for additional periods of up to three months. Temporary recommendations may not continue beyond the second World Health Assembly after the determination of the public health emergency of international concern to which they relate.

ARTICLE 16. STANDING RECOMMENDATIONS

WHO may make standing recommendations of appropriate health measures in accordance with Article 53 for routine or periodic application. Such measures may be applied by States Parties regarding persons, baggage, cargo, containers, conveyances, goods and/or postal parcels for specific, ongoing public health risks in order to prevent or reduce the international spread of disease and avoid unnecessary interference with international traffic. WHO may, in accordance with Article 53, modify or terminate such recommendations, as appropriate.

ARTICLE 17. CRITERIA FOR RECOMMENDATIONS

When issuing, modifying or terminating temporary or standing recommendations, the Director-General shall consider:

(a) the views of the States Parties directly concerned;
(b) the advice of the Emergency Committee or the Review Committee, as the case may be;
(c) scientific principles as well as available scientific evidence and information;
(d) health measures that, on the basis of a risk assessment appropriate to the circumstances, are not more restrictive of international traffic and trade and are not more intrusive to per-

412

sons than reasonably available alternatives that would achieve the appropriate level of health protection;

(e) relevant international standards and instruments;

(f) activities undertaken by other relevant intergovernmental organizations and international bodies; and

(g) other appropriate and specific information relevant to the event.

With respect to temporary recommendations, the consideration by the Director-General of subparagraphs (e) and (f) of this Article may be subject to limitations imposed by urgent circumstances.

ARTICLE 18. RECOMMENDATIONS WITH RESPECT TO PERSONS, BAGGAGE, CARGO, CONTAINERS, CONVEYANCES, GOODS AND POSTAL PARCELS

1. Recommendations issued by WHO to States Parties with respect to persons may include the following advice:

– no specific health measures are advised;
– review travel history in affected areas;
– review proof of medical examination and any laboratory analysis;
– require medical examinations;
– review proof of vaccination or other prophylaxis;
– require vaccination or other prophylaxis;
– place suspect persons under public health observation;
– implement quarantine or other health measures for suspect persons;
– implement isolation and treatment where necessary of affected persons;
– implement tracing of contacts of suspect or affected persons;
– refuse entry of suspect and affected persons;
– refuse entry of unaffected persons to affected areas; and
– implement exit screening and/or restrictions on persons from affected areas.

2. Recommendations issued by WHO to States Parties with respect to baggage, cargo, containers, conveyances, goods and postal parcels may include the following advice:

– no specific health measures are advised;
– review manifest and routing;
– implement inspections;
– review proof of measures taken on departure or in transit to eliminate infection or contamination;
– implement treatment of the baggage, cargo, containers, conveyances, goods, postal parcels or human remains to remove infection or contamination, including vectors and reservoirs;
– the use of specific health measures to ensure the safe handling and transport of human remains;

– implement isolation or quarantine;
– seizure and destruction of infected or contaminated or suspect baggage, cargo, containers, conveyances, goods or postal parcels under controlled conditions if no available treatment or process will otherwise be successful; and
– refuse departure or entry.

Part IV – Points of Entry

ARTICLE 19. GENERAL OBLIGATIONS

Each State Party shall, in addition to the other obligations provided for under these Regulations:

(a) ensure that the capacities set forth in Annex 1 for designated points of entry are developed within the timeframe provided in paragraph 1 of Article 5 and paragraph 1 of Article 13;
(b) identify the competent authorities at each designated point of entry in its territory; and
(c) furnish to WHO, as far as practicable, when requested in response to a specific potential public health risk, relevant data concerning sources of infection or contamination, including vectors and reservoirs, at its points of entry, which could result in international disease spread.

ARTICLE 20. AIRPORTS AND PORTS

1. States Parties shall designate the airports and ports that shall develop the capacities provided in Annex 1.

2. States Parties shall ensure that Ship Sanitation Control Exemption Certificates and Ship Sanitation Control Certificates are issued in accordance with the requirements in Article 39 and the model provided in Annex 3.

3. Each State Party shall send to WHO a list of ports authorized to offer:

(a) the issuance of Ship Sanitation Control Certificates and the provision of the services referred to in Annexes 1 and 3; or
(b) the issuance of Ship Sanitation Control Exemption Certificates only; and
(c) extension of the Ship Sanitation Control Exemption Certificate for a period of one month until the arrival of the ship in the port at which the Certificate may be received. Each State Party shall inform WHO of any changes which may occur to the status of the listed ports. WHO shall publish the information received under this paragraph.

4. WHO may, at the request of the State Party concerned, arrange to certify, after an appropriate investigation, that an airport or port in its territory meets the requirements referred to in paragraphs 1 and 3 of this Article. These certifications may be subject to periodic review by WHO, in consultation with the State Party.

5. WHO, in collaboration with competent intergovernmental organizations and international bodies, shall develop and publish the certification guidelines for airports and ports under this Article. WHO shall also publish a list of certified airports and ports.

ARTICLE 21. GROUND CROSSINGS

1. Where justified for public health reasons, a State Party may designate ground crossings that shall develop the capacities provided in Annex 1, taking into consideration:

(a) the volume and frequency of the various types of international traffic, as compared to other points of entry, at a State Party's ground crossings which might be designated; and
(b) the public health risks existing in areas in which the international traffic originates, or through which it passes, prior to arrival at a particular ground crossing.

2. States Parties sharing common borders should consider:

(a) entering into bilateral or multilateral agreements or arrangements concerning prevention or control of international transmission of disease at ground crossings in accordance with Article 57; and
(b) joint designation of adjacent ground crossings for the capacities in Annex 1 in accordance with paragraph 1 of this Article.

ARTICLE 22. ROLE OF COMPETENT AUTHORITIES

1. The competent authorities shall:

(a) be responsible for monitoring baggage, cargo, containers, conveyances, goods, postal parcels and human remains departing and arriving from affected areas, so that they are maintained in such a condition that they are free of sources of infection or contamination, including vectors and reservoirs;
(b) ensure, as far as practicable, that facilities used by travellers at points of entry are maintained in a sanitary condition and are kept free of sources of infection or contamination, including vectors and reservoirs;
(c) be responsible for the supervision of any deratting, disinfection, disinsection or decontamination of baggage, cargo, containers, conveyances, goods, postal parcels and human remains or sanitary measures for persons, as appropriate under these Regulations;
(d) advise conveyance operators, as far in advance as possible, of their intent to apply control measures to a conveyance, and shall provide, where available, written information concerning the methods to be employed;
(e) be responsible for the supervision of the removal and safe disposal of any contaminated water or food, human or animal dejecta, wastewater and any other contaminated matter from a conveyance;
(f) take all practicable measures consistent with these Regulations to monitor and control the discharge by ships of sewage, refuse, ballast water and other potentially disease-causing matter

which might contaminate the waters of a port, river, canal, strait, lake or other international waterway;

(g) be responsible for supervision of service providers for services concerning travellers, baggage, cargo, containers, conveyances, goods, postal parcels and human remains at points of entry, including the conduct of inspections and medical examinations as necessary;

(h) have effective contingency arrangements to deal with an unexpected public health event; and

(i) communicate with the National IHR Focal Point on the relevant public health measures taken pursuant to these Regulations.

2. Health measures recommended by WHO for travellers, baggage, cargo, containers, conveyances, goods, postal parcels and human remains arriving from an affected area may be reapplied on arrival, if there are verifiable indications and/or evidence that the measures applied on departure from the affected area were unsuccessful.

3. Disinsection, deratting, disinfection, decontamination and other sanitary procedures shall be carried out so as to avoid injury and as far as possible discomfort to persons, or damage to the environment in a way which impacts on public health, or damage to baggage, cargo, containers, conveyances, goods and postal parcels.

Part V – Public Health Measures

Chapter I – General provisions

ARTICLE 23. HEALTH MEASURES ON ARRIVAL AND DEPARTURE

1. Subject to applicable international agreements and relevant articles of these Regulations, a State Party may require for public health purposes, on arrival or departure:

(a) with regard to travellers:

(i)   information concerning the traveller's destination so that the traveller may be contacted;
(ii)   information concerning the traveller's itinerary to ascertain if there was any travel in or near an affected area or other possible contacts with infection or contamination prior to arrival, as well as review of the traveller's health documents if they are required under these Regulations; and/or
(iii)   a non-invasive medical examination which is the least intrusive examination that would achieve the public health objective;

(b) inspection of baggage, cargo, containers, conveyances, goods, postal parcels and human remains.

2. On the basis of evidence of a public health risk obtained through the measures provided in paragraph 1 of this Article, or through other means, States Parties may apply additional health measures, in accordance with these Regulations, in particular, with regard to a suspect or affected traveller, on a case-by-case basis, the least intrusive and invasive medical examination that would achieve the public health objective of preventing the international spread of disease.

3. No medical examination, vaccination, prophylaxis or health measure under these Regulations shall be carried out on travellers without their prior express informed consent or that of their parents or guardians, except as provided in paragraph 2 of Article 31, and in accordance with the law and international obligations of the State Party.

4. Travellers to be vaccinated or offered prophylaxis pursuant to these Regulations, or their parents or guardians, shall be informed of any risk associated with vaccination or with non-vaccination and with the use or non-use of prophylaxis in accordance with the law and international obligations of the State Party. States Parties shall inform medical practitioners of these requirements in accordance with the law of the State Party.

5. Any medical examination, medical procedure, vaccination or other prophylaxis which involves a risk of disease transmission shall only be performed on, or administered to, a traveller in accordance with established national or international safety guidelines and standards so as to minimize such a risk.

...

Chapter III – Special provisions for travellers

ARTICLE 30. TRAVELLERS UNDER PUBLIC HEALTH OBSERVATION

Subject to Article 43 or as authorized in applicable international agreements, a suspect traveler who on arrival is placed under public health observation may continue an international voyage, if the traveller does not pose an imminent public health risk and the State Party informs the competent authority of the point of entry at destination, if known, of the traveller's expected arrival. On arrival, the traveller shall report to that authority.

ARTICLE 31. HEALTH MEASURES RELATING TO ENTRY OF TRAVELLERS

1. Invasive medical examination, vaccination or other prophylaxis shall not be required as a condition of entry of any traveller to the territory of a State Party, except that, subject to Articles 32, 42 and 45, these Regulations do not preclude States Parties from requiring medical examination, vaccination or other prophylaxis or proof of vaccination or other prophylaxis:

(a) when necessary to determine whether a public health risk exists;
(b) as a condition of entry for any travellers seeking temporary or permanent residence;

(c) as a condition of entry for any travellers pursuant to Article 43 or Annexes 6 and 7; or
(d) which may be carried out pursuant to Article 23.

2. If a traveller for whom a State Party may require a medical examination, vaccination or other prophylaxis under paragraph 1 of this Article fails to consent to any such measure, or refuses to provide the information or the documents referred to in paragraph 1(a) of Article 23, the State Party concerned may, subject to Articles 32, 42 and 45, deny entry to that traveller. If there is evidence of an imminent public health risk, the State Party may, in accordance with its national law and to the extent necessary to control such a risk, compel the traveller to undergo or advise the traveller, pursuant to paragraph 3 of Article 23, to undergo:

(a) the least invasive and intrusive medical examination that would achieve the public health objective;
(b) vaccination or other prophylaxis; or
(c) additional established health measures that prevent or control the spread of disease, including isolation, quarantine or placing the traveller under public health observation.

ARTICLE 32. TREATMENT OF TRAVELLERS

In implementing health measures under these Regulations, States Parties shall treat travelers with respect for their dignity, human rights and fundamental freedoms and minimize any discomfort or distress associated with such measures, including by:

(a) treating all travellers with courtesy and respect;
(b) taking into consideration the gender, sociocultural, ethnic or religious concerns of travellers; and
(c) providing or arranging for adequate food and water, appropriate accommodation and clothing, protection for baggage and other possessions, appropriate medical treatment, means of necessary communication if possible in a language that they can understand and other appropriate assistance for travellers who are quarantined, isolated or subject to medical examinations or other procedures for public health purposes.

…

Part VI – Health Documents

ARTICLE 35. GENERAL RULE

No health documents, other than those provided for under these Regulations or in recommendations issued by WHO, shall be required in international traffic, provided however that this Article shall not apply to travellers seeking temporary or permanent residence, nor shall it apply to document requirements concerning the public health status of goods or cargo in international trade pursuant to applicable international agreements. The competent authority may request travellers to complete contact information forms and questionnaires on the health of travellers, provided that they meet the requirements set out in Article 23.

ARTICLE 36. CERTIFICATES OF VACCINATION OR OTHER PROPHYLAXIS

1. Vaccines and prophylaxis for travellers administered pursuant to these Regulations, or to recommendations and certificates relating thereto, shall conform to the provisions of Annex 6 and, when applicable, Annex 7 with regard to specific diseases.

2. A traveller in possession of a certificate of vaccination or other prophylaxis issued in conformity with Annex 6 and, when applicable, Annex 7, shall not be denied entry as a consequence of the disease to which the certificate refers, even if coming from an affected area, unless the competent authority has verifiable indications and/or evidence that the vaccination or other prophylaxis was not effective.

ARTICLE 37. MARITIME DECLARATION OF HEALTH

1. The master of a ship, before arrival at its first port of call in the territory of a State Party, shall ascertain the state of health on board, and, except when that State Party does not require it, the master shall, on arrival, or in advance of the vessel's arrival if the vessel is so equipped and the State Party requires such advance delivery, complete and deliver to the competent authority for that port a Maritime Declaration of Health which shall be countersigned by the ship's surgeon, if one is carried.

2. The master of a ship, or the ship's surgeon if one is carried, shall supply any information required by the competent authority as to health conditions on board during an international voyage.

3. A Maritime Declaration of Health shall conform to the model provided in Annex 8.

4. A State Party may decide:

(a) to dispense with the submission of the Maritime Declaration of Health by all arriving ships; or
(b) to require the submission of the Maritime Declaration of Health under a recommendation concerning ships arriving from affected areas or to require it from ships which might otherwise carry infection or contamination. The State Party shall inform shipping operators or their agents of these requirements.

...

Part VII – Charges

ARTICLE 40. CHARGES FOR HEALTH MEASURES REGARDING TRAVELLERS

1. Except for travellers seeking temporary or permanent residence, and subject to paragraph 2 of this Article, no charge shall be made by a State Party pursuant to these Regulations for the following measures for the protection of public health:

(a) any medical examination provided for in these Regulations, or any supplementary examination which may be required by that State Party to ascertain the health status of the traveller examined;
(b) any vaccination or other prophylaxis provided to a traveller on arrival that is not a published requirement or is a requirement published less than 10 days prior to provision of the vaccination or other prophylaxis;
(c) appropriate isolation or quarantine requirements of travellers;
(d) any certificate issued to the traveller specifying the measures applied and the date of application; or
(e) any health measures applied to baggage accompanying the traveller.

2. States Parties may charge for health measures other than those referred to in paragraph 1 of this Article, including those primarily for the benefit of the traveller.

3. Where charges are made for applying such health measures to travellers under these Regulations, there shall be in each State Party only one tariff for such charges and every charge shall:

(a) conform to this tariff;
(b) not exceed the actual cost of the service rendered; and
(c) be levied without distinction as to the nationality, domicile or residence of the traveler concerned.

4. The tariff, and any amendment thereto, shall be published at least 10 days in advance of any levy thereunder.

5. Nothing in these Regulations shall preclude States Parties from seeking reimbursement for expenses incurred in providing the health measures in paragraph 1 of this Article:

(a) from conveyance operators or owners with regard to their employees; or
(b) from applicable insurance sources.

6. Under no circumstances shall travellers or conveyance operators be denied the ability to depart from the territory of a State Party pending payment of the charges referred to in paragraphs 1 or 2 of this Article.

...

Part VIII – General Provisions

ARTICLE 42. IMPLEMENTATION OF HEALTH MEASURES

Health measures taken pursuant to these Regulations shall be initiated and completed without delay, and applied in a transparent and non-discriminatory manner.

ARTICLE 43. ADDITIONAL HEALTH MEASURES

1. These Regulations shall not preclude States Parties from implementing health measures, in accordance with their relevant national law and obligations under international law, in response to specific public health risks or public health emergencies of international concern, which:

(a) achieve the same or greater level of health protection than WHO recommendations; or
(b) are otherwise prohibited under Article 25, Article 26, paragraphs 1 and 2 of Article 28, Article 30, paragraph 1(c) of Article 31 and Article 33, provided such measures are otherwise consistent with these Regulations. Such measures shall not be more restrictive of international traffic and not more invasive or intrusive to persons than reasonably available alternatives that would achieve the appropriate level of health protection.

2. In determining whether to implement the health measures referred to in paragraph 1 of this Article or additional health measures under paragraph 2 of Article 23, paragraph 1 of Article 27, paragraph 2 of Article 28 and paragraph 2(c) of Article 31, States Parties shall base their determinations upon:

(a) scientific principles;
(b) available scientific evidence of a risk to human health, or where such evidence is insufficient, the available information including from WHO and other relevant intergovernmental organizations and international bodies; and
(c) any available specific guidance or advice from WHO.

3. A State Party implementing additional health measures referred to in paragraph 1 of this Article which significantly interfere with international traffic shall provide to WHO the public health rationale and relevant scientific information for it. WHO shall share this information with other States Parties and shall share information regarding the health measures implemented. For the purpose of this Article, significant interference generally means refusal of entry or departure of international travellers, baggage, cargo, containers, conveyances, goods, and the like, or their delay, for more than 24 hours.

4. After assessing information provided pursuant to paragraph 3 and 5 of this Article and other relevant information, WHO may request that the State Party concerned reconsider the application of the measures.

5. A State Party implementing additional health measures referred to in paragraphs 1 and 2 of this Article that significantly interfere with international traffic shall inform WHO, within 48 hours of implementation, of such measures and their health rationale unless these are covered by a temporary or standing recommendation.

6. A State Party implementing a health measure pursuant to paragraph 1 or 2 of this Article shall within three months review such a measure taking into account the advice of WHO and the criteria in paragraph 2 of this Article.

7. Without prejudice to its rights under Article 56, any State Party impacted by a measure taken pursuant to paragraph 1 or 2 of this Article may request the State Party implementing such a measure to consult with it. The purpose of such consultations is to clarify the scientific information and public health rationale underlying the measure and to find a mutually acceptable solution.

8. The provisions of this Article may apply to implementation of measures concerning travelers taking part in mass congregations.

Article 44. Collaboration and assistance

1. States Parties shall undertake to collaborate with each other, to the extent possible, in:

(a) the detection and assessment of, and response to, events as provided under these Regulations;
(b) the provision or facilitation of technical cooperation and logistical support, particularly in the development, strengthening and maintenance of the public health capacities required under these Regulations;
(c) the mobilization of financial resources to facilitate implementation of their obligations under these Regulations; and
(d) the formulation of proposed laws and other legal and administrative provisions for the implementation of these Regulations.

2. WHO shall collaborate with States Parties, upon request, to the extent possible, in:

(a) the evaluation and assessment of their public health capacities in order to facilitate the effective implementation of these Regulations;
(b) the provision or facilitation of technical cooperation and logistical support to States Parties; and
(c) the mobilization of financial resources to support developing countries in building, strengthening and maintaining the capacities provided for in Annex 1.

3. Collaboration under this Article may be implemented through multiple channels, including bilaterally, through regional networks and the WHO regional offices, and through intergovernmental organizations and international bodies.

ARTICLE 45. TREATMENT OF PERSONAL DATA

1. Health information collected or received by a State Party pursuant to these Regulations from another State Party or from WHO which refers to an identified or identifiable person shall be kept confidential and processed anonymously as required by national law.

2. Notwithstanding paragraph 1, States Parties may disclose and process personal data where essential for the purposes of assessing and managing a public health risk, but State Parties, in accordance with national law, and WHO must ensure that the personal data are:

(a) processed fairly and lawfully, and not further processed in a way incompatible with that purpose;
(b) adequate, relevant and not excessive in relation to that purpose;
(c) accurate and, where necessary, kept up to date; every reasonable step must be taken to ensure that data which are inaccurate or incomplete are erased or rectified; and
(d) not kept longer than necessary.

3. Upon request, WHO shall as far as practicable provide an individual with his or her personal data referred to in this Article in an intelligible form, without undue delay or expense and, when necessary, allow for correction.

...

Part X – Final Provisions

ARTICLE 54. REPORTING AND REVIEW

1. States Parties and the Director-General shall report to the Health Assembly on the implementation of these Regulations as decided by the Health Assembly.

2. The Health Assembly shall periodically review the functioning of these Regulations. To that end it may request the advice of the Review Committee, through the Director-General. The first such review shall take place no later than five years after the entry into force of these Regulations.

3. WHO shall periodically conduct studies to review and evaluate the functioning of Annex 2. The first such review shall commence no later than one year after the entry into force of these Regulations. The results of such reviews shall be submitted to the Health Assembly for its consideration, as appropriate.

...

Article 56. Settlement of disputes

1. In the event of a dispute between two or more States Parties concerning the interpretation or application of these Regulations, the States Parties concerned shall seek in the first instance to settle 34 the dispute through negotiation or any other peaceful means of their own choice, including good offices, mediation or conciliation. Failure to reach agreement shall not absolve the parties to the dispute from the responsibility of continuing to seek to resolve it.

2. In the event that the dispute is not settled by the means described under paragraph 1 of this Article, the States Parties concerned may agree to refer the dispute to the Director-General, who shall make every effort to settle it.

3. A State Party may at any time declare in writing to the Director-General that it accepts arbitration as compulsory with regard to all disputes concerning the interpretation or application of these Regulations to which it is a party or with regard to a specific dispute in relation to any other State Party accepting the same obligation. The arbitration shall be conducted in accordance with the Permanent Court of Arbitration Optional Rules for Arbitrating Disputes between Two States applicable at the time a request for arbitration is made. The States Parties that have agreed to accept arbitration as compulsory shall accept the arbitral award as binding and final. The Director-General shall inform the Health Assembly regarding such action as appropriate.

4. Nothing in these Regulations shall impair the rights of States Parties under any international agreement to which they may be parties to resort to the dispute settlement mechanisms of other intergovernmental organizations or established under any international agreement.

5. In the event of a dispute between WHO and one or more States Parties concerning the interpretation or application of these Regulations, the matter shall be submitted to the Health Assembly.

Article 57. Relationship with other international agreements

1. States Parties recognize that the IHR and other relevant international agreements should be interpreted so as to be compatible. The provisions of the IHR shall not affect the rights and obligations of any State Party deriving from other international agreements.

2. Subject to paragraph 1 of this Article, nothing in these Regulations shall prevent States Parties having certain interests in common owing to their health, geographical, social or economic conditions, from concluding special treaties or arrangements in order to facilitate the application of these Regulations, and in particular with regard to:

(a) the direct and rapid exchange of public health information between neighbouring territories of different States;

(b) the health measures to be applied to international coastal traffic and to international traffic in waters within their jurisdiction;

(c) the health measures to be applied in contiguous territories of different States at their common frontier;

(d) arrangements for carrying affected persons or affected human remains by means of transport specially adapted for the purpose; and

(e) deratting, disinsection, disinfection, decontamination or other treatment designed to render goods free of disease-causing agents.

3. Without prejudice to their obligations under these Regulations, States Parties that are members of a regional economic integration organization shall apply in their mutual relations the common rules in force in that regional economic integration organization.

...

ARTICLE 62. RESERVATIONS

1. States may make reservations to these Regulations in accordance with this Article. Such reservations shall not be incompatible with the object and purpose of these Regulations.

2. Reservations to these Regulations shall be notified to the Director-General in accordance with paragraph 1 of Article 59 and Article 60, paragraph 1 of Article 63 or paragraph 1 of Article 64, as the case may be. A State not a Member of WHO shall notify the Director-General of any reservation with its notification of acceptance of these Regulations. States formulating reservations should provide the Director-General with reasons for the reservations.

3. A rejection in part of these Regulations shall be considered as a reservation.

4. The Director-General shall, in accordance with paragraph 2 of Article 65, issue notification of each reservation received pursuant to paragraph 2 of this Article. The Director-General shall:

(a) if the reservation was made before the entry into force of these Regulations, request those Member States that have not rejected these Regulations to notify him or her within six months of any objection to the reservation, or

(b) if the reservation was made after the entry into force of these Regulations, request States Parties to notify him or her within six months of any objection to the reservation. States objecting to a reservation should provide the Director-General with reasons for the objection.

5. After this period, the Director-General shall notify all States Parties of the objections he or she has received with regard to reservations. Unless by the end of six months from the date of the notification referred to in paragraph 4 of this Article a reservation has been objected to by one-third of the States referred to in paragraph 4 of this Article, it shall be deemed to be

accepted and these Regulations shall enter into force for the reserving State, subject to the reservation.

6. If at least one-third of the States referred to in paragraph 4 of this Article object to the reservation by the end of six months from the date of the notification referred to in paragraph 4 of this Article, the Director-General shall notify the reserving State with a view to its considering withdrawing the reservation within three months from the date of the notification by the Director-General.

7. The reserving State shall continue to fulfil any obligations corresponding to the subject matter of the reservation, which the State has accepted under any of the international sanitary agreements or regulations listed in Article 58.

8. If the reserving State does not withdraw the reservation within three months from the date of the notification by the Director-General referred to in paragraph 6 of this Article, the Director-General shall seek the view of the Review Committee if the reserving State so requests. The Review Committee shall advise the Director-General as soon as possible and in accordance with Article 50 on the practical impact of the reservation on the operation of these Regulations.

9. The Director-General shall submit the reservation, and the views of the Review Committee if applicable, to the Health Assembly for its consideration. If the Health Assembly, by a majority vote, objects to the reservation on the ground that it is incompatible with the object and purpose of these Regulations, the reservation shall not be accepted and these Regulations shall enter into force for the reserving State only after it withdraws its reservation pursuant to Article 63. If the Health Assembly accepts the reservation, these Regulations shall enter into force for the reserving State, subject to its reservation.

ARTICLE 63. WITHDRAWAL OF REJECTION AND RESERVATION

1. A rejection made under Article 61 may at any time be withdrawn by a State by notifying the Director-General. In such cases, these Regulations shall enter into force with regard to that State upon receipt by the Director-General of the notification, except where the State makes a reservation when withdrawing its rejection, in which case these Regulations shall enter into force as provided in Article 62. In no case shall these Regulations enter into force in respect to that State earlier than 24 months after the date of notification referred to in paragraph 1 of Article 59.

2. The whole or part of any reservation may at any time be withdrawn by the State Party concerned by notifying the Director-General. In such cases, the withdrawal will be effective from the date of receipt by the Director-General of the notification.

...

Chapter 2. Public Health and Trade

2.1. The WTO Agreement on the Application of Sanitary and Phytosanitary Measures (SPS Agreement)

Reaffirming that no Member should be prevented from adopting or enforcing measures necessary to protect human, animal or plant life or health, subject to the requirement that these measures are not applied in a manner which would constitute a means of arbitrary or unjustifiable discrimination between Members where the same conditions prevail or a disguised restriction on international trade; Desiring to improve the human health, animal health and phytosanitary situation in all Members; Noting that sanitary and phytosanitary measures are often applied on the basis of bilateral agreements or protocols; Desiring the establishment of a multilateral framework of rules and disciplines to guide the development, adoption and enforcement of sanitary and phytosanitary measures in order to minimize their negative effects on trade; Recognizing the important contribution that international standards, guidelines and recommendations can make in this regard; Desiring to further the use of harmonized sanitary and phytosanitary measures between Members, on the basis of international standards, guidelines and recommendations developed by the relevant international organizations, including the Codex Alimentarius Commission, the International Office of Epizootics, and the relevant international and regional organizations operating within the framework of the International Plant Protection Convention, without requiring Members to change their appropriate level of protection of human, animal or plant life or health; Recognizing that developing country Members may encounter special difficulties in complying with the sanitary or phytosanitary measures of importing Members, and as a consequence in access to markets, and also in the formulation and application of sanitary or phytosanitary measures in their own territories, and desiring to assist them in their endeavours in this regard; Desiring therefore to elaborate rules for the application of the provisions of GATT 1994 which relate to the use of sanitary or phytosanitary measures, in particular the provisions of Article XX(b) (1);

Hereby agree as follows:

ARTICLE 1. GENERAL PROVISIONS

1. This Agreement applies to all sanitary and phytosanitary measures which may, directly or indirectly, affect international trade. Such measures shall be developed and applied in accordance with the provisions of this Agreement.

2. For the purposes of this Agreement, the definitions provided in Annex A shall apply.

3. The annexes are an integral part of this Agreement.

4. Nothing in this Agreement shall affect the rights of Members under the Agreement on Technical Barriers to Trade with respect to measures not within the scope of this Agreement.

ARTICLE 2. BASIC RIGHTS AND OBLIGATIONS

1. Members have the right to take sanitary and phytosanitary measures necessary for the protection of human, animal or plant life or health, provided that such measures are not inconsistent with the provisions of this Agreement.

2. Members shall ensure that any sanitary or phytosanitary measure is applied only to the extent necessary to protect human, animal or plant life or health, is based on scientific principles and is not maintained without sufficient scientific evidence, except as provided for in paragraph 7 of Article 5.

3. Members shall ensure that their sanitary and phytosanitary measures do not arbitrarily or unjustifiably discriminate between Members where identical or similar conditions prevail, including between their own territory and that of other Members. Sanitary and phytosanitary measures shall not be applied in a manner which would constitute a disguised restriction on international trade.

4. Sanitary or phytosanitary measures which conform to the relevant provisions of this Agreement shall be presumed to be in accordance with the obligations of the Members under the provisions of GATT 1994 which relate to the use of sanitary or phytosanitary measures, in particular the provisions of Article XX(b).

ARTICLE 3. HARMONIZATION

1. To harmonize sanitary and phytosanitary measures on as wide a basis as possible, Members shall base their sanitary or phytosanitary measures on international standards, guidelines or recommendations, where they exist, except as otherwise provided for in this Agreement, and in particular in paragraph 3.

2. Sanitary or phytosanitary measures which conform to international standards, guidelines or recommendations shall be deemed to be necessary to protect human, animal or plant life or health, and presumed to be consistent with the relevant provisions of this Agreement and of GATT 1994.

3. Members may introduce or maintain sanitary or phytosanitary measures which result in a higher level of sanitary or phytosanitary protection than would be achieved by measures based on the relevant international standards, guidelines or recommendations, if there is a scientific justification, or as a consequence of the level of sanitary or phytosanitary protection a Member determines to be appropriate in accordance with the relevant provisions of paragraphs 1 through 8 of Article 5.(2) Notwithstanding the above, all measures which result in a level of sanitary or phytosanitary protection different from that which would be achieved by measures based

on international standards, guidelines or recommendations shall not be inconsistent with any other provision of this Agreement.

4. Members shall play a full part, within the limits of their resources, in the relevant international organizations and their subsidiary bodies, in particular the Codex Alimentarius Commission, the International Office of Epizootics, and the international and regional organizations operating within the framework of the International Plant Protection Convention, to promote within these organizations the development and periodic review of standards, guidelines and recommendations with respect to all aspects of sanitary and phytosanitary measures.

5. The Committee on Sanitary and Phytosanitary Measures provided for in paragraphs 1 and 4 of Article 12 (referred to in this Agreement as the "Committee") shall develop a procedure to monitor the process of international harmonization and coordinate efforts in this regard with the relevant international organizations.

ARTICLE 4. EQUIVALENCE

1. Members shall accept the sanitary or phytosanitary measures of other Members as equivalent, even if these measures differ from their own or from those used by other Members trading in the same product, if the exporting Member objectively demonstrates to the importing Member that its measures achieve the importing Member's appropriate level of sanitary or phytosanitary protection. For this purpose, reasonable access shall be given, upon request, to the importing Member for inspection, testing and other relevant procedures.

2. Members shall, upon request, enter into consultations with the aim of achieving bilateral and multilateral agreements on recognition of the equivalence of specified sanitary or phytosanitary measures.

ARTICLE 5. ASSESSMENT OF RISK AND DETERMINATION OF THE APPROPRIATE LEVEL OF SANITARY OR PHYTOSANITARY PROTECTION

1. Members shall ensure that their sanitary or phytosanitary measures are based on an assessment, as appropriate to the circumstances, of the risks to human, animal or plant life or health, taking into account risk assessment techniques developed by the relevant international organizations.

2. In the assessment of risks, Members shall take into account available scientific evidence; relevant processes and production methods; relevant inspection, sampling and testing methods; prevalence of specific diseases or pests; existence of pest – or disease – free areas; relevant ecological and environmental conditions; and quarantine or other treatment.

3. In assessing the risk to animal or plant life or health and determining the measure to be applied for achieving the appropriate level of sanitary or phytosanitary protection from such risk, Members shall take into account as relevant economic factors: the potential damage in

terms of loss of production or sales in the event of the entry, establishment or spread of a pest or disease; the costs of control or eradication in the territory of the importing Member; and the relative cost-effectiveness of alternative approaches to limiting risks.

4. Members should, when determining the appropriate level of sanitary or phytosanitary protection, take into account the objective of minimizing negative trade effects.

5. With the objective of achieving consistency in the application of the concept of appropriate level of sanitary or phytosanitary protection against risks to human life or health, or to animal and plant life or health, each Member shall avoid arbitrary or unjustifiable distinctions in the levels it considers to be appropriate in different situations, if such distinctions result in discrimination or a disguised restriction on international trade. Members shall cooperate in the Committee, in accordance with paragraphs 1, 2 and 3 of Article 12, to develop guidelines to further the practical implementation of this provision. In developing the guidelines, the Committee shall take into account all relevant factors, including the exceptional character of human health risks to which people voluntarily expose themselves.

6. Without prejudice to paragraph 2 of Article 3, when establishing or maintaining sanitary or phytosanitary measures to achieve the appropriate level of sanitary or phytosanitary protection, Members shall ensure that such measures are not more trade-restrictive than required to achieve their appropriate level of sanitary or phytosanitary protection, taking into account technical and economic feasibility.(3)

7. In cases where relevant scientific evidence is insufficient, a Member may provisionally adopt sanitary or phytosanitary measures on the basis of available pertinent information, including that from the relevant international organizations as well as from sanitary or phytosanitary measures applied by other Members. In such circumstances, Members shall seek to obtain the additional information necessary for a more objective assessment of risk and review the sanitary or phytosanitary measure accordingly within a reasonable period of time.

8. When a Member has reason to believe that a specific sanitary or phytosanitary measure introduced or maintained by another Member is constraining, or has the potential to constrain, its exports and the measure is not based on the relevant international standards, guidelines or recommendations, or such standards, guidelines or recommendations do not exist, an explanation of the reasons for such sanitary or phytosanitary measure may be requested and shall be provided by the Member maintaining the measure.

ARTICLE 6. ADAPTATION TO REGIONAL CONDITIONS, INCLUDING PEST – OR DISEASE – FREE AREAS AND AREAS OF LOW PEST OR DISEASE PREVALENCE

1. Members shall ensure that their sanitary or phytosanitary measures are adapted to the sanitary or phytosanitary characteristics of the area – whether all of a country, part of a country, or all or parts of several countries – from which the product originated and to which the product is destined. In assessing the sanitary or phytosanitary characteristics of a region, Members shall

take into account, inter alia, the level of prevalence of specific diseases or pests, the existence of eradication or control programmes, and appropriate criteria or guidelines which may be developed by the relevant international organizations.

2. Members shall, in particular, recognize the concepts of pest – or disease-free areas and areas of low pest or disease prevalence. Determination of such areas shall be based on factors such as geography, ecosystems, epidemiological surveillance, and the effectiveness of sanitary or phytosanitary controls.

3. Exporting Members claiming that areas within their territories are pest – or disease-free areas or areas of low pest or disease prevalence shall provide the necessary evidence thereof in order to objectively demonstrate to the importing Member that such areas are, and are likely to remain, pest— or disease—free areas or areas of low pest or disease prevalence, respectively. For this purpose, reasonable access shall be given, upon request, to the importing Member for inspection, testing and other relevant procedures.

ARTICLE 7. TRANSPARENCY

Members shall notify changes in their sanitary or phytosanitary measures and shall provide information on their sanitary or phytosanitary measures in accordance with the provisions of Annex B.

ARTICLE 8. CONTROL, INSPECTION AND APPROVAL PROCEDURES

Members shall observe the provisions of Annex C in the operation of control, inspection and approval procedures, including national systems for approving the use of additives or for establishing tolerances for contaminants in foods, beverages or feedstuffs, and otherwise ensure that their procedures are not inconsistent with the provisions of this Agreement.

ARTICLE 9. TECHNICAL ASSISTANCE

1. Members agree to facilitate the provision of technical assistance to other Members, especially developing country Members, either bilaterally or through the appropriate international organizations. Such assistance may be, inter alia, in the areas of processing technologies, research and infrastructure, including in the establishment of national regulatory bodies, and may take the form of advice, credits, donations and grants, including for the purpose of seeking technical expertise, training and equipment to allow such countries to adjust to, and comply with, sanitary or phytosanitary measures necessary to achieve the appropriate level of sanitary or phytosanitary protection in their export markets.

2. Where substantial investments are required in order for an exporting developing country Member to fulfil the sanitary or phytosanitary requirements of an importing Member, the latter shall consider providing such technical assistance as will permit the developing country Member to maintain and expand its market access opportunities for the product involved.

ARTICLE 10. SPECIAL AND DIFFERENTIAL TREATMENT

1. In the preparation and application of sanitary or phytosanitary measures, Members shall take account of the special needs of developing country Members, and in particular of the least-developed country Members.

2. Where the appropriate level of sanitary or phytosanitary protection allows scope for the phased introduction of new sanitary or phytosanitary measures, longer time-frames for compliance should be accorded on products of interest to developing country Members so as to maintain opportunities for their exports.

3. With a view to ensuring that developing country Members are able to comply with the provisions of this Agreement, the Committee is enabled to grant to such countries, upon request, specified, time-limited exceptions in whole or in part from obligations under this Agreement, taking into account their financial, trade and development needs.

4. Members should encourage and facilitate the active participation of developing country Members in the relevant international organizations.

ARTICLE 11. CONSULTATIONS AND DISPUTE SETTLEMENT

1. The provisions of Articles XXII and XXIII of GATT 1994 as elaborated and applied by the Dispute Settlement Understanding shall apply to consultations and the settlement of disputes under this Agreement, except as otherwise specifically provided herein.2. In a dispute under this Agreement involving scientific or technical issues, a panel should seek advice from experts chosen by the panel in consultation with the parties to the dispute. To this end, the panel may, when it deems it appropriate, establish an advisory technical experts group, or consult the relevant international organizations, at the request of either party to the dispute or on its own initiative.

3. Nothing in this Agreement shall impair the rights of Members under other international agreements, including the right to resort to the good offices or dispute settlement mechanisms of other international organizations or established under any international agreement.

ARTICLE 12. ADMINISTRATION

1. A Committee on Sanitary and Phytosanitary Measures is hereby established to provide a regular forum for consultations. It shall carry out the functions necessary to implement the provisions of this Agreement and the furtherance of its objectives, in particular with respect to harmonization. The Committee shall reach its decisions by consensus.

2. The Committee shall encourage and facilitate ad hoc consultations or negotiations among Members on specific sanitary or phytosanitary issues. The Committee shall encourage the use of international standards, guidelines or recommendations by all Members and, in this regard,

shall sponsor technical consultation and study with the objective of increasing coordination and integration between international and national systems and approaches for approving the use of food additives or for establishing tolerances for contaminants in foods, beverages or feedstuffs.

3. The Committee shall maintain close contact with the relevant international organizations in the field of sanitary and phytosanitary protection, especially with the Codex Alimentarius Commission, the International Office of Epizootics, and the Secretariat of the International Plant Protection Convention, with the objective of securing the best available scientific and technical advice for the administration of this Agreement and in order to ensure that unnecessary duplication of effort is avoided.

4. The Committee shall develop a procedure to monitor the process of international harmonization and the use of international standards, guidelines or recommendations. For this purpose, the Committee should, in conjunction with the relevant international organizations, establish a list of international standards, guidelines or recommendations relating to sanitary or phytosanitary measures which the Committee determines to have a major trade impact. The list should include an indication by Members of those international standards, guidelines or recommendations which they apply as conditions for import or on the basis of which imported products conforming to these standards can enjoy access to their markets. For those cases in which a Member does not apply an international standard, guideline or recommendation as a condition for import, the Member should provide an indication of the reason therefor, and, in particular, whether it considers that the standard is not stringent enough to provide the appropriate level of sanitary or phytosanitary protection. If a Member revises its position, following its indication of the use of a standard, guideline or recommendation as a condition for import, it should provide an explanation for its change and so inform the Secretariat as well as the relevant international organizations, unless such notification and explanation is given according to the procedures of Annex B.

5. In order to avoid unnecessary duplication, the Committee may decide, as appropriate, to use the information generated by the procedures, particularly for notification, which are in operation in the relevant international organizations.

6. The Committee may, on the basis of an initiative from one of the Members, through appropriate channels invite the relevant international organizations or their subsidiary bodies to examine specific matters with respect to a particular standard, guideline or recommendation, including the basis of explanations for non-use given according to paragraph 4.

7. The Committee shall review the operation and implementation of this Agreement three years after the date of entry into force of the WTO Agreement, and thereafter as the need arises. Where appropriate, the Committee may submit to the Council for Trade in Goods proposals to amend the text of this Agreement having regard, inter alia, to the experience gained in its implementation.

ARTICLE 13. IMPLEMENTATION

Members are fully responsible under this Agreement for the observance of all obligations set forth herein. Members shall formulate and implement positive measures and mechanisms in support of the observance of the provisions of this Agreement by other than central government bodies. Members shall take such reasonable measures as may be available to them to ensure that non-governmental entities within their territories, as well as regional bodies in which relevant entities within their territories are members, comply with the relevant provisions of this Agreement. In addition, Members shall not take measures which have the effect of, directly or indirectly, requiring or encouraging such regional or non-governmental entities, or local governmental bodies, to act in a manner inconsistent with the provisions of this Agreement. Members shall ensure that they rely on the services of non-governmental entities for implementing sanitary or phytosanitary measures only if these entities comply with the provisions of this Agreement.

ARTICLE 14. FINAL PROVISIONS

The least-developed country Members may delay application of the provisions of this Agreement for a period of five years following the date of entry into force of the WTO Agreement with respect to their sanitary or phytosanitary measures affecting importation or imported products. Other developing country Members may delay application of the provisions of this Agreement, other than paragraph 8 of Article 5 and Article 7, for two years following the date of entry into force of the WTO Agreement with respect to their existing sanitary or phytosanitary measures affecting importation or imported products, where such application is prevented by a lack of technical expertise, technical infrastructure or resources.

Annex A Definitions (4)

1. Sanitary or phytosanitary measure – Any measure applied:

(a) to protect animal or plant life or health within the territory of the Member from risks arising from the entry, establishment or spread of pests, diseases, disease-carrying organisms or disease-causing organisms;
(b) to protect human or animal life or health within the territory of the Member from risks arising from additives, contaminants, toxins or disease-causing organisms in foods, beverages or feedstuffs;
(c) to protect human life or health within the territory of the Member from risks arising from diseases carried by animals, plants or products thereof, or from the entry, establishment or spread of pests; or
(d) to prevent or limit other damage within the territory of the Member from the entry, establishment or spread of pests.

Sanitary or phytosanitary measures include all relevant laws, decrees, regulations, requirements and procedures including, inter alia, end product criteria; processes and production methods; testing, inspection, certification and approval procedures; quarantine treatments including relevant requirements associated with the transport of animals or plants, or with the materials necessary for their survival during transport; provisions on relevant statistical methods, sampling procedures and methods of risk assessment; and packaging and labelling requirements directly related to food safety.

2. Harmonization – The establishment, recognition and application of common sanitary and phytosanitary measures by different Members.

3. International standards, guidelines and recommendations

(a) for food safety, the standards, guidelines and recommendations established by the Codex Alimentarius Commission relating to food additives, veterinary drug and pesticide residues, contaminants, methods of analysis and sampling, and codes and guidelines of hygienic practice;
(b) for animal health and zoonoses, the standards, guidelines and recommendations developed under the auspices of the International Office of Epizootics;
(c) for plant health, the international standards, guidelines and recommendations developed under the auspices of the Secretariat of the International Plant Protection Convention in cooperation with regional organizations operating within the framework of the International Plant Protection Convention; and
(d) for matters not covered by the above organizations, appropriate standards, guidelines and recommendations promulgated by other relevant international organizations open for membership to all Members, as identified by the Committee.

4. Risk assessment – The evaluation of the likelihood of entry, establishment or spread of a pest or disease within the territory of an importing Member according to the sanitary or phytosanitary measures which might be applied, and of the associated potential biological and economic consequences; or the evaluation of the potential for adverse effects on human or animal health arising from the presence of additives, contaminants, toxins or disease-causing organisms in food, beverages or feedstuffs.

5. Appropriate level of sanitary or phytosanitary protection – The level of protection deemed appropriate by the Member establishing a sanitary or phytosanitary measure to protect human, animal or plant life or health within its territory.

Note: Many Members otherwise refer to this concept as the "acceptable level of risk".

6. Pest – or disease-free area – An area, whether all of a country, part of a country, or all or parts of several countries, as identified by the competent authorities, in which a specific pest or disease does not occur.

Note: A pest – or disease-free area may surround, be surrounded by, or be adjacent to an area – whether within part of a country or in a geographic region which includes parts of or all of several countries -in which a specific pest or disease is known to occur but is subject to regional control measures such as the establishment of protection, surveillance and buffer zones which will confine or eradicate the pest or disease in question.

7. Area of low pest or disease prevalence – An area, whether all of a country, part of a country, or all or parts of several countries, as identified by the competent authorities, in which a specific pest or disease occurs at low levels and which is subject to effective surveillance, control or eradication measures.

Annex B Transparency of Sanitary and Phytosanitary Regulations

Publication of regulations

1. Members shall ensure that all sanitary and phytosanitary regulations (5) which have been adopted are published promptly in such a manner as to enable interested Members to become acquainted with them.

2. Except in urgent circumstances, Members shall allow a reasonable interval between the publication of a sanitary or phytosanitary regulation and its entry into force in order to allow time for producers in exporting Members, and particularly in developing country Members, to adapt their products and methods of production to the requirements of the importing Member.

Enquiry points

3. Each Member shall ensure that one enquiry point exists which is responsible for the provision of answers to all reasonable questions from interested Members as well as for the provision of relevant documents regarding:

(a) any sanitary or phytosanitary regulations adopted or proposed within its territory;

(b) any control and inspection procedures, production and quarantine treatment, pesticide tolerance and food additive approval procedures, which are operated within its territory;
(c) risk assessment procedures, factors taken into consideration, as well as the determination of the appropriate level of sanitary or phytosanitary protection;
(d) the membership and participation of the Member, or of relevant bodies within its territory, in international and regional sanitary and phytosanitary organizations and systems, as well as in bilateral and multilateral agreements and arrangements within the scope of this Agreement, and the texts of such agreements and arrangements.

4. Members shall ensure that where copies of documents are requested by interested Members, they are supplied at the same price (if any), apart from the cost of delivery, as to the nationals (6) of the Member concerned.

Notification procedures

5. Whenever an international standard, guideline or recommendation does not exist or the content of a proposed sanitary or phytosanitary regulation is not substantially the same as the content of an international standard, guideline or recommendation, and if the regulation may have a significant effect on trade of other Members, Members shall:

(a) publish a notice at an early stage in such a manner as to enable interested Members to become acquainted with the proposal to introduce a particular regulation;
(b) notify other Members, through the Secretariat, of the products to be covered by the regulation together with a brief indication of the objective and rationale of the proposed regulation. Such notifications shall take place at an early stage, when amendments can still be introduced and comments taken into account;
(c) provide upon request to other Members copies of the proposed regulation and, whenever possible, identify the parts which in substance deviate from international standards, guidelines or recommendations;
(d) without discrimination, allow reasonable time for other Members to make comments in writing, discuss these comments upon request, and take the comments and the results of the discussions into account.

6. However, where urgent problems of health protection arise or threaten to arise for a Member, that Member may omit such of the steps enumerated in paragraph 5 of this Annex as it finds necessary, provided that the Member:

(a) immediately notifies other Members, through the Secretariat, of the particular regulation and the products covered, with a brief indication of the objective and the rationale of the regulation, including the nature of the urgent problem(s);
(b) provides, upon request, copies of the regulation to other Members;
(c) allows other Members to make comments in writing, discusses these comments upon request, and takes the comments and the results of the discussions into account.

7. Notifications to the Secretariat shall be in English, French or Spanish.

8. Developed country Members shall, if requested by other Members, provide copies of the documents or, in case of voluminous documents, summaries of the documents covered by a specific notification in English, French or Spanish.

9. The Secretariat shall promptly circulate copies of the notification to all Members and interested international organizations and draw the attention of developing country Members to any notifications relating to products of particular interest to them.10. Members shall designate a single central government authority as responsible for the implementation, on the national level, of the provisions concerning notification procedures according to paragraphs 5, 6, 7 and 8 of this Annex.

General reservations

11. Nothing in this Agreement shall be construed as requiring:

(a) the provision of particulars or copies of drafts or the publication of texts other than in the language of the Member except as stated in paragraph 8 of this Annex; or
(b) Members to disclose confidential information which would impede enforcement of sanitary or phytosanitary legislation or which would prejudice the legitimate commercial interests of particular enterprises.

Annex C Control, Inspection and Approval Procedures

1. Members shall ensure, with respect to any procedure to check and ensure the fulfilment of sanitary or phytosanitary measures, that:

(a) such procedures are undertaken and completed without undue delay and in no less favourable manner for imported products than for like domestic products;
(b) the standard processing period of each procedure is published or that the anticipated processing period is communicated to the applicant upon request; when receiving an application, the competent body promptly examines the completeness of the documentation and informs the applicant in a precise and complete manner of all deficiencies; the competent body transmits as soon as possible the results of the procedure in a precise and complete manner to the applicant so that corrective action may be taken if necessary; even when the application has deficiencies, the competent body proceeds as far as practicable with the procedure if the applicant so requests; and that upon request, the applicant is informed of the stage of the procedure, with any delay being explained;
(c) information requirements are limited to what is necessary for appropriate control, inspection and approval procedures, including for approval of the use of additives or for the establishment of tolerances for contaminants in food, beverages or feedstuffs;
(d) the confidentiality of information about imported products arising from or supplied in connection with control, inspection and approval is respected in a way no less favourable than for domestic products and in such a manner that legitimate commercial interests are protected;
(e) any requirements for control, inspection and approval of individual specimens of a product are limited to what is reasonable and necessary;
(f) any fees imposed for the procedures on imported products are equitable in relation to any fees charged on like domestic products or products originating in any other Member and should be no higher than the actual cost of the service;
(g) the same criteria should be used in the siting of facilities used in the procedures and the selection of samples of imported products as for domestic products so as to minimize the inconvenience to applicants, importers, exporters or their agents;
(h) whenever specifications of a product are changed subsequent to its control and inspection in light of the applicable regulations, the procedure for the modified product is limited to what is necessary to determine whether adequate confidence exists that the product still meets the regulations concerned; and

(i) a procedure exists to review complaints concerning the operation of such procedures and to take corrective action when a complaint is justified.

Where an importing Member operates a system for the approval of the use of food additives or for the establishment of tolerances for contaminants in food, beverages or feedstuffs which prohibits or restricts access to its domestic markets for products based on the absence of an approval, the importing Member shall consider the use of a relevant international standard as the basis for access until a final determination is made.

2. Where a sanitary or phytosanitary measure specifies control at the level of production, the Member in whose territory the production takes place shall provide the necessary assistance to facilitate such control and the work of the controlling authorities.

3. Nothing in this Agreement shall prevent Members from carrying out reasonable inspection within their own territories.

2.2. Agreement on Technical Barriers to Trade (TBT Agreement)

Technical Regulations and Standards

ARTICLE 2. PREPARATION, ADOPTION AND APPLICATION OF TECHNICAL REGULATIONS BY CENTRAL GOVERNMENT BODIES

With respect to their central government bodies:

2.1 Members shall ensure that in respect of technical regulations, products imported from the territory of any Member shall be accorded treatment no less favourable than that accorded to like products of national origin and to like products originating in any other country.

2.2 Members shall ensure that technical regulations are not prepared, adopted or applied with a view to or with the effect of creating unnecessary obstacles to international trade. For this purpose, technical regulations shall not be more trade-restrictive than necessary to fulfil a legitimate objective, taking account of the risks non-fulfilment would create. Such legitimate objectives are, inter alia: national security requirements; the prevention of deceptive practices; protection of human health or safety, animal or plant life or health, or the environment. In assessing such risks, relevant elements of consideration are, inter alia: available scientific and technical information, related processing technology or intended end-uses of products.

...

2.8 Wherever appropriate, Members shall specify technical regulations based on product requirements in terms of performance rather than design or descriptive characteristics.

2.9 Whenever a relevant international standard does not exist or the technical content of a proposed technical regulation is not in accordance with the technical content of relevant international standards, and if the technical regulation may have a significant effect on trade of other Members, Members shall:

2.9.1 publish a notice in a publication at an early appropriate stage, in such a manner as to enable interested parties in other Members to become acquainted with it, that they propose to introduce a particular technical regulation;

2.9.2 notify other Members through the Secretariat of the products to be covered by the proposed technical regulation, together with a brief indication of its objective and rationale. Such notifications shall take place at an early appropriate stage, when amendments can still be introduced and comments taken into account;

2.9.3 upon request, provide to other Members particulars or copies of the proposed technical regulation and, whenever possible, identify the parts which in substance deviate from relevant international standards;

2.9.4 without discrimination, allow reasonable time for other Members to make comments in writing, discuss these comments upon request, and take these written comments and the results of these discussions into account.

2.10 Subject to the provisions in the lead-in to paragraph 9, where urgent problems of safety, health, environmental protection or national security arise or threaten to arise for a Member, that Member may omit such of the steps enumerated in paragraph 9 as it finds necessary, provided that the Member, upon adoption of a technical regulation, shall:

2.10.1 notify immediately other Members through the Secretariat of the particular technical regulation and the products covered, with a brief indication of the objective and the rationale of the technical regulation, including the nature of the urgent problems;

2.10.2 upon request, provide other Members with copies of the technical regulation;

2.10.3 without discrimination, allow other Members to present their comments in writing, discuss these comments upon request, and take these written comments and the results of these discussions into account.

Conformity with Technical Regulations and Standards

Article 5. Procedures for Assessment of Conformity by Central Government Bodies

5.4 In cases where a positive assurance is required that products conform with technical regulations or standards, and relevant guides or recommendations issued by international standardizing bodies exist or their completion is imminent, Members shall ensure that central government bodies use them, or the relevant parts of them, as a basis for their conformity assessment procedures, except where, as duly explained upon request, such guides or recommendations or relevant parts are inappropriate for the Members concerned, for, inter alia, such reasons as: national security requirements; the prevention of deceptive practices; protection of human health or safety, animal or plant life or health, or the environment; fundamental climatic or other geographical factors; fundamental technological or infrastructural problems.

5.6 Whenever a relevant guide or recommendation issued by an international standardizing body does not exist or the technical content of a proposed conformity assessment procedure is not in accordance with relevant guides and recommendations issued by international standardizing bodies, and if the conformity assessment procedure may have a significant effect on trade of other Members, Members shall:

5.6.1 publish a notice in a publication at an early appropriate stage, in such a manner as to enable interested parties in other Members to become acquainted with it, that they propose to introduce a particular conformity assessment procedure;

5.6.2 notify other Members through the Secretariat of the products to be covered by the proposed conformity assessment procedure, together with a brief indication of its objective and rationale. Such notifications shall take place at an early appropriate stage, when amendments can still be introduced and comments taken into account;

5.6.3 upon request, provide to other Members particulars or copies of the proposed procedure and, whenever possible, identify the parts which in substance deviate from relevant guides or recommendations issued by international standardizing bodies;

5.6.4 without discrimination, allow reasonable time for other Members to make comments in writing, discuss these comments upon request, and take these written comments and the results of these discussions into account.

5.7 Subject to the provisions in the lead-in to paragraph 6, where urgent problems of safety, health, environmental protection or national security arise or threaten to arise for a Member, that Member may omit such of the steps enumerated in paragraph 6 as it finds necessary, provided that the Member, upon adoption of the procedure, shall:

5.7.1 notify immediately other Members through the Secretariat of the particular procedure and the products covered, with a brief indication of the objective and the rationale of the procedure, including the nature of the urgent problems;

5.7.2 upon request, provide other Members with copies of the rules of the procedure;

5.7.3 without discrimination, allow other Members to present their comments in writing, discuss these comments upon request, and take these written comments and the results of these discussions into account.

2.3. General Agreement on Tariffs and Trade (GATT 1994 and ANNEX 1A)

ARTICLE XX. GENERAL EXCEPTIONS

Subject to the requirement that such measures are not applied in a manner which would constitute a means of arbitrary or unjustifiable discrimination between countries where the same conditions prevail, or a disguised restriction on international trade, nothing in this Agreement shall be construed to prevent the adoption or enforcement by any contracting party of measures:

…

(b) necessary to protect human, animal or plant life or health;

2.4. General Agreement on Trade in Services (GATS, ANNEX 1B)

ARTICLE XIV. GENERAL EXCEPTIONS

Subject to the requirement that such measures are not applied in a manner which would constitute a means of arbitrary or unjustifiable discrimination between countries where like conditions prevail, or a disguised restriction on trade in services, nothing in this Agreement shall be construed to prevent the adoption or enforcement by any Member of measures:

…

(b) necessary to protect human, animal or plant life or health;

2.5. Agreement on Trade-related Aspects of Intellectual Property Rights (TRIPS, Annex 1C)

ARTICLE 8. PRINCIPLES (PUBLIC HEALTH PROTECTION)

1. Members may, in formulating or amending their laws and regulations, adopt measures necessary to protect public health and nutrition, and to promote the public interest in sectors of vital importance to their socio-economic and technological development, provided that such measures are consistent with the provisions of this Agreement.

2. Appropriate measures, provided that they are consistent with the provisions of this Agreement, may be needed to prevent the abuse of intellectual property rights by right holders or the resort to practices which unreasonably restrain trade or adversely affect the international transfer of technology.

ARTICLE 30. EXCEPTIONS TO RIGHTS CONFERRED (RESEARCH EXCEPTION)

Members may provide limited exceptions to the exclusive rights conferred by a patent, provided that such exceptions do not unreasonably conflict with a normal exploitation of the patent and do not unreasonably prejudice the legitimate interests of the patent owner, taking account of the legitimate interests of third parties.

ARTICLE 31. OTHER USE WITHOUT AUTHORIZATION OF THE RIGHT HOLDER (GOVERNMENT LICENSING AND USE)

Where the law of a Member allows for other use of the subject matter of a patent without the authorization of the right holder, including use by the government or third parties authorized by the government, the following provisions shall be respected:

(a) authorization of such use shall be considered on its individual merits;
(b) such use may only be permitted if, prior to such use, the proposed user has made efforts to obtain authorization from the right holder on reasonable commercial terms and conditions and that such efforts have not been successful within a reasonable period of time. This requirement may be waived by a Member in the case of a national emergency or other circumstances of extreme urgency or in cases of public noncommercial use. In situations of national emergency or other circumstances of extreme urgency, the right holder shall, nevertheless, be notified as soon as reasonably practicable. In the case of public non-commercial use, where the government or contractor, without making a patent search, knows or has demonstrable grounds to know that a valid patent is or will be used by or for the government, the right holder shall be informed promptly;
(c) the scope and duration of such use shall be limited to the purpose for which it was authorized, and in the case of semi-conductor technology shall only be for public concommercial use or to remedy a practice determined after judicial or administrative process to be anti-competitive;
(d) such use shall be non-exclusive;

(e) such use shall be non-assignable, except with that part of the enterprise or goodwill which enjoys such use;

(f) any such use shall be authorized predominantly for the supply of the domestic market of the Member authorizing such use;

(g) authorization for such use shall be liable, subject to adequate protection of the legitimate interests of the persons so authorized, to be terminated if and when the circumstances which led to it cease to exist and are unlikely to recur. The competent authority shall have the authority to review, upon motivated request, the continued existence of these circumstances;

(h) the right holder shall be paid adequate remuneration in the circumstances of each case, taking into account the economic value of the authorization;

(i) the legal validity of any decision relating to the authorization of such use shall be subject to judicial review or other independent review by a distinct higher authority in that Member;

(j) any decision relating to the remuneration provided in respect of such use shall be subject to judicial review or other independent review by a distinct higher authority in that Member;

Note: "Other use" refers to use other than that allowed under Article 30.

(k) Members are not obliged to apply the conditions set forth in subparagraphs (b) and (f) where such use is permitted to remedy a practice determined after judicial or administrative process to be anti-competitive. The need to correct anti-competitive practices may be taken into account in determining the amount of remuneration in such cases. Competent authorities shall have the authority to refuse termination of authorization if and when the conditions which led to such authorization are likely to recur;

(l) where such use is authorized to permit the exploitation of a patent ("the second patent") which cannot be exploited without infringing another patent ("the first patent"), the following additional conditions shall apply:

(i)   the invention claimed in the second patent shall involve an important technical advance of considerable economic significance in relation to the invention claimed in the first patent;

(ii)   the owner of the first patent shall be entitled to a cross-licence on reasonable terms to use the invention claimed in the second patent; and

(iii) the use authorized in respect of the first patent shall be non-assignable except with the assignment of the second patent.

2.6. Consolidated versions of the Treaty on European Union and the Treaty on the Functioning of the European Union (2008/C 115/01)

Title XIV

Public Health

ARTICLE 168. (EX ARTICLE 152 TEC)

1. A high level of human health protection shall be ensured in the definition and implementation of all Union policies and activities. Union action, which shall complement national policies, shall be directed towards improving public health, preventing physical and mental illness and diseases, and obviating sources of danger to physical and mental health. Such action shall cover the fight against the major health scourges, by promoting research into their causes, their transmission and their prevention, as well as health information and education, and monitoring, early warning of and combating serious cross-border threats to health. The Union shall complement the Member States' action in reducing drugs-related health damage, including information and prevention.

2. The Union shall encourage cooperation between the Member States in the areas referred to in this Article and, if necessary, lend support to their action. It shall in particular encourage cooperation between the Member States to improve the complementarity of their health services in cross-border areas. Member States shall, in liaison with the Commission, coordinate among themselves their policies and programmes in the areas referred to in paragraph 1. The Commission may, in close contact with the Member States, take any useful initiative to promote such coordination, in particular initiatives aiming at the establishment of guidelines and indicators, the organisation of exchange of best practice, and the preparation of the necessary elements for periodic monitoring and evaluation. The European Parliament shall be kept fully informed.

3. The Union and the Member States shall foster cooperation with third countries and the competent international organisations in the sphere of public health.

4. By way of derogation from Article 2(5) and Article 6(a) and in accordance with Article 4(2)(k) the European Parliament and the Council, acting in accordance with the ordinary legislative procedure and after consulting the Economic and Social Committee and the Committee of the Regions, shall contribute to the achievement of the objectives referred to in this Article through adopting in order to meet common safety concerns:

(a) measures setting high standards of quality and safety of organs and substances of human origin, blood and blood derivatives; these measures shall not prevent any Member State from maintaining or introducing more stringent protective measures;
(b) measures in the veterinary and phytosanitary fields which have as their direct objective the protection of public health;

(c) measures setting high standards of quality and safety for medicinal products and devices for medical use.

5. The European Parliament and the Council, acting in accordance with the ordinary legislative procedure and after consulting the Economic and Social Committee and the Committee of the Regions, may also adopt incentive measures designed to protect and improve human health and in particular to combat the major cross-border health scourges, measures concerning monitoring, early warning of and combating serious cross-border threats to health, and measures which have as their direct objective the protection of public health regarding tobacco and the abuse of alcohol, excluding any harmonisation of the laws and regulations of the Member States.

6. The Council, on a proposal from the Commission, may also adopt recommendations for the purposes set out in this Article.

7. Union action shall respect the responsibilities of the Member States for the definition of their health policy and for the organisation and delivery of health services and medical care. The responsibilities of the Member States shall include the management of health services and medical care and the allocation of the resources assigned to them. The measures referred to in paragraph 4(a) shall not affect national provisions on the donation or medical use of organs and blood.

Medical Ethics

PART VII

1. World Medical Association International Code of Medical Ethics

Adopted by the 3rd General Assembly of the World Medical Association, London, England, October 1949 and amended by the 22nd World Medical Assembly Sydney, Australia, August 1968 and the 35th World Medical Assembly Venice, Italy, October 1983 and the WMA General Assembly, Pilanesberg, South Africa, October 2006

Duties of Physicians in General

A Physician shall
– always exercise his/her independent professional judgment and maintain the highest standards of professional conduct.
– respect a competent patient's right to accept or refuse treatment.
– not allow his/her judgment to be influenced by personal profit or unfair discrimination.
– be dedicated to providing competent medical service in full professional and moral independence, with compassion and respect for human dignity.
– deal honestly with patients and colleagues, and report to the appropriate authorities those physicians who practice unethically or incompetently or who engage in fraud or deception.
– not receive any financial benefits or other incentives solely for referring patients or prescribing specific products.
– respect the rights and preferences of patients, colleagues, and other health professionals.
– recognize his/her important role in educating the public but should use due caution in divulging discoveries or new techniques or treatment through non-professional channels.
– certify only that which he/she has personally verified.
– strive to use health care resources in the best way to benefit patients and their community.
– seek appropriate care and attention if he/she suffers from mental or physical illness.
– respect the local and national codes of ethics.

Duties of Physicians to Patients

A Physician shall
– always bear in mind the obligation to respect human life.
– act in the patient's best interest when providing medical care.
– owe his/her patients complete loyalty and all the scientific resources available to him/her. Whenever an examination or treatment is beyond the physician's capacity, he/she should consult with or refer to another physician who has the necessary ability.
– respect a patient's right to confidentiality. It is ethical to disclose confidential information when the patient consents to it or when there is a real

and imminent threat of harm to the patient or to others and this threat can be only removed by a breach of confidentiality.
– give emergency care as a humanitarian duty unless he/she is assured that others are willing and able to give such care.
– in situations when he/she is acting for a third party, ensure that the patient has full knowledge of that situation.
– not enter into a sexual relationship with his/her current patient or into any other abusive or exploitative relationship.

Duties of Physicians to Colleagues

A Physician shall   – behave towards colleagues as he/she would have them behave towards him/her.
– not undermine the patient-physician relationship of colleagues in order to attract patients.
– when medically necessary, communicate with colleagues who are involved in the care of the same patient. This communication should respect patient confidentiality and be confined to necessary information.

2. World Medical Association Declaration of Geneva

Adopted by the 2nd General Assembly of the World Medical Association, Geneva, Switzerland, September 1948 and amended by the 22nd World Medical Assembly, Sydney, Australia, August 1968 and the 35th World Medical Assembly, Venice, Italy, October 1983 and the 46th WMA General Assembly, Stockholm, Sweden, September 1994 and editorially revised at the 170th Council Session, Divonne-les-Bains, France, May 2005 and the 173rd Council Session, Divonne-les-Bains, France, May 2006

Physician's Oath

At the time of being admitted as a member of the medical profession:

I solemny pledge to consecrate my life to the service of humanity;

I will give to my teachers the respect and gratitude that is their due;

I will practise my profession with conscience and dignity;

The health of my patient will be my first consideration;

I will respect the secrets that are confided in me, even after the patient has died;

I will maintain by all the means in my power, the honour and the noble traditions of the medical profession;

My colleagues will be my sisters and brothers;

I will not permit considerations of age, disease or disability, creed, ethnic origin, gender, nationality, political affiliation, race, sexual orientation, social standing or any other factor to intervene between my duty and my patient;

I will maintain the utmost respect for human life;

I will not use my medical knowledge to violate human rights and civil liberties, even under threat;

I make these promises solemnly, freely and upon my honour.

3. World Medical Association Declaration of Helsinki

(see Medical Research)

4. Principles of Medical Ethics relevant to the Role of Health Personnel, particularly Physicians, in the Protection of Prisoners and Detainees against Torture and Other Cruel, Inhuman or Degrading Treatment or Punishment

Adopted by (UN) General Assembly resolution 37/194 of 18 December 1982

PRINCIPLE 1

Health personnel, particularly physicians, charged with the medical care of prisoners and detainees have a duty to provide them with protection of their physical and mental health and treatment of disease of the same quality and standard as is afforded to those who are not imprisoned or detained.

PRINCIPLE 2

It is a gross contravention of medical ethics, as well as an offence under applicable international instruments, for health personnel, particularly physicians, to engage, actively or passively, in acts which constitute participation in, complicity in, incitement to or attempts to commit torture or other cruel, inhuman or degrading treatment or punishment.

PRINCIPLE 3

It is a contravention of medical ethics for health personnel, particularly physicians, to be involved in any professional relationship with prisoners or detainees the purpose of which is not solely to evaluate, protect or improve their physical and mental health.

PRINCIPLE 4

It is a contravention of medical ethics for health personnel, particularly physicians:

(a) To apply their knowledge and skills in order to assist in the interrogation of prisoners and detainees in a manner that may adversely affect the physical or mental health or condition of such prisoners or detainees and which is not in accordance with the relevant international instruments;
(b) To certify, or to participate in the certification of, the fitness of prisoners or detainees for any form of treatment or punishment that may adversely affect their physical or mental health and which is not in accordance with the relevant international instruments, or to participate in any way in the infliction of any such treatment or punishment which is not in accordance with the relevant international instruments.

PRINCIPLE 5

It is a contravention of medical ethics for health personnel, particularly physicians, to participate in any procedure for restraining a prisoner or detainee unless such a procedure is determined in accordance with purely medical criteria as being necessary for the protection of the physical or mental health or the safety of the prisoner or detainee himself, of his fellow prisoners or detainees, or of his guardians, and presents no hazard to his physical or mental health.

PRINCIPLE 6

There may be no derogation from the foregoing principles on any ground whatsoever, including public emergency.

....

5. World Medical Association Declaration on Hunger Strikers

Adopted by the 43rd World Medical Assembly Malta, November 1991and editorially revised at the 44th World Medical Assembly Marbella, Spain, September 1992 and revised by the WMA General Assembly, Pilanesberg, South Africa, October 2006

Preamble

1. Hunger strikes occur in various contexts but they mainly give rise to dilemmas in settings where people are detained (prisons, jails and immigration detention centres). They are often a form of protest by people who lack other ways of making their demands known. In refusing nutrition for a significant period, they usually hope to obtain certain goals by inflicting negative publicity on the authorities. Short-term or feigned food refusals rarely raise ethical problems. Genuine and prolonged fasting risks death or permanent damage for hunger strikers and can create a conflict of values for physicians. Hunger strikers usually do not wish to die but some may be prepared to do so to achieve their aims. Physicians need to ascertain the individual's true intention, especially in collective strikes or situations where peer pressure may be a factor. An ethical dilemma arises when hunger strikers who have apparently issued clear instructions not to be resuscitated reach a stage of cognitive impairment. The principle of beneficence urges physicians to resuscitate them but respect for individual autonomy restrains physicians from intervening when a valid and informed refusal has been made. An added difficulty arises in custodial settings because it is not always clear whether the hunger striker's advance instructions were made voluntarily and with appropriate information about the consequences. These guidelines and the background paper address such difficult situations.

Principles

2. Duty to act ethically. All physicians are bound by medical ethics in their professional contact with vulnerable people, even when not providing therapy. Whatever their role, physicians must try to prevent coercion or maltreatment of detainees and must protest if it occurs.

3. Respect for autonomy. Physicians should respect individuals' autonomy. This can involve difficult assessments as hunger strikers' true wishes may not be as clear as they appear. Any decisions lack moral force if made involuntarily by use of threats, peer pressure or coercion. Hunger strikers should not be forcibly given treatment they refuse. Forced feeding contrary to an informed and voluntary refusal is unjustifiable. Artificial feeding with the hunger striker's explicit or implied consent is ethically acceptable.

4. 'Benefit' and 'harm'. Physicians must exercise their skills and knowledge to benefit those they treat. This is the concept of 'beneficence', which is complemented by that of 'non-maleficence' or primum non nocere. These two concepts need to be in balance. 'Benefit' includes respecting individuals' wishes as well as promoting their welfare. Avoiding 'harm' means not only minimising damage to health but also not forcing treatment upon competent people nor

coercing them to stop fasting. Beneficence does not necessarily involve prolonging life at all costs, irrespective of other values.

5. Balancing dual loyalties. Physicians attending hunger strikers can experience a conflict between their loyalty to the employing authority (such as prison management) and their loyalty to patients. Physicians with dual loyalties are bound by the same ethical principles as other physicians, that is to say that their primary obligation is to the individual patient.

6. Clinical independence. Physicians must remain objective in their assessments and not allow third parties to influence their medical judgement. They must not allow themselves to be pressured to breach ethical principles, such as intervening medically for non-clinical reasons.

7. Confidentiality. The duty of confidentiality is important in building trust but it is not absolute. It can be overridden if non-disclosure seriously harms others. As with other patients, hunger strikers' confidentiality should be respected unless they agree to disclosure or unless information sharing is necessary to prevent serious harm. If individuals agree, their relatives and legal advisers should be kept informed of the situation.

8. Gaining trust. Fostering trust between physicians and hunger strikers is often the key to achieving a resolution that both respects the rights of the hunger strikers and minimises harm to them. Gaining trust can create opportunities to resolve difficult situations. Trust is dependent upon physicians providing accurate advice and being frank with hunger strikers about the limitations of what they can and cannot do, including where they cannot guarantee confidentiality.

Guidelines for the management of Hunger Strikers

9. Physicians must assess individuals' mental capacity. This involves verifying that an individual intending to fast does not have a mental impairment that would seriously undermine the person's ability to make health care decisions. Individuals with seriously impaired mental capacity cannot be considered to be hunger strikers. They need to be given treatment for their mental health problems rather than allowed to fast in a manner that risks their health.

10. As early as possible, physicians should acquire a detailed and accurate medical history of the person who is intending to fast. The medical implications of any existing conditions should be explained to the individual. Physicians should verify that hunger strikers understand the potential health consequences of fasting and forewarn them in plain language of the disadvantages. Physicians should also explain how damage to health can be minimised or delayed by, for example, increasing fluid intake. Since the person's decisions regarding a hunger strike can be momentous, ensuring full patient understanding of the medical consequences of fasting is critical. Consistent with best practices for informed consent in health care, the physician should ensure that the patient understands the information conveyed by asking the patient to repeat back what they understand.

11. A thorough examination of the hunger striker should be made at the start of the fast. Management of future symptoms, including those unconnected to the fast, should be discussed with hunger strikers. Also, the person's values and wishes regarding medical treatment in the event of a prolonged fast should be noted.

12. Sometimes hunger strikers accept an intravenous saline solution transfusion or other forms of medical treatment. A refusal to accept certain interventions must not prejudice any other aspect of the medical care, such as treatment of infections or of pain.

13. Physicians should talk to hunger strikers in privacy and out of earshot of all other people, including other detainees. Clear communication is essential and, where necessary, interpreters unconnected to the detaining authorities should be available and they too must respect confidentiality.

14. Physicians need to satisfy themselves that food or treatment refusal is the individual's voluntary choice. Hunger strikers should be protected from coercion. Physicians can often help to achieve this and should be aware that coercion may come from the peer group, the authorities or others, such as family members. Physicians or other health care personnel may not apply undue pressure of any sort on the hunger striker to suspend the strike. Treatment or care of the hunger striker must not be conditional upon suspension of the hunger strike.

15. If a physician is unable for reasons of conscience to abide by a hunger striker's refusal of treatment or artificial feeding, the physician should make this clear at the outset and refer the hunger striker to another physician who is willing to abide by the hunger striker's refusal.

16. Continuing communication between physician and hunger strikers is critical. Physicians should ascertain on a daily basis whether individuals wish to continue a hunger strike and what they want to be done when they are no longer able to communicate meaningfully. These findings must be appropriately recorded.

17. When a physician takes over the case, the hunger striker may have already lost mental capacity so that there is no opportunity to discuss the individual's wishes regarding medical intervention to preserve life. Consideration needs to be given to any advance instructions made by the hunger striker. Advance refusals of treatment demand respect if they reflect the voluntary wish of the individual when competent. In custodial settings, the possibility of advance instructions having been made under pressure needs to be considered. Where physicians have serious doubts about the individual's intention, any instructions must be treated with great caution. If well informed and voluntarily made, however, advance instructions can only generally be overridden if they become invalid because the situation in which the decision was made has changed radically since the individual lost competence.

18. If no discussion with the individual is possible and no advance instructions exist, physicians have to act in what they judge to be the person's best interests. This means considering the hunger strikers' previously expressed wishes, their personal and cultural values as well as their

physical health. In the absence of any evidence of hunger strikers' former wishes, physicians should decide whether or not to provide feeding, without interference from third parties.

19. Physicians may consider it justifiable to go against advance instructions refusing treatment because, for example, the refusal is thought to have been made under duress. If, after resuscitation and having regained their mental faculties, hunger strikers continue to reiterate their intention to fast, that decision should be respected. It is ethical to allow a determined hunger striker to die in dignity rather than submit that person to repeated interventions against his or her will.

20. Artificial feeding can be ethically appropriate if competent hunger strikers agree to it. It can also be acceptable if incompetent individuals have left no unpressured advance instructions refusing it.

21. Forcible feeding is never ethically acceptable. Even if intended to benefit, feeding accompanied by threats, coercion, force or use of physical restraints is a form of inhuman and degrading treatment. Equally unacceptable is the forced feeding of some detainees in order to intimidate or coerce other hunger strikers to stop fasting.

6. The World Medical Association Declaration of Tokyo

Guidelines for Physicians Concerning Torture and other Cruel, Inhuman or Degrading Treatment or Punishment in Relation to Detention and Imprisonment. Adopted by the 29th World Medical Assembly, Tokyo, Japan, October 1975, and editorially revised at the 170th Council Session, Divonne-les-Bains, France, May 2005 and the 173rd Council Session, Divonne-les-Bains, France, May 2006

Preamble

It is the privilege of the physician to practise medicine in the service of humanity, to preserve and restore bodily and mental health without distinction as to persons, to comfort and to ease the suffering of his or her patients. The utmost respect for human life is to be maintained even under threat, and no use made of any medical knowledge contrary to the laws of humanity.

For the purpose of this Declaration, torture is defined as the deliberate, systematic or wanton infliction of physical or mental suffering by one or more persons acting alone or on the orders of any authority, to force another person to yield information, to make a confession, or for any other reason.

Declaration

1. The physician shall not countenance, condone or participate in the practice of torture or other forms of cruel, inhuman or degrading procedures, whatever the offense of which the victim of such procedures is suspected, accused or guilty, and whatever the victim's beliefs or motives, and in all situations, including armed conflict and civil strife.

2. The physician shall not provide any premises, instruments, substances or knowledge to facilitate the practice of torture or other forms of cruel, inhuman or degrading treatment or to diminish the ability of the victim to resist such treatment.

3. When providing medical assistance to detainees or prisoners who are, or who could later be, under interrogation, physicians should be particularly careful to ensure the confidentiality of all personal medical information. A breach of the Geneva Conventions shall in any case be reported by the physician to relevant authorities.

The physician shall not use nor allow to be used, as far as he or she can, medical knowledge or skills, or health information specific to individuals, to facilitate or otherwise aid any interrogation, legal or illegal, of those individuals.

4. The physician shall not be present during any procedure during which torture or any other forms of cruel, inhuman or degrading treatment is used or threatened.

5. A physician must have complete clinical independence in deciding upon the care of a person for whom he or she is medically responsible. The physician's fundamental role is to alleviate the distress of his or her fellow human beings, and no motive, whether personal, collective or political, shall prevail against this higher purpose.

6. Where a prisoner refuses nourishment and is considered by the physician as capable of forming an unimpaired and rational judgment concerning the consequences of such a voluntary refusal of nourishment, he or she shall not be fed artificially. The decision as to the capacity of the prisoner to form such a judgment should be confirmed by at least one other independent physician. The consequences of the refusal of nourishment shall be explained by the physician to the prisoner.

7. The World Medical Association will support, and should encourage the international community, the National Medical Associations and fellow physicians to support, the physician and his or her family in the face of threats or reprisals resulting from a refusal to condone the use of torture or other forms of cruel, inhuman or degrading treatment.

7. World Medical Association Declaration Concerning Support for Medical Doctors Refusing to Participate in, or to Condone, the Use of Torture or Other Forms of Cruel, Inhuman or Degrading Treatment.

Adopted by the 49th WMA General Assembly Hamburg, Germany, November 1997

Preamble

1. On the basis of a number of international ethical declarations and guidelines subscribed to by the medical profession, medical doctors throughout the world are prohibited from countenancing, condoning or participating in the practice of torture or other forms of cruel, inhuman or degrading procedures for any reason.

2. Primary among these declarations are the World Medical Association's International Code of Medical Ethics, Declaration of Geneva, Declaration of Tokyo, and Resolution on Physician Participation in Capital Punishment; the Standing Committee of European Doctors' Statement of Madrid; the Nordic Resolution Concerning Physician Involvement in Capital Punishment; and, the World Psychiatric Association's Declaration of Hawaii.

3. However, none of these declarations or statements addresses explicitly the issue of what protection should be extended to medical doctors if they are pressured, called upon, or ordered to take part in torture or other forms of cruel, inhuman or degrading treatment or punishment. Nor do these declarations or statements express explicit support for, or the obligation to protect, doctors who encounter or become aware of such procedures.

Resolution

4. The World Medical Association (WMA) hereby reiterates and reaffirms the responsibility of the organised medical profession:

1. to encourage doctors to honour their commitment as physicians to serve humanity and to resist any pressure to act contrary to the ethical principles governing their dedication to this task;
2. to support physicians experiencing difficulties as a result of their resistance to any such pressure or as a result of their attempts to speak out or to act against such inhuman procedures; and,
3. to extend its support and to encourage other international organisations, as well as the national member associations (NMAs) of the World Medical Association, to support physicians encountering difficulties as a result of their attempts to act in accordance with the highest ethical principles of the profession.

5. Furthermore, in view of the continued employment of such inhumane procedures in many countries throughout the world, and the documented incidents of pressure upon medical doctors to act in contravention to the ethical principles subscribed to by the profession, the WMA finds it necessary:

1. to protest internationally against any involvement of, or any pressure to involve, medical doctors in acts of torture or other forms of cruel, inhuman or degrading treatment or punishment;
2. to support and protect, and to call upon its NMAs to support and protect, physicians who are resisting involvement in such inhuman procedures or who are working to treat and rehabilitate victims thereof, as well as to secure the right to uphold the highest ethical principles including medical confidentiality;
3. to publicise information about and to support doctors reporting evidence of torture and to make known proven cases of attempts to involve physicians in such procedures; and,
4. to encourage national medical associations to ask corresponding academic authorities to teach and investigate in all schools of medicine and hospitals the consequences of torture and its treatment, the rehabilitation of the survivors, the documentation of torture, and the professional protection described in this Declaration.

8. World Medical Association Declaration on the Rights of the Patient

See patients' rights

9. World Medical Association Declaration of Ottawa on the Rights of the Child to Health Care

Adopted by the 50th World Medical Assembly Ottawa, Canada, October 1998

Preamble

1. The health care of a child, whether at home or in hospital, includes medical, emotional, social and financial aspects which interact in the healing process and which require special attention to the rights of the child as a patient.

2. Article 24 of the 1989 United Nations Convention on the Rights of the Child recognises the right of the child to the enjoyment of the highest attainable standard of health and to facilities for the treatment of illness and rehabilitation of health, and states that nations shall strive to ensure that no child is deprived of his or her right of access to such health care services.

3. In the context of this Declaration a child signifies a human being between the time of birth and the end of her/his seventeenth year, unless under the law applicable in the country concerned children are legally recognized as adults at some other age.

General Principles

4. Every child has an inherent right to life, as well as the right of access to the appropriate facilities for health promotion, the prevention and treatment of illness and the rehabilitation of health. Physicians and other health care providers have a responsibility to acknowledge and promote these rights, and to urge that the material and human resources be provided to uphold and fulfil them. In particular every effort should be made:

1. to protect to the maximum extent possible the survival and development of the child, and to recognise that parents (or legally entitled representatives) have primary responsibility for the development of the child and that both parents have common responsibilities in this respect;
2. to ensure that the best interests of the child shall be the primary consideration in health care;
3. to resist any discrimination in the provision of medical assistance and health care from considerations of age, gender, disease or disability, creed, ethnic origin, nationality, political affiliation, race, sexual orientation, or the social standing of the child or her/his parents or legally entitled representatives;
4. to attain suitable pre-natal and post-natal health care for the mother and child;
5. to secure for every child the provision of adequate medical assistance and health care, with emphasis on primary health care, pertinent psychiatric care for those children with such needs, pain management and care relevant to the special needs of disabled children;
6. to protect every child from unnecessary diagnostic procedures, treatment and research;
7. to combat disease and malnutrition;

8. to develop preventive health care;
9. to eradicate child abuse in its various forms; and
10. to eradicate traditional practices prejudicial to the health of the child.

Specific Principles

Quality of care

5. Continuity and quality of care should be ensured by the team providing health care for a child.

6. Physicians and others providing health care to children should have the special training and skills necessary to enable them to respond appropriately to the medical, physical, emotional and developmental needs of children and their families.

7. In circumstances where a choice must be made between child patients for a particular treatment which is in limited supply, the individual patients should be guaranteed a fair selection procedure for that treatment made on medical criteria alone and without discrimination.

Freedom of choice

8. The parents or legally entitled representatives, or the child herself/himself if she/he is of sufficient maturity, should be able: to choose freely and to change the child's physician; to be satisfied that the physician of choice is free to make clinical and ethical judgements without any outside interference; and to ask for a second opinion of another physician at any stage.

Consent and self-determination

9. A child patient and her/his parents or legally entitled representatives have a right to active informed participation in all decisions involving the child's health care. The wishes of the child should be taken into account in such decision making, and should be given increasing weight dependant on her/his capacity of understanding. The mature child, in the judgement of the physician, is entitled to make her/his own decisions about health care.

10. Except in an emergency (see par 12 below), informed consent is necessary before beginning any diagnostic process or therapy on a child, especially where it is an invasive procedure. In the majority of cases the consent shall be obtained from the parents or legally entitled representatives, although any wishes expressed by the child should be taken into account before consent is given. However, if the child is of sufficient maturity and understanding, the informed consent shall be obtained from the child herself/himself.

11. In general, a competent child patient and her/his parents or legally entitled representatives are entitled to withhold consent to any procedure or therapy. While it is presumed that parents or legally entitled representatives will act in the best interests of the child, occasionally this

may not be so. Where a parent or legally entitled representative refuses consent to a procedure and/or treatment, without which the child's health would be put in grave and irreversible danger and to which there is no alternative within the spectrum of generally accepted medical care, the physician should obtain the relevant judicial or other legal authorisation to perform such a procedure or treatment.

12. If the child is unconscious, or otherwise incapable of giving consent, and a parent or legally entitled representative is not available, but a medical intervention is needed urgently, then specific consent to the intervention may be presumed, unless it is obvious and beyond any reasonable doubt on the basis of a previous firm expression or conviction that consent to the intervention would be refused in the particular situation (subject to the proviso detailed in paragraph 7 above).

13. A child patient and her/his parents or legally entitled representatives are entitled to refuse to participate in research or in the teaching of medicine. Such refusal must never interfere with the patient-physician relationship or jeopardise the child´s medical care or other benefits to which she/he is entitled.

Access to information

14. The child patient and (except in the circumstances outlined in paragraph 18 below) her/his parents or legally entitled representatives are entitled to be fully informed about her/his health status and medical condition, provided this would not be contrary to the interests of the child. However, confidential information in the child's medical record about a third party should not be provided to the child, the parents or the legally entitled representatives without the consent of that third party.

15. Any information should be provided in a manner appropriate to the culture and to the level of understanding of the recipient. This is particularly important in the case of information provided to the child, who should have the right of access to general health information.

16. Exceptionally, certain information may be withheld from the child, or her/his parents or legally entitled representatives, when there is good reason to believe that this information would create a serious hazard to the life or health of the child or to the physical or mental health of a person other than the child.

Confidentiality

17. In general the obligation of physicians and other health care workers to maintain the confidentiality of identifiable personal and medical information of patients (including information about health status, medical condition, diagnosis, prognosis, and treatment) applies as much in the case of child patients as it does for those who are adult.

18. The child patient mature enough to be unaccompanied at a consultation by her/his parents or legally entitled representatives is entitled to privacy and may request confidential services. Such a request should be respected, and information obtained during such a consultation or counselling session should not be disclosed to the parents or legally entitled representatives except with the consent of the child, or in circumstances where adult confidentiality can be breached. In addition, where the attending physician has strong reason to conclude that, despite unaccompanied attendance, the child is not competent to make an informed decision about treatment, or that without parental guidance or involvement the child's health would be put in grave and irreversible danger, then in exceptional circumstances, the physician may disclose to the parents or legally entitled representatives confidential information gained during an unaccompanied attendance. However, the physician should first discuss with the child her/his reasons for doing so and attempt to persuade the child to agree to this action.

Admission to Hospital

19. A child should be admitted to hospital only if the care he/she requires cannot be provided at home or on an outpatient basis.

20. A child admitted to hospital should be accommodated in an environment designed, furnished and equipped to suit her/his age and health status, and a child should not be admitted to adult accommodation except in special circumstances dictated only by her/his medical condition, e.g. where the child is admitted for childbirth or termination of pregnancy.

21. Every effort should be made to allow a child admitted to hospital to be accompanied by her/his parents or parent substitutes, who should be provided, where relevant, with appropriate accommodation in or near the hospital at no or minimal cost and with the opportunity to be absent from their place of work without prejudice to their continued employment.

22. Every child in hospital should be allowed as much outside contact and visiting as possible consistent with good care, without restriction as to the age of the visitor, except in circumstances where the attending physician has strong reason to believe that visiting would not be in the best interests of the child herself/himself.

23. Where a child of relevant age has been admitted to hospital her/his mother should not be denied the opportunity to breast-feed, unless there is a positive medical contra-indication to such.

24. A child in hospital should be afforded every opportunity and facility appropriate to her/his age for play, recreation and the continuation of education. To facilitate the latter the provision of specialised teachers should be encouraged or the child afforded access to appropriate distance learning programmes.

Child Abuse

25. All appropriate measures must be taken to protect children from all forms of neglect or negligent treatment, physical and mental violence, coercion, maltreatment, injury or abuse, including sexual abuse. In this context attention is drawn to the provisions of the WMA's Statement on Child Abuse and Neglect (WMA Document 17.W).

Health Education

26. Parents, and children appropriate to their age and/or development , should have access to, and full support in the application of, basic knowledge of child health and nutrition, including the advantages of breast-feeding, and of hygiene, environmental sanitation, the prevention of accidents, and sexual and reproductive health education.

Dignity of the patient

27. A child patient should be treated at all times with tact and understanding and with respect for her/his dignity and privacy.

28. Every effort should be made to prevent, or if that is not possible to minimise, pain and/or suffering, and to mitigate physical or emotional stress in the child patient.

29. The terminally ill child should be provided with appropriate palliative care and all the assistance necessary to make dying as comfortable and dignified as possible.

10. World Medical Association Declaration on Ethical Considerations Regarding Health Databases

Adopted by the WMA General Assembly, Washington 2002

1. The right to privacy entitles people to exercise control over the use and disclosure of information about them as individuals. The privacy of a patient's personal health information is secured by the physician's duty of confidentiality.

2. Confidentiality is at the heart of medical practice and is essential for maintaining trust and integrity in the patient-physician relationship. Knowing that their privacy will be respected gives patients the freedom to share sensitive personal information with their physician.

3. These principles have been incorporated in WMA statements since the WMA was founded in 1947, in particular by:

1. The Declaration of Lisbon, that states: "The patient's dignity and right to privacy shall be respected at all times in medical care and teaching";
2. The Declaration of Geneva, that requires physicians to "preserve absolute confidentiality on all he knows about his patient even after the patient has died";
3. The Declaration of Helsinki, that states:

"It is the duty of the physician in medical research to protect the life, health, privacy, and dignity of the human subject"

"Every precaution should be taken to respect the privacy of the [research] subject, the confidentiality of the patient's information and to minimize the impact of the study on the subject's physical and mental integrity and on the personality of the subject"

"In any research on human beings, each potential subject must be adequately informed of the aims, methods, sources of funding, any possible conflicts of interest, institutional affiliations of the researcher, the anticipated benefits and potential risks of the study and the discomfort it may entail. The subject should be informed of the right to abstain from participation in the study or to withdraw consent to participate at any time without reprisal. After ensuring that the subject has understood the information, the physician should then obtain the subject's freely-given informed consent, preferably in writing"

4. The primary purpose of collecting personal health information is the provision of care to the patient. Increasingly, this information is held in databases. The database might hold the patient's health record or specific information from it, for example in the case of disease registries.

5. Progress in medicine and in health care is contingent upon the conduct of quality assurance and risk management activities and health and medical research, including retrospective epidemiological studies, which use information concerning the health of individuals, com-

munities and societies. Databases are valuable sources of information for these secondary uses of health information.

6. Care must be taken to ensure that secondary uses of information do not inhibit patients from confiding information for their own health care needs, exploit their vulnerability or inappropriately borrow on the trust that patients invest in their physicians.

7. For the purpose of this statement, the following definitions are used:

1. 'Personal health information' is all information recorded with regard to the physical or mental health of an identifiable individual;
2. A 'database' is a system to collect, describe, save, recover and/or use personal health information from more than one individual whether by manual or electronic means. This definition does not include information in the clinical record of any individual patient;
3. 'De-identified data' are data in which the link between the patient and the information has been broken and cannot be recovered;
4. 'Consent' is a person's voluntarily given permission for an action, based on a sound understanding of what the action involves and its likely consequences. In some jurisdictions, the law allows substituted consent to be given on behalf of minors, on behalf of adults who do not have the capacity to consent for themselves, or on behalf of deceased persons.

Principles

8. These principles apply to all new and existing health databases, including those run or managed by commercial organisations.

Access to information by patients

9. Patients have the right to know what information physicians hold about them, including information held on health databases. In many jurisdictions, they have a right to a copy of their health records.

10. Patients should have the right to decide that their personal health information in a database (as defined in 7.2) be deleted.

11. In rare, limited circumstances, information may be withhold from a patient if it is likely that disclosure cause serious harm to the patient or another person. Physicians must be able to justify any decision to withhold information from a patient.

Confidentiality

12. All physicians are individually responsible and accountable for the confidentiality of the personal health information they hold. Physicians must also be satisfied that there are appro-

priate arrangements for the security of personal health information when it is stored, sent or received, including electronically.

13. In addition, medically qualified person(s) should be appointed to act as guardian of a health database, to have responsibility for monitoring and ensuring compliance with the principles of confidentiality and security.

14. Safeguards must be in place to ensure that there is no inappropriate or unauthorised use of or access to personal health information in databases, and to ensure the authenticity of the data. When data is transmitted, there must be arrangements in place to ensure that the transmission is secure.

15. Audit systems must keep a record of who has accessed personal health information and when. Patients should be able to review the audit record for their own information.

Patients' consent

16. Patients should be informed if their health information is to be stored on a database and of the purposes for which their information may be used.

17. Patients' consent is needed if the inclusion of their information on a database involves disclosure to a third party or would permit access by people other than those involved in the patients' care, unless there are exceptional circumstances as described in paragraph 11.

18. Under certain conditions, personal health information may be included on a database without consent, for example where this conforms with applicable national law that conforms to the requirements of this statement, or where ethical approval has been given by a specially appointed ethical review committee. In these exceptional cases, patients should be informed about the potential uses of their information, even if they have no right to object.

19. If patients object to their information being passed to others, their objections must be respected unless exceptional circumstances apply, for example where this is required by applicable national law that conforms to the requirements of this statement or necessary to prevent a risk of death or serious harm.

20. Authorization from the guardian of the health database is needed before information held on databases may be accessed by third parties. Procedures for granting authorization must comply with recognised codes of confidentiality.

21. Approval from a specially appointed ethical review committee must be obtained for all research using patient data, including for new research not envisaged at the time the data were collected. An important consideration for the committee in such cases will be whether patients should be contacted to obtain consent, or whether it is acceptable to use the information for the new purpose without returning to the patient for further consent. The committee's deci-

sions must be in accordance with applicable national law and conform to the requirements of this statement.

22. Data accessed must be used only for the purposes for which authorization has been given.

23. People who collect, use, disclose or access health information must be subject to an enforceable duty to keep the information secure.

De-identified data

24. Wherever possible, data for secondary purposes should be de-identified. If this is not possible, however, the use of data where the patient's identity is protected by an alias or code should be used in preference to readily identifiable data.

25. The use of de-identified data does not usually raise issues of confidentiality. Data about people as individuals, in which they retain a legitimate interest, for example a case history or photograph, require protection.

Data integrity

26. Physicians are responsible for ensuring, as far as practicable, that the information they provide to, and hold on, databases is accurate and up-to-date.

27. Patients who have seen their information and believe there are inaccuracies in it have the right to suggest amendments and to have their comments appended to the information.

Documentation

28. There must be documentation to explain: what information is held and why; what consent has been obtained from the patients; who may access the data; why, how and when the data may be linked to other information; and the circumstances in which data may be made available to third parties.

29. Information to patients about a specific database should cover: consent to the storage and use of data; rights of access to the data; and rights to have inaccurate data amended.

Management

30. Procedures for addressing enquiries and complaints must be in place.

31. The person or persons who are accountable for policies, procedures, and to whom complaints or enquiries can be made must be identified.

Policies

32. National medical associations should co-operate with the relevant health authorities, ethical authorities and personal data authorities, at national and other appropriate administrative levels, to formulate health information policies based on the principles in this document.

11. World Medical Association Declaration on Patient Safety

Adopted by the WMA General Assembly, Washington 2002

Preamble

1. Physicians strive to provide the highest quality health and medical care to patients. Patient safety is one of the core elements of quality in health and medical care.

2. Progress in medical and allied science and technology has transformed modern medicine into an advanced and complex health system.

3. Inherent risks have always existed in clinical medicine. Developments in modern medicine have resulted in new and sometimes greater risks – some avoidable, others inherent.

4. Physicians should attempt to foresee these risks and manage them in the treatment of patients.

Principles

5. Physicians must ensure that patient safety is always considered during medical decision-making.

6. Individuals and processes are rarely solely responsible for producing errors. Rather, separate elements combine and together produce a high-risk situation. Therefore, there should be a non-punitive culture for confidential reporting healthcare errors that focuses on preventing and correcting systems failures and not on individual or organization culpability.

7. A realistic understanding of the risks inherent in modern medicine requires that physicians must go beyond the professional boundaries of health care and cooperate with all relevant parties, including patients, to adopt a proactive systems approach to patient safety.

8. To create such a systems approach, physicians must continuously absorb a wide range of advanced scientific knowledge and continuously strive to improve medical practice.

9. All information that concerns a patient's safety must be shared with all relevant parties, including the patient. However, patient confidentiality must be strictly protected.

Recommendations

10. Hence, the WMA recommends the following to national medical associations:

1. National medical associations should promote policies on patient safety to all physicians in their countries;

2. National medical associations should encourage individual physicians, other health care professionals, patients and other relevant individuals and organizations to work together to establish systems that secure patient safety;

3. National medical associations should encourage the development of effective models to promote patient safety through continuing medical education/continuing professional development;

4. National medical associations should cooperate with one another and exchange information about adverse events, including errors, their solutions, and "lessons learned" to improve patient safety.

12. International Council of Nurses (ICN) Position: Torture, Death Penalty and Participation by Nurses in Executions.

Adopted in 1998, Revised in 2003 and 2006

ICN Position:

The International Council of Nurses strongly affirms that nurses should play no voluntary role in any deliberate infliction of physical or mental suffering and should not participate, either directly or indirectly, in the preparation for and the implementation of executions. To do otherwise is a clear violation of nursing's ethical code of practice.

The nurse's primary responsibility is to those people who require nursing care.

Nurses have a duty to provide the highest possible level of care to victims of cruel, degrading and inhumane treatment, and should speak up against and oppose any deliberate infliction of pain and suffering.

While ICN considers the death penalty to be unacceptable, clearly the nurse's responsibility to a prisoner sentenced to death continues until execution.

ICN urges its member national nurses' associations (NNAs) to lobby for abolition of the death penalty; to actively oppose torture and participation by nurses in executions; and to develop mechanisms to provide nurses with confidential advice and support in caring for prisoners sentenced to death or subjected to torture.

ICN pledges to take appropriate action and urges NNAs and individual nurses to do the same in support of nurses who become victims of torture, cruel treatment or even death for upholding the professional ethical conduct and for their work in defending human rights.

ICN believes that all levels of nursing education curricula should include: recognition of human rights issues and violations, such as torture and death penalty; awareness of the use of medical technology including lethal injections for executions; and recognition of the nurse's right to refuse to participate in executions.

Background:

Violations of human rights are pervasive and scientific advances have brought about sophisticated forms of torture. ICN supports the United Nations Universal Declaration of Human Rights1 and advocates upholding the Convention Against Torture and Other Cruel, Inhuman or Degrading Treatment or Punishment, the Istanbul Protocol on Investigation and Documentation of Torture and Other Cruel, Inhuman or Degrading Treatment or Punishment.

The ICN Code of Ethics for Nurses states that …the fundamental responsibility of the nurse is to promote health, prevent illness, to restore health and to alleviate suffering. However we recognise that nurses are sometimes called upon to perform physical examinations before prisoners' interrogation and torture, to attend torture sessions in order to provide care, and/or to treat the effects of torture.

Efforts to regulate and 'humanise' the death penalty or even to 'medicalise' it have led to contradictory legal and ethical problems.

(Replaces previous ICN Positions "Nurses and Torture", adopted 1989 and "Death penalty and participation by nurses in execution" adopted 1989).

Index

A

acceptability 21
accessibility 21
accession 299
access to a doctor 75
access to contraceptives 28
access to information 175
access to quality health 40
accountability 36, 226
Additional Protocol 302
affordability 21
allocation process 333
amendments 129
anonymity 336
artificial feeding 456
asylum seekers 28
authorisation 281
authoritative interpretation 301
availability 20
available resources 126
avoiding harm 456

B

beneficiary 122
best interests 464
biological samples 362
biomedicine 46
blood transfusions 121
breach of confidentiality 452

C

CDBI 317
cell removal 296
child abuse 468
clinical independence 457
clinical trial 162, 240
clinical trial on minors 275
clinical trials on incapacitated adults 275
clinical utility 368

Q

R

S

solidarity 47
sponsor 273
standard minimum rules 69
states parties' obligations 19, 27
stem cells 304
sterilization 170
substitution 333
surveillance 404
systems of traceability 333

T

therapeutic benefit 121, 295
therapeutic necessity 112
therapeutic progress 120
third countries 340
tissue donor 339
tissues 305
to diminish infant and child mortality 81
traceability 339
transmissible diseases 310
transmission of diseases 333
transplantation centre' 343
transplantation chain 335
transplantation purposes 94
transplantation system 294
transportation of organs 346
travellers 418
treatment of illness 464

U

unconscious patient 150
undue damage 125, 299
undue inducement 245
undue influence 209
Universal Declaration 17
universal values 131
unusual public health event 407
use of placebo 289

V

vaccination 418
violations of the right to health 33
vulnerable population 287

W

X